The

American Story

Contributors

Agnes Rogers Allen
Paul M. Angle
John Bakeless
Leland D. Baldwin
Howard K. Beale
Whitfield J. Bell, Jr.
Ray A. Billington
Claude G. Bowers
Irving Brant
Carl Bridenbaugh
Carl Carmer
Bruce Catton
Thomas C. Cochran
Arthur C. Cole
David J. Dallin
George Dangerfield
Henry David
Philip Davidson
David Donald
James Thomas Flexner
Frank Freidel

John A. Garraty
Virginia C. Gildersleeve
Lawrence H. Gipson
Eric F. Goldman
Robert Selph Henry
J. D. Hicks
Irving Howe
Quincy Howe
Marquis James
Howard Mumford Jones
Waldemar Kaempffert
Bernhard Knollenberg
Oliver W. Larkin
Irving A. Leonard
Jay Leyda
Arthur S. Link
Dumas Malone
Earl Schenck Miers
Nathan Miller
Elting Morison
Richard B. Morris

Allan Nevins
Nathaniel Peffer
Dexter Perkins
Julius W. Pratt
Max Savelle
Nathan Schachner
Arthur Schlesinger, Sr.
Arthur Schlesinger, Jr.
James Shenton
Odell Shepard
Samuel R. Spencer, Jr.
Benjamin P. Thomas
Thomas J. Wertenbaker
Bell Irvin Wiley
George F. Willison
Charles M. Wiltse
Carl Wittke
Louis B. Wright

The

CHANNEL PRESS · GREAT NECK · NEW YORK

American Story

The Age of Exploration
to the Age of the Atom

Edited by Earl Schenck Miers
Introduction by Allan Nevins
Illustrated with contemporary
prints and photographs

TABLE OF CONTENTS

LIST OF ILLUSTRATIONS

THE PANAMA CANAL
> lithograph by Joseph Pennell, "Gates of Pedro Miguel." Library of Congress Collection, Prints and Photographs Division

SLOAN AND "THE ASH CAN SCHOOL"
> etchings from Library of Congress Collection, Prints and Photographs Division

WOODROW WILSON
> cartoon and photograph from Culver Collection

Following page 320

VOTES FOR WOMEN
> collection of buttons made by Mrs. Alice Park of Palo Alto, California; photograph from Library of Congress Collection, Prints and Photographs Division

LABOR ORGANIZES
> Office of War Information photograph, from Library of Congress Collection, Prints and Photographs Division

THE GREAT DEPRESSION
> photograph by Keystone View Company-Associated Press on October 31, 1933

FRANKLIN D. ROOSEVELT
> cartoon by Rollin Kirby, from New York *World-Telegram*, March, 1934
>
> cartoon by Luke Pease, Newark *Evening News*, March, 1937
>
> photograph made in Tunis, 1943, by United States Army

INTRODUCTION

THIS volume has certain unique qualities. Never before have so many historians and biographers of distinction united in writing a series of studies of this character. We possess a good many volumes in which a single author has dealt with the vital turning points and dramatic moments of our history. Carl Becker, for example, did this in his book *Our Great Experiment in Democracy;* Theodore Roosevelt did it in a more episodic way in the series of essays and addresses on American history collected after his death under the title *Men of Action;* and James Truslow Adams did it in a somewhat more analytical fashion in *The Epic of America.* In this book, however, three-score writers have had an opportunity to treat of those aspects of the national past in which they are most interested and proficient—or one of the aspects; and the result is remarkable in its combination of variety and expertness.

The book is unique, also, in that it grew out of an application of scholarly talent to the mass media, and its contents unite some of the virtues of the spoken word—directness, simplicity, human interest—with those of the written essay. These papers, now somewhat revised, first reached the public over the radio. They were heard by audiences which certainly aggregated millions of people, for hundreds of radio stations, from WNYC in New York to rural broadcasting units in the South and West, carried them. Probably no other series of narratives and essays (as distinguished from dramas) on the American past has ever had so extensive a currency. In this effort the Society of American Historians, which

13

was established to give history wider acceptance and better literary appeal, and which has been co-founder and co-sponsor of the magazine *American Heritage,* collaborated with Broadcast Music, Inc., and its imaginative and public-spirited president, Carl Haverlin. The Society wishes to express its appreciation to Broadcast Music, Inc., for sharing with it the proceeds of this book, thus assisting the Society's purposes of emphasizing the literary element in good historical writing, and securing a larger audience for sound presentation of history.

We wish also to thank the many radio stations throughout the nation for the way in which they have brought these chapters of history to the public. There has been an excellent response to these essays. Had the papers been prepared for ordinary book publication alone, they would have been somewhat different; they would have had less sparkle, less immediate appeal, and less relation to American life today.

Finally, this book of short essays was planned as a more catholic and variegated approach to American history than is readily accessible elsewhere. Our national story is becoming very long. Any really thorough study even of a single period must run into several volumes. A single volume must in general be either a condensed and therefore dry compendium of facts, or a selective work, choosing certain parts of the record for emphasis and omitting others. This book views our history primarily as a pageant, a series of events, scenes, and movements of striking color and dramatic force. The different writers strive to bring out the significance of each panel. But the volume as a whole is meant to be suggestive— to illustrate the immense range, heterogeneity, and vitality of life on our continental stage.

"America is opportunity," said Emerson—and how many different kinds of opportunity! "It is hard," wrote Lord Bryce in 1905, "to resist the temptation to express one's admiration for the richness and variety of the forms in which civilization has developed itself in America, for the inexhaustible inventiveness and tireless energy of the people." Those who do not understand the force of these statements miss the inner meaning of our national development. Not without blunders, failures, and suffering, as these pages show, did we seize our opportunities and display our tireless energy. But in breadth, variety, and color, as in underlying moral idealism, our history stands unsurpassed. Readers young and old, expert and inexpert, should here gain some fuller realization of the fact.

To give a precise statement of the truth, to stir the imagination, to furnish lessons for the future—these, apart from offering entertainment, are the main objects of historical writing. All three are difficult. To ascertain the truth is not simply a matter of grubbing for exact facts, and then putting them in accurate and meaningful sequence, challenging as that may be. The ground must be cleared of myth and error.

Indeed, a great part of a historian's time is spent in exploding fables, and dissipating the fog of old prejudices. What distorted ideas most people have, for example, about the Puritans! How hard it is to kill the mistaken idea that the British government in 1770 imposed a "tyranny" on Americans, or that the colonists as late as 1775 wanted revolution instead of mere reform! How difficult it is to get many people to dismiss the idea that we were crude aggressors in the Mexican War!

Truth escapes the conventional historian who does not closely question all received opinions. Perhaps the commonest temptation to error lies in being now-minded when we should be then-minded. We condemn those who paltered with slavery in 1850 because slavery today seems indefensible; we criticize those who opposed the League in 1919 as blind because international action and a world view are now imperative. But 1850 and 1919 were very different from our own time; what is reality to us was not reality to our ancestors. The essayists in this volume have taken great pains—some of them a lifetime of pains—to get at the truth. They have taken equal pains to apply ideas in understanding that truth. History and painting have often been compared, and the analogy has a profound truth. Sir Joshua Reynolds said that he mixed brains with his paints, and Macaulay and Parkman mixed brains with their ink. Superficial truth and inner truth are quite different entities. A photographic painting of a landscape, and a flat representational narrative of Wolfe's campaign against Quebec, may have truth, but not the truth of Reynolds and Parkman. Here, we hope, is some of the inner as well as the outer truth.

The appeal to the imagination is too often neglected by historians and teachers. The past has poetry—dramatic, lyric, and epic. Our American past is filled with matter that should stir the blood like ancient Hebrew poetry or Scottish border balladry. As our population grows, our callings, tastes, and ideas have become more varied, and specialism has increased, until the scientist, the governmental expert, the engineer, and the businessman seem almost to talk different languages. The country urgently needs a common denominator. Some one fund of knowledge, tradition, and emotion should be shared by all, as educated Englishmen, graduates of Rugby and Oxford, once shared the fund provided by the Greek and Roman classics.

What, then, should all master so that all can claim a common heritage? In part, the literary classics of our tongue. All should know the best of Shakespeare, Milton, Emerson, and Whitman. In part, unquestionably, the fundamental elements of our history. All Americans should know Roger Williams and William Penn, Valley Forge and Yorktown, "Don't give up the ship!" and "If any man hauls down the flag, shoot him on the spot!"; all should know the Gettysburg Address and the Emancipation Proclamation, the Fourteen Points and the Atlantic Charter; all should know Appomattox, El Caney, the Argonne, and the Battle of the Bulge. But all this should be taught not so much as fact, but as an appeal to the imagination. Much of it is so here presented, and those who master this volume will have learned a good deal of our ideal common denominator.

An imaginative approach to history has a double value. It stirs the emotions, and so feeds both our patriotism and our sense of the larger significance of life. It also stimulates curiosity. Through this gateway we hope many will walk to find their desire to learn truly quickened. The wars with the French when America was part of a world-wide empire, for example—three of them beginning in Europe, but the last and greatest starting in North America: were they not really world wars, and did we not return to an ancient pattern in our miscalled First and Second World Wars? Or take the farmers' rebellion in western Massachusetts in 1786, when rich Bostonians opened their purses to support the troops who killed several of the demonstrators: how much did this have in common with other farmers' uprisings, reaching down through the Grangers and Populists to the Non-Partisan League? The Reconstruction story after the Civil War offers some striking parallels, in its *mélange* of Northern reformers, striving Negroes, and Southerners determined to protect their old way of life, with the situation south of the Mason and Dixon line since the Supreme Court's decision against segregation. These essays contain some stimulating insights and parallels.

Readers of this volume will find themselves, we hope, coming to several conclusions which no reader of American history would have formed a generation ago. They concern patriotism, democracy, and the outlook for the future.

History is not merely a great teacher of patriotism, but the one indispensable teacher; the more we know about the struggles which made the nation, the great men who led it, and the principles which sustained its people in time of trial, the deeper will be our feeling for our country. But conceptions of patriotism change. Ours has broadened since Andrew Jackson's day, even since Lincoln's. Devotion to our own nation is combined with a stronger feeling of the fraternity of man, and the unity of the free world.

Simultaneously, our ideas of democracy have been enlarged. We used to say that the United States was unique in giving free self-government its largest and fullest test; that what Britain, Holland, and Switzerland did on a limited scale we did with tremendous sweep and amplitude. That was true. But political democracy is not enough. Social democracy, the abolition of race lines, class lines, and educational lines, is quite as important. So is economic democracy, the erasing of the old lines between rich and poor, the enactment of laws to make vast fortunes impossible, and the establishment of a welfare system which gives security to all.

And finally, the immense changes wrought by science and technology have given us a vision both of terrible new perils, and of dazzling vistas of comfort, happiness, and moral and intellectual growth. The wonders of mass production, of applied chemistry and physics, and of the tapping of nuclear energy have created for us a new world: a world in which America finds the problem of peace desperately urgent, but also faces the possibilities of a brighter era than was within the conception of our ancestors.

ALLAN NEVINS

Columbia University
September, 1956

The
American Story

ONE

Dawn and

the Morning Star

ONE SUMMER, around the year 1000 A.D., the high prow of a Viking galley pierced the cold mists of the North Atlantic. Some day a saga would tell of the voyage of this galley, sailing off into the unknown sea beyond Greenland under the leadership of Leif, son of Eric the Red. Of Leif, Norse father would relate to son: "He was a large and strong man, of noble aspect," and the boy, listening, would become Leif, peering through the icy haze and seeing at last the land—first the bleak, unfriendly shore of what was doubtless Labrador or Newfoundland, then the wooded coast of Cape Breton Island or Nova Scotia, and finally a country that was pleasant, mild, and inviting.

Here Leif and the Northmen disembarked, touching the dew with their hands, raising their fingers to their mouths, and deciding that "they never before had tasted anything so sweet." They caught salmon larger than they ever had seen; and because of the abundance of grapes they called the place Vineland. On a second voyage a year later (the brothers Ericson made three voyages) Thorvald, a brother of Leif, declared that "they found neither dwellings of men or beasts, except upon an island to the westward, where they found a corn shed of wood . . ." Thus, in the American Story, the curtains part briefly and a prologue is enacted; then almost five hundred years pass before the full drama begins.

These restless, barbaric men from the North, who had been to England, the Faeroe and Orkney Islands in the 8th Century and to

Iceland, Ireland, and Russia in the 9th, played other roles in re-shaping man's dimensions of the world he inhabited. It was reasonable that men who loved battle should learn also to love piracy, and, spurred by these affections, the Northmen by the 11th Century had traveled as far south as Sicily. Those who had come to plunder and to ravage discovered in time that they themselves had been made captives, not by force of arms but by force of a new concept called Christianity. So it was that men with Viking blood became part of the columns of fighting laymen who marched against the Infidel in the Crusades (1096–1270); and among the stories they brought back was evidence that the fabled wealth of the Indies, Cathay, and India had to be more than wild fancy. The missionary zeal of Christianity far outlived the Crusades; it spawned a new sort of adventurer in men like the Venetian trader, Marco Polo, who traveled widely in Cathay and Burma during the later years of the 13th Century. It spawned Nicolo de' Conti, who a hundred years later penetrated to Java. The travels of such men into Asia succeeded in producing an awakening perhaps as climactic as that which Columbus and the Age of Discovery would bring to the New World.

In other ways, in other areas, the 14th Century found an old, narrow world bursting at the seams. Ox-drawn wagons widened ruts into roads, and villages sprang up in many sections of Europe. Food that once had to be grown at home could be transported from ever growing distances; and the discovery of gold in the Black Forest gave freer circulation to money. Great changes began to touch the minds of men and to alter their habits. The local craftsman appeared, letting others grow his vegetables and tend the chickens and the cow while he perfected his skill in weaving or iron and leather work. Along village streets the figure of the middleman grew familiar, and his shadow, running into history, assumed the shape of the factory system. New ideas arose, and the worker thought of himself as worthy of his hire and deserving of his leisure.

Across Europe a freshening wind was blowing, bearing seeds that would fall, take root, and grow into the Protestant Reformation. In Germany a shy and secretive man, plagued by tax assessors and creditors whose bills he could not pay, understood the sounds this wind was murmuring. When this man was born no one knows; the best evidence is that he died some time around 1468. But the genius of Gutenberg was to become ageless, and so the dates do not matter. With the invention of printing from movable type all sorts of books and documents could be widely circulated—the Bible, tax receipts which saved countless hours of hand labor, the map of Claudius Ptolemy who almost thirteen hundred years ago had decided the world was round, and *The Book of Marco Polo*.

To Christopher Columbus, the dreamer-navigator named for the patron saint of sailors and travelers, the map of Ptolemy and the journal of Marco Polo possessed special fascination.

Toward the Setting Sun

IRVING A. LEONARD

The map of Ptolemy contained numerous mistakes, for which future generations could be thankful. Ptolemy curved the coast of Eastern Asia east and south instead of joining it to the Land of Linae, as seacoast China was then called. Then he made a lake of the Indian Ocean in order to extend Asia eastward to the limit of the habitable world, and thus reduced the unknown part of the globe between the points of easternmost Asia and westernmost Europe by some twenty-five hundred miles. Columbus, who believed that he could reach the Indies by sailing westward, saw little to frighten him in the Western Sea that Ptolemy charted. Before sunrise on August 3, 1492, Columbus set sail from Palos with some ninety men in a decked ship and two caravels. At the Canary Islands the ships were refitted, and the voyage resumed on September 6. Ahead twenty-four hundred miles, Columbus estimated, lay Japan. Irving A. Leonard, professor of Spanish American History and Literature at the University of Michigan, editor of the Handbook of Latin American Studies, *former editor of the* Hispanic American Review, *and author of many books on early American history, unfolds the background and meaning of the new era that Columbus would introduce—quite by accident.*

"THERE will come a time in the long years of the world when the Ocean Sea will loosen its shackles that bind things together and a great part of the earth will be opened up, and a new sailor such as Jason's guide, whose name was Thyphis, shall discover a new world, and then shall Thule no longer be the last of lands."

Long and earnestly a Genoese sailor known to history as Christopher Columbus pondered these prophetic words until they were indelibly woven into the texture of his dreams. For this half-mystical genius was a man of destiny whose name symbolizes a marvelous moment in world history, the Age of Discovery, which extended from the mid-15th Century far into the one following. Fate decreed that Columbus should be the "new sailor" to compel the vast ocean sea to yield up a new world to Renaissance Europe. By fulfilling the strange prediction of an ancient writer, this dreamer caused the small Mediterranean-centered world to explode suddenly into an immense globe of unsuspected dimensions. And by this act he unwittingly ushered into being the modern era of history, which records the spread of European influence in all its forms to the uttermost corners of the earth. Columbus thus pointed the way to many new worlds of human experience.

That dynamic intellectual and artistic movement called the Renaissance was in full bloom in the 15th Century. More and more it was emphasizing worldly living in contrast to the strict virtues stressed by the waning Middle Ages. This new spirit praised the dignity of the individual; it sharpened his curiosity about this world; and, incidentally, it whetted his appetite for the exotic goods of the East. From this last fact particularly came a growing urgency to re-establish contacts between the two then known centers of world civilization, the European West and the Asiatic East. During the late Middle Ages, connections between these two great regions had been increasingly close. Italian cities had prospered mightily from the rich trade in luxuries. But this communication was hampered after 1453 by intruders—the "terrible Turks"—who had captured Istanbul, once called Constantinople, and thus controlled much of the Near East. In addition, the Western nations were envious of the commanding position Venice held in trade with the Orient, and were determined to find other routes to the East to free themselves from her commercial domination. As a result, the Mediterranean center of gravity shifted from the Italian to the Spanish peninsula.

But why did Hispanic peoples thus become the first instruments of history in Europeanizing the globe through discovery, conquest, and colonization of its unknown parts? This question begs an answer that is not easy to reach. Periods of greatness of a people frequently arise from the coincidence of historic movements and of the circumstances of their surroundings. The position of the Hispanic lands, Spain and Portugal, at the western extreme of Europe, and the insistent demands for luxury goods, stimulated by the so-called Commercial Revolution, were compelling factors which now made these countries pioneers in a new epoch of history.

With the Turks threatening to dominate the entire Mediterranean, it was imperative to find new routes to the now isolated Orient. Not only these circumstances but the heavy demand for foreign goods required an all-water course. The former paths of commerce which led alternately by land and sea had made transportation slow and costly. There had been too many middlemen benefited along the way. Now, minds turned westward in quest of oceanic approaches to the glamorous kingdoms of the Indies and of the Great Khan. Fortunately, the technical advances in ship-building, in nautical instruments, and in the art of navigation made success likely. The geographic position of the Hispanic peninsula, together with the great imagination and extraordinary vitality of its people, were factors which prepared the Portuguese and Spaniards to meet the great challenge.

The Portuguese were first to seek an all-sea highway to the East. Fronting a vast, mysterious ocean, and serving so long as a way station of medieval trade between the Mediterranean and the ports of the Netherlands and Britain, the conquest of the watery wilderness was an ever-present incentive for this small nation. During the 15th Century their enlightened monarchs had experimented in maritime sciences. Systematic naval expeditions had been sent out into the Atlantic to discover the Azores, and along the African coast toward the forbidding waters of the Equator. Careful records of these undertakings provided the best scientific data on ocean navigation then available. With this enlarging knowledge, Portuguese navigators pushed ever more boldly southward. They scorned the superstitious perils popularly associated with the warmer seas and the Dark Continent until, shortly after the momentous voyage of Columbus, they rounded the Cape of Good Hope on the southern tip of Africa. In thus opening a waterway to India, to the spice-laden islands of the Far East, and the pearl-studded shores of Cathay, little Portugal enjoyed its brief moment of wealth and world power.

It is ironical, perhaps, that the land-minded Castilians, who occupied a large part of the interior of the Spanish peninsula, should win a greater prize across the seas and a more conspicuous place in history than their neighbors. To Isabella of Castile and her advisers, the proposal of Columbus to sail directly across the Atlantic Ocean to the shores of Cipango (Japan) and Cathay seemed fantastic. It was little more than a wild gamble compared to the systematic efforts of the Portuguese. Indeed had not the Portuguese, who had much more knowledge of such subjects, rejected this impracticable suggestion? In any event, Isabella chose to take part in the gamble with fortune which Columbus so persistently thrust upon her. Her heirs were to reap handsome returns on the long chance she had taken.

The Age of Discovery was the pursuit of the setting sun. From far back in antiquity the people of the Old World had watched the sun dip into the sea. Within them deepened the conviction that surely a better and brighter world existed in that mysterious realm behind the declining rays. There must lie the El Dorado where dwelt the eternal summer, the fairest women, the enchanted Eden. Travelers to the East, particularly Marco Polo, had given substance to these myths by highly colored descriptions of the land of the Great Khan and of misty Cipango. Hence it was, perhaps, that Christopher Columbus finally won support from the pious Queen of Castile; and why his feat, far less successful in its objectives than the Portuguese navigators, awakened such wide interest throughout Europe. The Great Discoverer was keenly aware that what he brought back from his voyages fell far short of expectations. But he bolstered these agelong beliefs by hints of the proximity of the Earthly Paradise to the newly discovered lands, of the existence of the Amazons, and of other rumored marvels.

Even before Columbus had concluded the last of his four voyages, a cloud of exploring expeditions was released from Europe. The Cabots sailed from England, the Corte-Reals from Portugal, and from Spain, Solís and Ojeda. The latter was accompanied by a Florentine, Amerigo Vespucci, who, through effective publicity, had his name attached to the New World.[1] In an astonishingly brief time, these and a host of others brought into view the pattern of the Western Hemisphere from Labrador to Patagonia. Columbus persisted to his death in the illusion that he had found the way directly west to the empire of the Great Khan and Cipango; but it was soon apparent that he had really discovered a vast land barrier to his real objective. Thus, in the hope of succeeding where Columbus had failed, other expeditions searched vainly up and down the long coastline for a water passage through this great obstacle. Only Magellan, another Portuguese argonaut in the serv-

[1] The name "America" was given to the new land by the geographer, Martin Waldseemüller, who read letters written by Amerigo Vespucci and believed him to be the discoverer.

ice of Spain, was able in 1520 to penetrate to the Pacific, which had been so recently glimpsed by Balboa as the isthmus joining the two continents. The strait through which Magellan passed, however, was so near the southern tip of the elongated New World that its discovery was of little benefit.

"It is undubitable, sovereign Princes," Columbus wrote in the report of his first voyage, "that in such countries there must be things of infinite value, and the profit that may be acquired here I am not able to describe." With the existence of an immense continental barrier to the Far East now established for all time, Spanish efforts shifted about 1520 to exploration and conquest of the lands about which the Great Discoverer was so hopeful. The Spaniards eagerly sought there those "things of infinite value" and the "profit" that Columbus had proclaimed.

The spectacular feats of sea captains now yielded to those of the Conquistador. The glittering exploits of the Spanish soldier-explorers adorn many luminous pages of the story of the Age of Discovery. By a series of bridgeheads successively established in the New World, these hardy adventurers swarmed over the immense hinterland of two continents. From the first foothold in the Caribbean, expeditions advanced into the Florida mainland, the Gulf of Mexico, and into the North coast of South America. From Cuba, Cortez made the spectacular conquest of Mexico, in turn a bridgehead for the exploration of Central America, the Pacific coast, and of the southwestern part of the United States. From another bridgehead in Panama, Balboa discovered the Pacific Ocean.

The Pizarros launched their bloody conquest of Peru, which then served as a point of departure for still further explorations into the Amazon basin, into Chile, and into the heartland of South America. With prodigious courage and endurance these tough sons of Spain fanned out from each center of concentration in eager quest of gold and treasures.

Their heads were full of the medieval lore which told of mysterious isles and lands inhabited by strange forms of life: gorgons, mermaids, weird Calibans, singing Ariels, and Amazons. And especially Amazons, for the recently introduced printing presses were pouring forth in type the earliest popular literature. Fantastic accounts of knights and chivalry were the Superman and Buck Rogers fiction of the day, and were all too often accepted as fact by the gullible. Impelled by these drives of greed, wonder, and fantasy, the Spanish Conquistadors, whose excesses in plunder and carnage are more highly advertised than their positive contributions to geographical knowledge, became the spearhead for Westernizing our globe. Almost the sole equipment of these adventurers was indomitable courage and will power. They lived on the borderland between the medieval and the modern age. They struggled in the hidden depths of unknown continents. They fought along the front line of clashing faiths and cultures. Though strongly conditioned by the traditions of the Middle Ages, they were men of action who personified the new Renaissance spirit of individualism. The Conquistador was, in short, a dynamic blend of medieval superstition and modern curiosity. Together with the great maritime discoverers, his was the chief glory in the Age of Discovery of unlimited expansion of knowledge of our physical world.

Experiment in Colonization

LOUIS B. WRIGHT

Within a generation after Columbus's first voyage, French, English, Portuguese, and Spanish fishing fleets were making annual journeys to Newfoundland for cod. By the middle of the 16th Century a considerable knowledge of the New World had been obtained. Woven into the American Story by then were the discovery of Florida by de León, and the three voyages by Cartier that carried the French up the St. Lawrence as far as the Lachine Rapids (1535–36). In 1541 Cartier returned and made a temporary settlement a few miles above Quebec. In that year deSoto and his followers were the first white men to look upon the mighty Mississippi (but the ripening corn that they needed so badly to survive was hardly the gold they had hoped to find).

Other events of good and evil portent for the New World filled the second half of the 16th Century. In 1562 the Englishman John Hawkins brought three hundred Negroes from the coast of Guinea to Haiti, trading them at a handsome profit for a cargo of ginger, sugar, and pearls. This hard-bitten seadog carried back to London stories of the Florida country, made two additional voyages, and was eventually knighted. Meanwhile the Spanish were not neglecting the New World, and by the beginning of the last quarter of the 16th Century they were firmly established in colonies from Mexico to Brazil. During the same period, the English had failed to capitalize upon the claim which John Cabot had given them by his voyage of discovery along the coast of North America in 1497. English corsairs, however, had raided the Spanish possessions, and Englishmen had acquired a greedy interest in the New World. The English were preoccupied rather than asleep, and now and then events occurred that foreshadowed the future—in 1553 the Muscovy Company, the first of England's great trading companies, was organized by a group of London merchants; two years later Richard Eden published his translation of Peter Martyr's Decades of the Newe World, a powerful stimulant to renewed English interest in America; and in 1558 Elizabeth ascended the throne. English explorers could not have asked for a more enthusiastic patroness than Elizabeth, though she sometimes had to encourage her mariners surreptitiously and occasionally she had to disown them; she bestowed a knighthood upon the slave-dealer Hawkins, encouraged Thomas Stucley's pretended colonizing expedition to Florida (but Stucley found piracy more to his taste), and sent Martin Frobisher in search of a northwest passage to Cathay (receiving at least a live Eskimo and samples of ore that proved to be fool's gold for her trouble). In 1579, Drake, sailing up the west coast of the Americas, claimed the California region in the name of the queen and named it Nova Albion.

Expansionists in England could take heart. Elizabeth had been twenty years a queen when Sir Humphrey Gilbert received from her patent to "discover, search, find out, and view such remote heathen and barbarous lands, countries, and territories not actually possessed of any Christian prince." Two voyages and five years later, Sir Humphrey managed to lay claim to Newfoundland, but he lost his life on the way back to England.

In the meantime, Sir Humphrey's half-brother, Sir Walter Raleigh, was beginning his own endeavors to colonize North America. In 1584 he sent out two captains, Philip Amadas and Arthur Barlow, to explore what is now the coast of North Carolina. To the whole coastal region, they gave the name of Virginia in honor of the Virgin Queen. Raleigh succeeded in planting a colony on Roanoke Island, but its inhabitants disappeared and left an enduring mystery.

To Elizabeth's successor, James I, belonged the real beginning of British colonization in America. By 1604 the long feud with Spain had ended; but the truly significant date for the English in the New World was April 20, 1606, when James I chartered the London and Plymouth Companies, giving to the Londoners the

*right to colonize the American coast between the 34th and 41st
parallels and to the Plymouth Company the right of colonization
between the 38th and 45th parallels. On December 20, members
of the London Company waved Godspeed to 144 men outward
bound under their auspices for Virginia. Louis B. Wright, distinguished director of the Folger Shakespeare Library, author of such
fine books as* The First Gentlemen of Virginia, *and editor of various
texts dealing with American history, tells the story of what befell
these bold adventurers.*

About the middle of May in 1607 three little ships under the command of Captain Christopher Newport sailed up the James River
and anchored off a grassy and wooded peninsula. The vessels
brought emigrants from England who would once more try to set
up a colony in North America. The men who came with Captain
Newport numbered a few more than a hundred souls. They were
weary with the long voyage, for they had sailed down the Thames
for the last time in the previous December. Ever since, they had
been buffeted by the North Atlantic. The earth of Virginia looked
good to them; indeed, any solid ground would have been a relief,
but Virginia in May was especially promising. Wild plums were in
bloom and the sailors reported the fragrance of strawberries
crushed under their feet as they came ashore. Surely this was an
auspicious beginning for the new adventure. They named the site
of their settlement Jamestown in honor of their sovereign.

Captain Newport's company had few qualifications for settling
a raw wilderness. Many had no knowledge of, or skill in, the labor
required to make homes in the woods. In fact, few of them had
any thought of staying in that uncouth waste; they had come for
adventure or in the hope of finding a hoard of gold such as Cortez
and the Pizarros had discovered. That gold had enriched Spain.
The Virginia adventurers hoped to seize wealth and hurry home.
When Captain Newport sailed back for England he carried a letter
from those left behind imploring reinforcements and supplies to
keep the "all devouring Spaniards," as they described them, from
laying "ravenous hands upon these gold showing mountains." The
hills which the settlers had dimly seen in the distance from their
camp by the river would, they believed, yield gold. They learned
better and they learned the hard way.

Unruly and not given to hard work, they were soon whipped into
shape by Captain John Smith, who gained command after the de-

parture of Newport. They soon learned that they had to work with their hands or perish. But they did not learn without quarrel and protest. Nevertheless, by the time winter had come they had cut trees, had erected mud and wattle houses, and had begun to make bricks for a church and other permanent structures. Smith, who was a stern disciplinarian, scorned soft-handed fellows and showed no sympathy for their troubles. When they swore at their blisters, he decreed that a can of cold water should be poured down the offender's sleeve, one can for each oath.

Captain Smith also explored the neighboring countryside and traded with the Indians. Had it not been for the corn which he obtained by barter, the colonists would have fared ill that first winter. The Indians were suspicious of the newcomers, and kept them in constant fear. On one of his expeditions Smith himself was made a prisoner by Powhatan, the chief of the local tribe, and that incident gave rise to a tale he later told in his *Generall Historie of Virginia* (1624) of his dramatic rescue by Pocahontas. Whether Pocahontas actually saved Smith in the manner which he described nobody knows for certain, but it is true that Pocahontas later married one of his group, John Rolfe, and left many descendants. Nearly a century later, Robert Beverley, one of the early historians of Virginia, lamented that more Virginians had not taken Indian wives, for thus they might have populated the country and made peace with the natives.

Jamestown's troubles were not over with the passing of the first winter and the arrival of additional settlers. The winter of 1609–10 was even worse. That season has gone down in history as the "starving time." The settlers ate rats, mice, and any roots they could dig. Fearful of the Indians, they dared not venture out to hunt or to cut firewood. They burned the timber of their houses rather than go into the woods. With the James River teeming with fish, it seems odd to us that they were so hard put to it for food. The answer is that these people were for the most part from the city of London; they had no capacity to adapt themselves to conditions and no equipment for, or skill in, fishing or hunting. They were about as ill-prepared as colonists have ever been.

By May, 1610, the little colony had been reduced to about sixty embittered and discouraged survivors who were ready to give up and return to England. Lord Delaware arrived with a relief expedition just in time to save them.

The colony survived but it found no gold. The backers of the venture, the Virginia Company of London, made no money out of the enterprise. This company had been organized with great fan-fare in 1606, and hundreds of Englishmen from all stations in life, from lords and bishops to simple London shopkeepers, had in-vested in it. They expected quick profits, for they had heard of in-vestments in voyages to the East Indies which had paid as much as 3,000 per cent on the subscription price of the stock. Unhappily, the stockholders in the Virginia Company were doomed to disap-pointment. The stock company idea was a failure and in 1624 the Crown took over Virginia as a royal colony, which it remained until the American Revolution.

One reason for the first failures was the lack of any product which could be turned quickly and profitably into money. The colonists shipped back a few cargoes of sassafras which had a contemporary vogue as a drug, but the European market for sassa-fras was soon glutted. The Virginians were not able to develop satisfactory trade with the Indians, as elsewhere adventurers were to turn the Indian trade in furs and skins to a profit. Their first attempts at farming were not successful. But about 1612, John Rolfe discovered that tobacco could be grown easily and would sell for a high price. Henceforth every ship's captain coming to Virginia was eager to buy this commodity.

The native tobacco of Virginia was a strong and bitter variety used by the Indians but not suitable for export. Then Rolfe ob-tained seed of a sweeter variety grown in the Caribbean and in South America. This latter type became the tobacco of commerce, though to this day the strong native tobacco of Virginia is grown in certain parts of the Balkans.

For a generation and more before John Rolfe's time, tobacco had been increasing in popularity throughout Western Europe. Many doctors of the day believed it to be a remedy for almost any ailment from gunshot wounds to epilepsy. A Spaniard named Monardes wrote a book on the remedies obtainable in America which an Englishman named John Frampton translated in 1577 as *Joyful News Out of the New Found World*. A large part of this book was devoted to description of the virtues of tobacco. Not every-body agreed with this view, however. King James himself in 1604 wrote a pamphlet entitled *A Counter Blast to Tobacco* in which he told of a great smoker who had died mysteriously. Upon his body being opened, it was found that it contained a bushel of soot. King James, a thrifty Scot, modified his views when he discovered that tobacco was a profitable commodity for his struggling Vir-ginia colony.

In three ships, with a crew of some 90 men, Columbus set sail on the first of the four voyages of discovery he was to make. In this early print the
Admiral is pictured on the deck of the *Santa Maria*.
The 100-ton vessel later went aground off Haiti, and
had to be abandoned.

After Columbus, there arose a wave of exploration. From Spain, England, Portugal, and France, small ships set out on many-month voyages to the New World. The crews returned with astonishing tales—including one pictured above, reproduced from a rare work on navigation published in 1671, showing how a band of sea-weary voyagers celebrated a religious holiday on the body of a living whale.

La Salle's landing at Matagorda Bay, Texas, in February of 1685. The illustration is a reduced facsimile from Father Louis Hennepin's *Nouveau Voyage d'un Pais plus Grand que l'Europe,* published in 1698. Hennepin, who sailed with La Salle, was the first to describe Niagara Falls, and was himself the discoverer of St. Anthony Falls— now known as Minneapolis.

A political cartoon which appeared in "Political Register," an English periodical, depicting the fury aroused by Lord Hillsborough's attempt to "Episcopize" the colonies by sending over Bishops appointed in England. Hillsborough, who was later (1768) appointed Secretary of State for the Colonies, opposed all concessions to the colonists.

So great was the popularity of tobacco in England that by 1614 England's annual tobacco bill amounted to two hundred thousand pounds sterling, roughly equivalent to about eight million dollars in our money today. Small wonder then that the Virginians had cause to thank John Rolfe. England had been forced to import most of its tobacco from Spain, and according to the economists of that day it was a national disaster to pay out so much money to a foreign country, especially to a potential enemy.

The growing of tobacco rescued the little Virginia colony, and several other factors helped to improve conditions. At first the colonists had been mere laborers for the Virginia Company. Then Governor Thomas Dale, who is remembered for his strict, almost martial "code," changed the system in 1613 so as to give every settler a few acres to farm for himself. This stimulation of self-interest proved a success. With this incentive, the colonists soon began to cultivate tobacco on a commercial scale, and within the next generation tobacco became the primary crop. So eager were Virginians to grow tobacco that they neglected other crops. In time they glutted the tobacco market to a point where crop restrictions had to be imposed.

Other things were happening in the little Virginia colony in these early years. The first representative assembly met in the church at Jamestown on August 9, 1619, a momentous date in the history of American democracy. On that day, Governor George Yeardley and his Council and twenty-two burgesses, two duly elected from each of the eleven settlements, met to make new laws for the colony. Ever after Virginians jealously guarded their rights to make their own laws. The Governor's Council served as both the upper house of the legislative body and the supreme court of the colony, though the home government in England might veto laws which it regarded as unfavorable. In actual fact, Virginia from this time onward was essentially self-governing.

Plans for schools and a university were also made in these early years. King James commanded the bishops to collect money for this endeavor, and on May 26, 1619, Sir Edwin Sandys, treasurer of the Virginia Company, reported fifteen hundred pounds sterling on hand for "that pious work." The Company also set aside ten thousand acres of land for the "university to be planted at Henrico" and it also allotted one thousand acres to establish a "college for the conversion of the infidels" (meaning Indians, of course). Other subscriptions were made to these educational enterprises, but the actual founding of the schools and colleges received a setback in the great Indian massacre of 1622. That tragedy darkened the prospects of the colony and once more placed its very existence in jeopardy.

From the time that Pocahontas had married John Rolfe, peace had reigned between white men and natives; Indians freely visited the settlements. White men went unarmed into the woods except for weapons needed in hunting. But a shrewd Indian chief, Opechancanough, who had succeeded Pocahontas's father Powhatan, was disturbed by the restrictions upon the hunting grounds which the white settlements were making. He determined to rid the land of the whites. On Good Friday, 1622, the Indians fell upon the isolated settlers and killed several hundred. Perhaps the whole colony might have been wiped out had not a Christian Indian warned his friends of the plot in time to save Jamestown itself and some of the other principal settlements. So devastating was the slaughter, however, that plans for erecting schools and the university were abandoned. When the news reached England, the Virginia Company employed preachers, as it had done in 1609 and at other times of crisis, to reassure the public about the safety of the English colony in Virginia. Thus propagandists induced the Englishmen at home to maintain their support of, and interest in, the colonial enterprise overseas.

The disaster was acute but the colony was too well established to perish. The survivors set to work to rebuild homes burned by the Indians and to wreak vengeance on the tribesmen. The old friendly days when white men and Indians lived in peace were over. Henceforth Virginians would war against the Indians until they drove them from the land.

Despite hardships and suffering, Englishmen gradually established themselves on all the Virginia rivers. There they grew tobacco and raised foodstuffs for their households. There in time they developed a civilization which brought over the best of the British tradition and bequeathed to Americans a legacy of law and liberty which we have guarded from that day to this.

The Fertile Germ of Democracy

GEORGE F. WILLISON

Sickness returned to Virginia in 1620, and that year more than one thousand persons died. Among the afflicted were some of the Negroes who had been brought to Virginia the previous August and sold into bondage as servants; others were part of a shipload of marriageable girls sent by the Virginia Company to be sold to planters at 120 pounds of tobacco each; and still others could be counted among one hundred children from London slums who had been shipped as apprentices to Virginia. On September 16, in that hard year for Jamestown and her neighbors, a new type of colonizer sailed from England for America. In such books as The Pilgrim Reader, *the story of the Pilgrims as told by themselves and their contemporaries, and* Saints and Strangers, *a lively chronicle of the Pilgrims, author-teacher-historian George F. Willison has demonstrated his special gift for telling the American Story, as he does in this fascinating chapter.*

LATE in 1620, with snow already flying, the now celebrated *Mayflower* dropped anchor off Cape Cod. She had on board only fifty men, plus twenty women and a number of children—thirty-four in all, down to babes in arms. One would have said that these weak and weary Pilgrims could not succeed, but succeed they did in a remarkably short time.

Who were these Pilgrims? The Saints, as they called themselves, were the core of the company. Because they demanded liberty of conscience, the right to worship as they pleased, they had been driven from England, and, crossing to Holland, had settled in Leyden, where they enjoyed religious freedom to the full. But they found life hard in a foreign land. They were farmer folk not used to city ways, and thus sank ever deeper into poverty. So they began looking to the New World as a place where they might live more easily by farming and fishing.

About forty Saints—some from the original Pilgrim congregation at Scrooby—crossed to Southampton, where the *Mayflower* was waiting. The vessel was loaded with what the Saints called Strangers, recruited in and around London by the merchant adventurers who financed the venture. After several delays, the *May-flower* set sail, but almost foundered in midocean.

The London Strangers had no interest whatever in the religious doctrine of Leyden Saints: the Strangers belonged to the Anglican Church or the established Church of England, and were content with it. Like the tens of millions who followed them to our shores during the next three centuries, these Strangers were not seeking spiritual salvation, but free land and a better chance to improve their worldly lot; and so long as they were willing to work hard, the merchant adventurers did not care how they prayed. But the Saints did; they prohibited the Anglican service, thus denying the Strangers the very liberty of conscience the Saints had so vigorously demanded for themselves.

If the Strangers wanted the consolations of religion, they were free to join the Saints' church; if not, they could go without. This contradiction was what religious freedom meant at Plymouth and throughout most of early New England. The fight for liberty of conscience and worship was won generations later when the Quakers, Baptists, Anglicans, and others broke the one-church rule of the Saints.

Mutiny was brewing among the Strangers as the *Mayflower* dropped anchor. To preserve unity, the Saints drew up the now famed Mayflower Compact and had all sign it. Under this remarkably democratic document, Saints and Strangers alike constituted themselves a civil body politic to be ruled, in the phrase of the Compact, by "just and equal laws."

By this charter of freedom, by this independent act, the Pilgrims created their own commonwealth. They chose a governor—Deacon John Carver—the first colonial governor in the New World, perhaps the first such governor in all history, to be chosen by the colonists themselves in a free election. Thus, the Pilgrims manifested a strong independent spirit and attained a remarkable degree of self-government from the start, passing what laws seemed good to them, stubbornly resisting all outside control and interference.

After some exploring, the Pilgrims chose to settle at Plymouth. Here on Christmas Day, they began hurriedly to throw up crude bough shelters. Bitter winter weather slowed up operations. Then work stopped altogether as the company lay prostrate under the General Sickness—a powerful combination of scurvy, ship's fever, and pneumonia. Whole families were wiped out, and by the time spring came half the Pilgrims were in their graves.

But fortune favored the Pilgrims in two respects. First, they won and kept the friendship of the Indians so that they could work in peace. Second, they were adopted by a local Indian, the renowned Squanto, who served them as guide, interpreter, and counselor. He taught them how to plant corn and tend it, how to build fish traps, how to stalk game in the woods. He introduced them into the beaver trade, long the base of Plymouth's economy. The Pilgrims gratefully acknowledged that without Squanto and his native skills all would have perished.

During the summer of 1621 the Pilgrims worked hard in their fields, but their crops came to little. Still, they decided to hold a harvest festival—New England's first Thanksgiving. The natives were invited, and for three days the whites and Indians played games and feasted themselves on venison, roast duck, shellfish, corn bread, and wild fruits and berries—all washed down with wine made of the wild grape, praised by the Pilgrims as "very sweet and strong."

Soon after the feast thirty-five more Pilgrims arrived—mostly men—a welcome addition of strength. But as they had come with few supplies, there were just that many more mouths to feed. A long, hard, hungry winter followed, but work went on. Promised supplies from England did not arrive. Life seemed to hang on the next harvest, and that harvest was as poor as the first, which reduced the Pilgrims to the utmost extremity.

The colonists prowled the woods for game, which was scarce. They laboriously gathered acorns, berries, and strange wild roots. They scoured the shore for clams, crabs, and other shellfish. They kept their small fishing boats constantly at sea, no matter how rough the weather. But all this food was little enough, and men staggered with hunger as they went about their chores. Yet the Pilgrims heatedly denied that they were reduced to eating toads and dogs that died in the street, saying that the Lord kept His people from such extremities.

The situation was desperate when two ships arrived in the summer of 1623. These crafts brought ninety more people, doubling the population and the demand upon the scanty supplies. The newcomers were aghast at the sight of those at Plymouth, who looked like skeletons clad in rags. There seemed no hope for any of them, for a severe summer drought was burning up their fields and gardens. But the Saints still had faith, praying harder and harder. And, said they, behold another providence of God! Presently, it began to rain and gentle showers continued for weeks, reviving not only the wilted corn but their drooping spirits. Reaping a bumper harvest that year, Plymouth never again knew any general want or famine.

It was an extraordinary achievement. Within three years, by their tireless efforts and against almost insuperable odds, the Pilgrims had succeeded in firmly establishing themselves in the wilderness along a rather barren and inhospitable coast. The work had been achieved by less than ninety men, both Saints and Strangers, who had one strong bond in common. All were definitely lower class . . . as has been well said, they were from the cottages and not the castles of England. They were humble men, used to hard work, and there was not among them any idle gentleman of fashion, or any blue blood who expected to live off the labor of others.

Plymouth was not yet on easy street. But it was secure, and life there was not so glum and drab as commonly represented. The Pilgrims were not sour ascetics. They liked to eat, and they liked to drink, and being very fond of beer, never complained more bitterly of their hardships than when necessity reduced them to drinking water. Nor did they ordinarily dress in funereal blacks and grays. These colors were reserved for the Sabbath. At other times, they wore the bright Lincoln green and the rich russet browns traditional among the common people in England, and they passed no laws against gay apparel. One of the saintliest of the Saints, Ruling Elder William Brewster, had in his closet a red cap, a white cap, a quilted cap, a lace cap, a violet coat and "1 paire of greene drawers for wear on occasion." The Pilgrims, too, were a remarkably enlightened and humane people for their day . . . they hanged no witches, they hanged no Quakers, they took life for only one offense—murder.

Plymouth, though a mere village with less than two hundred people, remained the metropolis of New England down to 1630 when the great Puritan migration to the Massachusetts Bay Colony really began. These Puritans still nominally belonged to the Church of England, though they grew increasingly critical of its way, but they had never had the courage to defy the law and separate from that church as the Plymouth Saints had done.

The first Puritan groups arrived sick, and many died. An appeal for help went to Plymouth, and the Pilgrims sent them Deacon Samuel Fuller, their doctor, who did far better than he could have expected. The good deacon tended not only the ailing bodies of his patients, but their puzzled souls as well. He persuaded them to renounce the Church of England and adopt the Pilgrim Church with its fundamentally democratic doctrine and ways. Every congregation, the Pilgrims held, should be a self-governing republic. It should choose its pastor and other officers, with all communicants voting. The church should be stripped of elaborate ceremonials. It should be restored to its "ancient puritie," to the originally simple and democratic form of Biblical days. Scripture was the law in all things.

The day when the Massachusetts Puritans took over the Pilgrim meeting house was a most important one in the American Story. With the Pilgrim saddle on the Bay horse, as the phrase went, the Saints at Plymouth had cause to rejoice. This was their hour of greatest triumph.

But the coming of the Puritans brought problems, too. Plymouth could not hope to compete with the well-financed Massachusetts Bay Colony. In the year 1630 alone, a thousand people came to the Bay Colony, more than three times as many as had come to Plymouth in a decade. The center of gravity shifted to Boston, which quickly became the hub of New England, as it has since remained. Plymouth's heroic days were over, and her relative importance shrank, down to the day in 1692 when the Colony lost its independence and was absorbed much against its will by the stronger Massachusetts Bay Colony. From being the proud but poor capital of the Pilgrim empire, Plymouth sank to a mere county seat, and not an important one at that.

But Mother Plymouth's day was not done. She would enjoy greater fame and influence than in her heyday of temporal power. She had given the Pilgrim meeting house, the Congregational faith, to the Puritans, and the principles of that meeting house radiated far and wide from Massachusetts and the rest of New England as restless Yankees moved westward, contributing as much as any other single influence to shaping the faith, ideas, manners, morals, and ways of life of millions of Americans.

Democratic equalitarianism was implicit in the Pilgrim faith. Both the Pilgrims and the Puritans repeatedly sinned against this basic concept, but it was never killed and constantly grew stronger. It was the *Mayflower* pioneers, to their eternal honor, who first brought the fertile germ of democracy to our shores.

Why the Dutch Failed

RICHARD B. MORRIS

Plagues, starvation, and Indian wars seemed in the end only to strengthen the will to survive among the English in Virginia and New England. The Dutch, however, were equally courageous, enterprising, and persistent, yet their efforts at colonization in the New World were doomed to failure. Why? To Professor Richard B. Morris of Columbia University the answer stems from "three conspicuous reasons"; it is an answer which reveals, upon reflection, some of the most essential characteristics of that impulse in the New World to which one day we would refer (a bit sheepishly on occasion) as the American Spirit. But the impulse existed—it was vital, compelling, and, as the Dutch discovered, sometimes devastating. Professor Morris is distinguished for many books, among them the editorship of the Encyclopedia of American History, *and the co-editorship of the multi-volume* New American Nation Series.

WHEN in 1609 that persevering and imaginative English navigator, Henry Hudson, yielded to his mutinous crew and turned the prow of the *Half Moon* westward, he was to make history, but of a very different sort from that he had anticipated. Engaging in this voyage for the Dutch East India Company, Hudson was seeking a Northwest Passage to the Indies and the spices and wealth of Asia. Entering New York harbor late that summer, he believed the majestic river which empties into the Upper Bay to be a fjord or strait. Not until he reached the vicinity of what is now Albany, and had sent an expedition somewhat farther north, did he realize that his quest was fruitless. But several facts were learned as a result of this voyage. Hudson and his crew found that the lands around the mouth of the river which now bears his name offered attractive possibilities for settlement; that the great valley itself was wonderfully fertile; that, at its northern extremity, the fur trade with the Iroquois Indians could be profitable.

Although the Dutch East India Company quickly lost interest in this freshly explored region, other Dutchmen immediately began a series of exploring and trading voyages to what is now New York, voyages that ultimately led to permanent settlement. Most

40

important of these early adventurers was Adrian Block, who sailed to Manhattan in the year 1613, braved the perilous strait named by him "Hellegat" or Hell Gate, and discovered the Housatonic and Connecticut Rivers, Rhode Island, and Block Island. The very next year a group of Dutch shipowners secured a trading monopoly over the area, and a few years later a permanent trading post was established at Albany.

All the early 17th Century settlements on territory now the United States were made through the direct efforts of private business firms, and not through the initiative of governments. New Netherland was no exception. In 1621 the Dutch government chartered the Dutch West India Company to trade and colonize that area. The company had the power to select the governor, known as the director-general, although that official had to be confirmed by the Dutch government. This private company proceeded to draw up rules of government, according to which the colonists were divided into two classes—free colonists, who received transportation and maintenance for the first two years and could own their own homesteads; and bound farmers, who were required to work for stated terms on the company's own farms or bouweries, or on those of company officials.

In the year 1624 some thirty families, mostly French-speaking Walloons, were permanently settled in the colony. They were to be found either on what is today Governor's Island in the Upper Bay, or across the East River near the Navy Yard (Wallabout), or on the Delaware, or at Fort Nassau (later known as Fort Orange, the present site of Albany). Quite possibly, too, some settled on Manhattan Island. The first official establishment on that island resulted from the efforts of Peter Minuit, a Rhinelander of Dutch or Walloon ancestry. Minuit arrived in May, 1626, and proceeded to purchase Manhattan from the native Indian chiefs for baubles and trinkets worth sixty guilders, the equivalent of twenty-four dollars in pre-1933 U.S. currency.

Whereas the Dutch had now secured the first beachhead along the middle Atlantic coast, they were destined to fail in their efforts toward establishing thereon the foundations of a lasting colonial empire. For this failure three conspicuous reasons stand out— their niggardly land policy, their inept leadership, and their reluctance to grant the colonists the kind of self-government which the English settlers were to enjoy elsewhere along the North Atlantic coast.

Although the Dutch were shrewd businessmen, they failed to

capitalize on the greatest of all impulses toward the colonization of America—the desire of the underprivileged people of Europe to secure a piece of land which they could call their own. A dramatic demonstration of their attempt to put the hands of the clock back was furnished by the Charter of Freedoms and Exemptions of 1629. Under this agreement the Dutch West India Company was empowered to grant those transporting fifty settlers huge estates fronting sixteen miles along rivers and extending inland as far as settlement would permit. The grantees were to be called patroons, and they were given feudal rights, including the right to hold courts as well as exemption from taxation for eight years. The Company immediately proceeded to grant five patroonships, but only one was successfully established. That was the patroonship of Rensselaerswyck, near Albany, granted to an Amsterdam diamond and gold merchant named Kiliaen Van Rensselaer, who ruled as an absentee proprietor over tenants holding perpetual leaseholds under him. Interestingly enough, that patroonship survived the English conquest of New Netherland and the social upheaval of the American Revolution. In fact, it was only terminated as a result of the Antirent War which raged in upstate New York from 1839 to 1846. The legislature was spurred by these struggles to curb perpetual leases and gradually replace them with fee-simple tenure.

But people did not flock to New Netherland to work in servitude to others. To lure the landless peasantry to the colony, a new Charter of Freedoms and Exemptions was issued in 1640. By its terms modest grants of two hundred acres were to be given those transporting five persons. However, the basic principle of free land to settlers, a principle upon which New England was founded, was never adopted in Dutch New Netherland nor in the successor colony of English New York.

A second roadblock to successful colonization was presented by the personality and character of the directors-general whom the Dutch West India Company sent to America to govern the colony. Immortalized by Washington Irving in his *Knickerbocker History of New York,* they were a quarrelsome, arrogant lot. With the exception of the irascible but able Stuyvesant, they put self-interest ahead of the public good. Peter Minuit has been described as a kind of early Dutch Aaron Burr, brilliant and unscrupulous, who was suspected of being too friendly to the patroons. When recalled, he quit the Dutch service and persuaded the Swedes to entrust him with the task of settling a colony for them on the Dela-

ware. A lover of skins and the sea, he finally went down with a
merchantman when it was trapped in a storm off the West Indies.

Following Minuit, a stopgap appointee was replaced by youth-
ful Wouter Van Twiller, who was fresh from a clerk's desk in the
Dutch West India House. His main qualification for the post seems
to have been the fact that he was the nephew of Van Rensselaer.
Surrounded by hostile officials, Van Twiller's vanity, weakness,
and ties to the patroon proved his undoing. In 1637 he was succeeded by William Kiefft, an Amsterdam merchant, who was expected to raise the tone of public morality and allow no special
favors to the patroon. But Kiefft's great weakness was his failure to
understand the Indians of the lower Hudson Valley who had come
to feel themselves hemmed in on all sides.

The Dutch had established a post on the Connecticut River, the
English had moved into Westchester and onto Long Island, and
colonization of the Jersey side of the Hudson and of Staten Island
was being pushed. Meanwhile the Iroquois in the north proved an
even greater threat to the Indians of New Netherland. In 1643,
the Mohawks, armed by traders at Rensselaerswyck and Fort
Orange, attacked the Indians of the lower Hudson and forced
them to seek refuge among the Dutch in Jersey and Manhattan.
In a treacherous attack launched by Kiefft's men, many of these
refugees were slaughtered. The inevitable Indian reprisals
brought terror and destruction to outlying Dutch settlements in
Westchester, on Long Island, and along the west bank of the Hudson. Peace was finally established, but not before most of the settlers south of Albany had retired behind a wall built across Manhattan Island. A thoroughly hated and discredited man, Kiefft was
replaced in 1646 by the tenacious and colorful one-legged Dutch
hero, Peter Stuyvesant.

A third basic reason for the breakdown of the Dutch colonial
effort was the failure of the authorities to recognize the positive
values of granting self-government, and their inveterate hostility
to anything that smacked of democracy. At the height of the
Indian reprisals Kiefft had been forced to seek counsel first from
a group of men called "The Twelve," and then from a group of
Eight chosen by the burghers and farmers. The opposition of the
latter group brought about his downfall. Stuyvesant found it expe-
dient to consent to an election of a group of eighteen men from
the Dutch householders of Manhattan, Brooklyn, and Flatlands,
who in turn chose Nine to advise the governor and council. When
The Nine demanded local self-government, Stuyvesant, on orders

from the Company, proclaimed New Amsterdam a municipality in 1653. In addition to the sessions of The Nine, Stuyvesant called three assemblies from towns adjacent to New Amsterdam. The first met during the Anglo-Dutch War in 1653,[2] the other two while the colony was in its last crisis, but this was a policy of too little and too late. The failure to confer broad legislative powers upon the representatives of the people certainly contributed to the gradual crumbling of the colony's morale.

Meantime the English had come to regard the Dutch beachhead as blocking their westward expansion and interfering with the enforcement of their trade laws. A task force of four English frigates reached New York harbor on August 29, 1664. Despite the frenzied efforts of Stuyvesant to rally support from the populace, he was obliged to surrender on September 7. Save for a brief period during 1673–74 when the Dutch, following the outbreak of another Anglo-Dutch war, reoccupied New York, the English crown retained control of the colony until the evacuation of the British army in 1783.

But Father Knickerbocker's cultural grip upon the colony persisted long after Dutch political rule had ended. So far as they could the Dutchmen in the Hudson Valley had duplicated the life of Holland. They had built their towns on the models of Amsterdam and Utrecht. They had established Dutch law, the Dutch Reformed Church, and the Dutch language, which continued to be spoken for generations after the area came under English rule. In New York City its use was largely abandoned by the eve of the Revolution, but the Dutch tongue lingered on well into the 19th Century along the upper Hudson Valley and among the Jersey Dutch in the Raritan and Hackensack Valleys.

The great fire which swept lower Manhattan in the fall of 1776 accomplished in a few hours what the English had not been able to do in a century. Gone was the New Amsterdam of Minuit, Kiefft, and Stuyvesant, gone the vividly tiled roofs, the stepped gables,

[2] The Anglo-Dutch Wars, growing out of commercial jealousies, first touch the New World in 1652–54; on June 30 of the latter year, recruits enlisted in New England are on the point of leaving Boston for New Amsterdam when news comes of peace between England and Holland. Again in 1664 hostilities are resumed and New Netherland is surrendered to the English and New Amsterdam is renamed New York. The usual dates of the Second Anglo-Dutch War, however, are 1665–67, and conclude with New Netherland surrendered to the English by the Treaty of Breda. A third Anglo-Dutch War is dated 1672–74, sees New York retaken from the English on July 30, 1673, but lost forever by the treaty ending this conflict.

the quaint and clean brick houses, the picturesque windmills. But no conflagration could destroy the Dutch spirit, a spirit exemplified by such great family names as the Schuylers, the Roosevelts, the De Peysters, and the Brevoorts. Into that great colonial melting pot which was New York poured the culture of the English, the Scots, the Scandinavians, the French, the Walloons, and the Jews, along with the Dutch. It was that cosmopolitan and liberal spirit which characterized both Dutch New Netherland and English New York that has left its indelible stamp upon the life and times of all later New Yorkers.

William Penn, Founder of Colonies

CARL BRIDENBAUGH

Following the conquest of New Netherland, the Duke of York granted to John Lord Berkeley and Sir George Carteret the region between the Hudson and Delaware Rivers. Ten years later Lord Berkeley sold his property rights to Edward Byllynge and John Fenwick, two English Quakers. Shortly thereafter the first Quaker settlement in New Jersey was founded at Salem; and a few months later Byllynge conveyed his rights in West Jersey to three Quakers, one of whom was William Penn.

For two decades Quakers in the colonies had led a troubled existence. When members of the sect reached Boston in 1656, they were quickly imprisoned or banished, and that year Connecticut passed a law to fine and then harry them out of the land. Five Quakers who arrived in New Amsterdam in 1657 fared no better before the anger of Governor Stuyvesant, who punished them harshly and banished them to Rhode Island (that shameless roost of rebels that already had taken a strong stand in favor of religious liberty). In the fall of 1658 the New England Confederation ordered the expulsion of Quakers, and death if they returned; and in 1660 Quaker Mary Dyer, who dared to reappear in Boston, was hanged for her courage.

Actually the period that an English Quaker named William Penn spent in America was brief; his impact upon the country could not be measured in time. Carl Bridenbaugh, who is Margaret Byrne Professor of American History at the University of

*California at Berkeley, and who was the first director of the Insti-
tute of Early American History and Culture at Williamsburg,
Virginia, writes of the great Quaker founder of colonies with the
affectionate warmth that even to this day characterizes the native-
born Pennsylvanian when he thinks of Penn.*

IT TOOK all kinds of people to make America. Most of them were
humble folk led by such sturdy members of the middle class as
Captain John Smith and John Rolfe of Virginia, and Miles Standish and William Bradford of Plymouth. Because of this fact, the
story of the New World called America is ordinarily a chronicle
of plain people seeking—and often achieving—a better life here
than the one they had known in the Old World. Or of persecuted
Pilgrims, Puritans, and Quakers seeking to establish a godly society wherein they might flourish spiritually and also get rich in
the Lord's service. But before these people could even set foot
on the western shores of the Atlantic, they had to have the encouragement and financial support of those whom the age labeled
the better sort—men of position and wealth, whose vision and
place in life enabled them to found and develop new plantations in
America.

No individual founder of a colony contributed more fruitfully
toward the noble end of assisting English men and women in the
attainment of their goal of a better life than William Penn. In
order to gauge with any degree of accuracy the importance and extent of William Penn's influence on American life and ideals, it is
essential that we first view against his Old World background this
man who has, with much reason, been called the greatest Englishman and one of the leading Europeans of the 17th Century. His
inheritance, education, and early experience combined to produce
the ideas and drives that made him also the foremost founder of
English colonies.

No humble commoner was William Penn. He was an aristocrat,
albeit a curious one; he was a virtually unique aristocrat to
emerge from the court life of that Restoration England which we
ordinarily associate with gaiety and licentiousness, with Rochester,
Shaftesbury, Charles himself, and Nell Gwyn, and with the daring
plays of Wycherly and Congreve. The son of Admiral Sir William
Penn grew to manhood like other young gentlemen. Athletic,
handsome, courtly in manner, he readily won friendship, respect,
and lasting influence in high places. That love of comfort and dig-

nified magnifience which accompanies the possessor of large landed estates became a part of the way of life to which he aspired, and long association with those who governed England afforded him the insights and supplied the knowledge that made him develop into a statesman of the first rank. Two years at Oxford, a sojourn at the Academy of Saumur in France, and a Grand Tour of the Continent provided William Penn with an education rivaled by few of his contemporaries, one which he topped off by naval service under his father and militia duty in Ireland. In these respects, Penn was a thoroughgoing product of his class—the gentry—and of his times.

But there were other sides of life and other classes of people in Restoration England, and, unlike most gentlemen, William Penn came to know these intimately too. Always serious, he found the easy way of conformity to the creed of the Church of England, into which he had been born, inadequate to his religious needs. For William Penn was a mystic, and the chance that brought him into contact with Thomas Loe, the Quaker preacher, imparted to him both a new faith—that of the persecuted Society of Friends —and a noble purpose in life.

Penn turned his back on the court, although not upon such close friends as James, Duke of York, and entered upon a career of preaching and writing to advance the teachings of the Quakers and to promote acceptance of the doctrines of political liberalism. He quickly became a powerful advocate of freedom of conscience, which progressed to religious toleration, and an incisive critic of current frivolity and luxury, an opponent of economic oppression of the many by the few, and, by virtue of his legal training at Lincoln's Inn, a successful defender of the security and property of Englishmen. In the famous Bushell's Case of 1670, for example, William Penn provided the classic argument for the freedom of juries from the dictation of judges. While in prison for his religious convictions, he wrote *No Cross, No Crown*, eloquently setting forth many of the principles we are likely to think of as strictly American. Between 1675 and 1680, Penn made several trips as a Quaker missionary to Holland and Germany; and in England he urged the Friends, without success, to enter politics and to work for liberal government. During these years he published several excellent political pamphlets exposing and condemning such abuses as uncontrolled Parliamentary elections. In this new phase of his life, he is again seen as a true child of his day, for Restoration England had also its sober and ideal aspects.

Thus by the age of thirty-three, when William Penn first became interested in America, his great convictions had been formed and developed. The opportunity to put them into effect presented itself when he was made one of the trustees to manage the property of West New Jersey, which the Society of Friends had acquired as a refuge for its members. In 1677, Burlington was founded under a charter of "Laws, Concessions, and Agreements" largely drawn up by Penn, guaranteeing religious freedom with the statement that "no Men, nor number of Men upon Earth, hath Power or Authority to rule over Men's Consciences in religious Matters." This instrument secured many specific "Fundamental Rights" of persons and property to the settlers, but, more portentous than these clauses was the liberal sentiment suffusing the whole, thereby proving, as Penn and his associates said of New Jersey, that "there we lay a foundation for after ages to understand their liberty as men and Christians, . . . for we put the power in the people." At his first opportunity, this privileged aristocrat had written his political liberalism into fundamental law and put it into practice in a new society. From such roots, indeed, freedom and its sister democracy could readily grow.

An even greater invitation to practical politics came to the Quaker statesman in 1681, when Charles II paid a long-standing debt to Admiral Penn by granting the son a huge tract of land north of Maryland. He named it Pennsylvania or Penn's Woods in honor of the late naval hero. The following year, William Penn's friend, the Duke of York (soon to be James II) transferred the territory known as Delaware to him. Now Penn could work out all of his social and political ideas in what he hopefully called a Holy Experiment. People of any faith, but especially his coreligionists, might henceforth dwell and worship there in peace. A society composed of great estates operated by landed gentlemen like himself could be nicely balanced by a numerous yeomanry tilling small farms acquired from Penn as proprietor at a very small cost; and a government of his own devising, liberal and representative of all ranks, could assure the common weal and stand as a model to all Christendom. This political and economic independence he embodied in a "Frame of Government" or constitution which he issued in 1682. It was not so democratic as the New Jersey "Concessions" because it made provisions for the landed gentry; but it did guarantee all fundamental liberties. The preface stated that "any Government is free to the People under it (whatever the Frame) where the Laws rule and the People are a

Party to those Laws." And the subsequent history of Pennsylvania and Delaware bore him out.

William Penn crossed to his colonies in 1682 and began at once the construction of a great estate on the Delaware above Bristol, which he named Pennsbury. Although he remained only twenty-two months, he saw to the laying out of Philadelphia, the sound and permanent establishing of the government, the attracting, by extraordinarily skillful advertising, of thousands of colonists from Holland and Ireland as well as from England, and the concluding of a lasting peace with the Indians. In striking contrast to these just and friendly arrangements with the Indians was the renewal of persecution of the Quakers in England, which forced his return in 1684.

Back home Penn persuaded James II to release 1,200 Quakers from prison, but his friendship with the Roman Catholic monarch led to the charges in 1689 that Penn was a Jesuit in disguise, and accordingly he was listed as a subversive when he applauded the King's Declaration of Indulgence or toleration, which he himself had strongly urged on James. From 1692 to 1694 Penn lost his governorship of Pennsylvania, but eventually he was cleared of all suspicion of treasonable activities. There never was the slightest case against him; indeed, the entire affair has a most familiar modern ring to it—that of guilt by association.

Undaunted by the treatment accorded by public authorities, Penn, in 1693, focused his attention on another great tenet of his sect, the prevention of war. He published an *Essay towards the Present and Future Peace,* which anticipated by more than two centuries an organization like the United Nations to compose international disputes before they reach the point of open hostilities. In 1697 he made the first proposal to join the English colonies for common purpose in his *Plan of Union.* Although these projects came to naught, they clearly demonstrate the broad wisdom and truly great statesmanship of the man and prove him to have been far in advance of his contemporaries.

From 1699 to 1701 the proprietor again visited his colonies, and in the latter year gave them a more liberal charter. This act completed his career as a constructive colonizer and liberal governor of provinces. That Pennsylvanians, Quaker and others, never quite lived in the state of brotherly love was not due to any lack of generosity on his part. "I am sorry at heart for your animosities . . . ," he once cried out. "For the love of God, me, and the poor country, be not so governmentish, so noisy, and open, in your dissatisfactions."

In all, William Penn spent less than four years in the colonies. Yet his influence on their development in his day and his legacy to the future United States were as important a contribution as that made by any settler or other English promoter of the 17th Century. He shared prominently in establishing three colonies— New Jersey, Delaware, and Pennsylvania. He saw that humble folk got a chance to start their lives anew under favorable conditions; he practiced and preached religious freedom; he was a great humanitarian in an inhumane age; and he wrought so well that his ideals have in the long course of time become primary ingredients in the tradition of democracy in America. When we think of William Penn, we ought to visualize him both as the lord of now-restored Pennsbury, landing at the foot of his garden from the barge in which his servants rowed him up the Delaware from his "greene countrie Towne," and also as the responsible aristocratic champion of ordinary people, as exemplified by the statue atop Philadelphia's City Hall. Penn's hand rests on an open book wherein we read: "Lo, I go to prepare a place for thee."

Roger Williams, a Minority of One

MAX SAVELLE

The true revolutionist in America often has been the solid citizen with firm conservative background, and surely Roger Williams, educated at London's Charterhouse School and at Cambridge University, fell within that definition. In his mid-twenties this stalwart Puritan was ordained a minister, but the concept of religious tolerance and liberty that colored his sermons forced him to flee an England that stubbornly, sternly insisted upon conformity to the established church. So one of the greatest of our colonial statesmen—who would found the first genuinely democratic state of modern times and provide in large measure a model for the country that one day would be called the United States of America—reached Salem. As much as anything, Williams's belief that the Massachusetts Bay Company should have paid the Indians for their lands provided a practical reason for his banish-

*ment. A cold winter spent among the Narragansetts revealed the
stature of Williams the leader—the man who could mend differences between tribes, who was a beloved peacemaker and trusted
friend. The Indians gave him land on which to remain, and under
his guidance tiny Rhode Island became the atom that shattered
the philosophical foundations of the Old World. It is this chapter
in the American Story that we are now told by Max Savelle, professor of American History at the University of Washington, a
former Fulbright fellow, and the author of several authoritative
works about the colonial period.*

ROGER WILLIAMS was the true morning star in the galaxy of the
American great. For not only was he the most brilliant architect
among the builders of the colonial societies that were to become
the United States of America, but in him there flamed those ideals
of individual freedom and social democracy that were to inspire
this new people and make it unique among the nations of the
world.

Yet to most of the men of his own generation, Williams was a
dangerous, subversive, revolutionary radical. He had been welcomed to Massachusetts in 1631 as one of the most brilliant and
promising young dissenters fleeing the Anglican persecution—as,
indeed, he was. But almost immediately the leaders of the colony
had discovered that, if he was a brilliant dissenter from the
Anglican way in England, he was just as irrepressible a dissenter
and critic in America. So they "investigated" him, and the Massachusetts General Court—which at that time was both legislature
and court—found that he was spreading "newe and dangerous
opinions, against the authoritie of magistrates." On September 13,
1635, therefore, the General Court ordered that he be banished
from Massachusetts.

Why was it that the government and the leaders of Massachusetts considered Williams so dangerous?

It was because, by temperament and by conviction, Williams
was a nonconformist and a courageous, trenchant critic of the
status quo in Massachusetts. It was because, if they had allowed
this unique radical to continue to spread his "newe and dangerous
opinions," their own work would be overthrown.

The first of the revolutionary convictions that distinguished
Roger Williams from most of his contemporaries was his highly
positive religious and intellectual individualism. For in that age,

religious conformity was the general rule. Even the Puritans who founded Massachusetts took it for granted; although they had fled England to escape having to conform to the Church of England, when they came to America they set up in Massachusetts a religion-dominated state even more authoritarian and even less tolerant of dissenters than the England from which they had fled. Sincerely convinced that they knew exactly what God wished them to do, they had made it a requirement that to be a full-fledged "freeman," or citizen with the right to vote, a man had first to be a member of a Puritan congregation. Then they had required all the colonists, whether "freemen" or not, to take an oath of submission to the regime they had created, and to attend church regularly.

To Williams, such religious regimentation, such use of the church as a foundation and support for the state, was intolerable. For him, the most precious privilege of any man or woman was that of worshiping God in his own way. He even stopped trying to convert the Indians, when he apparently became convinced that their religious practices were their own way of worshiping God, and that God would not reject such worship. And in his own personal religion, he seems to have moved from being a Puritan Anglican, to become first a Separatist, then a Baptist, and finally a Seeker, always moving away from set religious rules and forms toward complete simplicity and directness in his relationship, as an individual, with his God.

It was this point of individual religious freedom that Williams most fiercely defended in his famous pamphlet, *The Bloudy Tenent of Persecution for the Cause of Conscience* (1644). How ghastly and unbelievable, he cried, was the damage done and the number of innocent human beings slaughtered in the effort to make men and women worship God in some certain way!

But Williams's dissent was not, by any means, confined to his rebellion against religious regimentation. For he criticized the leaders of the colony on economic and political grounds as well. In the first place, he criticized the builders of the Massachusetts colony on the ground that they had taken the Indians' lands without permission and without payment—a criticism that was both economic and moral. At the same time, he criticized the identification of the Puritan church with the government, especially the use of the government to enforce the Ten Commandments as part of the colony's basic law, along with the decisions of the meetings of preachers, called "synods." The first he criticized because the government was enforcing religion, and the second because it interfered with the freedom of the separate congregations to believe and teach without dictation or interference from anybody. He also criticized the law requiring everybody to go to church and the requirement of the oath of loyalty because it commanded loyalty to a religious system in which many of the people did not heartily concur.

Religion, or the enforcement of a certain form of religion, is none of the government's business, Williams proclaimed. And since men are bound to differ from each other in what they believe, he said,

> The permission of other consciences and worships than a state professeth, only can (according to God) procure a firme and lasting peace, (good assurance being taken according to the wisdome of the civill state for uniformity of civil obedience from all sorts of men). . . . True civility and Christianity may both flourish in a state or Kingdome, notwithstanding the permission of divers and contrary consciences, Jew or Gentile.

Thus Williams's second basic idea, which followed logically from the first, was the double idea of separation of church and state and complete toleration, by the government, of all sorts of religion.

Yet significant as these two ideas were for the future growth of the American way of life, of still greater significance, if possible, was Williams's philosophy of democracy, political as well as religious. Already, while he was a pastor at Salem, he had begun to teach his congregation the ideals and practices of democracy. But by the time he was banished, he was ready to apply his democracy to government as well as to church affairs. Thus, if as a Seeker he was an extreme individualist in religion, as a political philosopher his equally strong political individualism made him a democrat in politics (small "d").

He believed that every individual man has certain rights by natural law; that government is created by a group of individuals bound together by what was then called a "social compact"; and that the government, created by the people, is always their servant, responsible to them, and can be changed whenever they wish.

This was strong doctrine for those days. Some political philosophers, such as Williams's contemporary, Thomas Hobbes, were indeed beginning to explain the origin of the state as derived from the people in terms of some sort of "social compact." But almost none, as yet, had been so bold as to proclaim that since the people created the government they could also limit it or change it at will.

How could the founders and leaders of Massachusetts tolerate such a man?

The state they had set up tolerated only one form of religion, and it forced all the people to conform to it. There was no room for religious individualism in Massachusetts Bay. Their state was identified with the church; in fact, it was impossible to say whether the church was an arm of the state or the state was an arm of the church. Far from admitting the principle of the separation of church and state, the Massachusetts leaders believed with most of their contemporaries that everybody in a state should worship alike. Anybody who insisted upon some other form of religion must stay away from Massachusetts, and they made no bones about it.

Finally, the Massachusetts government was anything but democratic. Its leaders abhorred democracy; their system concentrated political power in the hands of a select, self-appointed few; and its will was imposed upon the people as authoritative, even absolute. The idea that the people could change the form of the government was to them unthinkably revolutionary.

What would happen to the "Godly Commonwealth" of Massachusetts Bay if Williams's ideas of religious individualism, of separation of church and state, and of an elementary democracy were allowed to get a foothold there? Their utopia would be destroyed. The state they had built would be overthrown. Worst of all, such a catastrophe would be a destruction not only of their work, but of God's. They simply could not tolerate him. So they banished him.

In the winter of 1636 Williams made his way to Narragansett Bay and there, having bought the land from the Indians, he and his followers built the town of Providence. There they founded their society on the principles for which Williams had fought. Each head of a family was to have an equal voice with all the others in the government. In religion, every individual was to be completely free to worship as he thought best; and there was a complete separation of church and state. The activities of the state were strictly limited to civil affairs.

In 1647, when the town of Providence united with the towns of Warwick, Portsmouth, and Newport to form the colony of Rhode Island, these principles were written into the constitution of the colony, establishing "a government held by the free and voluntarie consent of all, or the greater parte of the free inhabitants," and providing for freedom of conscience and separation of church and state. Thus Rhode Island, under the inspiration and guidance of Roger Williams, became the great pilot experiment in American democracy and religious toleration.

The men who banished Roger Williams from Massachusetts were sincere and godly men. But their faces were turned backward, and they stood for religious regimentation, for the identification of the church with the state, and for absolute, authoritarian government from above. Given their convictions, they had, logically, to get rid of him. Yet the passage of time has shown that they were wrong and he was right, that the nation yet to rise upon the foundations they were unwittingly laying would follow the plan that Williams laid down, and not theirs.

America has much for which to thank Roger Williams: for his religious and intellectual individualism, for his principles of religious toleration and the separation of church and state, and for the precious principle of democracy as a way of life. Above all, perhaps, America—and other democratic peoples everywhere—may be deeply grateful to him for his courage—the courage to think straight and to fight for the ideals he knew were right, even though he were in a minority of one; the courage to face persecution, banishment, and suffering for his convictions; and the courage to build firmly the first society in the world dedicated to the proposition that all men are free and equal.

A Red Sinking Sun

THOMAS J. WERTENBAKER

In Virginia, a century before the Declaration of Independence, another Englishman of impeccable conservative background fired what seems, in the imaginative view of history, to have been the opening shot of the American Revolution. Indian massacres and oppressive taxation were the immediate causes that drove Nathaniel Bacon and his Virginia rebels toward this "false dawn" of American freedom, but there were deeper passions stirring in the land that led Bacon, the uncommon aristocrat, to champion

the common man. With the publication in 1940 of Torchbearer of
the Revolution, *Thomas J. Wertenbaker rescued this hero of that
prophetic struggle of 1676 and gave him a proper and deserved
focus in the American Story. Professor Wertenbaker began his
brilliant career as a member of the Princeton University faculty
in 1910 and retired from active teaching in 1947; he has served as
visiting professor at many educational institutions, including
Munich and Oxford.*

I⊤ is strange that the leader of the first American revolt against
English authority was a young English aristocrat who lived in
America less than three years. Nathaniel Bacon was born January
2, 1647, at Friston Hall, Suffolk, England, the only son of a wealthy
squire. Surrounded by every luxury, the favorite of his aunt and
sisters, accustomed to the homage of servants and tenants, he little
dreamed that he was destined to lead a desperate rebellion in far-
off Virginia.

This rebellion grew out of the misgovernment of the King's governor, Sir William Berkeley. Berkeley had been a liberal and
popular executive during his first term of office. But when he was
driven out by the English Civil War he became the opponent of
anything tending to self-government. With the restoration of
Charles II to the throne, Berkeley again became governor of Virginia, and soon changed into a petty despot whose chief aim was
to build up a system of personal rule by corrupting the Lower
House of the Assembly through the use of the appointing power.
When the Burgesses met in the little statehouse at Jamestown in
1661 the governor made clear that they were the objects of his
favor. This man he made a collector of taxes, this one a sheriff, this
one a justice of the peace, this one a captain in the militia. To one
or two he hinted at a seat in that august body, the Council of State.
The Burgesses were duly grateful, and henceforth voted for whatever Sir William proposed.

What he proposed was no less than tyranny. Vast areas of un-
occupied land were granted to his favorites, and the taxes which
bore down with crushing weight upon the poor were levied in
part for their private benefit. The estates of Sir William's enemies were confiscated. Bacon declared that the common people
were "curbed and oppressed . . . in all manner of ways," and
that the perpetual breach of laws, prosecutions, excuses, and eva-
sions showed that things were carried "as if it were but to play a

booty, game, or divide a spoil." Had the governor called for a new election, the men who had thus betrayed their trust would have been kicked out in short order. But Berkeley, having obtained a subservient House, continued it for no less than sixteen years by extending it in office from year to year. As Bacon pointed out: "Consider what hope there is of redress in appealing to the very persons our complaints do accuse."

After years of oppression the people turned their thoughts to open resistance. Many took down weapons from their places on the wall in preparation for a march on Jamestown. "They speak openly that they are in the nature of slaves, so that the hearts of the greatest part of them are taken away from his Majesty," said one observer. Twice they assembled in arms, and were with difficulty persuaded to disperse.

Though misrule and the repression of liberty were the fundamental causes of Bacon's Rebellion, the occasion which touched it off was an Indian war. In the summer of 1675 hostilities broke out between the English and the Susquehannocks, who had entrenched themselves on the north bank of the Potomac, opposite the site of Mt. Vernon. When a detachment of Marylanders and Virginians forced the Indians to evacuate their fort, they crossed the river in canoes and carried fire and death through the Virginia frontier. Scores of helpless men, women, and children were captured and tortured to death. As the fugitives from the Indian terror streamed into the older settlements, the cry went up for an immediate expedition of revenge. And when Governor Berkeley refused, the people decided to take matters into their own hands.

This uprising differed from the others in that now the people had a leader. When Nathaniel Bacon migrated with his wife to Virginia, Berkeley did his best to win Bacon's support. Although Bacon was a mere boy in years, Berkeley gave him the most important post in the colony next to the governorship itself, a seat in the Council of State. But Bacon was unhappy from the first in Sir William's official family, and frequently absented himself from the meetings. So, when the small farmers of the frontier assembled in arms and asked him to be their commander, Bacon defied Berkeley's orders by leading them out against the Indians.

When the governor heard of Bacon's action he was so infuriated that he sent out a call for troops to intercept him. But Bacon's men had disappeared into the forest. Berkeley had to content himself with proclaiming Bacon a rebel and suspending him from his offices, though he thought it wise to appease the people by dissolving the old Assembly and calling for a new election. In the meanwhile, Bacon had won a victory over the Indians on an island in the Roanoke River and was on his way back to the settlements. When he arrived, the people of his country rewarded him by electing him one of their Burgesses. This action proved unwise, for though he was guarded by an armed band when he went down to take his seat, he was arrested and brought before the governor. Berkeley again tried to win Bacon over by pardoning him and restoring him to his seat in the Council, but he refused to give him a commission to continue the war against the Indians.

Bacon went back to the frontier and, after collecting a force of several hundred men, marched on Jamestown. Here he forced Berkeley to give him a commission, and the Assembly to pass a series of laws which struck at the roots of the governor's power. Councillors were no longer to be exempt from taxation; officials must not charge for their services more than the fees prescribed by law; the justices of the peace were to be restrained in assessing taxes; sheriffs were not to succeed themselves; no man was to hold more than one public office at a time. Most important of all was a law, at least a century and a half in advance of its time, giving the right to vote to all freemen. Having seen these remarkable laws through the Assembly, and having forced Berkeley to sign them, Bacon marched away with his ragged army to repel new Indian attacks. When he heard that Berkeley had again proclaimed him a traitor and was trying desperately to raise an army to fight him, Bacon came storming back. The governor with a few of his followers already had fled across Chesapeake Bay to the eastern shore.

Civil war ensued. Many leading planters took their indentured servants and followed Berkeley, so that the governor eventually had a force of considerable size. He also strengthened himself enormously when he secured a number of merchant ships and armed them, thus making himself master of the network of waterways of eastern Virginia. But on the mainland, Bacon remained in control. When Sir William sailed up the James and took possession of Jamestown, the rebels streamed down and forced him to retire. They then deliberately burned the town, with its picturesque church, the old statehouse, and the cluster of cottages, to keep him from returning.

Berkeley took advantage of his "sea power" to make a series of raids on Bacon's outposts which stretched along the banks of the great Virginia rivers. When these raids had netted a number of captives, the merciless old man held a Council of War and sentenced them to death. The first martyr to the cause of American freedom was Thomas Hansford.[3] As he stood on the scaffold, he made a brief address denying that he was a rebel and swearing that he died a lover of his country.

In the meanwhile, Charles II had learned of the "uproars" in the colony and sent an army to restore peace. Bacon was resolved to fight on. "May not five hundred Virginians beat them," he asked, "we having the same advantages against them the Indians have against us?" But he was destined not to fight the redcoats. Worn out by his forced marches, hunger, sleeping in the open under the forest trees, exposure to heavy rains, violent disputes, and anxieties, he became ill and died. His faithful followers, fearing that the governor might expose the body on the gibbet, buried it secretly; no one knows where.

> While none shall dare his obsequies to sing
> In deserv'd measures, until time shall bring
> Truth crown'd with freedom, and from danger free,
> To sound his praises to posterity.

The rebellion continued for several months after Bacon's death, but the result was inevitable. As the rebel forces melted away, some of the leaders fled into the forest and were never heard of again. A harder fate awaited the others. They were captured, dragged before Sir William, given hasty trials, and hanged. Most of them merely bowed their heads before a cruel fate. One man, Anthony Arnold, boldly defended the right of the people to resist oppression and injustice. Kings had no right but what they got by conquest and the sword, he said.[4] For this the court ordered that he be hanged in chains. When Charles II heard of these wholesale executions he was reported to have remarked to his courtiers: "That old fool has hanged more men in that naked country than I for the murder of my father."

[3] Hansford declared that he had taken up arms only for the defense of Virginia against the Indians. A passionate plea "that he might be shot like a soldier and not hanged like a dog" failed to move Sir William, who saw Hansford simply as "a rebel taken in arms against the King." Wertenbaker, Thomas J.: *Torchbearer of the Revolution*, pp. 187–88.

[4] It was Arnold's contention that "he who can by force of the sword deprive them [Kings] thereof has as good and just a title to them as the King himself." To the horror of those who listened, Arnold declared: "If the King should deny to do me right I would think no more of it to sheath my sword in his heart or bowels than of my mortal enemies." *Ibid.*, p. 205.

The more one studies Bacon's Rebellion, the more its kinship with the American Revolution becomes apparent. As the Sugar Act brought distress in 1764, so the Navigation Acts undermined prosperity in Virginia a century before. As the Stamp Act threatened representative government by wresting the control of taxation from the Assemblies, so it was Berkeley's corruption which turned representative government into a farce in Virginia. As the Revolution was partly a civil war, so the uprising in Virginia found class arrayed against class, and to some extent, section against section.

Nathaniel Bacon has never received the recognition due him as a true American patriot. One looks in vain for his statue at Jamestown, or Richmond. We have no right to ignore his memory merely because the movement he championed ended in failure. Let us not forget that though the sun of liberty sank blood red across the James as one patriot after the other went to the gallows, it was the same sun which rose a century later to shine down upon the triumph of the man we call the Father of his Country.

TWO

Toward a

Common Cause

TWO CENTURIES after Columbus had stumbled upon the New World, colonial life had assumed a distinct definition. Patterns of group motivation, of group behavior, of group thought, of group necessity were beginning to shape an American individuality. The efforts of English kings to force upon their subjects acceptance of the teachings of the Church of England had been a powerful colonizing force among Puritans, Quakers, Baptists, and Separatists; and after 1680 the same force operated in France, where Huguenots preferred religious peace in the wilderness to Catholic persecution at home; and in Germany, where the members of many sects sought a land that would allow them to separate church and state.

Coupled with this intellectual revolt was an equally strong desire to find in the New World an economic freedom that the Old World no longer could provide. For the lower and middle classes, England in the 17th and 18th Century offered a miserable standard of living; conditions were even worse in Germany, where wars had wasted the land and created a vast tax burden; large numbers of Rhinelanders, unable to secure work, emigrated to Pennsylvania; and the Scotch-Irish, finding their woolen industry ruined by an England that stopped at no end to crush competition, fled overseas to escape a bleak, impoverished future.

In essence, what these colonists were seeking through religious

61

and economic freedom would one day be described as man's inalienable right to life, liberty and the pursuit of happiness; and
this search for political freedom was also an intrinsic part of the
motivating force behind the development of the New World.
Thus, leaders like William Penn, Roger Williams, and Nathaniel
Bacon were truly representative men; and so, too, at the other
extreme, was stubborn and vindictive Governor Berkeley, who
clung to an ideal of government and society that hated to admit its
prime had passed and age had hardened its arteries. Before the
struggle between the ideals of the Old World and the New could
be consummated, a century had still to pass after Bacon's Rebellion.

Colonial America had its classes, ranging from the aristocratic
plantation owner to the indentured servant and the captive
slave. But the New World bred a belief (of which Benjamin Franklin was the ardent spokesman and glowing example) that energy
and ability could achieve miracles in altering these barriers among
freemen. People worked hard in Colonial America. By 17th and
18th Century standards they built good towns and cultivated
excellent farms. In such crafts as furnituremaking, glassware,
metalware, clockmaking, and needlework, the colonial level of
achievement was impressive; as early as 1648 taxation was used
in Dedham, Massachusetts, as a legitimate means of supporting a
public school system; and conspicuous examples of well organized
industries included fishing and whaling, lumbering and shipbuild-
ing, ironmaking and leather tanning. A domestic commerce existed
from Maine to Florida; and every schoolboy or girl becomes fas-
cinated at the kind of perpetual motion in foreign trade that grew
up whereby the West Indies produced the molasses and sugar for
New England to make the rum that bought the slaves in Africa to
trade in the West Indies for more molasses and sugar.

Inevitably disputes arose among the colonies. It was reasonable,
to the degree there ever is reason in such matters, that Old World
religious disputes should develop into New World hostilities, and
the animosity between Catholic Maryland and Protestant Virginia was an example. Until the formation of the New England
Confederation (1643–84), smaller colonies like Plymouth, New
Haven, and Connecticut distrusted the grasping domination of
the Massachusetts Bay Colony; and with grants that extended to
the Pacific coast, Virginia, Massachusetts, and Connecticut bickered over rights in the western lands where Scotch-Irish and Germans, unable to obtain land or compete with slave labor in the

South, already were forging frontier settlements. Not one colony showed the slightest real disposition to surrender its power of taxation or control of western lands, and so Franklin's Albany Plan (1754), which might have provided greater harmony through a form of central government, failed. Yet where reason would not draw together the colonies, fear could—specifically, the fear of the Indians and the French.

The Great War for the Empire

L A W R E N C E H . G I P S O N

The epic struggle for North America had many phases. The Dutch had lost New Netherland by 1664, and the Spanish, who in St. Augustine claimed the oldest settlement on the continent (1565), were chiefly concerned with solidifying their positions in Central and South America. The Swedes, who gained a foothold in the valley of the Delaware River, collapsed as a factor in the battle for North America as early as 1655 when the Dutch captured their forts. So by the middle of the 18th Century, the lines of conflict in the Great War for the Empire were tightly drawn between the English and the French. Both coveted control of the Atlantic fisheries and the lucrative fur trade. Both coveted the western lands, and it was no consoling knowledge to the English that the French were stringing their trading posts and forts across the Great Lakes region and southward through the Illinois country. Meanwhile, the French displayed great adeptness at getting along with the Indian and in keeping him supplied with the means and the will to raid and destroy English settlements in the west.

Lawrence Henry Gipson, research professor emeritus at Lehigh University, and the author of the monumental multi-volume work, The British Empire Before the American Revolution, *sets the stage as the colonies moved toward a common cause.*

T HE French and Indian War was the American phase of a worldwide, nine-year war that was waged between the years 1754 and 1763. It was called by many names, but it is most accurately termed "the Great War for the Empire." It involved at first only the empires of Great Britain and France, then the German Electorate of Hanover, of which the King of England was head. Two other western German states were drawn into it when France attacked Hanover, and still later Spain and Portugal became participants.

The Great War for the Empire began over the specific issue as to whether the upper Ohio Valley was a part of the British Empire or part of the French Empire. But behind this issue loomed the infinitely greater one—the question which language, form of government, and social pattern was to dominate the heart of the continent of North America.

British territorial claims rested upon the Cabots's discovery of the North American continent in the latter part of the 15th Century. In the early part of the 17th Century, English royal charter had granted to the Virginia Company and to the Grand Council for New England all the land within certain limits between the Atlantic and Pacific Oceans. Further, in 1663, there was created the colony of Carolina. Out of this grant, North Carolina, South Carolina, and Georgia were later formed. Thus, all lands south of French Canada and north of Spanish Florida, stretching from sea to sea, were claimed by England.

In conflict with this claim were those of France to the whole of the Mississippi Valley, including the Ohio Valley, based upon the discoveries of La Salle who, starting from Canada, moved through the Great Lakes. After descending the Mississippi River in 1682, he took possession in the name of the King of France of all lands drained by this river and its tributaries.

For some sixty years, the issue as to which nation had the better right to lands in the great Mississippi Basin was to remain unresolved. The English gradually settled all along the Atlantic seaboard to the south of the Gulf of St. Lawrence, where some fourteen colonies, including Nova Scotia, came into existence and flourished.

By the middle of the 18th Century, small clearings were to be found even to the west of the Appalachians. By the end of the period, hundreds of Pennsylvania traders had likewise settled in the villages of Indian tribes of the upper Ohio Valley. On the other hand, the French had been firmly in control of Canada from the early part of the 17th Century. Gradually, they began the exploitation of the Great Lakes region, establishing permanent settlements at Detroit, at the mouth of the Mississippi, and at Biloxi and Mobile Bay.

Philad^a July 5. 1775

Mr Strahan,

You are a Member of Parliament, and one of that Majority which has doomed my Country to Destruction. — You have begun to burn our Towns, and murder our People. — Look upon your Hands! — They are stained with the Blood of your Relations! — You and I were long Friends: — You are now my Enemy, — and

I am,

Yours,

B Franklin

For eighteen years Ben Franklin served abroad, working to preserve the relationship between England and the colonies. Then, when war supplanted peace, the calm philosopher became an ardent partisan, and addressed this letter to a former friend.

A rare recruiting poster of the Revolution showing soldiers going through drill. The text offers "a truly liberal and generous . . . bounty of Twelve dollars" plus the prospect of spending "a few happy years in viewing the different parts of this beautiful continent . . . returning with pockets FULL of money and . . . head COVERED with laurels."

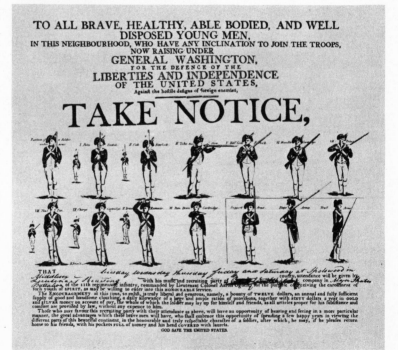

Illumination.

COLONEL TILGHMAN, Aid de Camp to his Excellency General WASHINGTON, having brought official acounts of the SURRENDER of Lord Cornwallis, and the Garrifons of York and Gloucefter, thofe Citizens who chufe to ILLUMINATE on the GLORIOUS OCCASION, will do it this evening at Six, and extinguifh their lights at Nine o'clock.

Decorum and harmony are earneftly recommended to every Citizen, and a general difcountenance to the leaft appearance of riot.

October 24, 1781.

When news came that 8,000 men under Cornwallis had surrendered at Yorktown, American patriots knew that final victory was within reach. The jubilant citizens were permitted three hours in which to "illuminate on the Glorious Occasion" in a handbill issued at the request of General Washington.

Books may be classed from the Faculties of the mind, which being

I. Memory.   II. Reason.   III. Imagination

are applied respectively to

I. History.   II. Philosophy.   III. Fine Arts.

				Chap.
			Antient.	Antient hist.	1.
		Civil proper.		foreign	2.
	Civil.		Modern.	British.	3.
				American.	4.
		Ecclesiastical		Ecclesiastical	5.
History.				Nat. Philos.	6.
				Agriculture	7.
		Physics.		Chemistry	8.
				Surgery.	9.
				Medicine	10.
	Natural.		Animals	Anatomy.	11.
				Zoology.	12.
		Nat. hist. prop.	Vegetables	Botany.	13.
			Minerals.	Mineralogy	14.
		Occupations of Man		Technical arts	15.

In 1776 Jefferson proposed four reforms as essential to a Virginia government which would be "truly republican," one of which called for free elementary education, a state college, and a free state library. For his personal library he devised a classification scheme which reveals Jefferson's wide-ranging interests—from aeronautics and agriculture to religion, surgery, and zoology.

A conflict between the two nations over their rival North American claims was doubtless inevitable, but it might have been delayed for many years had not the Governor General of New France forced the issue. In 1749 he sent troops into the upper Ohio Valley to compel Pennsylvania traders to lower the British flag and, as trespassers on the King of France's lands, to retreat to the eastern slopes of the Appalachians. When this move did not have the desired effect, force was applied. In 1752, the French destroyed the very important British colonial trading center on the upper Great Miami River. This act was followed by an all-out war against every English-speaking trader or settler in the region that the French and their Indian allies could find.

For a long time the government of Virginia had taken the position that the lands of the upper Ohio were clearly included in the colony's charter grant of 1609. Under that charter the governor and council had, by the end of 1752, made conditional grants of about a million and a half acres of Ohio Valley land. Almost every important Virginia family, including the Washingtons, Lees, and Randolphs, was vitally interested in the fate of the Ohio Valley. Late in 1753 the news reached Virginia that the French were not only driving out English traders and others but building forts on the headwaters of the Allegheny as well. Young George Washington was sent to warn the French that they were occupying lands that belonged to Virginia. After that daring mission failed, the Ohio Company of Virginia decided to build a fort at the place where the Allegheny and Mononagahela Rivers join to create the Ohio River (where Pittsburgh now stands), with the understanding that Virginia troops would support the undertaking.

The French, however, moved first. Descending the Allegheny River in numbers in the spring of 1754, their troops, commanded by French regular officers, overwhelmed the little force of woodcutters and carpenters busy with the construction of a palisaded log fort. The French had acted before the arrival of Virginia troops and a company of South Carolina Independents under Colonel Fry and Lieutenant Colonel Washington. Upon the death of Fry, Washington took command and decided to entrench himself at Fort Necessity. There he was attacked and, in the face of great odds, compelled to surrender.

It was this clash between British and French armed forces that brought on the Great War for the Empire which ultimately spread from the Ohio Valley to every part of the world where either of the two nations had territorial interests.

The government of Virginia appealed to the King for assistance. They asked particularly for two British regiments so that regulars could be pitted against regulars in this wilderness contest. Fearing the outbreak of a new war with France, George II at first stubbornly refused to consider the request. He agreed with the position taken by his minister, the Duke of Newcastle, who said: "Let Americans fight Americans" in distant New World clashes. But when it became clear that raw militia could not be expected to stand against seasoned regulars, he finally agreed to order troops to Virginia to clear the French invaders from the forks of the Ohio.

During the first four years of the fighting that followed, the overall advantage was with the French. It seemed that they would succeed in enclosing the British colonials firmly to the east of the Appalachian Mountain barrier, thus condemning them to remain for the future simply an Atlantic seaboard people. During those years British regulars and American colonials suffered one stunning reverse after another. Braddock was defeated in 1755 at the new Fort Duquesne that the French had erected at the forks of the Ohio. Fort Oswego and Fort William Henry in upper New York fell to the French. Lord Loudoun's expedition against the great French fortress Louisbourg, on Cape Breton Island, ended in dismal failure; General Abercrombie, in attacking the French Fort Ticonderoga in 1758, had his army almost destroyed. The frontier settlements in what is now central New York, central Pennsylvania, western Maryland, and western Virginia were deserted. Thousands of families fled in panic from the torch, sword, and tomahawk carried by the French and their Indian allies.

But in a conflict of this character, which involved such a tremendous stake as the future of a continent, other factors were to play a decisive role. William Pitt, the English prime minister, saw correctly that, despite the spread of the Anglo-French War to other parts of the world, the winning of it in North America was the supreme task at hand. With almost fanatical zeal he dedicated himself to that end. He found first class military leaders in such men as Generals Amherst, Wolfe, and Forbes; he recruited new regiments of regulars to replace or to reinforce the old, shattered ones; he persuaded Parliament to grant him almost unlimited funds; he promised the colonies a liberal reimbursement of their expenses, if they would do their part in furnishing soldiers; and finally, every important detail with respect to operations in North America came under his personal direction. Pitt, in a very true sense, was the organizer of victory in the Great War for the Empire.

In Pitt's favor were three things that were destined to permit him to overwhelm his opponents. One was the growing superiority of the British navy. Slowly but relentlessly, it swept French merchantmen, ships of war, and troop transports from the seas, thus shutting off the enemy's means of bringing reinforcements of troops and munitions to Canada. Second, Great Britain had vastly greater financial and industrial resources than France. Toward the end of the struggle, France faced the dangers of national bankruptcy and economic paralysis. Finally, both British regulars and American colonials became seasoned fighters.

In time, the tide turned in North America. Amherst captured Louisbourg in 1758, closing the Gulf of St. Lawrence; Fort Frontenac, Fort Duquesne, and Fort Niagara were compelled to surrender; and Wolfe won the Battle of the Heights of Abraham, which led to the fall of Quebec. Amherst completed the conquest of Canada when, with the fall of Montreal in 1760, all parts of that great French possession and its dependencies were surrendered to him. Although this series of victories did not terminate the Great War for the Empire, the French and Indian phase of it was thus ended. With the ratification of the Peace of Paris in 1763, the supreme issue was definitely settled as to whether the English-speaking people or the French-speaking people would assume the chief responsibility for shaping the destinies of the North American continent.

"The Father of All Yankees"

WHITFIELD J. BELL, JR.

Climactic though the French and Indian Wars would be in turning the future struggle for North America into a quarrel between Englishmen of the New World and Old, other events of the first half of the 18th Century could not be ignored in giving impetus to the emerging American Story. In the years from 1700 to 1710 the first law in the colonies supporting a library was passed by the assembly of South Carolina, Yale College was founded (Harvard was chartered in 1636 and William and Mary in 1693), The Boston News-Letter was established as the first regularly

*issued newspaper in America, Virginia enacted a law requiring a
master to teach an apprenticed orphan to read and write (and
the fifth revision of its slave code declared slaves to be real estate),
and the extremely effective Pennsylvania rifle introduced the spiral
bore to colonial marksmen. The second decade of the 18th Century
found the town records of Boston complaining that too much Latin
and Greek was taught in its free schools, New York City had a
slave revolt and burned or hanged twenty-one Negroes, Pennsylvania banned the importation of Negroes, an American-type sailing
schooner was built in Gloucester, Massachusetts, the first play-
house in America was built in Williamsburg, Virginia, and Bostonians read with fascination an anonymous publication entitled*
Hoop Petticoats, Arraigned and Condemned by the Light of Nature and the Law of God.

*Midway through the third decade of the 18th Century John
Peter Zenger was acquitted of seditious libel, and another freedom
in the colonies—that of the press—won a great victory. The 1740's
opened with Jonathan Edwards haranguing the citizens of
Connecticut on "Sinners in the Hands of an Angry God"; the
following year citizens of Philadelphia, less harassed by fears of
brimstone, began to enjoy puppet shows advertised in* The Pennsylvania Gazette; *and in 1746 the Presbyterians established the
College of New Jersey (Princeton). At mid-century bituminous
coal was first mined in America in Virginia's Richmond Basin and
a Pennsylvanian named Jacob Yoder invented a flatboat for inland
water. Also in that year of 1750 an Iron Act was passed by Parliament which prohibited colonial manufacture of iron beyond pig
and bar stage, although the entry of pig and bar iron into England
was allowed duty free. A small grumble could be heard; and even
a small frown can linger and grow.*

*In even this kaleidoscopic view, with its inevitable distortion,
the years from 1700 to 1750 were an age of excitement, of living, of
a maturing community spirit. The most representative man of that
age began life as the son of a poor tallow chandler and soapmaker;
he ended it as one of the great men of the world. "Debby,"
Benjamin Franklin once said to his wife, "I wish the good Lord
had seen fit to make each day just twice as long as it is. Perhaps
then I really could accomplish something." Whitfield J. Bell, Jr.,
visiting professor of history at the College of William and Mary
and assistant editor of* The Papers of Benjamin Franklin *sum-
marizes what was accomplished by "the most American of all the
Americans of the 18th Century."*

When Benjamin Franklin was born in Boston in 1706, the British North American colonies contained 350,000 persons clustering along the Atlantic seacoast and the broad tidewater rivers. The great interior valleys—Mohawk, Susquehanna, and Shenandoah—were far beyond the limits of settlement. There had been one clash with the French in New York and Canada, but the issue of who was to control the Great Lakes and the Ohio and Mississippi Rivers was hardly joined; and, in any case, the colonies had neither the strength nor the discipline to decide it alone. At the beginning of the 18th Century almost any tiny sugar island in the West Indies or steaming slave castle on the Guinea Coast was worth more to Britain than any of the mainland colonies.

When Franklin died in Philadelphia in 1790, all this was changed. The population of the United States exceeded four million. There were farms in Ohio. Flatboats on the western waters floated down to New Orleans. Only twenty-five years after Daniel Boone had learned the way into Kentucky, that region was ready for statehood. A dozen colleges were educating a new generation of Americans; there were even three medical schools in the country; and at Pittsburgh and Lexington, newspapers appeared weekly. The colonies Franklin knew in his youth had achieved political independence; at his death they were forming a nation on principles Europeans viewed with mingled awe and approbation.

Franklin's life thus covered the years when the colonies matured and the American political union was formed. His actions reflected those great movements; he strengthened and directed them. Developing as the nation grew, Franklin provided new answers to its changing needs; and so, perfectly integrated with his time, he seems to have been the most American of all the Americans of the 18th Century. At the same time he was always the least limited in scope. "The father of all the Yankees," as Thomas Carlyle called him, was also the citizen of a country and a world, a cosmopolitan who moved with ease and competence whether to negotiate an Indian treaty on the Pennsylvania frontier, explain some physical phenomenon to the philosophers of France, or dine with a king.

Perhaps it is this supreme adaptability to circumstances—it is reflected in his flexible literary style, so admirably suited to any occasion—that makes Franklin the most agreeable and instructive of all American heroes: he has something for every generation. But just because he seems to belong to every age and place as well as his own, he is the most consistently authoritative of our heroes. He can tell us, as well as he told his neighbors, how to save a pound a year; and his wise observations on the follies of mankind might have saved any of us time, trouble, and pain had we not insisted on learning for ourselves that "experience keeps a dear school, but fools will learn in no others, and scarce in that." The continued relevance of Franklin's character and achievement, the universality of his appeal, are the most significant things about him.

The American colonies where Franklin passed the first half of his very long life were a place where, for the most part, necessities of individual subsistence and community life had still to be provided. The relentless struggle to keep alive and make a living was uppermost. Any slackening might mean suffering for the individual and, in the case of poor settlements, for the entire community as well. Franklin felt these pressures too; and, significantly, it is as a tradesman and a practicing economist that he first appears to us.

Franklin's father intended that the boy should follow him in the soapmaker's trade; but Benjamin was an unwilling learner who preferred his brother James's printing shop. Here he learned his trade and had some gratifying success as an author and editor. Eventually, believing himself undervalued, he ran away to seek his fortune. He found it soon enough in Philadelphia, the fastest-growing city in the colonies. By 1729, when he was twenty-three, Franklin was established as the publisher of the *Pennsylvania Gazette*. He was a good workman, who carefully advertised his industriousness. He "dressed plain," he tells us in the *Autobiography*, "and was seen at no place of idle diversion . . . never went out a-fishing or shooting." And, just to show his customers that he was not above his work, he sometimes rolled a barrow of paper through the streets to his shop.

As profits increased, Franklin invested them in promising journeymen whom he set up in business in other towns. He supplied part of the capital and took part of the profits; and his profits were the larger because the printers bought their paper, ink, and printing supplies from him. To the printing of a paper Franklin added all kinds of job printing, and published books, school texts, and almanacs. So well did he keep his shop that when he was forty-two, only twenty years after he set up as an independent master, his shop could keep him, as Poor Richard promised it would.

Poor Richard's Almanac, with a sale of ten thousand copies annually, was certainly the best known of Franklin's many publications. Like Franklin's private industry and frugality, the maxims of Poor Richard came out of the circumstances of American society. They were addressed to a people whose survival and prosperity both as individuals and a community depended on prudence and self-reliance. "A fat kitchen, a lean will" was a social doctrine as well as a principle of conduct.

The community, however, as Franklin knew better than most, needed more than industry and thrift in its citizens to succeed. From the beginning of his career Franklin was a citizen as well as a tradesman.

When a group of artisans intent on self-improvement discovered they lacked books and the means to buy them, Franklin suggested they club together for the purpose; and so the Library Company came into being. When Philadelphians projected a college in 1749, Franklin drafted a model curriculum. Perfectly adapted to the needs of a mercantile community, it emphasized English and practical mathematics. A fire company, a hospital, a city police were all established wholly or partly by his leadership and ingenuity. They were just what Philadelphia needed at the time.

"The first drudgery of settling new colonies . . . is now pretty well over," wrote Franklin in 1743, "and there are many in every province in circumstances that set them at ease, and afford leisure to cultivate the finer arts and improve the common stock of knowledge." What Franklin was saying is that the struggle for survival had been won; the economic problem had been solved; and American energies might now turn in other directions. For Franklin, soon to retire from active business, a period followed during which he could devote himself to science, especially to electricity. To cultivate the liberal arts and sciences was now no less important to colonial America than to "plough deep, while sluggards sleep."

In the role of natural philosopher, Franklin was every bit a child of the 18th Century, the last age of the brilliant amateurs, when an English dissenting clergyman, Joseph Priestley, discovered a new chemical element, oxygen; a German bandmaster, William Herschel, found a new planet, Uranus; and a Philadelphia printer, Franklin, established the science of electricity.

Utilitarian though he was, Franklin was interested in science out of pure curiosity. He wanted to know what and why. If, after that, the knowledge he obtained had some practical usefulness, so much the better; but utility was the result rather than the reason for his investigations of scientific problems. He made a lightning rod because the nature of electricity puzzled him; he did not study electricity because he wanted to protect houses from lightning bolts.

Franklin found electricity something of a spectacular parlor game; he left it a science, with a body of observations, a series of experiments, some proven laws, and a nomenclature. Of all his experiments the most memorable, for it had the perfect simplicity of great genius, was that which proved the identity of lightning with electricity. Franklin's iron points drawing fire from the sky excited the imaginations of men everywhere, and won Franklin—and, through him, America—recognition from European men of learning. It also laid the basis of his international reputation. "He had snatched lightning from the skies; soon," declaimed Turgot[1] in a tremendous epigram, "he would snatch the scepter from the tyrant's hand."

Franklin's leisure for scientific inquiries soon ended. Hitherto Americans' problems were personal ones, like making a living (which Franklin had done); or local ones, like organizing the community (Franklin had showed his fellow citizens how to get their streets lighted and their incurables cared for). Now Americans' problems were political; they involved the imperial connection itself. Leaving others to preside over Philadelphia's civic institutions, putting aside his Leyden jars and friction machine, Franklin was increasingly occupied in the last half of his life with intercolonial, imperial, and, finally, national political questions. He emerged as an intercolonial statesman in 1754, proposing a plan to unite the colonies under an American legislature.

Three years later, Pennsylvania sent him to England as its agent at the seat of government in London. There Franklin remained, with but a single visit home, for eighteen years. Not only was he the official representative of Pennsylvania, but also the unofficial but authentic spokesman of British North America, striving to preserve the imperial union between England and her American colonies. His mission ended in failure and he returned home in the

[1] Anne Robert Jacques Turgot (1727–1781), French statesman, who encouraged industry by enlarging the rights of individuals and abolishing the exclusive privileges of companies and corporations; bitterly opposed by the clergy and the nobility, he was dismissed from office as comptroller-general in 1776.

spring of 1775. War had already broken out; Franklin was put in the Continental Congress, helped draft the Declaration of Independence, tried to win over Canada as a fourteenth colony. Late in 1776, at the age of seventy-one, he set out to Europe once more, this time to negotiate a treaty of commerce and friendship with France.

The treaty of alliance was drafted. French supplies and troops were sent to America to aid the rebels. With John Adams and John Jay, he negotiated the treaty by which Britain recognized American independence and ceded British territory east of the Mississippi to the new republic. Franklin's personal success was even more spectacular. While Adams grumbled helplessly, Frenchmen lionized the aging philosopher, who epitomized to them many of the most cherished principles of the 18th Century enlightenment. At a time when all the world seemed to move in harmonious balance, and moderation was the best rule of conduct, Franklin was the man of eminent reasonableness. His skepticism and genial tolerance were expressed in deceptively homely wit. Though he accepted men pretty much as they are, the bad with the good, he was a humanitarian whose efforts had measurably promoted the comfort and happiness of men in this world. Even his homespun appearance seemed proof to the French that their dream of a "natural man" was realized.

The Boston-born printer, Poor Richard of the *Almanac*, the colonial of 1756, had come a long way. Though he retained his American quality and spoke in the American idiom, Franklin had assumed the role which his country's new status now demanded: he was the citizen of a nation risen among the nations. Like others of his generation—Voltaire, Tom Paine, Joseph Priestley, for example—he belonged to his own country and to others. He told Lord Kames that he would be happy to settle in Scotland except that he had so many connections in Pennsylvania; and he would have been as content and effective a citizen of Edinburgh as he was of Philadelphia.

But he came back to Pennsylvania. His last five years, like the preceding sixty, were filled with work of the kind America needed to have done. He was president of the Executive Council of Pennsylvania and sat in the Federal Convention, considering its work moderately satisfactory. He was president of one society to study the new political questions of republican government and of another to promote the abolition of slavery and improve the condition of free Negroes. He presided over meetings of his fellow scientists in the American Philosophical Society. And, though neither he nor his country would again be held to strict accountability by Poor Richard, he ended his life as he began, in the firm, bold words of his will, "I, Benjamin Franklin, of Philadelphia, Printer . . ."

Apostles of Freedom

PHILIP DAVIDSON

In 1760, when the population of the thirteen colonies had grown to an estimated 1,600,000, George III ascended to the throne of England. Thereafter another pattern emerged:

> *1763—Patrick Henry, arguing the Parsons' Cause in Virginia, challenges the authority of the Crown to disallow colonial statutes.*
>
> *1764—The Sugar Act, passed by Parliament as a means "toward defraying necessary expenses of defending, protecting and securing said colonies," stirs up numerous colonial memorials of protest.*
>
> *1765—The Stamp Act, providing taxes on newspapers, legal papers, pamphlets, playing cards, etc., is made a law and colonial merchants sign nonimportation agreements while bells toll in muffled tones and flags fly at half-mast.*
>
> *1766—Stamp Act repealed and joyous New Yorkers vote to build statues of George III and William Pitt.*
> *Declaratory Act passed; Parliament declares its power to bind the colonies "in all cases whatsoever."*
>
> *1767—Townshend Revenue Act levies import duties on glass, lead, paint, tea, paper, etc.*
>
> *1768—John Dickinson's "Song for American Freedom" is published in the* Boston Gazette *and reprinted as "The Liberty Song."*
>
> *1769—Virginia Resolves, drawn up by George Mason, protests ministerial policy in England.*
>
> *1770—The Boston Massacre.*

Indeed, times had come to North America that would try the souls of men. Yet, in crisis, the colonies proved rich in leadership.

*In Boston emerged an Adams, troubled by a speech impediment
growing out of palsy that made him a hesitant public speaker but
a vigorous wielder of that mightiest of weapons, the pen. In Philadelphia a thirty-seven-year-old Englishman arrived in 1774,
plagued by a sense of frustration in his inability to alleviate the
conditions of the poor in England. In the New World a new start
was the last hope for Tom Paine. There were many "Apostles of
Freedom," but none of stronger will than Adams and Paine. Now
Philip Davidson, president of the University of Louisville and
author of* Propaganda and the American Revolution *captures the
true roles played by these men in the American Story.*

THE American Revolution was the product of powerful forces
rooted deep in the colonial past. Inspired leadership put those
forces to work for the freedom of the colonies from Great Britain.
National monuments today testify to the power of Thomas Jefferson and George Washington in declaring the independence of this
country and in winning it from the most powerful empire in the
world at that time. But behind these two great figures were others
without whose work the first shots would never have been fired
at Lexington and Concord. Without them the Declaration of Independence would never have been adopted, and Cornwallis
would never have been defeated. These were the men whom today we might call "propagandists." But that word has an evil
sound, and these men were patriots of sincerity and devotion to
their country. "Apostles" is perhaps the better word—"apostles of
freedom," men who sensed the popular but unexpressed opposition to Great Britain and her acts, men who made that opposition
articulate and provided the machinery through which it could
be expressed in concrete action.

Within a generation after 1750, the settlers had first united with
England to destroy the power of France on the continent of North
America. They then completely nullified British legislation within
the colonies, and revolutionized their own governments. Finally
they joined with their ancient enemy, France, to defeat the mother
country and establish themselves as an independent nation. Within
a generation, a revolution in thought and institutions had crystallized that was not accomplished by chance. The evidences of a
conscious, systematic effort on the part of certain colonial leaders
to gain public support for their ideas are unmistakable. "By their
fruits ye shall know them."

Of all the leaders of the American Revolution there are two, Sam Adams and Tom Paine, who have almost been unequaled in human history in their ability to arouse people to action. At hand for their use was the accumulated discontent of a hundred and fifty years' restive development under English control. There existed also the turbulent forces creating the Americanism they were beginning to perceive, and the 18th Century compact philosophy that was to make them free. To unite all America in one pulsating hope, to vitalize that hope with the new philosophy, was their task. They could succeed, for they had a secret knowledge of what the people thought, wished, feared, and hated. They had as well the power to interpret for the public "its own conscience and its own consciousness"—therein lay their strength.

Sam Adams owned no superior as a propagandist. No one in the colonies realized more fully than he the primary necessity of arousing public opinion; no one set about it more persistently. His entire life up to 1763 had equipped him perfectly for the work. Harvard training grounded him in the classics and gave him an equally profitable acquaintance with Locke and the liberal writers of the 18th Century. He read theology and abandoned the ministry. He read law and abandoned the bar. He entered business and lost a thousand pounds. Each experience narrowed the field of his future endeavors. He was finally forced into the one field in which he had any real interest and for which he had any real talent— politics. But these experiences did more; they gave him a substantial background for his later efforts. He had absorbed the political implications of the 18th Century nonconformist thought. He had learned the legal approach to the rights of his colony. He had seen the effects of British interference on the colony's internal economic and political affairs. Academically, he had been thoroughly interested in the 18th Century discussions of liberty. But he became realistically concerned when an act of Parliament ruined a very promising venture of his father—the ill-fated Massachusetts Land Bank—an event which nearly resulted in the complete loss of the family fortune.

His varied career and intimate knowledge of so many aspects of New England's life made him almost a composite of the aggrieved American. He could speak with assurance for the clergyman, the lawyer, and the merchant. In addition to this sureness of knowledge and complete identity of himself with his times there were the will and such qualities to do the task as tremendous physical energy, inexhaustible patience, a burning zeal for the doctrines of liberty, and religious fervor for the tenets of Puritanism. "I will oppose this tyranny at the threshold, though the fabric of liberty fall, and I perish in its ruins," he said.

To the task of opposing British encroachments on colonial rights, Adams brought his every ability. "All are not dead; and where there is a Spark of patriotic fire, we will enkindle it," he said. From the first issue of the *Independent Advertiser* in January, 1748, to the Declaration of Independence, he was constantly writing for the press under a variety of pseudonyms. At least twenty-five have been recognized as his. The number of his essays and controversial articles must have run into the hundreds. During the height of the pre-Revolutionary struggle he practically filled the pages of the *Boston Gazette*. Writing essays, clipping items from other papers, extracting pertinent bits from his private correspondence, editing news items—all this he did with the one idea of arousing anti-British feeling. He carried on a voluminous correspondence with leaders in England and America, insinuating his ideas and gaining support for his policies. He was instrumental in forming revolutionary organizations, such as committees of correspondence. He was a member of many of the more important Boston and Massachusetts committees. His activities were directed toward preparing opinion. He wrote James Warren that, as it could not be foreseen what the British ministry might do, "it will be wise for us to be ready for all Events, that we may make the best Improvement of them." When James Otis objected to publishing in the *Boston Gazette* a letter to Lord Hillsborough in England before he could possibly receive it, Sam Adams retorted, "What signifies that? You know it was designed for the people, not for the minister."

Adams was at his best in writing and in political manipulation. Public oratory was never his real field although he could speak with force and distinction at times. He was no social incendiary, nor was he a mob leader. Although he probably inspired the group which destroyed the tea in Boston Harbor, he took no part in mob violence. His contribution lay in his superb organization of the movement in New England, and in the unity of opinion he achieved throughout the colonies by his ceaseless agitation against the colonial policies of Great Britain.

Thomas Paine, agitator and propagandist supreme, was not connected with the revolutionary movement by the facts of his condition and environment, as were the great majority of the

American leaders. His association with it was almost an accident. Introduced to Philadelphia printing circles by Benjamin Franklin after a drab and undistinguished career in England, he began unimportant writing for *The Pennsylvania Magazine* shortly after his arrival in November, 1774. This writing was for the most part not political in character, although Paine did write a poem, "The Liberty Tree," which was published in its pages. *Common Sense* and *The Crisis* letters, written during the war, established sufficiently his claims as a propagandist. He sensed as did few others the radical temper, and could express to people what they themselves thought and felt in striking, popular language. He was not an original thinker. As Adams said of *Common Sense*, there was nothing in it that had not been frequently urged on the floor of the Continental Congress.

Common Sense appeared early in January, 1776, and caught hold immediately. A small pamphlet, it was printed and reprinted in every colony. It plainly stated the case of the colonies against the mother country and demanded independence as the only solution. "The period of debate is closed," said the author, first thought to be Franklin. "Arms as the last recourse must decide the contest." The bold, even harsh words of the argument simply said what everyone had been thinking. Timed as it was, it carried the cause of independence forward with a rush.

Paine was far more radical in his social theories than the other leaders of the revolution. He was, of course, not identified with their interests except in the revolutionary movement. His Northern compatriots did not share his religious notions. His Southern friends did not share his antislavery ideas. But these were ideas and concepts immaterial to the immediate problem of independence. Puritan New Englanders, the slave-holding Southerners, and the propertied leaders everywhere had no compunctions about using the crude vigor of Paine's English to further their own objectives. There is still power in the famous essay called *The Crisis*. Read by Washington's order to his troops, it begins "These are the times that try men's souls. The summer soldier and the sunshine patriot will in this crisis, shrink from the service of his country; but he that stands it NOW, deserves the love and thanks of man and woman." The stirring sibilants, the epigrammatic vigor of these lines heartened the discouraged little band of winter patriots left with Washington. So it was with all his writings, each one perfectly timed, perfectly adapted to the needs of the moment.

Throughout the long war Adams and Paine were indispensable in keeping up the spirits of the people. Tom Paine's *Crisis* letters appeared at frequent intervals, and Sam Adams kept up his ceaseless efforts in New England. Every instance of American bravery or success was magnified, for, as Tom Paine said, "It is always dangerous to spread an alarm . . . unless the prospect of success be held out with it." American resources, they said, American manpower, American generals could never be overcome. Independence was inevitable. Adams and Paine, the apostles of freedom, had led their people well. They knew that before the finishing blow to British power in America could be given, courage must rise with danger and hope with fear. They knew that they and their fellows alone could so inspire the people, for they had possessed for themselves the words of St. Paul, "For if the trumpet give an uncertain sound, who shall prepare himself to the battle?"

A Virginia Gentleman

BERNHARD KNOLLENBERG

Today's visitor to beautifully reconstructed Colonial Williamsburg, Virginia, steps back into the 18th Century world that so strongly influenced the mind and life of the Father of the Country. Here, at the age of seventeen, Washington accepted public office as a county surveyor; here, ten years later, he was seated in the House of Burgesses and became the intimate of political leaders who fanned the embers of liberty into the flame of Revolution; here, on an autumn day in 1781, he arrived to plan the final assault on the British at Yorktown. To stroll the Duke of Gloucester Street in Williamsburg is to walk through a corridor of history and to feel the breathing spirit of the Virginia patriots who helped "turn the world upside down," as the British said. Who can say which of these patriots was greatest? But one can say that none was greater than Washington, and the reason why is explained by Bernhard Knollenberg, member of the Council of the Institute of Early American History and Culture at Williamsburg, and author of many books, including Washington and the Revolution, A Reappraisal.

I n temper and outlook, George Washington had little in common with such radicals of the Revolution as Samuel Adams and Thomas Paine. He was a well-to-do planter who, along with other planters of his class, felt the pinch of British imperial control in matters involving his daily activities. As exporters of tobacco, planters felt the hardship of Britain's restrictive trade laws which wholly prohibited the export of British colonial tobacco to any place outside the colonies except Great Britain. These laws even taxed shipments of tobacco from one colony to another. The planters thought themselves shabbily treated by the British merchants who handled their exports and attended to their orders for British imports. They saw the English policy of prohibiting the taking up of Western lands as the end of one hope of lifting themselves out of a burden of debt which had weighted them down after many years of poor markets for their produce.

Furthermore, beginning in 1759, the Privy Council in England exasperated the Virginians by interfering more than before in the internal affairs of the colony. Parliament added to their discontent, as well as that of the rest of the colonists, by levying colonial taxes and thus invading a field of the highest importance; one previously reserved, with few exceptions, for the colonial legislatures.

Though Washington's greatness of character emerged, perhaps was forged, only as he faced and surmounted the trials of eight years of Revolution, his ability was outstanding from an exceptionally early age.

In 1747, when only fifteen years old, he began earning money as a surveyor. Two years later, the President and Masters of William and Mary College, acting for the government of Virginia, appointed him official Surveyor of Culpeper County. A few months after this he became surveyor for Lord Fairfax, the greatest landowner in Virginia. Washington's career was doubtless assisted by the marriage of his older half-brother, Lawrence Washington, to the daughter of Colonel George William Fairfax, first cousin of Lord Fairfax and one of the most influential residents of Virginia. But great landowners were not likely to entrust the security of their land titles, nor a colonial governor his reputation and the safety of his people, to a young man who had not proven his worth.

When not yet twenty-one, Washington began his remarkable military career. He was appointed adjutant, with the rank of major, of one of the four districts into which the militia of Virginia was divided. The following year he was delegated by Governor Din-widdie of Virginia to carry to the commander of the French forces on the Ohio the momentous message which precipitated the French and Indian War by demanding, in the name of King George II, that the French withdraw from the Ohio Valley. Washington's report of his dangerous and arduous trip through ice and snow to deliver the Governor's summons has long been in print. But only recently French reports of Washington's mission have come to light corroborating and amplifying the young emissary's own version.

The story of young Washington's important part in the French and Indian War, his defense of Fort Necessity, his heroism in the attack on General Braddock's army on the Monongahela, and his participation as colonel of a Virginia regiment in the taking of Fort Duquesne is, of course, well-known. Lesser known, perhaps, is his career as planter and land speculator following his retirement from the army in 1758 up to the outbreak of the Revolution in 1775.

After the British took Fort Duquesne, foreshadowing the destruction of French power on the Ohio and ensuring the safety of Virginia from French invasion, Washington resigned his command. He married Martha Dandridge Custis, a rich widow with two children. The family settled down at Mount Vernon, which he had inherited from his brother Lawrence. Here he tried various experiments to grow crops more profitable than tobacco. He also gave much attention to the purchase and development of wild land in the Ohio Valley, in which he was greatly assisted by the wealth placed at his command by his marriage to Martha.

The nucleus of Washington's land claims was a certificate for 15,000 acres of land on the Ohio. This he acquired under a proclamation issued by Governor Dinwiddie to encourage enlistments in Virginia. The grants from this and from similar certificates, purchased by Washington from fellow officers, were still unissued when the War of the Revolution broke out. Transfer of dominion over the land from the British Crown to the government of the new state of Virginia finally removed all barriers to the grants. So was laid the foundation for the ample fortune in western lands left by Washington to numerous relatives at his death.

Washington took a relatively unimportant part in the agitation against British measures adversely affecting the colonies from 1759 to 1774. However, when the British "Intolerable" Acts of

1774,[2] directed chiefly against Boston and Massachusetts but threatening the freedom of all the colonies, led to the assembling of the Continental Congress at Philadelphia, Washington was one of the Virginia delegates. When war broke out, a commander-in-chief of the united colonial forces was required. Washington was the logical choice because of the outstanding importance and prestige of Virginia, and because he alone, of all the delegates in Congress, had had extensive military experience.

As commander-in-chief, Washington's greatest feat probably was keeping his men together despite inadequate support from the states (whose representatives in the Continental Congress were the ambassadors of thirteen independent, distracted and, in some respects, rival little nations); despite the apathy of the people after many years of indecisive fighting; and despite the dissatisfaction among many of his men, and strong suspicion of a standing army.

Washington's trials at Valley Forge during the winter of 1777–78 have been high lighted by many historians and biographers. But to my mind, his supreme period during the war was the year before. Then, after the shattering disaster at Fort Washington on upper Manhattan Island and the insubordination and capture of General Charles Lee, his second in command, Washington never flagged in determination. He gathered together the remnants of his army and victoriously struck the British at Trenton and Princeton.

When the War ended in 1783, Washington resumed his life as planter and land promoter at Mount Vernon, though not so quietly or economically as he wished. Multitudes of visitors were eager to make or renew the acquaintance of the distinguished and successful leader of the Revolutionary army. Then in less than four years he was called from his comfortable life as private citizen. This time he was asked to lead the Virginia delegation to the Convention at Philadelphia, called to strengthen the Articles of Confederation under which the national government (such as it was) limped along. On his arrival, he was chosen to preside. And almost as a matter of course he was subsequently elected President of the government established under the Constitution framed at the Convention.

[2] It was not within the nature of George III to permit the Boston Tea Party (December 16, 1773) to pass without reprisal. The Boston Port Act, first of the coercive measures, received royal approval the following March 31; the Massachusetts Government Act, nullifying the charter, came in May as well as the Administration of Justice Act; in June the Port of Boston was closed and the Quartering Act passed.

As President for eight years, Washington's recognized disinterest in personal gain and his integrity made it possible for him to command general respect; and as a Federalist, a believer in strong central government, and a conservative in matters of credit and finance, he helped to establish the young republic firmly in the eyes of its own citizens as well as of Europe.

In 1797 he returned to Mount Vernon only to be occupied in public service again a year later. On the threat of war with France, he accepted appointment by President John Adams as commander-in-chief of the provisional army voted by Congress for national defense. The war scare blew over, and Washington was at home again tending to private affairs at Mount Vernon, when in December, 1799, he caught cold and died—truly first in war, first in peace, and first in the hearts of most of his countrymen.

Prophet of the American Way

DUMAS MALONE

Washington came to Williamsburg in 1759 to begin his service in the House of Burgesses; and the following year along Duke of Gloucester Street strolled a gangling, reddish-haired boy beginning his education at William and Mary College. Young Tom Jefferson was from "up country," the wilderness around Charlottesville, and his spirit and mind never ceased to soar like the eagles he watched in this beloved mountain homeland. Later as a law student under the gifted George Wythe (pronounced to rhyme with Smith), Jefferson heard Patrick Henry present his resolves against the detested Stamp Act; here he defended a slave and told the court that under the law of nature "we are all born free"; later still, taking his seat in the House of Burgesses, he, too, became the intimate of men like Peyton Randolph and George Mason. So in the same atmosphere that nurtured the Father of the Country, the mind of the Father of its Declaration of Independence was largely shaped. Dumas Malone, professor of history at Columbia University and author of such distinguished volumes as Jefferson the Virginian *and* Jefferson and the Rights of Man, *evaluates the significance of this hero from the past whom he knows so well and loves so dearly.*

On any list of famous Americans, the name of Thomas Jefferson must appear near the top. He may not be so universally revered as Washington, whose monument towers above all others, but he seems less remote than that stately gentleman. Jefferson's form is not so familiar as that of Lincoln, since he lived before the time of photographs. He is probably a less beloved figure than the martyred President, but his words are even more often quoted. Of all our historic public men, only Ben Franklin can match him in versatility.

Besides being a statesman of the first rank, Jefferson was notable in law and agriculture, in science and invention, in religion and philosophy, in education and architecture. One reason why his fame has kept on growing is that he has something important to say on so many subjects, and appeals to so many different sorts of minds. His fame has probably reached its highest point in our own day, and there is a special explanation for this. More than any other American, Jefferson is a symbol of the freedom of the individual, and he represents a complete antithesis to totalitarianism in any form. He is the best single champion whom we can summon from the past and enter in the lists against contemporary dictators; and if the Communists can quote Karl Marx, we can quote Thomas Jefferson.

This prophet of the American way of freedom and democracy was born to a considerable estate, and received the best education that his times afforded. He was a recognized member of the landed aristocracy of Old Virginia, but he was a lifelong foe of every form of special privilege and a champion of the interests of the common people. To him, aristocracies of birth and wealth were artificial; what he believed in was the natural aristocracy of talent and virtue which would inevitably rise under conditions of general freedom. Shy and studious in his youth, and unprepossessing in appearance though strong in body, Jefferson would have preferred to devote himself to the tranquil pursuits of science which so delighted his eager and omnivorous mind. But, as he said, he was drawn into public affairs by emergencies which threatened his country with slavery, and ended by leaving it free. Responding to the challenge of his times, he was for forty years almost continuously in the public service. No other American ever did more to make his country free and keep it free.

The first great struggle of his career was against the mother country. Great Britain had given her colonies more liberties than any other imperial power had, but in Jefferson's young manhood she was threatening these liberties. If he had done nothing more, he would have gained clear title to immortal fame as the author of the Declaration of Independence, with which the history of the United States as a nation began. That document, as it came from his pen in 1776, was far more than the assertion of the rights of these states to be self-governing; it was also a charter of the liberties of Americans and all other men as individuals. It was a manifesto of human rights against any and every sort of tyranny. Jefferson was only thirty-three when he wrote it as a member of the Continental Congress, but at the end of his long life he still placed it first among his achievements.

Next after the Declaration Jefferson placed his authorship of the Statute of Virginia for Religious Freedom, which was adopted several years later and has been regarded ever since as one of the noblest expressions of the freedom of the human spirit. He carried on the struggle against intolerance throughout his life, and no saying of his better reveals the essence of the man than the one which can now be seen on the walls of the memorial to him in Washington: "I have sworn on the altar of God eternal hostility against every form of tyranny over the mind of man."

The third service of his which he thought most memorable was the founding, in his old age, of the University of Virginia. Earlier efforts of his in behalf of public elementary schools had been only partially successful, but he stands in our national history as the most eminent early apostle of education for everyone according to his abilities. He regarded universal education as a necessary corollary of political self-government. "If a nation expects to be ignorant and free," he said, "it expects what never was and never will be."

Jefferson's greatest services in his own eyes were to freedom and enlightenment, and he appears to have set little store on his political honors. That he should have been successful in politics is somewhat surprising, for he was no orator and was unhappy in any crowd. In his case, the office nearly always sought the man, not the man the office. After serving in the American Revolution as a legislator and, under very difficult circumstances, as the war governor of his state, he succeeded the most famous of early American diplomats, Benjamin Franklin, as minister to France. There he witnessed the beginnings of the French Revolution. Appointed by President George Washington as the first Secretary of State, he expected to devote himself to foreign affairs, in which he was well versed and which were exceedingly important in his time. It was because of his opposition to certain policies of his colleague, Alexander Hamilton, first Secretary of the Treasury, that he was drawn into domestic controversy; and the differences between them have been reflected in the division of American political opinion until this day.

These two brilliant and stanchly patriotic men were agreed on some of the most important issues of the time, such as the necessity for creating orderly government under the new Constitution and establishing the credit of the new nation. But they sharply disagreed about some of the means to be employed, and with respect to the ends of government they differed in emphasis. The freedom and happiness of individuals was the main concern of Jefferson, and he believed that Hamilton was going too far in his effort to increase the power of the national government. Perhaps Jefferson would not have gone far enough if things had been left wholly to him. The consensus of historical judgment is that the country needed both men. Jefferson felt that Hamilton was catering to a relatively small group—especially the commercial and financial interests—without sufficient regard for the great body of the people, who were mostly farmers. Hence Jefferson, whose background was aristocratic, came to be regarded as a prophet of democracy and of agrarianism. In his own day, however, his financial views were conservative, not radical. He feared public debt and favored and practiced economy. He was no advocate of mob rule; he insisted on an educated electorate and expected the people to choose trained leaders. But he will always stand forth in history as a champion of majority rule against the rule of the privileged few, and he had a faith in the character and good sense of the ordinary citizen which has been an inspiration to all succeeding generations.

Jefferson's description of his own election to the Presidency as a "revolution" was exaggeration, but unquestionably it marked a victory for liberty over potential despotism. Freedom of speech and the press had been endangered by the Alien and Sedition Acts, and the government did seem to be trying to enforce uniformity of political opinion in a time of hysteria over foreign danger. Jefferson checked the tide of political reaction, restored calm common sense to the public counsels, and, in a time when repression was the rule in European countries, gave the United States a liberal government in which men might differ in opinion without being stigmatized as unpatriotic.

Jefferson's own political philosophy was a compound of faith in individual human beings and distrust of governmental power as liable to abuse. It seemed to him that a vigorous national government was necessary only in the field of foreign relations; what was most to be desired within the country itself was the freedom of all men to avail themselves on equal terms of the unparalleled opportunities that a relatively undeveloped continent afforded. He set himself against any sort of special favor and, during his Presidency, he enormously increased opportunities by means of the Louisiana Purchase, which practically doubled the area of the country.

In practice he was by no means a weak executive. He objected to legislative omnipotence as much as to any other form of tyranny; he strongly upheld the prerogatives of the President; and he exerted influence on legislation which was all the more efficacious because it was so tactful. As President, he was the acknowledged leader of his party. He had been very critical of the formalism of official society during the administrations of his predecessors, Washington and Adams, and in reaction he went to the extreme of informality in his own dress and in indifference to protocol, with results which were often amusing. He was a bountiful host and fascinating conversationalist, however, and he fully maintained the dignity of his high office in his own person and character.

After the Louisiana Purchase, when general war was resumed in Europe, Jefferson was confronted with practically insoluble problems in his efforts to maintain American neutrality. He aroused the bitter hostility of important commercial groups, especially in New England. His popularity suffered during his second term, and he was under something of a cloud when he retired in 1809 at the age of sixty-six. But this cloud lifted during the years of peace that followed the War of 1812. His famous mansion, Monticello, was then in its present form, after a generation of building and rebuilding. The thousands of visitors who now ascend his little mountain can see not only the buildings he planned and erected and the grounds he laid out, but also numerous gadgets that he invented and delighted in. It was during his seventeen years of retirement that his fame as the Sage of Monticello came into full flower. He spent his mornings at his writing desk, corresponding with all manner of men on an infinite variety of subjects. His favorite correspondent was ex-President John

Adams; with him his old friendship had been most happily restored.

His last years were clouded by financial disaster, but Jefferson retained extraordinary health and serenity. He rode horseback every day, and the vigor of his mind was shown in the far-reaching plans he made for the University of Virginia. That institution remains his architectural and intellectual monument. In his native community, it is said, people still talk as though Mr. Jefferson were in the next room. He continues to speak to his countrymen and indeed to all mankind in his writings. No American of his age left such voluminous papers; they are now being published in an authoritative edition of more than fifty volumes. Few of us can read all of these, but anybody can quote some of his immortal sayings:

> "The God who gave us life gave us liberty at the same time."
> "Though the will of the majority is in all cases to prevail, that will, to be rightful, must be reasonable."
> "Error of opinion may be tolerated where reason is left free to combat it."
> "The earth belongs always to the living generation."
> "Nothing is unchangeable but the inherent and inalienable rights of man."

He died on July 4, 1826, at the age of eighty-three. On that same day John Adams, unaware that his old friend had gone, spoke his last words: "Thomas Jefferson still survives."

Alexander Hamilton

NATHAN SCHACHNER

With Washington, Jefferson, and Franklin, Alexander Hamilton was ranked as one of the four leading Americans of his day. Above his grave in Old Trinity Churchyard in New York City a monument bears this tribute: "The patriot of incorruptible integrity; the soldier of approved valor; the statesman of consummate wisdom." Evaluating Hamilton's contribution to the country, Daniel Webster said: "He smote the rock of the national resources, and abundant streams of revenue gushed forth. He touched the dead corpse of Public Credit, and it sprang upon its feet."

*Among the Founding Fathers none possessed a more complex
personality than Hamilton. His own passions burned so intensely
that he wedded controversy to unquenchable bitterness—in
Thomas Jefferson, who opposed him fiercely; in Aaron Burr, who
killed him on the duelling ground. Yet Hamilton, in his own right,
was a man of lasting greatness, a fact that adds much appeal to this
portrait of him by the late Nathan Schachner, eminent attorney-
at-law whose well-known, authoritative books include* Alexander
Hamilton, Nation Builder *and* The Founding Fathers.

PERCHED on a high stool, the small boy was alone in the counting
house of merchant Cruger at St. Croix in the West Indies. Only
the scratch of his pen disturbed the quiet. Suddenly he stopped,
seized another sheet of paper, and began to write.

"To confess my weakness, Ned," his pen raced along, "my ambition is prevalent, so that I contemn the grovelling condition of
a clerk or the like, to which my fortune condemns me, and would
willingly risk my life, though not my character, to exalt my station . . . I wish there was a war!"

He folded the sheet, addressed it to his friend Edward Stevens,
King's College, New York. Then with a sigh, he returned to his
ledger.

The name of the warlike little boy was Alexander Hamilton.
His age was twelve. And the year was 1769.

Alexander Hamilton was born, according to his own account, on
January 11, 1757 on Nevis in the West Indies. His mother was
beautiful Rachel Fawcett; his father James Hamilton, who had
come from Scotland to the West Indies to make his fortune. Instead, he met Rachel.

But James was a shiftless sort, and after a second child was
born, deserted his family. Heartbroken, Rachel died not long after.
At eleven, young Alexander was an orphan.

Relatives took charge of the boy and apprenticed him to merchant Cruger, who traded in molasses, rum, flour, and mules.
Young Alexander proved himself so able in business that Cruger
left him in charge during his frequent absences. A fine future
beckoned. But, as we have seen, the boy had other ambitions. He
panted for the great world—and for glory.

Then opportunity knocked in a strange disguise. A great hur-
ricane almost destroyed the island. Many died. The boy—now
fifteen—wrote an account which was published in a newspaper.

It made a sensation. The governor was impressed; so were others. Such a genius, they said, deserved an education on the mainland of America.

And so, the young lad soon found himself in New York and, within a year, a student at King's College (now better known as Columbia). Alexander did very well at his studies. But the times were in a turmoil. The British had tried to tax the colonies, to be met with the slogan: "No taxation without representation." The climax was the Boston Tea Party.

The students at Columbia paid more attention to the political disputes than to their books; and Hamilton was their leader. He wrote pamphlets which attracted wide attention. Then came Lexington and the Revolution had begun.

Aged nineteen, Hamilton volunteered as a captain of artillery. The war of which he had dreamed had become a fact; and the glory for which he panted was just around the corner. The war went on . . . Harlem Heights, the disaster of Long Island, the stand at White Plains, where Hamilton's artillery halted the attacking British long enough to enable Washington's ragged troops to withdraw and retreat to New Jersey. He raked the surprised Hessians at Trenton. He forced a company of redcoats to surrender at Princeton.

Washington needed an aide who could take over the burden of correspondence. Hamilton was known for his ready pen. And so he was now Colonel Hamilton. Morristown, Brandywine, Monmouth—the tide of battle moved on. Valley Forge, Saratoga. Hamilton hated being an aide. He wanted to lead troops, sword in hand. Yet he realized that war also required money, and there was no money. There must be an efficient government, and there was only a loose Confederation. He wrote long letters to members of Congress setting forth his views. They said: "Here is a young man with great talents and ideas." But the times were not yet ripe. The war dragged on.

Hamilton married Betsy Schuyler, the daughter of the wealthy and influential New York general. In disgust at being just a penman, Hamilton resigned his commission and studied law. He returned to the army only to join in the final assault on Yorktown. And then the war was over. Independence was won. A new nation had to be made.

Back in civilian life, Hamilton became a brilliant lawyer. He entered politics. But he was alarmed at the way the Confederation was drifting. There was no real central power, no money. The states bickered among themselves, held on to separate finances, separate tariffs. Revolt flared in Massachusetts. How long, he thought, could such a quarreling combination exist in a world of predatory powers?

For Hamilton, to think was to pick up his pen. No American has ever surpassed the power of his language, the sweep of his logic, the clarity of his ideas. Again and again he hammered his points: there must be a strong, stable government; a regular source of income for that government; and a Constitution granting such powers.

Almost single-handed, he initiated the Constitutional Convention. There, the others listened to him with respect, but thought his scheme too strong for popular approval. The final Constitution was a compromise; but even so, it met with widespread objections. Though Hamilton considered it too weak, he fought for ratification. He wrote *The Federalist Papers,* in which Madison and John Jay joined. They are still the most masterly exposition of the Constitution and of our government ever produced, and they helped swing the reluctant states into line. The Constitution was ratified, and Washington took office as President. The United States was born.

Washington chose Hamilton to head the Treasury. No office in the country was more important, for the new government was starting out bankrupt. Millions were owed in war debts here and abroad, and there was no money.

Hamilton evolved a series of far-reaching measures. First, a tariff on imports and an excise tax on certain domestic products. Second, a funding system by which the outstanding debts would be called in, and interest-bearing bonds issued in their place, dollar for dollar. In this way only, he insisted, could the credit of the nation be sustained. But the plan evoked a storm of opposition. The old soldiers who held most of the debt had long ago sold their certificates for back pay to speculators at a fraction of face value. Hamilton's opponents cried that his scheme would enrich the already rich, and grind down the poor veterans with taxes to pay again for what they had already lost. And it also meant, they said, a centralized government. That way lay monarchy, dictatorship. Was it for this they had fought the Revolution?

Hamilton remained adamant. The only way, he replied frankly, to gain peace, strength, and stability was through a powerful central government. And the only way to get such a government was to interest the rich—through their pocketbooks—in its support. He added privately that he preferred the rule of the wise, the rich, and the well-born to the rule of the masses. Look at what was happening in France! Revolution, bloodshed, anarchy!

In spite of the clamor, Hamilton forced the funding through Congress. Point three of his plan was to set up a Bank of the United States, to establish a free flow of currency, to aid business, and to furnish a reservoir from which the government could borrow in times of need. This proposal aroused even more alarm. It meant a money monopoly in the country, the strangling of agriculture, and it was unconstitutional. But Hamilton won again; and in doing so, laid down the doctrine that the Constitution must be liberally interpreted.

Point four in his plan was to encourage manufacturing through government bounties and a protective tariff. Thereby, he said, the country would never again be dependent on the wars or whims of Europe. This time he failed; and the industrial age in the United States was delayed for at least a generation.

The battles over Hamilton's proposals led to the formation of parties—the Federalists and the Republicans. Hamilton headed the Federalists; Jefferson the Republicans. In varying forms these political divisions have lasted to the present day. Hamilton called for a nation strong at home and respected abroad. He believed in economic planning, a manufacturing economy, and a rule of the elite. Jefferson feared centralization and government intervention in private affairs, thought agriculture the true basis for freedom, and pinned his faith on the instincts and votes of the common man. They fought even on foreign relations. Hamilton favored England and Jefferson France. Only on one thing did these great antagonists agree. America must keep out of war as long as possible.

Both men finally resigned from the Cabinet in disgust. Hamilton returned to his law practice. Jefferson eventually came back as Vice President and, in 1801, gained the Presidency. The Federalist party went down in decisive defeat.

Hamilton was in despair. All his great plans, he thought, had miscarried. His life had been a failure. Even his own followers had deserted him. And so even the fates seemed to indicate. For, in 1804, at the age of forty-seven, he fell on the duelling ground, slain by a bullet from the pistol of Aaron Burr, whom he had politically and personally denounced.

Yet history had belied his gloomy forebodings. In spite of temporary failure, the foundations he laid proved enduring. The world we now live in is, in effect, Hamilton's world. His financial schemes saved the nation from perishing. His dream of an industrial system has come startlingly true. We have a government with powers and an economy that is being increasingly planned. The Constitution has been extended and interpreted to meet the needs of a modern age. In one instance only might the present scene evoke a shudder from Hamilton—universal suffrage and the rule of all rather than of a select few. In this the Jeffersonian philosophy has triumphed, and properly so.

Yes, Hamilton and his ideas live on; and America is proud and grateful to own him as a Founding Father.

Establishing a Government

IRVING BRANT

When news of the surrender of Cornwallis at Yorktown reached England, a distracted Prime Minister, Lord North, cried: "Oh God! It is all over!" For the thirteen colonies along the Atlantic seaboard, however, simply another ordeal was beginning. The war had left the colonies with a debt, in round figures, of $40,000,000, one fifth of which was owed to foreign powers. A Congress that could not levy taxes to cover current running expenses had to appeal for contributions from the states to meet its debt—a slow, agonizing, ineffective situation in its most optimistic view. Moreover, each state acted as a sovereign nation, passing its own tariff laws and creating hardships that were as trying for the rich as for the poor.

In time, an order of enduring strength was evolved from this chaos—true, not until after an abortive movement like Shays' Rebellion in Massachusetts with its frightening implications had shaken the wealthy classes. Many played their part in the remarkable drama of forging the colonies into "We, the People"; and, of course, that achievement became the shining hour for James Madison, who has been called the "Philosopher of the Constitution"—a shy, sensitive Virginian of very limited oratorical gifts (a quality he shared with raspy-voiced Jefferson), who behind the closed doors of the Constitutional Convention carried point after point by his eloquence of reasoning and his unreserved charm of personal manner.

In illustrating the effectiveness of the democratic process to the world, as author-editor-historian Irving Brant soon tells us, the establishing of a government became a testament to what in the American Story truly informed statesmanship could achieve. Formerly an editorial writer for some of the nation's leading newspapers, Mr. Brant presently is at work on a five-volume biographical study of James Madison, most recently published of which is James Madison, The President, 1809–1812.

THE American people have had three systems of central government since they rebelled against King George in the spring of 1775. The first was that of the wartime Continental Congress appointed by the thirteen individual colonies; it governed the general affairs of the Union for six years.

The second system began in 1781, shortly before fighting ended in the Revolutionary War. The Continental Congress continued to govern, but it operated now under the Articles of Confederation, the first written constitution of the nation.

The third system of government is the one we have today—that of the Constitution of 1787, put into effect in 1789.

Some historians say that the Continental Congress wasn't really a government. Actually, in the early years, it governed boldly and powerfully. In 1775, it established a Continental Army and Navy. It issued paper money. It authorized individual colonies to set up civil government. It adopted a national Declaration of Independence and made a treaty of alliance with France.

The Continental Congress drew its early strength from two things: the united determination of the people, and the Congressional power to print money and make treaties. The paper money carried a pledge that it would be redeemed in gold or silver. But hard money could be obtained only through taxation. "No taxation without representation" was the war cry, and to a lot of people that meant "No Taxation. Period." With Congress unable and the states unwilling to levy taxes, Continental currency began to slide down hill. Prices soared. More money was printed. Inflation swept the land.

Finally, late in 1779, Congress stopped printing money and called on the states to pay for the war. That didn't settle the financial problem, but it finished Congress as a powerful governing body. Before the money presses were shut down, wrote James Madison, Congress had the whole wealth and resources of the continent within its command, and could do as it pleased. Since this power was given up, it had become "as dependent on the states as the King of England is on the Parliament."

Meanwhile, the Articles of Confederation were before the state legislatures for ratification. These articles were drafted in a period of national strength and unity, but they did not reflect that spirit. Written for peace time use, they were weakened by sectional jealousies, by errors due to inexperience, and by the all-pervading dislike of taxation.

In foreign affairs, war and peace, treaty making, and so forth, federal authority was of a sweeping nature. There were, however, three defects which utterly ruined the new form of government.

The most serious was the absence of taxing power, leaving Congress completely dependent on the states. Coupled with this weakness was the inability of Congress to regulate commerce.

The second defect was procedural. With each state delegation having one vote, the Articles required nine state votes for many decisions, and seven for all the rest. As a result, to be absent was the same as voting No—a system that paralyzed Congress.

The third handicap was a declaration that each state retained every power not expressly delegated to the Confederation. The purpose was moderate, to prevent the exercise of unlimited power by implication. However, it came close to excluding implied powers altogether, and the absence of a federal judiciary made the situation worse. Ratification of the Articles was delayed for four years, while Maryland, New Jersey, and other small states demanded that the unpopulated western lands be recognized as the property of the entire nation. They won that fight. But in the meantime, lack of taxing power caused federal authority to slump disastrously. Since that was not remedied in the Articles of Confederation, they were outdated even before they went into effect.

A handful of Congressmen, led by Madison, tried desperately to wipe out these defects by interpretation. Had they succeeded, the Articles of Confederation might have produced a powerful central government. But they failed. The new government, born with one foot in the grave, dragged the other one after it.

With the coming of peace, desperate trade rivalry took the place of vanishing wartime unity. States set up trade barriers against each other. When Congress demanded money, each state complained that others were paying too little, so each retaliated by paying less. The federal government defaulted on its debt to France and Holland. Unpaid war veterans sold their pay certificates to speculators for a tenth of their value. Virginia and New York brazenly violated the treaty of peace on payment of British debts and return of seized property. New England, to obtain a Spanish market for fish, was willing to give up the American claim to the Mississippi River, vital to western agriculture. American prestige, gloriously high at the close of the Revolution, slumped throughout the world.

During this time, valiant efforts were made to amend the Articles of Confederation. Twelve states voted to give Congress power to tax imports. But unanimity was required, and Rhode Island blocked the plan. A new amendment was submitted. New York defeated it.

Madison, who had entered the Virginia legislature, proposed there that the states give Congress power to regulate commerce. Patrick Henry's followers cut this resolution to pieces. Thereupon, Madison shifted to a call for a national convention on regulation of commerce—and a most lucky shift it was, for it led to the famous Annapolis Convention of 1786. The handful of men who met there, led by Hamilton and Madison, did not even form a quorum of the states. But instead of giving up, they drove boldly forward and asked Congress to summon a general convention to revise the federal government. Otherwise, they all felt, the American Union was doomed to break to pieces.

At this moment an unwelcome ally came to their aid. Financial depression struck the nation. In Massachusetts, mortgage-ridden farmers got out their Revolutionary muskets and closed the courts (Shays' Rebellion). Elsewhere, debts were stayed by law or wiped out by a flood of paper money. Tax collections were postponed, cancelled, or forcibly resisted. Alarm spread everywhere, among men of property and other sober citizens, and it took the form of a rush of support for the proposed constitutional convention.

So the framers of our present Constitution gathered in Philadelphia in the spring of 1787—men whose roster is almost a roll call of heroic figures in statecraft—George Washington, chairman of the convention; Franklin, the eighty-one-year-old diplomat; Madison, Hamilton, Gouverneur Morris, James Wilson, George Mason, Roger Sherman, Rufus King, the Pinckneys of South Carolina. Conspicuously absent were Thomas Jefferson and John Adams, who were then our ministers in Paris and London.

For three months the framers worked in utter secrecy. Then their work was submitted to state conventions. In a virtual act of revolution, the framers disregarded the unanimity clause of the old Articles, and authorized nine states to bring the new Constitution into effect. Titanic efforts were needed to win the key states of Massachusetts, Virginia, and New York. Opponents conjured up imaginary terrors and pointed to a real weakness—the absence of a Bill of Rights. Supporters offset that objection by promising later amendments. In Virginia, after a terrific verbal combat, the frail, weak-voiced Madison vanquished the mighty orator Patrick Henry. In New York, Hamilton triumphed over state-minded Governor Clinton. It was during this campaign that Hamilton, Madison, and Jay wrote *The Federalist Papers,* which have won enduring fame as a commentary on the Constitution.

What were the framers really aiming at? Were they disinterested statesmen? Or, as some say, were they big property owners protecting their own interests? Were they nationalists or states' righters? Were they aristocrats, republicans, or defenders of democracy? What was in their minds?

To begin with, the Constitution was framed after thirty years of colonial and national ferment, of armed revolution and political experiment, during which every intelligent American had become a student of government. As a result, this convention brought together the best informed group of statesmen that ever was assembled by democratic processes in the world's history.

Being revolutionists, these men were not afraid of drastic change. They wanted a strong government, but they did not want tyranny, whether by a king, a President, a Congress, or a mob. So they separated the executive from the legislative branch, and apart from both they set a strong and independent judiciary.

The framers desired to protect property. But if you will read the Constitution carefully, you will find that the provisions safeguarding property are directed against the states. The framers trusted the federal government and left it free; but the Bill of Rights, adopted soon after the establishment of the new government, placed certain curbs upon the federal government in its relations with both persons and property.

Why did these men of property trust Congress and the President? Because, at bottom, they had confidence in the people. Hamilton had no such confidence. He wanted a President and Senate chosen for life. The convention said No. Charles Pinckney argued in vain against elections by the people and in favor of huge property qualifications for officeholders. The convention followed Franklin's advice: Do not debase the spirit of the common people.

However, it was Madison who put a solid foundation under democratic self-government. The abuses of democracy, he said, were at their worst in small republics. The only remedy was to enlarge the sphere of government. That would divide the community into so great a number of interests and parties that it would be difficult to organize a majority for the oppression of the minority. There was, said Madison, no other defense consistent with the democratic form of government. "It was incumbent on us then to try this remedy and with that view to frame a republican system on such a scale and in such a form as will control all the evils which have been experienced." The state governments, being inclined to oppress minorities, must be held in check by federal authority. But the federal government, being continental in extent, could safely have large powers, if those powers were checked and balanced among the branches of the government.

The framers, men of property, accepted that view, and built on it the democratic institutions under which we operate today.

THREE

The Ideal

and the Fact

THE CONSTITUTION of the new Republic made the people sovereign. They created the government. They could both give and reserve "rights." Moreover, they could limit these rights so that a state could not usurp the functions of the central government and the national legislature could not infringe upon the purely internal affairs of the states. When conflicts arose, the courts were empowered to decide where authority properly belonged.

Yet, taking a hard look at this revolutionary document which required only ratification to become the supreme law of the land, many Americans could not conceal their disappointment, their dissatisfaction, their distrust. Wasn't this constitutional plan a form of watered-down democracy, for all the arguments of Hamilton, Madison, and Jay in *The Federalist Papers?* How did the Constitution protect the people against possible oppressions of the national government? Where—where, indeed—was its Bill of Rights? With such questions the opposition spoke scornfully—in Massachusetts through the raspy throat of Sam Adams, in Virginia through the now thundering, now dulcet voice of Patrick Henry.

The colonial constitutions of Virginia, Pennsylvania, Maryland, Vermont, New Hampshire, North Carolina, and Massachusetts contained a Bill of Rights; and the constitutions of the other colonies included some form of protection for civil liberties. For

99

too long had the New World struggled toward an ideal of human freedom not to understand the deep Old World origins of its aspirations. The struggle antedated even the Age of Discovery, for when in 1215 in the meadow at Runnymede the Magna Carta had been wrung from King John such stipulations that justice must not be sold, or that no one should be deprived of property and imprisoned without due process of law, or that taxes should be collected by legal means and not by force were terms reaffirming the dignity of the individual. By 1690, when John Locke published his *Second Treatise on Government,* the concept of individual dignity had grown to include "inalienable rights" that no man, out of a decent respect for his descendants, could ever surrender. In the Declaration of Independence Jefferson borrowed and adapted Locke's phrase, and "life, liberty, and the pursuit of happiness" became "inalienable rights" to which all men were "endowed by their Creator."

Thus a divine right of the individual superseded the divine right of kings, and a new complication was added to what Abraham Myerson calls the "underlying and fundamental principle in human life" whereby man becomes "a creature who builds up contradictory, hostile, and opposite patterns of life and attempts to live them simultaneously." To Dr. Myerson the tragedy of all human idealism rests in the necessity that "each idealism must utilize the weapons of battle to establish itself. What it wins is a successful war rather than a successful idealism."[1]

Undoubtedly man's strength and sanity are sorely taxed by this schizophrenic ambivalence; yet patterns of life change and there is a continuity to man, a history. Each generation makes its own struggle, within the microcosm of its own problems. The conflicts that arise take many names—rich against poor, white against black, Federalist against Republican, mercantile North against agricultural South, capital against labor, reformer against conservative—but there is a basic denominator to all: man against man. Out of a rough and brutal background, from feudalism and darkness into Renaissance and Reformation, man had learned this much about himself whether he be prince or pauper, poet or plodder.

The genius of the American governmental structure was based on this one tear of wisdom that had worn at the rock of eternity; that genius placed a system of checks and balances in the Consti-

[1] Myerson, Abraham: *Speaking of Man* (New York, 1950) pp. 13, 26-7.

tution and then won eventual ratification by making a Bill of Rights of its first ten amendments. A government of a people, dedicated to existing in reasonable harmony, thus was fashioned as a means to the end of compromise between opposing groups, prejudices, ambitions, and opportunities. The ideal was older than the experiment but that fact made neither less hazardous. There were few precedents upon which the young nation could lean, and its early struggle became raw and harsh and bruising—upon Washington, who would see a hostile Senate refuse to pass a resolution congratulating him on his birthday; upon Alexander Hamilton and Jefferson and John Adams, each of whom would flinch and squirm under the lash of the public whip. There were of course perils older by far than the ideal—the peril of lust for power or the peril of expediency. Could these destroy the dream behind the new Republic? In the administration of our second President both perils became dangerously real.

The Alien and Sedition Acts

C L A U D E   G .   B O W E R S

John Adams was a short, stout, ruddy-faced man, nervous and hasty, fearless and stubborn, with little of the warm personality that drew people to his second cousin, Sam Adams. Born in Braintree, Massachusetts, Puritan in a square-jawed way, educated at Harvard (as had been his father), John developed one of the best legalistic minds in the Bay Colony. The Stamp Act of 1756 found him snarling that "this tax was set on foot for my ruin as well as that of Americans in general"; thereafter he became a steadfast patriot, and whereas others might view the Boston Tea Party as rash and shocking, he called it "the most magnificent movement of all."

Elected to the Continental Congress, John Adams was one of the most powerful voices supporting the Declaration of Independence. He was a leading figure in gaining the appointment of Washington as commander-in-chief of the 16,000 New England Minute Men who, under the persuasion of Adams, Congress now incorporated into the "Continental Army." Later he was a prominent American emissary, serving in Holland where he secured recognition of

American independence, in France where he became known as "the Washington of Negotiations," and in England where his sharp opinions and antagonistic attitudes sometimes were anything but diplomatic.

Twice John Adams served as Vice President under Washington, bitter that he had been forced to accept second choice and seeing his office as "the most insignificant . . . ever the imagination of man contrived." During this period Adams published his Discourses of Davila, *revealing the mind of an arch conservative. Where Jefferson applauded the French Revolution as a people's movement, Adams detested it. The old patriot, in these later years, had grown sharp-tongued, bull-minded, and contumaceous to the point of irascibility. No one who ever crossed wits with him denied these difficult traits—least of all Alexander Hamilton, whose feud with Adams split the Federal Party into irreconcilable factions. When Washington, weary of the slurs and the abuse, refused to serve a third term, Adams opposed Jefferson for the Presidency and won by a scant three electoral votes.*

During the administration of John Adams the Navy Department was created (and war with France was narrowly averted), the nation's capital was moved to Washington (and Abigail Adams dried the family wash in the East Room of the White House), George Washington died at Mount Vernon (1799) and John Marshall became Chief Justice (1801). Yet overshadowing these events in influencing the American Story was the Alien Act and the Sedition Act. Claude G. Bowers, who served as United States Ambassador to Spain from 1933 to 1939 and whose widely read works of history include The Tragic Era *and* Jefferson and Hamilton, *describes the "reign of terror" that resulted.*

T<small>OO</small> FEW Americans realize that our freedom did not come to us like manna from heaven, but only after a bitter struggle. Despite the ideals and aspirations of the vast majority of the people, powerful forces were determined to crush government by the people in its infancy. It was not because of oversight that the Constitution came from the Convention that framed it with no provision for the protection of the people against the abuse of power. Shocked by this omission, Thomas Jefferson demanded and forced the incorporation of the first ten amendments. Thus was laid the cornerstone of our American democracy.

During the first decade of the Republic, the Federalist Party was in power. It represented wealth and the aristocracy, scorned democracy, and looked with contemptuous indifference on the mass of men. The Federalists were brilliantly led by Alexander Hamilton, who was at best lukewarm toward democracy.

Hamilton's party hated the French Revolution as a democratic movement against privilege. Taking advantage of its excesses, the Federalists made desperate efforts to force this country into a war against its one-time ally. Conditions were favorable for such a move because of the strained relations existing between the two nations. During the greater part of the French Revolution, Gouverneur Morris had continued as American minister to France. Aristocratic, monarchistic Morris aligned himself militantly with conspirators to return the King and the nobility to power. When decency demanded his recall, James Monroe, an opponent of the Federalists and sympathetic to the purpose of the Revolution in France, was sent in his place. Harassed and attacked by Federalists, he was soon recalled, much to the displeasure of the French. To succeed him, the Federalists sent C. C. Pinckney, another foe of the French Revolution. Pinckney was not received by the French government, a move made to order for the Federalists. Their spokesmen raised the hue and cry that we had been insulted. Their extremists demanded war. But President John Adams, unanxious for war, sent a commission of three men to iron out diplomatic wrinkles in Paris.

Again fate seemed to align itself with the enemies of democracy in America. The notoriously corrupt French foreign minister, Talleyrand, acting on his own, demanded a bribe as the price for receiving the American commission. The group indignantly spurned the demand and hurried home.[2] Demagogues worked the people into a state of hysteria over this move. The war hawks multiplied. The time seemed ripe for the extermination of democracy and freedom in the name of "patriotism."

The hour apparently had struck to make liberalism and democracy a crime. The conspiracy took form in a struggle to legislate the Alien and Sedition Laws. Swaggering rowdies made a mockery

---

[2] The notorious X Y Z affair that wrote into American legend the slogan: "Millions for defense, but not one cent for tribute." Warring France and England insisted they had the right to seize American ships on the high seas. Adams, honestly trying to remain neutral, sent a commission to France to arrange a treaty. Not only was the attempt at bribery by the French foreign minister reported, but, it was said, a further price for peace demanded by France was a loan of $10,000,000. War feelings reached the point where Washington was called from Mount Vernon to resume command of the army.

of the debate on these bills on the floor of Congress. Men like Madison and Gallatin, speaking against the measure, could not be heard for the loud laughter, talking, and scraping of feet on the floor. The conspirators could not afford to let the people hear what was being said against the bills. They could not let them hear men like Edward Livingston, who shouted against the clamor: "Do not let us be told that we are to excite a fervor against a foreign aggression to establish a tyranny at home; and that like the arch traitor, we cry 'Hail Columbia' at the moment we are betraying her to destruction; that we sing 'Happy Land' when we are plunging it in ruin and disgrace."

The Alien and Sedition Laws were intended to serve a party purpose. There were few Frenchmen in America, and the Alien bill was not aimed at them. One real object was to exclude the Irish, who were seeking refuge from tyranny at home. Coming to America in search of freedom, they aligned themselves with the followers of Jefferson. The hue and cry against so-called "aliens" went to desperate lengths. Demagogues demanded the expulsion of Albert Gallatin, a militant anti-Federalist and one of the foremost statesmen of the early Republic, because he was born a Swiss.

But the fighters against democracy and basic freedoms relied more for their purpose on the Sedition Law than on the Alien bill. The first draft of this measure was viciously savage. As passed by the House of Representatives, the bill declared every Frenchman an enemy of the United States, though the two nations were not at war. It provided that anyone who gave aid and comfort to a Frenchman was guilty of treason, punishable by death, an act that could have resulted in the executions of Jefferson, Madison, Monroe, and Livingston. Under provisions of this act, combinations opposing execution of the laws, or attacks on Administration policies were punishable by fines and prison. The bill would have made democracy a mockery and freedom a memory. So infamous were the law's provisions that Hamilton, leader of the Federalists, begged the Senate not to establish despotism by passing the House measure. The bill was moderated by the Senate, but it remains one of the most tyrannical laws ever to blacken American statutes.

With the passage by narrow margins of the Alien and Sedition Laws, the demagogues once more took the field against democracy. The Federalist press demanded the arrest of liberals and anti-Federalists as traitors. Federalist judges, taking their cue from party caucuses, denounced opponents of the laws as seditious. One Federalist paper in New York declared that any man criticising the Sedition Law "deserves to be suspected." Soon men were being condemned and damned on suspicion without any proof. A Boston Federalist paper smugly reminded critics of the laws that "Benedict Arnold complained bitterly about the treason law." And so, everyone opposing the Sedition Law and evoking the guarantees of the Bill of Rights was labeled a "traitor."

Mobs roamed through the country pulling down liberty poles. A demand was made that anyone who did not subscribe to the creed of the Federalist Party should be dismissed from factories making war material. Jefferson's followers were to be dismissed from the army. Federalist judges, in open court, denounced as traitors distinguished lawyers who defended victims of the Sedition Law.

Thomas Jefferson was pictured as the arch traitor, for, the demagogues pointed out, had he not said that the laws were "merely an experiment on the American mind to see how far it will bear an avowed violation of the Constitution"? On many nights Jefferson was disturbed by hoodlum gangs who played the "Rogues' March" beneath his window. His mail was opened in the hope of finding some phrase on the strength of which he could be arrested for sedition. Ignorant mobs, inflamed by the "Big Lies" of irresponsible demagogues, covered the statue of Ben Franklin with slime from the gutters.

A reign of terror was now in full blast. Scores of editors of anti-Federalist papers were awakened at night and dragged from their beds. Thrown into jails unfit for human habitation, they were hurried before packed juries and sentenced to prison for daring to speak out against the Sedition Law.

With demagogues bullying, threatening, and denouncing defenders of freedom as traitors, with drunken mobs smashing the presses of anti-Federalist papers and beating their editors, with rowdies stoning members of the anti-Federalist party, with men screaming for "heads . . . more heads," the weak and the timid were frightened into silence. Free speech had become a crime.

And then came the climax of this sorry story. The Constitution had been ignored. The Bill of Rights had become a measure of sedition. Now the conspirators against freedom actually proposed to make it an act of treason to speak against the Sedition Law on the floor of the House or Senate. With suppression of papers that might have told the truth, one Virginia Congressman was forced to write a letter to his constituents, describing the scenes at the

Capitol. A Federalist judge promptly laid a copy of the letter before a grand jury with a demand for an indictment for sedition.

Now, assured that the people had been bullied into silence, the enemies of freedom went further and planted their heels on the Bill of Rights. It was time, they thought, to deny the people the sacred right of petition. John Armstrong, author of the Newburgh Address which urged the officers of the Revolution to defy Congress in order to obtain moneys due them, wrote a powerful petition for the repeal of the Sedition Law.[3] The man who circulated it for signatures was arrested as a common criminal. Surrounded by armed horsemen, he was paraded two hundred miles through the rain to a mockery of a trial in New York City. There he was sentenced to prison for circulating a petition.

Thus, with the Bill of Rights brushed aside, it became a criminal act for a citizen to petition his representatives in Congress.

Citizens expressed their opinions at their peril. The freedom of the press had become a mockery. Party conclaves, and not courts, determined the guilt or the innocence of the accused. Any man accused by an irresponsible demagogue was presumed to be guilty. Lawyers defending victims of the Sedition Law were tongue-lashed by Federalist judges as "traitors." For two years the Bill of Rights was anathema, and an arrogant despotism had its heel on the neck of American democracy.

It was under these conditions that Thomas Jefferson formed a party of opposition to awaken the people to their peril, to mobilize them in defense of their freedoms, to revive their courage and fighting spirit. With consummate skill and daring he led the people. The foulest abuse was heaped upon him; the most atrocious lies were circulated against him. To avoid insults, Jefferson retired from social circles.

There were Federalists, and among them the greatest, who had no sympathy with the Alien and Sedition Laws. Hamilton, who was no demagogue, found the Sedition Law repugnant. When the Federalists hoped through terrorism to win the Congressional election in 1798 and persuaded John Marshall to accept a nomination, there was jubilation in their camp. But the jubilation was short-lived. Marshall's first act after his nomination was to issue a statement against the Sedition Law.

[3] John Armstrong (1758–1843) had kindled Washington's displeasure with his "Newburgh Addresses," intended to arouse Congress to redress army grievances. Later he served as United States Minister to France (1804–1810) and as Secretary of War (1813–1814).

This era of fascism and fakery, so strikingly like that in any totalitarian state, continued for two years. Then, in the Presidential election of 1800, the people arose in defense of their freedoms and swept Jefferson into the Presidency. The vicious Alien and Sedition Laws passed from the statutes. Their victims were released from prison. The Constitution and the Bill of Rights again became sacrosanct. American democracy was definitely proclaimed the system of the nation.

And the Federalist Party, responsible for these despotic laws and the crimes that came from them, passed from power never to rise again.

History's Greatest Real Estate Bargain

JOHN BAKELESS

During the early weeks of 1801 about the calmest person in Washington City was Thomas Jefferson. Persons who saw him lounging at Conrad's boarding house in the plain, somewhat mussed clothes that had become a political symbol of his democratic faith in the people would have thought him almost disinterested in the nation's most bristling controversy. A deadlock in the electoral college gave both Jefferson and Burr seventy-three votes and threw into the House the election of a President to succeed John Adams. Congressmen toiled up the hill to the Capitol through a swirling snowstorm on February 11; after twenty ballots Jefferson still held eight states, one less than necessary for election, with Vermont and Maryland divided. Days later the result was unchanged; an unruly spirit swept Washington and mobs roamed the streets; but behind the scenes Hamilton, who thoroughly detested Burr, worked to elect Jefferson. On the thirty-sixth ballot the Federalist Congressmen from Vermont and Maryland declined to vote, and Jefferson was elected.

To the office of President the author of the Declaration of Independence carried more than a belief that he understood, respected, and represented the so-called "common man." As minister to France, as Secretary of State under Washington and Vice President under Adams, Jefferson had proved that he was an astute student of statecraft. Moreover, he knew the ticklish implications posed by the French political situation. In 1801 Spain transferred its Louisiana territory to France, and a large area basic to the growth of continental North America came under the control of Napoleon. "The day that France takes possession of New Orleans, we must marry ourselves to the British fleet and nations," wrote Jefferson, who might have contemplated smallpox with equal relish. With two million dollars secured from Congress for "extraordinary expenses," Jefferson hurried James Monroe to France to assist our minister there, Robert R. Livingston, in arranging for the purchase of New Orleans and Florida (or at least to secure perpetual freedom of navigation of the Mississippi).

Meanwhile Napoleon was having troubles—the revolt under Toussaint l'Ouverture in Haiti and Santo Domingo (1801), another war impending with England (about 1803), and a pressing need for money. So Talleyrand, who had a way of catching Americans by surprise, asked bluntly: "What will you give for the whole of Louisiana?" To explain what, once we recovered our wits, the purchase signified, John Bakeless, lecturer in journalism at New York University, brings the sharp insight gained from authorship of such books as Lewis and Clark, Partners in Exploration *and* The Eyes of Discovery.

T HE Louisiana Purchase has been called "the greatest real estate bargain in history." That estimate is probably correct. At any rate, it would be hard to think of a better one, though the United States has always done pretty well in its real estate deals. Manhattan Island wasn't a bad buy. Neither was Alaska nor the Gadsden Purchase.

But the Louisiana Purchase was a good deal more than a smart bargain in real estate. It was really the making of the modern United States; or, if that is putting it too strongly, it was one of half a dozen events, without which there would never have been anything like the present United States of America.

The Louisiana Purchase made possible the destiny of America as a two-ocean world power. It gave us control of some of the most fertile territory and some of the richest mines in the world. It gave us control of the Mississippi River, which, in the days before transportation by air and rail, was a vital commercial route. Thus the Louisiana Purchase united our country as nothing else could have done. The West—in those days that meant Kentucky and the country around it—decided to stick with the United States.

Before the Purchase there had been continual trouble because farm products could be sold only by sending them down the Mississippi, with the Spaniards in control at New Orleans. Western Pennsylvania even staged an armed rebellion, which had to be suppressed by the father of Robert E. Lee! There was always the chance that the Westerners might leave the United States entirely and throw in their lot with Spain. Even so sterling an American as Daniel Boone had been forced to leave the country he had opened up, and settle in Missouri, then part of "Louisiana." Boone was even, for a time, an official of the Spanish government in Missouri.

But when the Louisiana Purchase made the Mississippi firmly American, as well as the vast stretch of country reaching to the Rockies, the United States could turn its back on the Atlantic world and forget the squabbles of Europe for at least a century. We could devote ourselves to developing our own immense resources and immense internal market, unhampered by tariffs between the states, or frontier jealousies. We could provide for a growing population.

The queer thing is that in 1803 nobody quite knew what the United States had bought. North America had already been crossed, overland, but not through this territory. Clearly, Mr. Jefferson thought, the thing to do was to send an expedition up the Missouri River to its source. Nobody knew where the source was, but it simply had to be somewhere in the Rocky Mountains. Then, if the expedition crossed the Rocky Mountains alive, it could go beyond the Purchase territory, down the Columbia River to the Pacific Coast—that is, if it could find the Columbia. White men knew where the river's mouth was. A few of them had gone some miles up its length. Beyond that—no one knew.

The Lewis and Clark Expedition was almost ready to start even before the Louisiana Purchase was made. Western exploration had been on Mr. Jefferson's mind for years. As early as 1783, he had asked General George Rogers Clark, hero of the Revolution in the Northwest, if he would like to lead an expedition. Mr. Jefferson wanted to get ahead of the British, now that the Revolutionary War was ending, but the scheme never did work out. Yet William Clark, youngest brother of George Rogers Clark, became one of the two leaders of the Lewis and Clark Expedition, and it was General George Rogers Clark who advised him to go.

The Lewis and Clark Expedition came near not being a Lewis and Clark Expedition at all, for Mr. Jefferson really meant it to be

the Lewis Expedition. For years he had watched Meriwether
Lewis grow up on a neighboring plantation. When Jefferson was
elected President, he asked young Captain Lewis, then on duty
with the army in the wilderness beyond Pittsburgh, to become his
secretary and live in the White House with him.

Mr. Jefferson certainly did not select Captain Lewis for any
special secretarial talents. For one thing, he was one of the worst
spellers who ever lived. It is reasonably clear that Mr. Jefferson
had already settled on his young Albermarle County friend to explore the West. Allowed to select another leader to go with him,
Lewis's first choice was red-headed Billy Clark, with whom he had
served in the army a few years before.

Until Lewis and Clark crossed the Continent and came back
with the facts, people had some very odd ideas of what was in the
new and unknown land they had bought. Mr. Jefferson himself
rather expected the Corps of Discovery, as the expedition liked
to call itself, to find mammoths still alive. Whatever the scientific
men may say about it, the Indians had stories about mammoths.[4]
Daniel Boone and others found their tusks and bones lying on, or
just under, the ground in Kentucky. An English sailor who walked
across eastern North America in the middle 1500's insisted he had
actually seen "elephants"—which must have meant mammoths.

[4] Jefferson recorded the following Indian story: ". . . the Mammouth, or big
buffalo, as called by the Indians, must certainly have been the largest. Their
tradition is, that he was carnivorous, and still exists in the northern part of
America. A delegation of warriors from the Delaware tribe having visited the
governor of Virginia, during the present revolution, on matters of business,
after these had been discussed and settled in council, the governor asked them
some questions relative to their country, and, among others, what they knew
or had heard of the animals whose bones were found at the Saltlicks, on the
Ohio. Their chief speaker immediately put himself into an attitude of oratory,
and with a pomp that he suited to what he conceived the elevation of his subject, informed him that it was a tradition handed down from their fathers, 'that
in ancient times a herd of these tremendous animals came to the Big-bone
licks, and began a universal destruction of the bear, deer, elks, buffaloes, and
other animals, which had been created for the use of the Indians; that the
Great Man above, looking down and feeling this, was so enraged that he seized
his lightning, descended on the earth, seated himself on a neighboring mountain, on a rock, on which his feet and the print of his feet still are to be seen,
and hurled his bolts among them till the whole were slaughtered, except the
big bull, who presenting his forehead to the shafts, shook them off as they fell;
but missing one at length, it wounded him in the side; whereon, springing
round, he bounded over the Ohio, over the Wabash, the Illinois, and finally
over the great lakes, where he is living at this day.'" Jefferson, Thomas: *Notes
on the State of Virginia* (London, 1787), pp. 64–5.

Mr. Jefferson also believed that there was a huge mountain, all of rock salt, somewhere in the West. Apparently he had been hearing distorted rumors of the great salt deserts. His enemies scoffed. Probably, they said, there was also a great big American eagle, also carved in rock salt, sitting on top of Mr. Jefferson's mountain.

But the things that the Corps of Discovery really found in the Louisiana Purchase were stranger and more valuable than anything imagined: the wonderful stretch of fertile land, the enormous plains, the towering Rockies—"Shining Mountains," the Indians called them—buffalo herds, grizzly bears, trees towering two hundred feet in air (though the expedition never saw the big sequoias of California), new rivers, strange plants. The Lewis and Clark Expedition did not see everything. They never noticed, for instance, that there was gold in the sands of Montana's rivers over which their canoes passed.

Nevertheless, the exploration of the Louisiana Purchase—and beyond—was a wonderful achievement. Lewis and Clark went from St. Louis to Oregon without losing a man in battle and with only one Indian fight. A sergeant died of illness, probably appendicitis. Captain Lewis was accidentally shot by one of his own men, who deserves a small niche in military history (he is the only private in the history of the U.S. Army who ever shot his commander in the seat of the britches and got away with it). Lewis and Clark were the first army officers to put enlisted men on courts martial. It probably wasn't legal, but the army has followed their example since World War II.

The expedition even took a baby along, and brought it back, alive and healthy. The baby belonged to the admirable little Shoshone squaw, Sacagawea, and her husband, who made the trip as interpreters. It is sometimes said that Sacagawea "guided" the expedition, which is nonsense. While the explorers were on the rivers they needed no guide. In the mountains, Sacagawea knew nothing about the country. But to cross the Rockies they had to get pack horses, and it was Sacagawea who interpreted when they were bargaining with the Shoshone Indians. Moreover Lewis and Clark had the luck to run into the very band from which she had been kidnaped, years before, and of which her brother was now chief.

The Lewis and Clark Expedition told America for the first time what it had acquired by its great Purchase. After them came trappers, traders, soldiers, settlers, farmers, cattlemen—and laid the foundations for the America of today.

Pioneer of Technological Change

NATHAN MILLER

Quickly the new Republic discovered that independence is a relative term. Actually America was far from being economically free from its old status as a colony of Europe. The habit of raising raw materials and buying British merchandise carried over from colonial days, and a post-Revolution depression left its mark. When Hamilton's financial policies produced a more fluid capital, the speculative wave that followed depended on immigration and foreign money, both of which began to disappear about 1793 as Europe braced for a general war. Finally, the overwhelming interest of the population in agriculture hardly brought the economic independence that must come through manufacture, better transportation, the development of real estate, and wider trade.

In the South especially this preoccupation with agriculture developed deep roots that, spreading, intensified the struggle for American economic independence and became a factor in producing a national catastrophe. Yet this result might never have followed except for an imaginative Yankee, and the story of Eli Whitney now is related by Nathan Miller, an economic historian at Rutgers University.

WHEN THE shore batteries of Charleston opened fire on Fort Sumter in April, 1861, and began the four-year struggle between North and South, Eli Whitney had been dead for thirty-five years. Whitney's achievements, however, lived on after him. The cotton gin that he invented played a significant part in the rise of the Cotton Kingdom in the South. In the North, Whitney's principle of interchangeable parts in manufacturing, no longer restricted to muskets, was being applied to clocks, watches, locks, sewing machines, and agricultural implements. North and South of the Mason-Dixon line the consequences of this inventor's labors were felt, and would continue to be felt long after the guns were permanently silenced at Appomattox.

Eli Whitney was born in Westboro, Massachusetts, in 1765. During the years when our nation was being established, Whitney grew up on his father's farm. There he showed less interest in the routine chores of a farm boy than in working with the tools and lathe in his father's shop. During the Revolutionary War, while still in his teens, Whitney established his first modest business enterprise, the manufacture of nails, which at the time were commanding high prices. When the war ended and prices fell, Whitney, with the shrewdness of an experienced man of affairs, shifted to the more profitable production of pins for ladies hats. Clearly, before Whitney was fully grown, he had displayed the two characteristics that would shape the course of his adult life—an interest in manufacturing and an adeptness in business matters. In 1789, Whitney entered Yale College after several years of teaching in country schools. Upon graduation, Ezra Stiles, president of Yale, recommended him as a tutor in the family of a Southern planter.

He made the long sea voyage to Savannah, there to find that the terms of his employment had, inadvertently, been misrepresented. Uncertain as to what course to take, he bided his time on the estate of Mrs. Catherine Greene, the widow of the Revolutionary War general, Nathanael Greene. There, during his brief stay, he may have learned of the precarious condition of the Southern economy, for rice and indigo no longer yielded profits, and tobacco was a glut on the market. Some spoke hopefully of the short-staple, green-seed cotton, which grew well in the Southern uplands, as a possible marketable crop that could lift the section out of its economic doldrums. This hope was based on more than wishful thinking. A series of spectacular inventions had so mechanized the British textile industry that in the brief period between 1783 and 1790 its capacity to consume raw cotton had increased more than threefold. Moreover, there were signs that the demand for raw cotton would continue to mount. Despite British efforts to prevent it, new improvements in cotton manufacturing had been carried across the Atlantic. At Providence, Rhode Island, Samuel Slater, a British mechanic, had succeeded in reproducing from memory the complicated machinery in use by the British spinning mills.

What mechanical invention had done for spinning and weaving, it might well do for processing raw cotton. The chief obstacle that prevented the South from reaping great profits in the booming market for cotton was the stubborn way that the cotton fiber clung to its seed. At Mrs. Greene's, Whitney heard some "very respectable gentlemen" agree "that if a machine could be invented which would clean the cotton with expedition, it would be a great thing to the country and the inventor." Whitney solved the problem quickly. A model was immediately followed by a large-scale machine. The tutorship was forgotten; Whitney went into partnership with Phineas Miller; and the inventor returned to New Haven to devote all of his time to the manufacture of cotton gins.

There was nothing especially complicated about Whitney's gin. The machine's utter simplicity accounted for its usefulness and efficiency, as well as for Whitney's extreme caution in warning his father "to keep the whole matter a profound secret"—at least until a patent was obtained. But no patent could protect the inventor of a machine which, according to Whitney, would do the work of a hundred men in a day and seemed capable of turning depression into prosperity for many planters. Too much was at stake. Besides, as the planters reasoned their situation, were not Whitney and Miller setting up a monopoly which was contrary to the traditions of the American Revolution?

Within a year after Whitney's gin was patented, illegal gins were springing up throughout the South. The firm of Whitney and Miller was busily instituting lawsuits against infringers. The patent law, which required proof that illegal gins were actually in operation, created great hardship for the inventor when he resorted to court action to protect his rights. The operation of illegal gins was conducted in secrecy, so successfully that on one occasion Whitney found it difficult to prove in court that such gins were in use despite the fact that their rattling could be distinctly heard from the courthouse steps.

The turning of the tide came when South Carolina, North Carolina, and Tennessee bought the rights to Whitney's gin, and after the federal government had amended the patent law in favor of the inventor. Even in Georgia, where resistance to the so-called ginning monopoly had been greatest, justice was done to Whitney. A court ruling clearly assigned credit for the invention to him, and credit for the South's economic revival to the invention. One statistic tells the story. Shortly after Whitney patented his gin in 1795 the total cotton crop of the United States was eight million pounds; in 1807, it was ten times that amount.

If the gin failed to enrich Whitney, as it had enriched some planters, it yielded unsuspected profits in terms of industrial experience. As a manufacturer of gins, Whitney tried to substitute the machine for the skilled artisan, of whom there were too few at that time in the United States. However, it was as a manufacturer of muskets for the government that the inventor had the opportunity to make extensive use of machinery in manufacturing. Up to that time, the skilled gunsmith made muskets which resembled each other outwardly, but which showed slight but distinct differences in the construction of their parts and in the way they fitted together. Each musket was produced as a single unit. No part of one musket could be transferred to another. Only the manufacture of uniform parts by machinery could make possible the successful use of interchangeable parts.

Whitney's reputation as an inventor—along with the threat of war with France in 1798—helped him win a government contract to make ten thousand muskets, the largest order for one man to fill given up to that time. Only an order of this size, however, could make an arms factory feasible, and only the government's large need could justify mass production methods.

The government contract paid for Whitney's "experiment" in his new method of manufacturing and proved to be his financial salvation. "Bankruptcy and ruin were constantly staring me in the face," wrote the inventor. "I was miserable . . . without resources and without any business . . . An opportunity offered to contract for manufacturing muskets for the United States. I embraced it . . . By this contract I obtained some thousands of dollars in advance which saved me from ruin."

Whitney chose the site for his arms factory outside of New Haven on the Mill River. Heavy snowfalls in the winter of 1798 interfered with the construction of his shops. But such accidental difficulties were of small significance when compared with those imposed by the new production methods, whose costs in time and money even Whitney had not foreseen. Repeatedly, the inventor explained to officials in Washington the delay in meeting his schedule of delivery, and, on occasions, requested an advance of funds. Only men of independent judgment and a willingness to act according to their beliefs would have backed Whitney as loyally as they did. By 1801 their confidence in the man was vindicated. Early that year, Whitney went to Washington to present several muskets for inspection to President John Adams and various department heads of the national government. The impression he made was obviously great. Speaking of the inventor, one observer reported that "men of all parties agree that his talents are of immense importance and must be . . . devoted to the means of defense." It was Jefferson, however, who best explained the full details of Whitney's method of manufacturing. He informed Governor Monroe of Virginia that Whitney "invented moulds and machines for making all pieces of his musket locks so exactly equal, that take one hundred locks to pieces and mingle their parts, and the hundred locks may be put together as well by taking the first pieces that come to hand."

The outbreak of the War of 1812 found Whitney once again manufacturing arms for the government. With justification he declared at this time that his "new method" was "practically useful and highly important"; and so it was. His methods were adopted by the government and used in armories.

Whitney's inventions were of great consequence. His cotton gin revived the Southern economy, but at a fearful expense. Increasingly, the section became tied to the annual fate of the cotton crop. And the crop depended, so Southern planters believed, on the maintenance of slavery.

Mass production and interchangeable parts became a commonplace feature of modern manufacturing. By lowering costs of production, wide distribution of innumerable products of industry were made possible, transforming luxuries into necessities and affecting the tastes and habits of a whole nation. The origins of the methods of manufacture used in the automotive and aircraft industries, and in the manufacture of vacuum cleaners and washing machines, may be traced back to Whitney's shops on the Mill River outside of New Haven.

"Mr. Madison's War"

GEORGE DANGERFIELD

A small, frail man, quiet in manner, studious in habits, modest by nature, James Madison came to Williamsburg, Virginia, as a member of the Governor's Council in 1778. Here he formed the warm friendship with Thomas Jefferson that endured through the remainder of his lifetime. Madison's calmness, his great gift for tact, his practical judgment, his interests in history, politics, law, Hebrew, and philosophy were all capacities that drew Jefferson to him. The struggle for the separation of church and state in Virginia, started by Jefferson, was completed by Madison with the enactment in 1786 of Virginia's Statute for Religious Liberty—a document that in Virginia, declared Madison, "extinguished forever the ambitious hope of making laws for the human mind." Madison's

role in the Constitutional Convention and his share in writing
The Federalist Papers *added to his reputation.*

*Jefferson turned naturally to this gifted fellow Virginian to
serve as his Secretary of State during his eight trying years in the
Presidency; and when a weary Jefferson, aware of his waning
popularity, decided to retire after two terms, he chose Madison for
his successor as the Republican candidate. The situation that
Madison inherited was far from happy; and George Dangerfield,
who in 1953 won both the Bancroft Prize and the Pulitzer Prize
for his book* The Era of Good Feelings *(which had been preceded
by other distinguished volumes), explains how Madison influenced
Americans to realize "they were no longer a tail to the European
kite."*

On June 18, 1812, the United States of America declared war on
Great Britain. The War of 1812, as it is now called, was sometimes
known in those days as "Mr. Madison's War"—a title which, need-
less to say, was the invention of President James Madison's political enemies. For the War of 1812 was not a war of President
Madison's choosing. It was forced upon him—partly by Great
Britain, partly by France, partly by the farmers and planters of
the American West and Southwest, partly by desperation, and
partly by destiny.

But however mixed its origins may have been—whether it was
fought for the freedom of the seas, or for independence, or out of
frustration, or for the sake of Canadian farming lands—the War of
1812 was not, properly speaking, just a private quarrel between
America and England. It was an episode, almost a final episode, in
the great drama of the Napoleonic Wars, and its causes ran deep
into the old quarrel between Great Britain and France.

The Napoleonic Wars, beginning in 1803, might be described as
a contest between the French and British for the control of the
vital trade routes between America and India. The wars were
really one gigantic trade war, and, like a whirlpool of uncontrol-
lable dimensions, they sucked in fragment after fragment of the
civilized world.

How could America escape? She was in the fatal position of
being a neutral with something attractive to offer. She may have
been poor, young in years, and the occupant of an inconspicuous
place in the family of nations, but she had a fine merchant marine
and a marvelously profitable carrying trade. It was not possible

that this trade should escape the attention of England and of France. Each began to woo the United States; and, as is usually the case with great and desperate belligerents, it was not with kind words and seductive promises that they wooed her, but with insults and with menaces.

By the Berlin and Milan Decrees of 1806 and 1807, Napoleon declared that he would confiscate all neutral shipping that came within his grasp if it had had relations of any kind with the British. If he could have enforced these Decrees, the merchant marine of the United States would simply have vanished. By Orders-in-Council of 1807, the British announced that all neutral shipping must submit itself entirely to their illegal system of license and toll. Napoleon, in other words, tried to cut English commerce off from the continent of Europe, while the British hoped to defeat Napoleon by compelling neutral shipping to pay tribute to their government. Caught between these two policies, the United States might well find it impossible not to enter the war upon one side or the other.

Whether the Decrees were more piratical than the Orders-in-Council, or the Orders-in-Council more savage than the Decrees, has never been decided. The British, however, piled insult upon insult by their system of impressment—that is, by seizing foreign seamen and forcing them to serve in the living hell of their navy. It is estimated that as many as 6,000 American sailors were enslaved in this way.

Here, surely, was a cause for war. Yet the United States had tried by every means to keep out of the war; and her system of peaceful coercion through Embargo and Nonintercourse came, in the end, miraculously close to success. Just two days before the United States declared war, Great Britain repealed her offensive Orders-in-Council. If only the Americans could have waited a few weeks longer—but they could not wait. World wars have their own momentum, which single nations cannot arrest; and their own corruption, which human nature cannot resist. It is an ironical fact that the shipping and mercantile interests of Americans—in New England, for example, and in New York City—were totally opposed to a war with Great Britain. The impressment of their seamen, and the confiscation of their tonnage and cargoes, meant little to them when compared to the immense profits which were obtained from a single successful voyage. On the other hand, the Congressional leaders of the farming interests—the representatives of men who lived in the shadow of remote forests and by the shores of almost legendary rivers, and who had never seen the sea—began to clamor for war in the name of "Free Trade and Seaman's Rights."

These leaders, known as the War Hawks, were all young men who had never agreed with the pacific policy of Jefferson and Madison. They came either from the West or from the frontier districts of the older sections. The most famous of them were Henry Clay of Kentucky and John Caldwell Calhoun of South Carolina. Certainly men like Clay and Calhoun were ardent and patriotic. Certainly their high spirit had been affronted by England's violation of America's neutral rights on the high seas, no less than by her sinister relations with the Indians on their borders. But what is more to the point is that they controlled the Twelfth Congress, sitting from 1811 to 1813, and in the Twelfth Congress they represented not only pride, but hunger.

Of all early American appetites, land hunger is historically the most basic and universal; and the West had long been yearning for the farm lands of Canada and the undeveloped real estate of Spanish Florida. A successful war with England would undoubtedly be the quickest way of securing this territory for American expansion.

What surprises us is the innocence, or infatuation, of the War Hawks. They could not expect to win such a war. All they could reasonably hope was not to lose it.

The invasion of Canada was a failure from the start. The War Hawks believed that this immense task could be accomplished chiefly through the efforts of half-trained militia and raw recruits. The government did not exactly share this delusion, but it never seems to have realized, until it was too late, that the British could be defeated only if their one supply route of the St. Lawrence could be cut off as near the source as possible. Instead the invasion took the form of three or four unco-ordinated assaults, led by generals whose incompetence was positively startling. Only Master Commandant Perry's great victory on Lake Erie in 1813, and General William H. Harrison's consequent triumph at the Battle of the Thames, saved the West from disaster.

In 1814, to be sure, under new generals like Jacob Brown, Alexander Macomb, and Winfield Scott, the Americans fought with a ferocious valor at the small but bloody Battles of Chippewa and Lundy's Lane, thus proving that, properly trained and led, they were formidable fighting men. But the battles were, strategically, quite inconclusive in general result.

The invasion of Spanish Florida, properly speaking, never took place at all. Madison's enemies in the Senate saw to it that he was forbidden to move any army east of the Perdido River. In 1814, General Andrew Jackson made a brief and successful and quite unauthorized attack upon Pensacola, but this was a raid and nothing more. Only in single-ship battles with units of the British navy, only in the daring of their privateers who raided in the English Channel itself, did the Americans enjoy a dazzling success. This hit-and-run action was highly mortifying to British pride, but it made scarcely a dent on the British navy or British commerce. Indeed, if the Americans can be said to have accomplished anything it was the expulsion of the Creek Indians from some of their rich farming lands in the Southwest.

The British meanwhile, after Napoleon's defeat at Moscow in the winter of 1812, became more at liberty to turn their attention to the United States. Their naval blockade tightened its grip on our long and helpless coastline. With Napoleon's abdication in 1814, they had the United States at their mercy. Yet the British were singularly merciful; or, to put it more accurately, they were singularly inept. Their invasion by way of Lake Champlain was halted by American Captain Macdonough's magnificent naval victory over British Commodore Downie in Plattsburg Bay. Their diversionary movement in Chesapeake Bay culminated in the burning of the White House and Capitol, a piece of senseless vandalism which even they could not explain away (but which at least inspired Francis Scott Key, as a result of the defense of Baltimore's Fort McHenry, to write "The Star-Spangled Banner"). And their great assault upon the vital waterway of the Mississippi was hurled back by Andrew Jackson's riflemen in the horrible bloodbath of the Battle of New Orleans.

And yet the government of the United States was by this time thoroughly discredited. Its treasury was empty. In New England the leaders of the mercantile and shipping interests were openly talking of secession. But the British, it seems, no longer pressed for victory. Thus, we come, as surely we must, to the trading features of this indecisive war. From the beginning, both sides had been trying to make peace; and at Ghent, in 1814, commissioners from both sides eventually met to try to decide upon terms. As one examines these negotiations, one realizes that the British had undergone a significant change of mind. They had realized that, as an industrial and exporting nation, they needed free access to

American markets far more than they needed control of the American merchant marine. Friendship was more profitable than enmity; victory was less important than trade.

When a treaty of peace was signed at Ghent on December 28, 1814—ironically enough, before the Battle of New Orleans was even fought—it said nothing about the grave issues which underlay the war. It was silent about impressment, it was silent about neutral rights. These and other problems were left to the arbitration of time. And time—if there is enough of it—is the best of arbitrators. As the century advanced all the great issues between America and England were peacefully settled; and Anglo-American friendship, at least in trade relations, became finally one of the firm realities of the modern world.

No doubt the War of 1812 had something to do with this, and it had another and more immediate result. Once it had been won, or at any rate not lost, the Americans realized that they could no longer be considered a weak sideline republic, clinging precariously to the fringes of Christendom. Still less could they be considered a mere tail to the European kite. They had gained a respectable place in the family of nations. They entered at once upon an era of exuberant nationalism and, with a superb confidence, turned toward the vast, the beckoning, the almost unimaginable West.

The Factory Comes to New England

THOMAS C. COCHRAN

Perhaps there was not a single concrete gain to credit to Mr. Madison's War, yet at least two indirect results had a tonic effect upon the future. First, the strengthening of patriotism, as Mr. Dangerfield concludes, found young America entering upon "an era of exuberant nationalism"; and, second, a war that cut off imports from Britain provided powerful stimulation to the creation of domestic manufactures. Soon in New England an experiment would be tried that brought travelers from overseas to inspect and to marvel at this achievement of Yankee ingenuity. Thomas C. Cochran, professor of American History at the University of

Pennsylvania, editor of the New York University Business History Series, and author of numerous books, unfolds this climactic episode in America's progress toward economic independence.

W<small>HEN</small> "Mr. Madison's War" in 1812 hit a hard blow at overseas trade, New England merchants reluctantly turned to new ways for employing their capital. Many possibilities beckoned, for canals were needed, Western lands awaited development, and high grade ores might still be found in the Eastern states. But all these involved new and unexplored risks. More familiar to the merchants of eastern New England was the trade in textiles.

Rhode Islanders had already established small factories for spinning yarn, but no one had successfully duplicated the completely mechanized cotton mills of Great Britain. Power weaving was the crux of the technological problem. Could Americans build a successful power loom? Could they keep it operating profitably after it was built?

Francis Cabot Lowell, who was to give a final affirmative answer to these questions, had been familiar with them since his youth. While he was a student at Harvard his uncle had built one of the first spinning mills. Consequently, when disputes with Great Britain hurt Lowell's business as a Boston merchant, his thoughts turned to the possibilities of weaving cotton by machinery.

In 1811 he went to England for what he called a vacation to study the textile industry. He steeped himself in the details of cotton manufacture, watching looms, asking questions, comparing various factories. All these observations had to be made without attracting too much attention, for British laws prohibited the export of plans and models or the emigration of skilled technicians. Nevertheless, when Lowell returned to Boston in the spring of 1812, he was convinced that he could design a successful cotton factory.

Needing a practical mechanic to build a machine Lowell turned to Paul Moody of nearby Amesbury. Much of the ensuing success depended on Moody, who proved to be an inventor and designer of high ability. Working from Lowell's amateurish drawings and inexact recollections, the two re-invented the power loom. Their machine was bigger and bulkier than its British contemporaries, but in some respects it was better. Nathan Appleton, one of the newer merchants of Boston and a cautious investor in the enterprise, wrote: "I well recollect that state of admiration and satisfaction with which we sat by the hour, watching the beautiful movement of the new and wonderful machine, destined as it was to change the character of all textile industry."

Meanwhile, Lowell had interested his wealthy brother-in-law, Patrick Tracy Jackson, in his plans, and they purchased a water power site at Waltham, on the Charles River, a few miles west of Cambridge, and secured a corporate charter for the Boston Manufacturing Company. With the model loom in working order, and the legal details attended to, Jackson and Lowell readily interested their rich friends and relatives in shares of the $300,000 capital deemed necessary for a start. This abundance of capital was a major element in their success. Unlike small mills that lived from hand to mouth, the Boston Company could pay cash for what it wanted, and buy anything that promised to improve efficiency.

The Waltham factory, opened in 1815, began a new era of American production. All previous uses of power had been small-scale. Makers of hardware and firearms had used a few power tools in their machine shops; cotton spinners had built only small mills because they were limited to the amount of hand-weaving that could be done in the neighborhood. But Waltham was a true factory. Every stage of production from raw cotton to finished cloth was under one roof, and each stage was mechanized to keep pace with the next. More machines could be added indefinitely as demand increased. Here was the realization of mass production.

Not least among the achievements of Lowell and his group, who came to be called the Boston Associates, was their solution of the labor problem. Earlier American textile plants had moved whole families from farms to squalid mill towns. In good times all members of the family above five years old found work at spinning, carding, or weaving, but in bad times unemployment and hunger plagued these company towns. And at all times, they, like their English prototypes, were wracked by poverty.

From studying these mill towns at home and abroad, Francis Lowell evolved a better plan. He wanted well-brought-up farm girls to tend his machines. He guessed correctly that these vigorous young women would welcome the chance to get away from home, earn some money, and partake of the cultural advantages of the city. They would constitute a fluid labor supply, able to return home without hardship when out of work, and anxious to bring in younger sisters and friends when more hands were needed. The plan depended on two essentials: the conditions must be attractive to the girls, and appear safe to puritanical fathers and mothers.

Pursuing such thoughts, Lowell and Jackson established the famous boarding house system. The girls lived in company-regulated homes as thoroughly supervised by matrons as at any fashionable boarding school. Wages were high enough to save a dollar or two a week beyond necessary expenses, and ultimately entertainment and learning were supplied by libraries and lecturers. The plan worked. The girls came and liked it, making the Associates proud not only of their efficient workers, but also of an achievement in mass education.

In other departments, Lowell, Jackson, and Moody had improved upon Lowell's British observations. No foreign factory was so completely integrated. Like Henry Ford a century later they understood the American market for cheap, standardized goods. No fancy cottons came from the looms at Waltham. One grade only of strong coarse sheeting was produced at a price to sell to the poorest Western farmer.

These shrewd men of Boston saw their problems in broad terms. They realized that with the close of the war the time was ripe to secure a protective tariff. Accordingly Francis Lowell journeyed to Washington. There he talked to men like John C. Calhoun of South Carolina about the great future of American textile production in the South as well as in the North. To these Southerners he pointed to the statistics of cotton consumption that showed the ties between plantation and mill. To Daniel Webster, who spoke for the merchants of Massachussetts (Lowell's own relatives) he emphasized that he wanted only a moderate tariff duty that would keep out foreign products made of "very inferior" materials. He returned in triumph to Boston with just the kind of protection he had asked for: a minimum high enough to allow Waltham handsome profits on their coarse sheeting, and low enough to permit British trade in all better grade textiles. But just when every problem seemed solved, and a vast fortune only a matter of time, this forty-two-year-old industrial statesman died, worn out by his own relentless energy.

However crucial Lowell's ideas may have been in the beginning, the Associates were now well able to carry on without him. In spite of a general depression from 1819 to 1821, the dividends from Waltham paid back the initial investment within six years. By 1820 the men who had joined together to create Waltham were ready for still larger ventures. The Charles River could not supply enough power so they purchased a site on the broad and swift Merrimac, reverently christened the spot Lowell, and secured a charter for the Merrimac Company with $600,000 in capital. The demand for cheap textiles seemed unlimited and the Associates had the capital necessary for continual expansion. By 1831 they had created seven more companies on the Merrimac, with from $500,-000 to $1,350,000 in capital. Some 2,500 girls were in the mills of Lowell, and it had become the textile center of the nation.

Each new mill erected by the Associates copied Francis Lowell's boarding house plan. While the number of girls in all boarding house mills were never a majority of the employees in cotton textiles, the Lowell girls became far more famous than any other group. Foreign visitors regarded Lowell as one of the sights that must not be missed, and famous Americans lectured there to audiences composed mainly of mill girls. For daughters of back country New England farmers, the mills of Lowell were a finishing school or college where they could learn the ways of the world and make money in the process.

The companies made the change from farm to factory easy by sending agents in long black covered wagons to explain the rules to hesitant parents, and to bring the girls and their baggage direct to the boarding houses. No doubt the agents talked more of lectures and libraries, clothes and smart shops than of the twelve to thirteen-hour work day. Or they held out the goal of four dollars a week, two dollars and seventy-five cents more than the cost of board, without mentioning that few girls ever worked fast enough to achieve such pay. But to girls used to hard work on poor farms, to big families in little houses, the realities were not too bad. Six girls sleeping in a small room might seem crowded to an upper class visitor, but to the girls it was just like home.

For similar reasons the strict regulations seem to have been acceptable. Disobedience led to immediate dismissal. Group efforts to protest regarding pay, hours, or other conditions were treated as "mutiny." Church had to be attended on Sunday. The curfew tolled nightly at ten. But parents, relatives, or schoolmasters would have imposed equally strict discipline, and the girls expected it. In fact, standards of morality seem to have been preserved more by group attitudes toward offenders than by the vigilance of the company police. As a French traveler noted in 1835: "Lowell is not amusing, but Lowell is clean and decent, peaceful and sober."

The success of the Boston Manufacturing Company started a chain reaction that spread far beyond textiles. The Associates not only continued to build cotton mills wherever New England water power beckoned, but also to finance the ventures needed for general industrial growth. The profits of Massachusetts textile mills were thus transformed into railroad tracks in Michigan, Illinois, and Iowa, into buildings in Cleveland or Chicago, and into hundreds of other new American enterprises.

"Clinton's Ditch"

CARL CARMER

By 1821 statehood had been achieved in Ohio, Illinois, Indiana, Kentucky, Tennessee, Missouri, Alabama, and Mississippi, and the potential colossus that was taking shape in the West began to cause concern among Eastern and Southern politicians. Cheap land in the West was draining off population from both of the older sections, and the South viewed with particular concern the trend toward creating "free" states in the territories. The only policy of major importance in Congress on which it appeared possible to obtain national unanimity was the belief that the Indians should move out of the white man's way. The sale of public lands produced bitter debates; and so also did every proposal to facilitate adequate transportation to the growing West.

During Jefferson's administration Albert Gallatin had made extensive plans for a canal system, but the best Congress would provide was a modest start on the great National Road. Madison spoke strongly of the need for a system of transportation to draw "more closely together every part of our country" and to increase "the share of every part in the common stock of national prosperity," but then Madison lost his nerve on constitutional grounds and decided that he needed an amendment rather than an act of Congress. On the national level throughout the administrations of Monroe and Jackson, transportation was a warm political potato that no one in real authority wished to juggle.

Yet where the national government hesitated, the states did not. With "Clinton's Ditch," New York threatened very quickly to gain a commercial leadership that set off a flurry of canal building in other states. Carl Carmer, whose Stars Fell on Alabama *and* Listen

For a Lonesome Drum *are widely read and enjoyed, carries the American Story through that eventful October 2, 1825, when cannons boomed all the way from Buffalo to New York.*

FOR A decade the waters of New York State had offered a thought-provoking pattern to the nation-builders at the beginning of the 19th Century. Their dreams of moving the riches of the West to ports on the shores of the Atlantic were troubled. There was the possibility that the prized cargoes might move from Lake Erie into Lake Ontario and thence down the St. Lawrence River to British-Canadian markets. There was a stronger chance that the Mississippi might prove the major channel for transporting the treasures of the midlands to New Orleans. If the vast grain and beef producing plains and the ore-laden mountains were to be profitable to the East, home of the majority of the people, it would be necessary to conceive and execute a plan by which Lake Erie could be connected with other navigable waters that led to Atlantic ports. That this link must be forged as soon as possible was made very clear by President George Washington as early as 1784: "The Western settlers," he said, "stand as it were upon a pivot. The touch of a feather would turn them any way . . . smooth the road and make the way easy for them, and then see what an influx of articles will be poured upon us; how amazingly our exports will be increased by them, and how amply we shall be compensated for any trouble and expense we may encounter to effect it."

The situation involved problems more important to ambitious New York State than to the nation as a whole. Pennsylvania and Maryland were advocating a canal that would connect the Great Lakes with little Lake Otsego, from which the Susquehanna River would float Western cargoes to Chesapeake Bay. Philadelphia and Baltimore would profit by this arrangement and, since they were both larger seaports than New York, they felt that they deserved the advantage it would furnish them.

New Yorkers opposed this idea because it would bypass their biggest city at the mouth of the Hudson and, although it provided for passage from north to south through the middle of their state, the major benefits would be derived at the Philadelphia and Baltimore terminals. Many of the leading citizens of New York had therefore advocated the building of a canal which would cross the state from west to east. It would make use of such waters as might prove available and practicable, including the Finger

Lakes and the Mohawk River, and it would connect Lake Erie with the deep current of the Hudson River sweeping south to Manhattan Island.

New York made a strong effort to persuade the federal government to finance this project but many of the nation's leaders looked upon it as impractical. Indeed, Thomas Jefferson had written that "talk of making a canal three hundred and fifty miles through a wilderness is little short of madness," and political enemies of its advocates scorned the scheme as absurd, impractical, ridiculous.

Realizing then that unless the canal were built immediately, either the Mississippi or the Susquehanna might capture the bulk of the Western trade, New York under the leadership of its governor, De Witt Clinton, who had been one of the most ardent supporters of the plan, undertook to build the Erie Canal at its own expense. At once the governor's opponents scornfully labeled the canal "Clinton's Ditch" and prophesied its failure.

Digging began at Rome, New York, on July 4, 1817. This site had been selected because it was a part of what was known as the "Long Level"—a stretch of many miles of level ground where the work would be comparatively easy. At the ceremonies attendant on the first turning of the earth, De Witt Clinton's spoken prophecy seemed to echo the hopes and needs discussed by President Washington more than three decades before. Said the Governor: "As a bond of union between the Atlantic and Western States, this canal may prevent the dismemberment of the American Empire. As an organ of communication between the Hudson, the Mississippi, the St. Lawrence and the Great Lakes of the North and West and their tributary rivers, it will create the greatest inland trade ever witnessed."

The impetus obtained from the swift completion of the first section of the canal did much to encourage the builders toward the accomplishment of engineering feats hitherto regarded as impossible. The invention of an underwater cement by Canvass White of Utica, New York, proved an advantage of incalculable worth. The hiring of work gangs of native Americans and of immigrant Irish, Welsh, and other nationalities increased employment across the state. Gradually a canal four feet deep, twenty-eight feet across at the bottom, and forty feet at the top crossed the three hundred and fifty mile width of the state. Here and there along the way, elevations delayed completion by necessitating the construction of locks. When the job was done eighty-one locks had annihilated differences in level amounting to approxi-

When this map of New Orleans appeared in a
Dutch history in 1769, the city was already the
capital of the vast province of Louisiana. Within
four decades it had grown from a settlement of
less than a hundred wretched hovels; and before
it became a part of the young American Republic
in 1803, New Orleans had passed from French to
Spanish and then back to French rule.

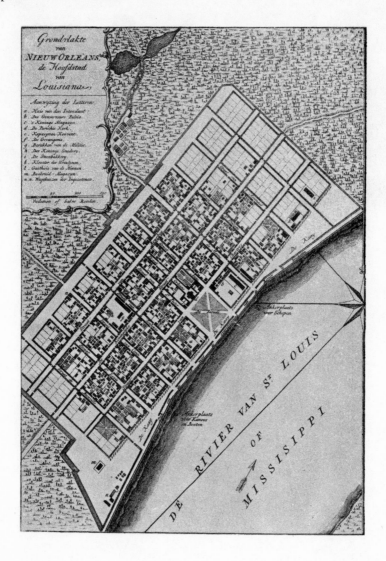

The Treaty of Ghent—here allegorized by engraver Alexis Chataigner—was as indecisive as the War of 1812 itself, mentioning none of the issues which had caused the conflict: impressment, blockades, maritime seizure. America's greatest victory was won after the signing of the peace, but before news of it arrived. British losses in the Battle of New Orleans were 2,000 killed and wounded; American losses were eight killed, thirteen wounded.

It was a time of enthusiastic celebration and elegant ceremony when the Erie Canal was officially opened to traffic along its entire 360-mile route on October 2, 1825. Members of trade associations paraded, officials danced at civic functions, and fire companies competed with each other in contests of skill. The illustration above is from an official program.

Charles Dickens was a critical visitor, and his *Notes* on his first trip to America wounded national pride. But he had little other than praise for the New England factory system and the famed "Lowell girls," seen above at "belltime"—the end of the working day. Mr. Dickens commented that he "walked through three miles and a half of these young ladies, all dressed out with parasols and silk stockings," and could not recall one "young face that gave . . . a painful expression."

mately seven hundred feet. The diggers had fought their way through thick woods, rocky barrens, and miasmic swamps, and the long channel of the waters was ready for their admission.

Even as the work was in progress, the canal gave promise of its ultimate success. When sections were completed they were opened to limited local trade between ports along the banks, and this surpassed the dreams of the most optimistic supporters of the enterprise. In 1823, two years before the opening of the full length of the canal, more than thirteen hundred craft traveled its waters on short haul voyages. In 1825, though use of the entire waterway was available only a short part of the season, the increase in the number of craft at work numbered many thousands.

On October 2, 1825, salvos of cannon, set within earshot of each other all the way from Buffalo to New York, boomed the news of the opening of the entire waterway to rejoicing throngs along the banks. They also proved the starting guns of one of the greatest and swiftest developments in the history of commerce. So successful was the canal that in the first decade of its history—and before Western produce, on which the builders had counted for profits, had begun to move east in substantial amounts—the seven millions of dollars which New York State had put into its construction had been repaid.

At once the raw products of rural New York began moving on canal waters toward the cities where machines, operated through water power, might turn them into factory-made goods. This trade caused an immediate demand for labor, and Rochester and Buffalo, which had less than a thousand inhabitants in 1820, held about twenty thousand by 1840. Syracuse, Rome, Utica in the same period grew from villages to cities. Frontier settlements that had been scatters of log houses assumed the dignity of ports on a teeming waterway—Weedsport, Spencerport, Brockport, New Port (now Albion), Port Byron, Adam's Basin, Eagle Harbor. The population west of the center of the state was growing twice as fast as in the eastern half. Frame houses replaced cabins. Church spires gleamed above the trees on high ground. Below them, taverns, saloons, boat yards, harness shops lined the new man-made river. The cost of freight per ton from Buffalo to New York had dropped from a hundred dollars to six dollars. Upstate poured a golden flood of grain into New York, and in five years' time that city went ahead of both Philadelphia and Buffalo as a flour market.

More important even than the cheap shipment of produce along the waterway, which had suddenly lost its nickname of

"Clinton's Ditch" and assumed the august title of "The Grand Canal," was the movement of people. In the first full year of its operation, 1826, Utica reported that forty thousand people had passed her docks on freight boats and passenger packets. The latter by 1831 had become elegant vessels eighty feet in length and fourteen feet wide, and furnished accommodations for twenty to thirty passengers. They moved at an average of about four miles an hour and charged their patrons a half cent a mile. Meals, sleeping berths, and other charges brought the cost per mile up to about four cents.

As a result of such cheap passage the Western states began to fill up. A guidebook of 1825 reported five hundred persons a day going west. Ohio, which had been rated seventeenth in population at the beginning of the century, was third in 1840. Indiana, which had been twentieth in the early listing, rose in the same period to tenth. As for the Western cities, five years after the canal opened Cleveland had increased in population more than 400 per cent and Detroit more than 300 per cent above their 1820 listings. Considerably more than half of the Western emigrants, it was discovered, had come by the water route.

For about a decade after the opening of the canal the greater part of the Western produce continued to move in the ways to which its shippers were accustomed toward Philadelphia and Baltimore. After that period of adjustment, however, the canal became the favored means of transport. Buffalo, which had received a million bushels of grain and flour in 1836, received fifteen years later an astonishing seventeen million, seven hundred thousand. The whole country was profiting by the joining of Lake Erie with the Atlantic.

Commercial profits were not the only benefits derived from the three hundred and sixty mile canal. Among the long processions of neat boxlike grain boats, odoriferous pig boats, and passenger packets, there were occasional library boats, theatre boats, waxwork boats which in their separate ways sought to educate and entertain the people of the canal towns. A folklore was also growing up along the towpaths where drivers, known to canallers as "hoggies," sang songs and told tall tales, all of which were based on their jobs and the peculiarities of life along the waterway. The canal introduced a way of life less inhibited and less dignified than most Americans had known. There was a free atmosphere, much joking, fighting, and roistering.

On the other hand, the highly imaginative and unusual religious cults which sprang up along the course of the canal—the Shakers, the Spiritualists, the Oneida Community Perfectionists, the Mormons—also accepted the opportunity for freer thought than New England would allow, and settled groups of earnest converts across the state. Standards of living became higher as trade made more Americans prosperous. There had been very rigid differentiations in America between the rich aristocrats and the common people. As the latter became more prosperous these disappeared, and true democracy won more ground. Real estate and personal property rose in value along the canal. Pillared "Greek Revival" houses proved an impressive advance in architecture.

The canal brought money—and in its wake a more leisurely and more cultural life. Many of the passengers bound west took with them ideas on living which they had obtained from observations on their journey. Thus the canal made its impression on the life of the United States as a nation, an impression that Americans realize today has had a lasting and ennobling effect.

Cornerstone of American Policy

DEXTER PERKINS

James Monroe gave fifty years of service to the nation. Member of the Virginia Assembly, delegate to the Confederate Congress, United States Senator, governor of Virginia, minister to France, Great Britain, and Spain, Secretary of State, Secretary of War, fifth President of the United States—these were the public offices of one who, by outward appearance, looked anything but distinguished.

The eight years of Monroe's administration are known as "the era of good feelings"—that is to say, the Federalists had disappeared, the Whigs had not yet risen, and the Republicans had things pretty much their own way. Nationalism—the "American System," Calhoun named it—and sectionalism were rubbing shoulders in a hard contest to dominate the political scene. Population and wealth grew rapidly; a flourishing country flexed its muscles and began to recognize its strength.

Monroe's two terms sparkled with diplomatic achievements— the Rush-Bagot Agreement in 1817, providing for the practical dis-

armament of the Great Lakes; agreement with Spain (1819) and Russia (1824) whereby they renounced any claim to the Territory of Oregon; an agreement with Great Britain in 1818 to a boundary line between the United States and Canada. But the most important of all Monroe's diplomatic triumphs—the doctrine that lives on bearing his name—would be pronounced in December of 1823. Dexter Perkins, John L. Senior Professor of American Civilization at Cornell University, author of numerous books on American foreign policy, and an active laborer in the cause of international understanding, gives his authoritative estimate of what the Monroe Doctrine has contributed to the American Story.

T<small>HE</small> <small>FAMOUS</small> declaration of December 2, 1823, that has come to be known as the Monroe Doctrine, had a double purpose and a double origin. On the one hand, it originated in a dispute between Russia and the United States, with regard to trading rights on the northwest coast of America, in the region known as Alaska, then under Russian sovereignty. Referring to this dispute, President Monroe laid down the principle in his message to Congress "that the American continents, by the free and independent condition which they have assumed and maintain, are henceforth not to be considered as subjects for future colonization by any European powers." On the other hand, the declaration was provoked by the fear existing in Washington in the fall of 1823 that the Continental European powers would intervene by force of arms to restore to Spain her lost colonial dominion in America. "With the governments [that is, of the Spanish American republics] who have declared their independence and maintained it," wrote the President, "and whose independence we have, on great consideration and just principles, acknowledged, we could not view any interposition for the purpose of oppressing them, or controlling in any other manner their destiny, by any European power in any other light than as the manifestation of an unfriendly disposition towards the United States."

While it is the second of these two pronouncements that raises the most interesting and important questions, some attention must be paid to the first. The so-called "Doctrine" relating to the Russian matter is almost entirely the work of John Quincy Adams, Monroe's Secretary of State. It was Adams who, from the very first, conducted with Russia the negotiations arising out of the Russian government's decree of September 16, 1821, which excluded American trading vessels from the shores of the Northwest down to the line of 51 degrees. Adams saw "an abuse of government" in measures of colonial exclusion of this kind, and as early as November, 1819, was disposed to challenge completely Russian claims in the Northwest. By the summer of 1823 there had taken form in his mind the idea which was later to be incorporated in the message of the President. It formed a part, at that time, of his instructions to Richard Rush, our minister in London, and it was explicitly stated to Baron Tuyll, the Russian diplomatic representative at Washington. "I told him specially," wrote Adams in his diary about the interview on July 17, 1823, "that we should contest the right of Russia to *any* territorial establishment on this continent, and that we should assume distinctly the principle that the American continents are no longer subjects for *any* new European colonial establishments." Though Adams did not instruct the American minister at St. Petersburg to press the point, he reiterated the view expressed to Tuyll in a draft presented to the President for the preparation of the annual message. Monroe took it over virtually in the form in which his Secretary of State drafted it.

The noncolonization principle springs in part from Adams's interest in trade. It was directed against limitations on this trade, but it rests upon a shaky legal basis. Adams's own defense of it was on the ground that the American continents in 1823 "consisted of several sovereign and independent nations, whose territories covered their whole surface." Such a statement appears hardly true, in the light of the conditions that then existed. There were certainly unsettled areas in both South and North America in 1823, to which title had not been definitely determined. Adams also sought to rest his case on the claim that the United States had derived a valid claim to all the Northwest by virtue of the treaty of February 22, 1819 with Spain. In that treaty, Spain renounced all territorial claims north of 42 degrees. But the weakness of the original Spanish title to this region makes this argument as unconvincing as the previous one.

The noncolonization principle played no great part in the actual settlement of the dispute over the Northwest. The Russians preferred to ignore it, "to waive all discussion upon abstract principles of right," as Nesselrode[5] put it. An agreement was reached which

[5] Count Carl Robert von Nesselrode (1780–1862), Russian statesman who, as the chief contriver of the "Holy Alliance," made Russia virtually supreme in Europe. Nesselrode's power lessened under Emperor Nicholas; he retired after the accession of Alexander II.

restricted Russian claims to the line of 54 degrees and which granted to American citizens rights of trade for a ten-year period. The only effect of the pronouncement was to cool the interest of Great Britain (who also had claims in this area) for joint negotiation with the United States against Russia.

With regard to the other part of the message, the most important facts are these. In the summer of 1823, the administration in Washington received word from Richard Rush of talks that Rush had had with Canning, the British prime minister. These conversations suggested that the Continental European powers, having set about the suppression of revolution on the European continent, and having, through France as their agent, stamped out a revolutionary movement in Spain, might turn their attention to Latin America. A little later, two communications from the Russian government accentuated the apprehensions of Monroe and his advisers. In October, 1823, momentous discussions in the Cabinet took place. Canning had suggested joint action in behalf of the Latin Americas. The President, who had consulted Madison and Jefferson, was disposed to accede to this suggestion. But Adams stoutly maintained that "it would be more candid as well as more dignified, to avow our principles explicitly to Russia and France, than to come in as a cock-boat in the wake of the British man-of-war," and his view of the matter prevailed. It was not Adams, however, who had the idea of broaching the warning in the forthcoming Presidential message. This idea was Monroe's own. The famous pronouncement was read with dismay by those who had hoped for the suppression of revolution in Spain and Greece, as well as in Latin America. He wished to "make an American cause, and adhere inflexibly to that." Here again he got his way.

Canning, who had in October been reassured by the French government with regard to intervention in Latin America, was by no means delighted with Monroe's declaration. The United States had stolen a march on Great Britain in competition for the favor of the Latin Americans. It was Canning's object, following 1823, to redress the balance; and in 1825 Britain, first of all European governments, recognized the independence of the new states.

Monroe's declaration was variously received in Latin America. The plain truth of the matter is that the material power of the United States was not such as to furnish a very impressive guarantee of the independence of the new states, without British support. When, moreover, in 1824, various of the Latin American republics approached the government at Washington with a view to translating Monroe's generalizations into binding pledges, they found no disposition on the part of the administration to commit itself. The debates in the American Congress in 1826 underlined the determination of most Americans to refrain from pledges of any kind. The significance of the message, so far as Latin America was concerned, remained, therefore, largely moral.

The warning to Europe, like the noncolonization principle, is open to substantial criticism on grounds of logic. Monroe sought to place his admonition on the principle that European intervention would be dangerous to our peace and safety. Yet it is difficult to believe that in the conditions of 1823 the re-establishment of a colonial regime in some remote part of Latin America would have been a source of peril to the United States. Indeed, so true is this, that for many years to come, the practical application of the doctrine was restricted to the region of the Caribbean. The sweeping language of the President outran the facts of his own time.

Nonetheless, the Monroe Doctrine is of the highest historic significance. In the first place, it is an interesting, if not a decisive, episode in the clash of two points of view—the principle of intervention on the one hand and the principle of nonintervention on the other. In the history of the self-determination of peoples, it will long have a place as a resounding expression of a theory that has had wide influence in the past, and that has wide influence today.

In the second place, the technique of the message gives it substantial importance. The United States was, from an early period, a practitioner of that open diplomacy that has played an increasing role in our own time. There are few more striking examples of that diplomacy than the message of 1823. Rarely, too, has the weapon of open diplomacy been more effectively used. Granted the premises on which Monroe and Adams acted, what could have been more skillful than this public assertion of principle? How much more gratifying to the national pride, how much more productive of prestige in Latin America, how much more disconcerting to Europe than an unostentatious diplomatic protest!

Thirdly, it hardly needs to be stated that almost no other document in American diplomatic history has had a more pronounced effect in the long run. Enunciated with a view to a special situation, it was to grow into a guiding principle of action, powerful in its appeal and far-reaching in its influence.

Finally, it symbolized the thought of an era. It was a declaration of the separation of the New World from the Old. The idea has become outmoded. But it exercised a powerful influence on policy for many generations, and did much to shape the diplomatic action of the United States.

FOUR

The Rise of

the Common Man

A FTER the War of 1812, America entered a period extending well into the middle years of the 19th Century when its people were free to expend their creative powers and enthusiasm upon an opportunity without equal in history.

Before them stretched a land teeming with resources—a land 80 per cent vacant and waiting to be occupied by those with the energy and the gumption to harness its fertility and wealth. The one dynamic, dominant force of the new era was people moving, the home-seekers, the pioneers, the modern men and women of that age—restless human waves rolling from Virginia and North Carolina into the land between the Appalachians and the Mississippi; from New England across the central New York river valley and the Great Lakes (or across western Pennsylvania and down the Ohio River) into Ohio, Indiana, Michigan, Illinois; or through the Cumberland Gap, into Kentucky, Tennessee, Mississippi, Louisiana, southern Ohio, Indiana, Illinois . . . streams of people seeking land, a newer life in the New World, and somehow finding it for all the hardships of nature and the rougher human nature of speculator and extortioner.

Swamp fever, Indian raids, animals of the forest—the trials were many. The heavy, burdensome toil of wilderness survival beat

137

many men into premature wrecks. But they began to win the land, the future. As people, they began to know their strength.

At the same time—more slowly, and yet just as irresistibly—urban life entered the new age counting its own gains. In the 1840's New Yorkers bragged about their uniformed police, and up in Hartford residents wondered about that dentist, Horace Wells, who eased the pain of extractions by using nitrous oxide gas; both Boston and Cincinnati introduced paid fire departments, and in Georgia a Dr. Crawford N. Long used ether to quiet patients during operations. Wherever one turned, people as individuals taking the devil by the tail had never seemed more important.

The Common Man's Hero

ARTHUR SCHLESINGER, JR.

Naturally there were political repercussions. The War of 1812 left the Federalist Party gasping its death rattle. Yet political differences had not vanished nor personal ambitions disappeared. A new kind of political partisanship was in the making—the least, perhaps, that an evolving society should expect. Rather impatiently, youngsters waited for the oldsters to get out of the way. The struggle for succession was inevitable, once Monroe had the grace to finish his term.

For four years John Quincy Adams (to his father's delight) managed to hold the reins—no credit to the scoundrel, said his enemies, who saw his election as the result of a corrupt bargain between Adams and that blackleg, Henry Clay. Arrayed against Adams was a force that never surrendered easily. A new political party was being born, heir to the old Democratic-Republican label that belonged to Jefferson, but even more the party of the people.

So onto the American political scene came Andrew Jackson, and no one in our generation understands him better than Arthur Schlesinger, Jr., associate professor of history at Harvard University and winner of the Pulitzer Prize for his historical study, The Age of Jackson.

THE American Republic was founded, in the main, by gentlemen. The men who gathered in Philadelphia to devise the new Constitution, the men who organized and staffed the new government, the men who dominated politics during the first half century of independence—they were nearly all men of superior station. In 1789, for example, the property and other qualifications for suffrage were such that only about 25 per cent of the adult males had the right to vote in the elections. And you could tell gentlemen by the clothes they wore—their knee breeches, their satin waistcoats, their frilled laced shirts, their powdered wigs, their buckled shoes.

This was the way the Republic began, but, in a sense, it was against the logic of the new nation. For the Declaration of Independence had declared that all men were created equal before the law. It could be only a matter of time before the people of the country gained equality in the voting booth and in the administration of government.

The election of Thomas Jefferson in 1800 was the first step in the conquest of the government by the people. Though Jefferson himself was a Virginia gentleman, his party, the Democratic-Republican party, as it was then called, stood for the common people of the day, as against the Federalist Party, which stood for the bankers, merchants, and businessmen. In the years after Jefferson, states began to reduce property qualifications on voting and thus to admit more and more ordinary people to voting rights. At the same time, new states were added to the West—by 1821 the original thirteen states had grown to twenty-four. As a consequence of these changes, the common man began to increase in political power. But he still felt himself excluded from government by the aristocracy, and he chafed increasingly under this sense of exclusion.

Jefferson was succeeded by Madison, and Madison by Monroe, good Virginia gentlemen all. In 1824, at the end of Monroe's second term, there were a number of eminent candidates for the Presidency—John Quincy Adams of Massachusetts, Andrew Jackson of Tennessee, Henry Clay of Kentucky, and William H. Crawford of Georgia. When the votes were counted, it was clear that Jackson was the popular favorite. But no one received a majority of the electoral votes, and the choice therefore went to the House of Representatives. In the House, a shift of the Clay votes to Adams resulted in Adams's election. The victory, widely ascribed to a bargain between Adams and Clay, made the common people feel bitterly that they had been cheated of their rightful choice.

Four years later, they had another chance. This time Jackson received a decisive majority, both in popular vote and in the electoral college. The people had spoken, and their voice had at last been heard. On Jackson's inauguration in 1829, ordinary men and women crowded Washington, cheered the new President, and stormed the official White House reception, standing on damask-covered chairs with muddy boots, breaking glass and china, and elbowing the rich and fashionable to the side. It was an omen: the people at last felt they had their own President.

Who was the new President? General Andrew Jackson was sixty-two years old, a tall, gaunt man, standing straight as a ramrod, his face wrinkled with pain and age, his thick gray hair, pushed straight back from his forehead, turning snow white. To the nation he was known primarily as a picturesque military hero. In the Revolution, an English officer had slashed him with a saber for refusing to clean a pair of boots. In the War of 1812, he had shown great energy and resource in putting down Indian uprisings in the Southwest; and in 1815, after the treaty of peace had been signed but before news of it had reached America, he had won at New Orleans the greatest American victory of the second war with England. In quieter intervals, he had lived the life of a Tennessee gentleman on his fine plantation, the Hermitage, near Nashville, entertaining his friends, racing his horses, and heatedly talking politics. He had served in the Senate, the House of Representatives, and as a judge in Tennessee.

Jackson was hardly the uncouth, semiliterate backwoodsman of legend. He was actually an urbane and dignified gentleman with distinguished manners and bearing. But, though a country squire himself, he had no sense of commitment to the old ruling aristocracy; he had a commanding eye and a gift for decision; and there surged through him a sense that the people had made him their trustee in the use of the powers of government. "They were his blood relations," said his close associate Martin Van Buren, "the only blood relations he had." He believed that "to labour for the good of the masses was a special mission assigned to him by his Creator and no man was ever better disposed to work in his vocation in season and out of season."

Jackson's first spectacular act as President expressed his sense of devotion to the people. This was the redistribution of federal jobs, which Jackson and his supporters regarded as a reform measure and called "rotation-in-office" and which his opponents decried as the "spoils system." Whatever the results of this practice —and some results were certainly deplorable—Jackson's intent was clear enough. It was to destroy what seemed to him a monopoly of office-holding by a certain class (and one cannot forget that in this period some federal offices were regarded almost as hereditary); it was to open up the United States government to the man in the street.

This measure was only the first of a series designed to serve the political, social, and economic aspirations of the common man. His greatest fight was against the Bank of the United States, a privately controlled banking corporation, enjoying unique and profitable powers over the whole system of currency and credit. Jackson felt that so great a concentration of power in private hands was incompatible with democracy. He further felt that this power was being used to benefit those who were already well-to-do and to restrict economic opportunity for the men who had their way to make. Nicholas Biddle, the president of the Bank, anticipating Jackson's opposition, forced a bill to recharter the Bank through Congress in 1832. But he did not anticipate the vigor and eloquence of Jackson's veto. "It is to be regretted," said Jackson in memorable language, "that the rich and powerful too often bend the acts of government to their selfish purposes . . . When the laws undertake . . . to make the rich richer and the potent more powerful, the humble members of society—the farmers, mechanics and laborers—who have neither the time nor the means of securing like favors to themselves, have a right to complain of the injustice of their Government."

It was the humble members of society—farmers, merchants, laborers—to whom Jackson appealed; and they answered his appeal with enthusiasm and adoration. Four months after the Bank veto, with the full force of the Bank's power thrown against Jackson in the Presidential election, Jackson was triumphantly re-elected for his second four years in the White House.

Jackson continued his fight for popular rights. Throughout the states Jacksonian Democrats followed his example. It was a tremendous period of release and reform. The Jacksonians called for laws ending the system of incorporations by special charter and making corporate privileges available on equal terms for all. They demanded regulation and inspection of banking practices. They fought for the right of workers to organize, helped establish the legality of trade unions, and worked closely with the labor leaders of the day. They called for a ten-hour working day and for the secret ballot. They urged codification of the law, and Jackson's Supreme Court, under Chief Justice Roger B. Taney, liberalized the interpretation of the Constitution. They worked to open the public lands in the West to settlement. They stood for freedom of religious faith and of intellectual expression. They introduced a great new ferment of liberation for the individual and reform for society.

This was part of Jackson's legacy: the great democratic revolution that came in his wake, as he asserted the rightful powers of the common man in the American government. Another part of his legacy was the transformation he wrought on the office of the Presidency. Up to this time, the Presidents of the United States had been essentially passive in their attitude toward the powers of their office. But Jackson perceived with great clarity what we now know so well to be the case: that our system can work effectively only if a strong President provides initiative and leadership. He saw that it was his responsibility to formulate policies, to rally his own party behind those policies, and, if Congress would not enact his measures, to appeal over the heads of Congress directly to the people. The President, as the one officer of government elected by all the people, was responsible to all the people: his commitment was to the *national interest and welfare*—as Jackson showed when he asserted the federal authority against the attempt of the state of South Carolina to nullify an act of Congress.

Naturally so positive an affirmation of democratic principle and executive power provoked bitter opposition. The conservatives of the day, the leading businessmen, the newspapers, the college presidents, the fashionable ministers—in short, the men of wealth and prominence and those who served them—were united in their hatred of Jackson. They called him a dictator; they accused him of stirring up the poor against the rich; they spread false and scurrilous stories about his character and even his sanity. But, as so often happens in our history, the conservatives savagely fought reforms which a few years later, when in power themselves, they would unquestionably accept.

In retrospect, for all the anger and acrimony of the day, the place of Andrew Jackson seems secure in our history. This fine old man, with his long, seamed face, his lean, erect figure, his sharp blue eyes, his fire and devotion, expressed the indomitable conviction of the American people that this was their country and their government. He gave new vitality to the methods, the purposes, and the faith of our democratic society.

Sam Houston, Statesman

MARQUIS JAMES

Americans, pushing back the wilderness, came to believe that any part of the North American continent from Alaska to the Rio Grande was theirs for the taking. Washington could sign treaties, if it liked; the man on the frontier often fitted diplomatic reality to what he considered personal necessity. Grudgingly, under the treaty of 1819, Spain relinquished her claim to Florida, and in return the United States agreed not only to pay $5,000,000 in damages due Americans from Spain, but also to renounce its claim to Texas. A boundary from the Sabine River north and west over an uneven course to the forty-second parallel and then running westward to the Pacific defined the territory belonging to Spain. Soon, Spain's sister republic, Mexico, acquired this land by revolution.

In the year that Spain and the United States drew up their agreement on Florida and Texas, a Connecticut Yankee who had lived for twenty years in Spanish-controlled Missouri was ruined by a panic. Thus circumstances forced Moses Austin to travel deeper into the South and to strike a bargain with friends in the officialdom of Mexico City: he obtained a charter granting lands for colonization to 200 American families. Moses died and his son Stephen won a similar agreement. American colonists were to receive land tax free for seven years in return for becoming Mexican citizens and faithful Catholics. By 1827 twelve thousand Americans had settled in Texas. Southern cotton-growers brought their slaves with them.

Constant friction between the Mexicans and their empresarios resulted. In the Fredonian uprising of 1827, Americans tried unsuccessfully to gain their independence. Then Mexico abolished slavery and prohibited the importation of slaves. Only Catholics might settle in Mexican territory henceforth, for American promises to embrace the church had counted for little. The seven years stipulated in the grants expired and heavy taxes were levied. Worst

of all was the rise of General Antonio Lopez de Santa Anna to
power; he joined Texas to the Mexican state of Coahuila, sought
to cut off imports by excessive duties so as to force the frontiers-
men to buy from Mexican merchants, and in other ways fanned
the rebellious spirit that these Americans had inherited from fa-
thers who in 1776 had thrown off British bonds.

Thus the stage was set for the revolution of 1835, when aroused
Texans seized San Antonio. Now in the spotlight of the American
Story stepped Andrew Jackson's old friend, the soldier-statesman
Sam Houston. The late Marquis James, twice a Pulitzer Prize win-
ner, distinguished biographer of Sam Houston and Andrew Jack-
son, sees in Houston much more than "a swashbuckling frontier
captain."

THE frontier looms large in the panorama of American history,
and it has produced many arresting figures. In the Southwest, the
greatest of these was Sam Houston. More than any other man,
Houston won the independence of the province of Texas from
Mexico. More than any other man he created and sustained through
ten years of its turbulent life the Republic of Texas. More than
any other man he brought Texas into the Union—and this was not
so easily done in 1846 as one might suppose. The consequences
were great. The annexation of Texas proved a stepping stone to
the acquisition of California, just as Houston had long intended.

Sam Houston had all the qualities of a frontier leader. He was
six feet, six inches tall, and a prodigy of physical strength and endurance. He was physically brave, sometimes to the point of recklessness. He had the gift of chieftainship. On the frontier, titles
counted for little. It was the man who counted. There were occasions when, in desperate situations, the very presence of Sam
Houston in a room or in a camp was enough to quell opposition.
He could inspire men to follow him, when, by all rational calcula-
tions, the cause seemed hopeless.

And he had other qualities—moral qualities. Sam Houston was
a great deal more than a swashbuckling frontier captain. He was
a farsighted statesman. His spiritual integrity gave him the courage to take the unpopular side of causes whose advocacy would
have ruined another border leader. He was a friend of the American Indian, and so found himself in opposition to 95 per cent of
his white frontier compatriots. In an age when our policy toward
the Indians was frankly scandalous, Houston stood undeviatingly

for honesty, decency, and justice toward the original occupants of American soil.

Another thing that helped to attract attention to Houston during his early days on the frontier was the mystery surrounding the romantic incident—a tragic love affair and marriage—that had driven him there. In 1829 when Andrew Jackson journeyed from Tennessee to begin his luminous term as President of the United States, Sam Houston was the gifted young governor of Tennessee, Old Hickory's home state. He had distinguished himself as a boy soldier under Jackson in the War of 1812. Entering public life, he stood high in the Jackson political hierarchy. With his patron in the White House, loftier honors than the governorship of Tennessee seemed possible for Sam Houston. Then, overnight, his immediate career was wrecked.

Sam Houston's bride of twelve weeks left her husband and took refuge in her father's house. In bitterness and heartbreak, Houston resigned the governorship of Tennessee and fled to the Indian country. In what is now Oklahoma he joined a tribe of Cherokee, with whom he had once spent four years. For a time The Raven, as Houston was known by the Indians, refused to speak English. He was often drunk. The downfall could not have been more complete.

For four years Houston remained with the Indians, alternately behaving as an inspired leader of his adopted people and as a tribal vagabond. Clad in beaded buckskins and a blanket, he made two journeys to Washington to represent the Indians. He helped them as much as anyone could. On the occasion of Houston's second visit to Washington, President Jackson persuaded his old friend to lay aside his Indian garb and buy a suit of civilized clothing.

What else Houston and Jackson talked about is not known, though it is impossible to believe that the future of Texas was not one of the subjects. American emigrants formed the bulk of the sparse population of the vast province, which Jackson was trying to purchase from Mexico. And he was getting nowhere. Some of the Americans were talking about establishing the independence of Texas by force. Sam Houston left Washington in 1832 with a commission from the War Department to hold talks with nomadic Indians who roamed both the American and the Texas sides of the Red River. There he signed a treaty with the Indians; yet the affair has the look of an excuse to cover a reconnaissance of Texas for the confidential use of General Jackson.

In 1835 Americans in Texas drove the weak Mexican garrisons south of the Rio Grande. Early in 1836, the rebellious province declared its independence of Mexico and elected Sam Houston commander-in-chief of the armies of the Republic of Texas. The army consisted of widely scattered bands of American adventurers, numbering in all less than a thousand men. The first news the commander-in-chief received was that Santa Anna, president of Mexico, had crossed the Rio Grande at the head of 7,000 troops. Houston ordered a general retreat and concentration. The leaders of the Texan bands refused to obey on the assumption that one American could account for about twenty Mexicans. Santa Anna surrounded the Alamo and slew its 188 defenders to a man. Then he finished off all but one of the other bands. The result was panic in Texas, precipitating a flight of the government and civil population toward United States soil. But for Sam Houston, the Texas Republic would have ended then and there.

Houston got hold of the one surviving band, numbering 374 men, and began a retreat, the most difficult of all military maneuvers. Fleeing refugees gave him as much concern as the enemy. Whenever he could, he saw to their safety. He kept a cool head when nearly everyone else had lost his. For thirty-seven days he zigzagged eastward. Santa Anna divided his forces in pursuit, and thought everything was over but the shouting. Houston's force swelled and then shrank as whole companies would march off, with or without orders, to join their own frightened families. That the commander kept anyone with him at all was a testimonial to his leadership.

On April 20, 1836, Houston, with 800 men, intercepted Santa Anna, with 1,450, at a ferry over the San Jacinto River near the present city of Houston. After a campaign that had brought him nothing but victory, the Mexican leader did not believe that Houston would fight, much less attack. The following day he rested his army. Houston attacked and caught half of the enemy asleep. All the Mexicans were killed or captured. The Texans lost sixteen killed and twenty-four wounded, including General Houston. But with Santa Anna a prisoner, Texan independence had been won after everyone had given it up for lost.

Thus the Republic of Texas, with Sam Houston as president, began its ten-year history. Few Texans, least of all Houston, thought it would last that long. Houston had gone to Texas to play a part in its annexation to the United States—also Andrew Jackson's idea. But times had changed. The slavery question was dividing the United States. Jackson hesitated to inflame the North and East by adding to slave territory.

The disappointed Houston turned to the task of making Texas, with a white population of 30,000, strong enough to stand alone. He succeeded marvelously well. The Republic became the embodiment of its chief magistrate. The constitution of Texas, however, forbade a president to succeed himself. Sam Houston was followed in office by a shallow man with grandiose ideas. Within three years, the machinery of the Republic had all but ceased to function. Currency was worthless, Indians were on the warpath, Santa Anna gathered forces for invasion. For the second time annexation had been refused by the United States. Resuming the presidency in 1841, Sam Houston became, once more, virtually the only asset of the Republic of Texas.

Prospects improved at once. Houston obtained favorable treaties with England and France. The diplomatic representatives of those countries in Texas were treated with marked respect. The United States minister was treated coolly. This attitude had its effect on our Northern and Eastern statesmen, who feared a Texas under obligation to England and France even more than they feared an extension of slavery. In 1843 President Tyler offered to reopen negotiations for annexation. Houston declined the offer and spoke of the friendly attitude of the European powers. Tyler renewed his bid, promising immediate annexation. Houston raised difficult conditions. Old Jackson, in retirement in Tennessee, tried in vain to find out what was in Houston's mind.

In a masterpiece of diplomacy Texas had turned the tables on the United States. We were now the supplicants and Texas the one to hold aloof. Texas became a national issue, with support for annexation in every part of the country. Sam Houston had decided to guarantee the future of Texas by one means or another. He preferred annexation, but this time there must be no slip. He played the diplomatic game to agonizing lengths until, certain there would be no mishap, he gave his consent to furl the flag of the Lone Star. On February 16, 1846, Texas became a state of the Union.

Sam Houston went to the United States Senate. The slavery question, which had kept Texas out of the Union so long, was the most serious issue before the country. Senator Houston's resolute stand against the Southern extremists cost him so much in popularity that Texas administered him an unprecedented rebuke. In those days Senators were elected by state legislatures. Two years before Houston's term expired, the Texas legislature chose his successor—a rabid pro-slavery man. It was difficult, however, for Texas to resist the magic of Sam Houston. In 1859, he ran for governor of Texas, and was elected.

Then came the final magnificent drama of his life—Houston's hopeless fight to prevent Texas from joining the Confederacy. He stumped the state against secession. His life was threatened when he declared that secession would mean war and that the North would win that war. Most Southerners thought the Yankees would not fight.

When secession was voted, Governor Sam Houston was summoned before the secession convention to take the Confederate oath. He declined in these words:

"In the name of my own conscience and my own manhood I refuse to take this oath. It is perhaps meet that my career should close thus. I have seen the patriots and statesmen of my youth one by one gathered to their fathers, and the government they reared rent in twain. I stand the last almost of my race, stricken down because I will not yield those principles I have fought for. The severest pang is that the blow comes in the name of Texas."

In the midst of the Civil War, in 1863, and with his popularity beginning to return, Sam Houston died, still without having sworn allegiance to the Confederacy. Thus, at seventy, ended the career of a great frontiersman and a great American.

War with Mexico: An Inescapable Step

ROBERT SELPH HENRY

The young Congressman from Illinois had the floor. Intense political feeling dominated this first session of the Thirtieth Congress, arising from President Polk's message that fixed the blame on Mexico for starting a war and the introduction of a resolution justifying the conflict and demanding indemnity commensurate with Mexico's persistence in continuing the struggle. This resolution was more than Whig strategy intended to swallow, and young Abe Lincoln, rising to make his first major speech as a Congressman, was a loyal Whig to the marrow of his bones.

Lincoln's speech was a long and skillful one, biting, rich in idiom, and reflective of an attitude against the war that many held. A representative passage follows:

". . . As to the mode of terminating the war, and securing peace, the President is equally wandering and indefinite. First, it is to be done by a more vigorous prosecution of the war in the vital parts of the enemy's country, and, after apparently talking himself tired on this point, the President drops down into a half-despairing tone, and tells us that 'with a people distracted and divided by contending factions, and a government subject to constant changes, by successive revolutions, the continued success of our arms may fail to secure a satisfactory peace.' Then he suggests the propriety of wheedling the Mexican people to desert the counsels of their own leaders, and trusting in our protection, to set up a government from which we can secure a satisfactory peace; telling us, that 'this may become the only mode of obtaining peace.' But soon he falls into doubt of this too; and then drops back on to the already half-abandoned ground of 'more vigorous prosecution.' All this shows that the President is, in no wise, satisfied with his own positions. First he takes up one, and in attempting to argue us into it, he argues himself out of it; then seizes another, and goes through the same process . . . His mind, tasked beyond its power, is running hither and thither, like some tortured creature, on a burning surface, finding no position, on which it can settle down, and be at ease."

The war that the President had expected to end in three or four months now had lasted almost twenty; American arms, Lincoln said, "have given us the most splendid successes"—but when would the struggle terminate? Clearly the President—"a bewildered, confounded, and miserably perplexed man"—didn't know, and Lincoln could only comment: "God grant he may be able to show, there is not something about his conscience, more painful than all his mental perplexity!" It was difficult to accuse Mr. Lincoln of dullness. He voted the resources for war but he had no belief in its necessity. Robert Selph Henry, author of The Story of the Mexican War and The Story of the Confederacy, takes a less partisan view than that held by the Illinois Congressman during those days of passion in 1848.

Occupation by a single people of that belt of the North American continent that is the United States is an established and accepted fact in the world today. Yet, for most of us, it is hard to realize how recent was the time when the western half of the present area of the nation was not part of this country.

When the year 1845 opened, the United States had only a claim to the Pacific Northwest, a claim vigorously disputed by Great Britain, then in substantial occupation of the area. The present states of California, Arizona, New Mexico, Utah, Nevada, and most of Colorado were Mexican territory. The present state of Texas was an independent republic.

Two years later the British were out of the Oregon country and the present northwestern boundary had been established. The hold of Mexico on California and the Southwest had been replaced by United States possession. The Republic of Texas had become a state of the Union.

The first step in this amazing expansion was the offer of annexation by the United States made to Texas and accepted on July 4, 1845. Texas had won her independence nine years before, and for nearly a decade had maintained it. But in much the same way as Spain had long refused to recognize that Mexico had won its independence, so Mexico had refused to accept the fact of Texan independence. Instead the Mexican government kept alive the threat of war against what she still thought of as a province in revolt.

Annexation was proffered to Texas for good reasons of geography and racial kinship. But with annexation the United States inherited the smoldering state of war between that nation and Mexico. Indeed, according to the Mexican government, the fact of annexation was to be regarded by Mexico as a declaration of war to be acted upon accordingly without any further formality.

This threat from across the border called for prompt measures for protection of the newly acquired territory. Accordingly, Brigadier General Zachary Taylor was ordered to move his forces to the vicinity of the Rio Grande, the boundary claimed by Texas and thus the new southwestern frontier of the United States. By the end of July, 1845, Taylor's Army of Observation of about 4,000 men was in camp at Corpus Christi, the most southerly settlement of the Texans.

There they remained throughout the winter. During this time President James K. Polk sought to re-establish the diplomatic relations which had been broken by Mexico when the United States offered annexation to Texas. This attempt to reopen negotiations failed. President Herrera of Mexico was driven from office by a revolution, chiefly because he had appeared to be willing to treat with the United States. The new president, General Paredes, took office as 1846 began. Mexico's intentions were made plain with a ringing assertion of her continued and undiminished claim to all of Texas. Paredes further declared he would defend the national territory and began to strengthen his forces in the north of Mexico.

In March, Taylor moved his forces to the north bank of the Rio Grande. There, on April 25, 1846, occurred the first clash of arms between reconnoitering forces, with severe losses to the United States cavalry. "Mexico," in the words of President Polk, had "shed American blood upon the American soil"—an interpretation which was rejected by Mexico, of course, and also by many of those in the United States who objected to the annexation of Texas. It was upon this issue, however, that America declared war.

The United States entered the war with Mexico all but totally unprepared. We had an army of fewer than 8,000 men. Not since the War of 1812 had there been a concentration of forces for maneuvers or other training. Infantry companies had been reduced to forty-two men, and not all these skeleton compaines were filled to authorized strength. Supplies and transportation wherewith to haul them were both woefully lacking, so that the United States was forced to improvise and, in the phrase of Quartermaster General Jesup, "to pay for time"—as it has so often done since.

The opening Battles of Palo Alto and Resaca de la Palma, fought north of the Rio Grande in May, were won by a handful of United States regulars, including a few batteries of what was then called "flying artillery." Obviously, though, the war could not be fought to a conclusion by these forces, so volunteers—some for terms of three months, some for six, and most for twelve months—were enlisted.

The original plan of operations of the United States Army called for advances in three directions. Colonel Stephen W. Kearny was to march from Fort Leavenworth with a force of 1,700 men—the Army of the West—with which he was to occupy Santa Fe and press on to California with a small part of his force. Brigadier General John E. Wool was to organize an Army of the Center at San Antonio and then march on Chihuahua. The main effort was to be made from the lower Rio Grande, where Taylor's Army of Occupation was to cross the river and occupy the northern province of Mexico.

The difficulty with these operations in so far as effecting the purpose of "conquering a peace" was that none of them were directed at the true seats of Mexican population and power. To correct this failing, Major General Winfield Scott, commanding the Army, soon ordered Taylor to take up the march on the "high road to the capital of Mexico." Secretary of War William L. Marcy, however, raised practical questions as to the feasibility of supply and transportation on an overland march of nearly one thousand miles. Instead, he suggested using the naval superiority of the United States to shift its main forces by sea to Vera Cruz, whence the advance could be made to the capital by the shortest route.

It was not until the following year, however, that this plan was put into effect. Meanwhile, the United States Navy had occupied the coast of California, and the Californians had at first accepted and then risen against the new authority. Kearny's handful of dragoons had reached the vicinity of San Diego. Remnants of the Mexican forces capitulated, accepting the Treaty of Cahuenga, in January, 1847. In the same period, Taylor captured the city of Monterey in northern Mexico and advanced beyond Saltillo. There Wool's Army of the Center, which had been diverted from its original destination of Chihuahua, joined him in time to help win the great battle of the northern operations when, on Washington's Birthday of 1847, at Buena Vista, Taylor repulsed the attacks of the Mexican commander, General Santa Anna.

On March 9, in America's first D-day amphibious landing on a foreign shore, General Scott and the Home Squadron, under command of Commodore David Conner, put 10,000 men ashore on the beach below Vera Cruz. The landing was followed by the siege and capture of that seaport, the march up the heights to do battle at Cerro Gordo, and the occupation of Jalapa, half-way up the mighty mountain wall which rises between the coast and the plateau of Mexico. There the time of enlistment of the twelve-month volunteers expired and almost to a man they demanded their discharges and return to the States. With the half of the army which remained, Scott marched on to Puebla, where he awaited reinforcements. Upon their arrival he cut loose from his Vera Cruz base and marched into the Valley of Mexico. There, after the double victories of Contreras and Churubusco, the fruitless attack on Molino del Rey, the storming of the fortress of Chapultepec, and the battles on the causeways leading into the capital, Scott occupied the "Halls of the Montezumas" on September 14, 1847.

Heavy fighting was over but it was not until February of 1848 that the Treaty of Guadalupe Hidalgo was signed, and not until the end of May that it was finally ratified. The treaty confirmed the Rio Grande up to El Paso and a line drawn thence to the Pacific Ocean as the boundary between the two nations.

No one would now undo the annexation of Texas, which led to the war with Mexico. That war added to the United States the immense Southwest—another result which no one would today undo. These results were due, basically, to the same cause which brought the Northwest into the Union—the westward push of an expanding population into lands which were almost empty of settlement. When directed north of the Missouri Compromise line of 36 degrees 30 minutes north latitude, this push was accepted as part of a mission to civilize a continent. When south of that line, the westward push frequently has been regarded as the result of a plan to extend the range of slavery. Actually, the movements were in both instances essentially those of individuals, few of whom held slaves in any number, acting in the familiar patern of the frontier.

The Mexican War was a small affair by modern standards of combat. There was never a time when a United States commander could put into action more than 10,000 men and rarely a time when a Mexican commander could muster many more. But it was a war big with consequences.

To Mexico, the war meant finally giving up its claim to Texas and its precarious hold on Upper California, and losing its far northern outpost of New Mexico. But it meant also gaining a new sense of nationality with a common tradition of brave, even heroic, resistance.

To the United States, the war meant new territory and new problems. One of these was the flaming-up of antislavery agitation in the dispute over the disposition of the newly acquired lands. In this respect the Mexican War has been regarded as a spark which fired the train of events leading up to the American Civil War. But it should be noted that not a square mile of the territory which it added to the United States was opened to slavery, and that the sectional controversy did not come to a head in the newly added territory but in Kansas, which had been American since the purchase of Louisiana, half a century before.

To the world, the Mexican War meant that the United States was rounded out to truly continental proportions, thereby precluding any possible further European occupation of territory on the American continent. The War with Mexico was an inescapable and a not inglorious step in the historical process by which the United States of America was brought to its present place in the world.

Utopia in America

ODELL SHEPARD

In this age of the common man, American individualism took many forms. In New Harmony, Indiana, in 1826, a British social reformer named Robert Owen was endeavoring to set up a co-operative community affording time for education and recreation (and failing because the devil also had a way of finding amusements for idle hands). Owen was one of many who sought Utopia—a part of that spirit in the land sensing a need for forms of sweeping social reorganization. True, there was often an element of regimentation in such social experimentation that went against the grain of American individualism. The community groups devised by the Frenchman, Charles Fourier, and called phalanxes, were to be equal in size, similar in program. Yet while the Utopia-movers could be ridiculed as faddists, the times had produced them, and aspirations of the common man echoed behind the language they spoke.

Odell Shepard, one of our finest biographers and historical novelists, winner of the Pulitzer Prize for his biography of Bronson Alcott, tenderly treats this instinct that developed in America as man hoped for—and sought to shape—a better world.

WITH the discovery of America four centuries and a half ago, old Europe began to think young thoughts. Wearied by the strife and tyranny of a thousand years, she had come to think that happiness lay far behind her in a Paradise forever lost, or else far ahead in a life beyond the grave. But then came news of another Eden, deep in the west, where mankind might perhaps build on solid earth something more like heaven than the world had yet known. Humanity was to have a great second chance. The creative imagination—the source of all human progress—awoke once more. To the old men there came grander visions, and the young men had bolder dreams.

We know, of course, that in the occupation and exploitation of this western Eden the baser elements of human nature have been fully represented. Selfishness and cruelty and greed have done their work here, as elsewhere, from the beginning until the present moment. And yet it is also true that our country is the child of audacious dreaming and exalted vision. We shall never understand her until we realize that she was born of a union between hard cold facts as they are and an ideal of what they should be.

An example of the intellectual awakening caused by the discovery of America is seen in the book called *Utopia,* which was written by Sir Thomas More of England only twenty-four years after the voyage of Columbus. It does not mention America, and indeed the title of the book, which was made out of two Greek words, means "nowhere." Yet, probably, More thought of his imaginary island—crescent-shaped and two hundred miles across—as lying in the region of the West Indies. The word "Utopia" was adopted long ago into the English language as signifying a place or a social and economic condition regarded as ideally perfect. In our day it is commonly used in derision, as though there were something ridiculous in all efforts to imagine a state of affairs closely corresponding to the heart's and mind's desire. However that may be, there is nothing laughable in this famous book by Sir Thomas More, the first thing of its kind since Plato wrote *The Republic* nearly two thousand years before.

More's plan for ensuring human happiness is admirable in some ways but not in all. In his Utopia there are no people hugely rich and none who are desperately poor. In that country everyone works with his hands, part of the time at a trade, and then, for a change, works on the land. No one, however, works for more than six hours a day, and when that labor has filled the market everyone takes a vacation. Thus full provision is made for leisure, and this is regarded not as preparation for more work but as work's reward. Just here the Utopians have something to teach us—and yet we should find life on their island quite intolerable because it left no room for the development and expression of individuality. The fact is that More's plan was founded upon distrust, even fear, of the individual. He regarded freedom as a dangerous thing. For that reason every detail of Utopian life was strictly regulated, like the monotonous ticking of a clock. Every precaution was taken against change in the laws and customs of the island. Privacy was not allowed, even in family life. The people of that island were directed to wear a uniform, to eat what they were told was good for them, to marry according to rule, and to bring up their children under strict supervision of the magistrates. After all, their leisure was not free time. At best, the happiness supposed to result from their conformity was that of contented cows. It was a happiness forced upon them, and so indistinguishable from pure misery.

Sir Thomas had essentially a medieval mind in spite of his ability to spell out the Greek language. His ideal community suggests the severe and cautious and prudish regulations of monastic life in the Middle Ages. Not only does he try to wipe out all distinctions of rank and property, but he strives to obliterate everything that Walt Whitman meant by "the single, separate person." He has no place, therefore, in the development of truly American life, which is committed once and for all to the perils and the exalted aspirations of an individualism reaching toward the heights from which Saint Teresa spoke when she said that a single soul is worth more than all the material universe.

Because Sir Thomas More, whom many now call Saint Thomas, was a devout and resolute Roman Catholic, it seems natural that his Utopia should be like the monasteries of the Middle Ages. The surprising thing is that the same monastic pattern should recur in the many communities founded by Protestants in America. This fact seems to hint that monasticism answers to some deep need of human nature which is independent of time and place and creed. American Utopians withdrew from the world to devote themselves to the life of the mind and the spirit. They too were convinced that no one profits by gaining the whole world if he loses his own soul. Like the monks, these people were highly industrious, and they were at times economically successful, yet they held all their worldly goods in common, taking from each according to his ability and giving to each according to his need.

On account of this equal sharing the American Utopians have sometimes been called "Communistic." They were that in the pre-Marxian sense of the word, and they drew their example from the practice of the early Christians as recorded by Saint Paul. But between them and the Communists of our day we find nothing but sharp contrasts. The followers of Karl Marx are avowedly materialistic while the American Utopians lived almost solely for spiritual and intellectual values. Furthermore, they wished to remain small. It was never their intention to overwhelm the minds of others. They never felt that they were in possession of all the truth. They often said that their ways of life were experimental, tentative, and exploratory. It was perhaps their deepest wish that they might be pathfinders on the way to a world more kindly and sensible and warm than the one they knew. We do not find that they made any effort, by force or by guile or by propaganda, to increase their number or their power. Indeed it was always easier to leave one of their communities than to enter it. In these respects they were sharply distinct from the Communists of our time.

And the differences between them and the medieval monasteries are perhaps equally numerous. For one thing, they seldom excluded women. In both the theory and practice of equality between the sexes these communities were well in advance of America as a whole. Another difference lay in the fact that each community wished to be completely independent, acknowledging no external authority, enacting and administering its own laws, admitting and excluding whomsoever it pleased, setting up its own codes of conduct. Furthermore, they were not bound together, like the monasteries, as parts of a greater whole. Each one was a separate unit, going its own way and managing its own affairs.

In America, since the beginning, we have had at least a hundred of these ideal communities. They have been the homes, for periods long or short, of at least a hundred thousand men and women and children. They have often been ridiculed, and at times they have been persecuted, but in their quiet withdrawal from the main-traveled roads they have been quite as American as those of us who have kept the middle of the way. Some of them, like Bronson Alcott's "Fruitlands" in Massachusetts, have lasted for only a few months, and some—the Shakers, for example, and the still-flourishing Amana community of central Iowa—have existed for more than a century. Because they have always preferred the frontier to established towns and cities, the many places of their residence reach from the Atlantic to the Pacific, mostly north of Mason and Dixon's line. By their own choice they have seldom been mentioned in the news, and our historians do not usually take them into account. Nevertheless, they have laid a stone in the wilderness which, though thus far rejected by the builders, may some time become an American cornerstone.

There is a possibility that the America of our day is growing unduly conservative and cautious. There may come a time when these who lived for the mind and the spirit—the Shakers, the Harmonists, the Separatists of Zoar, the Owenites, the Perfectionists, the Brook Farmers, the Phalangists, the Icarians—will shine in our national calendar as pathfinders of the future. For America was born of a dream, and without a vision we should long since have perished. These Utopians helped to build our castle in the clouds. As Henry Thoreau once said, that is where it belongs. Now it is our task to build its foundations.

The American Renaissance

JAY LEYDA

With the rise of the common man came the finest flowering of American culture. With a foothold firmly secured in the wilderness, with business finding stable patterns that suited the times and its opportunities, with leisure setting more easily upon the American conscience (especially in the cities) books appeared in increasing numbers, magazines and newspapers flourished, and literary societies, museums, academies, libraries, and lyceums mushroomed. Independence also was being won for an American intellect that was now daring to strike out along its own high road to adventure. In the decade before the Civil War, in these "golden years," the American Story acquired, then, this deeper dimension. Jay Leyda, who relates that fascinating chapter, is an authority on Herman Melville (The Melville Log is among his notable books) and Emily Dickinson.

THE American Story has brought us now to a period of our history that more and more we tend to look back on as the richest and fullest period of American thought and imagination—the middle of the last century. We never seem to tire of asking why those few years before the Civil War should have produced a more glorious crop of thoughts and books than has any other time in our nation's life.

One remarkable aspect of this rich period is that the men who made it supreme were themselves unusually aware of their responsibilities and their privileges. They spoke of it as an American Renaissance—an American rebirth—not as a second birth of an American culture, but as the maturity on a new soil of arts and culture inherited from Europe. It had been conceived in New England, but was now spread to every part of the United States where books were read. There were, of course, many resemblances to the several mother countries in the ideas behind this new birth, but more easily noticed in the works of the period was an aspiring new voice that could only be called "American."

In the very mid-year of the century, in 1849, Ralph Waldo Emerson, moral and intellectual guide for the era, published a statement first announced in his lectures: "There is a moment in the history of every nation, when, proceeding out of this brute youth, the perceptive powers reach their ripeness. . . ." Emerson called this "the moment of adult health," and in the literature of Emerson and his followers we can watch that perception reach in all directions, exalting the joys of clear sight, clear understanding, and clear challenges to all that seems wrong or blind. To produce this splendid moment, every element in American life—even some that seem, at first glance, remote from literature—made its contribution.

With an untouched frontier still on the horizon, the old farming majority of the coastal states was moving into business, changing the character of American society. The young democracy was being tested on all fronts. More citizens of all classes demanded and claimed a voice in the government. Even in religion and science a democratic factor provoked change—old unquestioned forms of religion experienced tremendous upheavals; broadened educational facilities, both in genuinely public schools and in a greater number of institutions of higher learning, encouraged an expansion of the teaching and practice of the natural sciences. A new consciousness of nationalism summoned, involuntarily, new writers. Even the negative particles of these elements were necessary and useful, for this entire environment had to demonstrate not only "opportunity" but also imperfections enough to make the artist want to speak for himself.

Who, then, of that period, stands beside Emerson? Next to him —but a little apart—will always stand the man who admired him best and doubted him most, Henry David Thoreau—a bolder, sterner, and more uncompromising thinker than his teacher. We know him as a man who would never hesitate to perform an act, or refuse to perform an act, in accordance with his beliefs, no matter where the logic led him. Thoreau's long meditation beside Walden Pond was a test of principles: "I went to the woods because I wished to live deliberately, to front only the essential facts of life, and see if I could not learn what it had to teach, and not, when I came to die, discover that I had not lived."

Emerson had an almost irrational antipathy to all forms of fiction, but that did not alter Nathaniel Hawthorne's gratitude to Emerson for his stimulation and affection. Hawthorne's stories and novels were his expression of the same faiths and probings that Emerson expressed in essays and poems.

The relation of Herman Melville to Emerson was almost totally impersonal. It was Emerson as thinker and writer that influenced Melville, who sometimes met friends of Emerson's, but never the man himself. As Melville wrote fiction, it is possible that Emerson was no more than aware of his existence.

Walt Whitman lived the longest of this group, yet his work was well begun in 1855 when he published his first edition of *Leaves of Grass*. With all these men, there were difficulties in public acceptance, but the daring substance and form of Whitman's poetry made round him the tallest barrier from the public. Abraham Lincoln's place among the thinkers of the American Renaissance must be fixed also. He was as much a product and a creator of the period's philosophy as any man, transcending party politics.

It is often said that the one art vigorously developed in America's early years was that of oratory. Certainly the artistic eloquence of these men derives from the art of the vivid, direct oral communication of abstract ideas. Two of this group stemmed from earlier careers in oratory—Emerson in the pulpit (and later on the lecture platform), Lincoln on the political stump. The rhythms of Whitman, the prose style of Hawthorne and Melville were born out of the language of personal persuasion, whether practiced before a Calvinist congregation or a Tammany Hall crowd.

Such a source would have seemed and sounded strange in any other country's cultural history, but such a workaday inspiration was a cause for pride among these artists, glad to have their works distinguished from the traditions of England and Europe. None of them boasted any ridiculous separation from the literature and culture of the mother countries; but they all, even in the detached mild voice of Hawthorne, demanded recognition for their own fresh merits and asked that new standards of critical measurement be applied to their work.

It was at home that critics and readers hesitated longest to accept this new group and its aims. To the English publisher who had just accepted his masterpiece, Herman Melville wrote, "This country is at present engaged in furnishing material for future authors, not in encouraging its living ones."

By the time Sam Houston posed for this daguerreotype, he had served in Congress, successfully fought for and secured the independence of Texas from Mexico, and had twice been president of the new Republic of Texas.

A plan for Utopia in Indiana—"New Harmony," an association framed upon principles advocated by Robert Owen. The architecture and geography were to be "so regulated . . . to form . . . greater physical, moral and intellectual advantages than have ever yet been realized in any age or country."

In the South the "peculiar institution" had existed since August of 1619; in the North, organized antislavery movements began in April, 1688. Perhaps the most dramatic manifestation of abolitionist sentiment was John Brown's Raid at Harper's Ferry in 1859. Brown—seen here in a photograph which has only once before appeared in print (in 1898)—was hanged soon after his capture by a force of U. S. Marines commanded by Colonel Robert E. Lee.

"The skepticism of the statesmen, the despotism of tyranny and the carping of political croakers to the contrary, a new people, a free nation, a sovereign independence, lives and has its being in THE CONFEDERATE STATES OF NORTH AMERICA." Thus, in February of 1861, was the inauguration of Jefferson Davis as provisional president of the Confederacy hailed by the Memphis *Appeal* in an editorial titled "The Birth of a Nation."

I have mentioned "Emerson and his followers," but I don't want to leave the impression that this was a "school" or a group. The writers who made major contributions to the American Renaissance had only one characteristic in common—they were all, distinctly, individualists. No equal collection of great writers, living and working in one time and country, saw so little of each other as did Emerson, Thoreau, Hawthorne, Melville, and Whitman. Some were not even acquainted with the others, and at no time did they all ever find themselves in one room together, even for a public occasion. Within the collection there were admirations, but little intimacy and life-long friendships. For some years Thoreau felt a deep personal friendship for Emerson, and always acknowledged his debt to him. But Thoreau was too frank to be tolerant of Emerson's later inability to face whole truths. Without Hawthorne, Melville would not have written *Moby Dick* as we know that book, but this friendship, too, expired within a few years. Melville may never have met, personally, any of the other men. Whitman, the most outwardly sociable of these, caught only glimpses of the men with whose names his would be linked forever. No comparable group of literary contemporaries, in England or France or Germany, lived and worked so much to themselves, measuring their work against their individual consciences, rather than against the desire of their audience.

The chief themes of all these men were those that need solitary and profound contemplation, more than lively social converse. The nature of good and evil is by no means a theme unique to this group, but it is a theme that gripped each of them, from Emerson with his essay on nature, to Melville with his white whale and Captain Ahab. Their other chief theme, the relation of the individual to his society, was explored in all its conflicts more searchingly than it is today, when those conflicts appear more violently conspicuous than they did a hundred years ago. "The mass of men," in Thoreau's words, still "lead lives of quiet desperation." It was Lincoln, who claimed no art, who had the toughest duty of giving practical form to all that this group learned and felt. A tragic tone dominates this renaissance, despite—perhaps because of—the optimism and confidence in which the country as a whole then seemed so secure.

The Artist in the 19th Century

OLIVER W. LARKIN

In prose, in poetry, in drama, America became an image so clearly caught that it could be translated into emotions its people recognized as true of themselves. So, too, for the man with palette and brush, sketch pad and pen was there an image of America that haunted mind and heart. Oliver W. Larkin, professor of art at Smith College, and winner of the Pulitzer Prize for his splendid Art and Life in America, *tells how America began to capture and to foster a native art.*

"AMERICA is a poem in our eyes; its ample geography dazzles the imagination." Thus wrote Ralph Waldo Emerson in 1843, observing the swift and turbulent life of the nation. Foreign travelers complained that America was barbarous, noisy, and crude; but Emerson advised the artists of our country to celebrate this dramatic spectacle—the Northern trade, the Southern planting, the Western clearing—in their poems and their paintings. Alive to this challenge, our writers achieved what has been called the American Renaissance. During the middle years of the century, between 1840 and 1860, they produced their masterpieces: *Representative Men, The House of the Seven Gables, The Deerslayer, Walden, Moby Dick, Leaves of Grass.*

The American painters, too, were inspired to choose new subjects and to represent them in new ways. One by one, the men who had pictured the days of Revolution and of the first years of the new republic had passed on—Charles Willson Peale, John Trumbull, Gilbert Stuart, and their like. New men were taking their places, men who worked for a much wider public. Where there had been a few men of wealth before to buy pictures, there were now dozens of bankers, merchants, and politicians who took an especial pride in fostering a native art. The young artists of the previous age had been obliged to study in Europe; now they could learn their profession in Boston or Philadelphia, or at the National Academy in New York, a thoroughly democratic institu-

162

tion which had been founded and was managed by artists themselves, which exhibited the work of living Americans, and which offered free instruction and prizes to its students. Further encouragement was afforded in the 1840's by the American Art Union, a nationwide organization which came to number almost twenty thousand members. For five dollars per year, each member received a fine engraving from the work of a native artist and a share in the annual lottery where he could, if he were lucky, win an original painting. With its funds the Union bought, exhibited, and gave away by lot hundreds of canvases by our foremost artists.

The painters were quick to respond to such favorable conditions. In the field of landscape there arose what historians have called the Hudson River School. Thomas Doughty gave up the leather business in Philadelphia to paint quiet pastoral scenes along the Delaware and the Hudson. Asher B. Durand turned from making skillful engravings to study the foliage of American woods, which he painted in fresher greens than Doughty had dared to use. Another artist of this group was John Kensett, who caught the glowing colors of rocky shore and deep blue water at Newport, Rhode Island, and the golden sunlight of the valleys near Chocorua in the White Mountains. It was the still whiteness of New England winter that appealed to George Durrie of Connecticut, and his sturdy farmhouses among snow-laden trees under gray December skies earned him the title, "the Whittier of American painting." The art of Durrie entered a good many homes when the firm of Currier and Ives made colored prints of his snowbound scenes for sale throughout the nation. George Inness was younger than these other landscape artists, but already gave promise in his Lackawanna Valley that he could construct the solid planes of earth and fill his spaces with atmosphere and sunshine.

The most popular of this group was the romantic Thomas Cole, who won praise from William Cullen Bryant for his scenes of wild grandeur, his majestic mountains wreathed in storm clouds, his mighty forests which no axe had ever touched, his flaming sunset skies and the terrifying shapes of his great rocks and writhing trees. Cole was versatile enough to paint the sunny calm of the Connecticut valley in his work, *The Oxbow*, where a broad stream wanders among rich farmlands and meadows, but also to portray the crash and turbulence of a thunderstorm in the Catskills. People flocked to see his series called *The Course of Empire*, a painted sermon on the fate of nations which become too proud, too wealthy, and too powerful. And people hailed his landscapes because they knew that the progress of civilization would soon destroy the primeval grandeur of his forests.

That grandeur was still to be found in the Far West; and as the explorer, the frontiersman, the hunter, the road builder, the homemaker pushed into the vast region beyond the Mississippi, many an American artist went along with his sketchbook to record the appearance and habits of the vanishing redskin. George Catlin journeyed from St. Louis up the Missouri River. His subjects ranged from prairie fires to a buffalo hunt on snowshoes, and his observation and daring broke through the limitations of his technique. Audiences here and in Europe marveled at Catlin's traveling exhibition, which included not only his many canvases but also a group of live Indians. Many others followed Catlin: John Mix Stanley painted from Texas to Oregon; Alfred J. Miller made fresh and brilliant water colors of the Rockies; Seth Eastman illustrated the six volumes of Henry Schoolcraft's work on the Indian tribes; a German-born artist named Albert Bierstadt joined the surveying expedition of General Lander and made the first of those great panoramic pictures of towering canyons, mighty waterfalls, redwood forests, and stupendous mountain peaks for which American millionaires were to pay fantastic prices.

Thus was the natural setting of America presented in fresh, bold colors to its inhabitants. But those inhabitants also demanded pictures of themselves. To be sure, the portrait painter now faced a competitor—the camera.

A Frenchman named Daguerre had made images on a copper plate, and in this country people could sit in rigid postures for daguerreotypes. The makers of painted likenesses had somehow to match the vaunted realism of this new device. Some of them learned from the Düsseldorf school how to render their subjects with sharp detail and a smooth finish; others relied on their own keen eyesight. Chester Harding by the mid-century was manufacturing portraits with a firm and sometimes harsh presentation of the facts before him. Another realist was Thomas Hicks, who preferred to show his subjects the size of life on big canvases. In his study of Hamilton Fish, the shrewd patron stands aggressively at his desk and stares at the observer, his rugged features and baggy clothes painted without a trace of flattery—a symbol of self-reliance. And other men made equally vigorous characterizations—men like Charles Elliott, William Page, Daniel Hunting-

ton, Wyatt Eaton, and Thomas Buchanan Read. A young Irish-
man from Boston named George Healy, who had earned his first
pennies by holding gentlemen's horses, made his first bid for
reputation with a sober and solid portrait of Abraham Lincoln in
1864, and was soon famous as a painter of the world's most celebrated people.

Not all the portraits of this period were signed with well-known
names. Through the back-country regions moved the artisans who
had just enough skill to outline a head and body and then fill in its
colors. These were the so-called "primitives" whose direct and
honest vision took the place of a sophisticated technique, and
whose instinct often produced an effective design. They put colors
together which convention would have forbidden. Sometimes they
modeled a head as though carving it from granite; sometimes they
reduced the sitter to the flatness of a map. These traveling limners
stayed long enough in one place to paint the few who could pay
ten or fifteen dollars for a likeness, and then moved on. Their
work has the vigor of something freshly seen, and as directly set
down by the brush.

As we now look back on those middle years of the century, their
most characteristic art seems to be of the type called "genre"
painting. A few men like Emanuel Leutze executed pompous
scenes from American history—scenes like Leutze's huge *Washington Crossing the Delaware,* in which every cake of ice and
every fold in a costume were done with a painful precision. But
these grand occasions of the past were less interesting to the
Americans of the 1840's and 1850's than the daily scene of life
as it was being lived. Emerson had once said, "I embrace the common . . . and sit at the feet of the familiar." Out of the common
and the familiar, a host of talented genre painters made their
vivid anecdotes, and the sum total of their work is a fascinating
record of the age.

In the small panels of David G. Blythe we come to know the
brawling and grimy life of frontier Pittsburgh, its dim saloons,
its outdoor horse markets where men haggle over broken-down
nags, its coal miners and crowded omnibuses, all rendered with a
grotesque humor which reminds us of the Dutch and Flemish
masters.

In the paintings of William Sidney Mount we recapture the
genial warmth of country life on Long Island, where a Negro
woman spears eels in the calm waters of Setauket, where farmers
and their wives dance on the barn floor to a fiddler's tune.

On the canvases of George Caleb Bingham is spread before us the raucous pageantry of the frontier, the rough and picturesque life of the traders and boatmen which was to inspire some of Mark Twain's best pages. Bingham had grown up in Missouri and had observed every detail of its life when in 1844 he painted two men paddling their dugout along mist-laden waters in his *Fur Traders Descending the Missouri.* In later works—*The Jolly Flatboatmen, Raftsmen Playing Cards, The Country Election*— Bingham toiled, as he said, "to assure us that our social and political characteristics . . . will not be lost in the lapse of time for want of an Art record rendering them full justice." To know his paintings is to know life on the great Western rivers.

Fortunately for us, these genre painters not only knew how to assemble pictorial facts, but also knew how to make pictures. Blythe's crowded canvases always tell their story clearly. Mount framed his figures effectively in the doorways of barns; Bingham's multitudes are kept in order by ingenious devices which lead the eye from one group to another, and by the harmony of his bright, clear colors. For these painters, necessity was the mother of invention, and they let the subject determine its own form.

After these landscapists, these portrait makers, and these genre painters of the mid-century would come men of greater sophistication and a riper skill—Hunt, Eakins, Homer. Yet these masters of the Gilded Age built on the foundation laid by the earlier painters, whose tribute to the beauty of their native land, to the character of its representative men, and to the humor and pathos of its daily life, forms one of the finest chapters in the history of our art.

FIVE

The Blue

and the Gray

S INCE the terrible days from 1861 to 1865, when the Republic was torn apart by civil war, historians have attributed many causes to the bloodiest conflict between brothers the world has ever witnessed. For a long time strong emphasis was put upon the economic background of the war, and yet the conflict between a predominantly mercantile North and a predominantly agricultural South does not give a satisfying reason for war. True, the South in 1861 tended in its thinking toward remaining more or less a colony of Europe, and in this respect continued a struggle for American economic independence that had been going on since the years following the Revolution.

But a great deal more was involved in a phenomenon as extremely complicated as the American Civil War. Along with economic differences were factors of politics, of mass psychology, of constitutional law, of manners and customs and morals, and each contributed its share to producing the dismemberment of the Union. Between the North and the South, however, there existed one undeniable distinction—in one the "peculiar institution" did not function, in the other it did. Said Lincoln in his Second Inaugural: "One eighth of the whole population was colored slaves. . . . These slaves constituted a peculiar and powerful interest. All knew that this interest was, somehow, the cause of the war." And Lincoln's architect of ultimate military victory, Ulysses S. Grant,

167

wrote in the closing months of his life: "For some years before the war began it was a trite saying among some politicians that, 'A state half slave and half free cannot exist.' . . . I took no part myself in any such view of the case at the time, but . . . I have come to the conclusion that the saying is quite true."

Remove the "peculiar institution" and the American Civil War becomes unthinkable; with it, there is motivation for all the emotion, the suspicion and hatred, the contradiction of logic, the thundering clash of sectional and personal interest that produced those years of despair. No other crisis before or since has had a power to draw apart Americans over so wide an area; and all the arguments employed to explain secession amounted, in the end, to justifying slavery as absolute and untouchable. Certainly great sectional ambitions were in conflict between North and South, and between both of these regions and the West; such struggles long had existed, and continue to exist, but without conscience to question and defend they do not mean disunion and war. States' rights was the legal argument, but slave rights was the defendant before the bar of history. On July 4, 1861, an appropriate day for a man who through a lifetime had revered the Declaration of Independence, Lincoln addressed a special message to Congress. The legal argument of the Confederacy he ridiculed as a sophism, declaring that "the little disguise that the supposed right [of secession] is to be exercised only for just cause, themselves to be the sole judge of its justice, is too thin to merit any notice." Then, contemplating the moral basis of the war, Lincoln said:

"This is essentially a people's contest. On the side of the Union, it is a struggle for maintaining in the world, that form, and substance of government, whose leading object is, to elevate the condition of men—to lift artificial weights from all shoulders—to clear the paths of laudable pursuit for all—to afford all, an unfettered start, and a fair chance, in the race of life. Yielding to partial, and temporary departures, from necessity, this is the leading object of the government for whose existence we contend."

In an age distinguished for the rise of the common man—an age in which that man had proved he could get ahead on the frontier as an empire builder, in the city as a man of business who also possessed culture and refinement, in arts and letters as an individual intellect with something to say, with experiences worthy of portrayal, with emotions that were valid to fellow human beings—Lincoln used a true idiom. First Bull Run followed; the years of bleeding ran on; and when at last Grant emerged, the prime maker

of the victory, he was called, in a tremendous triumph of historical perception, "the uncommon common man."

Today a part of family folk legend, the American Civil War
exerts an enormous fascination upon the national imagination. Its
causes and its events are pondered and studied with an immediacy
of interest as though they occurred yesterday. In a sense, they did;
the today we have, the tomorrow we hope for, stem from them.

Voice of Northern Industrialism

A R T H U R   C.   C O L E

*"Sectionalism as a divisive force in American History," Professor
Thomas P. Govan recently warned his colleagues, "has had more
importance as a subject for historians than it ever has had in the
life of the nation."[1] Truly, the loose use of the term creates a ridiculous mental image of boiling sectional geysers bursting at stated
intervals through the crust of the nation. The more dramatic reality
is that many times the giants of conflicting interest, whom the cartoonist sees at dagger point, actually are seeking ways to become
comfortable, if grudging, bedfellows.*

*To northern industrialism in the decade preceding the Civil
War, Daniel Webster was the man with a golden voice in national
politics. He, too, was an uncommon common man. From humble
beginnings, he went ahead in the rosiest American tradition: knowing what talent and character and enterprise could achieve, dedicated to the stanch belief that property and the Constitution were
good for New England (and therefore the country), Black Dan
was as natural to his age as any of its figures who grew into legends
—a man of intellectual power and spiritual resourcefulness who
tried from the bottom of his fine conservative heart to travel the
middle road. Yet there were principles which Webster would not
surrender; legends are not hung on weak spinal columns. He was
dead in October of 1852. Arthur C. Cole, now retired, was long
chairman of the history department of Brooklyn College and*

[1] Govan, Thomas P., "Was the Old South Different?", *The Journal of Southern
History*, November 1955, Vol. XXI, No. 4, p. 451.

chairman of the Academic Freedom Committee of the American Civil Liberties Union. With telling insight, he evaluates the niche that Webster deserves in the American Story.

W ITH many forces in American life—including its budding artistic genius—betokening a rising and even lusty sense of nationalism, the voice of Daniel Webster rang out to proclaim a devotion to the great American Union excelled by none of his contemporaries.

Middle-class revolutionary New England folk, Daniel Webster's parents sacrificed to send him to Dartmouth College. There he won laurels for his eloquence and was graduated in 1801. He showed an early concern about the claims of "talent . . . character . . . property" which he found among the "bigwigs" of New England; a resulting fear of the spread of French revolutionary egalitarian ideals aroused in him an ardent devotion to "the bonds of our Federal Union." The Jeffersonian victory of 1800 seemed "an earthquake of popular commotion." He sought in a humble way—in Fourth of July orations and in occasional political pamphleteering —to arouse his fellows to resist the "contagion of democracy." He soon became a "defender of the Constitution," suspicious of innovation and fearful of change.

Studying law in Boston and later practicing it in Portsmouth, New Hampshire, Webster became sensitive to the desires of the shipping mercantile interests of New England. As their champion he not only condemned the retaliatory policies of Great Britain and France in their efforts at commercial domination, but even denounced the embargo and the other Jeffersonian countermeasures of "peaceable coercion."

In a Fourth of July oration in 1812 Webster condemned the administration for having led the nation into an unjustifiable war. Unlike some of his compatriots, however, who contemplated recourse to disunion, he was content to seek "the peaceable remedy of election" and was sent to Congress from New Hampshire on an antiwar platform.

In Congress he labored diligently to promote various New England interests and attitudes, lamenting that "the events of the times . . . have bereft us of our commerce, the great source of our wealth." Admitted to practice before the Supreme Court, he soon made a brilliant record in some of the great cases presided over by Chief Justice John Marshall. His oratorical powers won additional acclaim for his performances in his Plymouth Oration celebrating the landing of the Pilgrims, his appeal for Greek independence, and his Bunker Hill address.

Returned to Congress from Massachusetts in 1822 to represent the commercial interest of Boston, Webster opposed the increasingly popular movement for a protective tariff. For over a dozen years he deemed the tariff question "a tedious, disagreeable subject." He publicly condemned Henry Clay for stating that protection was part of a great "American system" when it was a practice that America had never tried, and which was urged in imitation of a questionable British example.

But Webster denied that he was an enemy of manufacturers— generally; he merely opposed rearing them in hotbeds. There were proposed duties of which he approved; about others he was acquiescent. But he found most of them too "burdensome" and "too dangerous to that interest which has steadily enriched, gallantly defended, and proudly distinguished us."

The Webster of this period was less satisfied with economic theories and more concerned with the realities of life. The tariff of 1824 was followed by increased investments in wool manufacturing. Webster had taken a small block of stock when the Merrimac Manufacturing Company was incorporated in 1822. In due course he developed close associations with mill owners in his state. He was soon frank in stating that nothing was left for New England "but to consider that the government had fixed and determined its own policy: and that policy was protection."

By 1828 Webster had become a stalwart champion of the interests of the textile mill owners and of manufacturers generally, and spoke out firmly for tariffs that would protect the domestic economy. By this time Webster was an established Bostonian of a dozen years standing and the acknowledged head of the local, if not the American, bar. "Black Dan," he was called, with his sturdy frame, wide-awake, deep-set eyes, and lionlike head. He became widely admired for the rich, sonorous voice, the effective command of language, and the dignified, impressive personality that he devoted to the national interest and its advancement.

When the spokesman of the Southern planters, smarting under a tariff burden that seemed to benefit only the manufacturing areas, proclaimed that a state could—and, if necessary, would—nullify a federal law continuing this system, Webster made his famous reply to Senator Robert Y. Hayne of South Carolina. In it he affirmed that the Union had been created by the national popular will. In a ringing summation he declared himself for "Liberty and Union, now and forever, one and inseparable."

In the nullification crisis of 1832, he stood squarely behind President Andrew Jackson in his defiance of the Southern forces led by John C. Calhoun. But true to his protectionist faith, he refused to accept the "compromise tariff" that resolved the controversy, although he found some satisfaction that the outcome had "tended to strengthen the union of the States, and to uphold the government." His four-hour speech in reply to Calhoun closed with the words: "I shall exert every faculty I possess in aiding to prevent the Constitution from being nullified, destroyed, or impaired. . . ."

In another year Webster became the leading New England exemplar and lion of the new Whig Party, a combination of anti-Jackson forces held together by a common interest in vested property rights. Any temptation toward continued co-operation with Jackson was removed by the latter's war on the Bank of the United States. Webster supported the Bank both on principle and as a profitable client. In due course the Whigs of the Massachusetts legislature named him as their Presidential favorite. He was regularly thereafter a potential Whig Presidential nominee.

At a sacrifice to personal and political fortunes, Webster rendered distinguished services as Secretary of State in the Harrison-Tyler administrations. In the winter of 1844–45 he allowed himself to be returned to the Senate. Devoted to the vested interests of his state—indeed, virtually dependent upon their bounty—Webster deemed it his "especial business to look to the preservation of the great industrial interests of the country." All his efforts, however, could not prevent the reductions under the Walker Tariff of 1846. While the New England industrialists were learning to adjust themselves to these reductions, national politics turned increasingly around the slavery controversy.

Webster had from an early day condemned Negro slavery as "a great moral and political evil," subject however to the exclusive control of the states. Its extension was another matter and he voted consistently both against acquiring additional territory and for the Wilmot Proviso to restrict the spread of slavery. With the triumph of the expansionists he saw nothing in the future but "contention, strife, and agitation." This seemed at hand when in December, 1849, Congress convened to face a most serious crisis in the sectional controversy, with passions on both sides at a white heat. Like other conservative statesmen, Webster came to feel that the preservation of the Union was at stake, and was determined to do all in his power to avert the danger.

As a champion of protection Webster was alarmed to find the continued agitation of the slavery question an obstacle to Whig efforts at tariff revision. It seemed to him that the more important issue of the tariff was being sacrificed to the slavery controversy. Southern Whigs as slaveholders could not be expected to vote protection to the interests of Northerners while their own rights, property, and feelings were being constantly assailed. Moreover, the antislavery forces were becoming increasingly militant and unreasonable. They will not believe, wrote Webster, that "I am an antislavery man unless I repeat the declaration once a week."

With Clay's famous compromise proposals under consideration, Webster rose on March 7, 1850 "to beat down the Northern and Southern follies, now raging in equal extremes." He spoke "not as a Massachusetts man, nor as a Northern man, but as an American." Slavery was an evil, but not so great an evil as disunion. There could be no peaceable secession, he informed the South. On the other hand, he condemned the unnecessary severity of the antislavery forces and admitted that Northerners had not lived up to their obligations to return fugitive slaves.

Congressional prohibition of slavery in the territories was useless since a law of nature had ordained "beyond all terms of human enactment, that slavery cannot exist in California or New Mexico." To the conservative element of the country Webster's performance seemed "Godlike," but the antislavery forces, including those in his own party, could see him only as a fallen star.

Becoming Secretary of State under President Fillmore, Webster supported the legislation that substantially covered the ground of Clay's compromise proposals and followed with concern the storm that raged. His Presidential aspirations were revived in 1852 when many Southern Whigs favored his candidacy, but he failed to secure the nomination and, sick in mind and in body, he succumbed on October 24, 1852, murmuring, "I still live."

Two score years in the political arena revealed in Daniel Webster an eloquent champion of the American Union and a special advocate of the industrial interests then so rapidly forging to the fore in the national economy. The Presidential office was reserved for men of less distinction. Yet perhaps no Northerner left so strong an impress upon the political life of this "middle period" or made a more substantial contribution toward the preservation of the Union in the supreme test of the Sixties.

Calhoun and Nullification

CHARLES M. WILTSE

In those years when Webster was the thundering voice of Northern industrialism, the Cotton Kingdom found its own eloquent spokesman in John C. Calhoun. The man from the North and the man from the South shared one frustration: time and again both coveted the Presidency and time and again both were thwarted. Calhoun started life as the son of a small planter in the up-country of his beloved South Carolina; a good marriage into Charleston's aristocracy advanced his future and his fortunes; but the greatest asset Calhoun claimed was the mind of a brilliant political philosopher.

History—in terms of the emotions that motivate it—betrayed Calhoun. In his doctrine of "concurrent majority," which the secessionists perverted into a basis for war, the great South Carolinian actually sought means of preserving the authority of the central government without destroying the rights (or liberties) of minorities. Calhoun thus began as a sound Jeffersonian, and when later he apparently strayed from the fold of the Virginia dynasty of former days, the change can be dated from his quarrels with Jackson. Here, indeed, is one of the most compelling figures in the American Story; and Charles M. Wiltse, whose three-volume biography of Calhoun is an authoritative and indispensable source, deals with the Calhoun who became both symbol and catalyst to the tormented South.

JOHN C. CALHOUN was a master of defensive strategy in politics: the resourceful, obstinate, and single-minded champion of a minority interest and of an obsolescent way of life. His public career began in the House of Representatives in 1811, when he was only twenty-nine years old. It ended in the Senate in 1850, in the midst of the historic debate that was to bring California into the Union as a free state. In the intervening years he held two Cabinet posts, served two terms as Vice President of the United States, and was twice a serious contender for the Presidency. He lived to see the frontier advance from the Mississippi to the Pacific; to feel the impact of the steamboat, the railroad, the telegraph; to see war

174

and industrial revolution irrevocably alter the pattern of American life.

In the course of those forty years, Calhoun changed also—changed from exuberant nationalist, sure of his country's destiny, to a conservative critic of the changing scene. His views as to the nature of man and society, and his analysis of the political process became the intellectual justification for Southern secession, and so it has been easy to lay upon the gaunt South Carolinian's shoulders more than his share of responsibility for the tragedy of civil war. Yet he himself sought only to preserve a familiar way of life, and to advance what he conceived to be the best interests of his constituents. No conscientious believer in representative government could do more; none ought to do less.

In Calhoun's early Congressional years he was one of the young War Hawks who forced a second war with Great Britain upon a reluctant administration. He supported the tariff of 1816 to protect the warborn manufacturing enterprises of New England and the Middle States. But aside from this special case he towered above all class and sectional bias. In six short years he achieved the reputation that won him a seat in Monroe's Cabinet as Secretary of War.

In this new role Calhoun brought his fine mind, his energy, his liberal views to bear on new problems. He reorganized both the War Department and the Army along modern lines. In the give-and-take of Cabinet discussion with such men as James Monroe, John Quincy Adams, and William H. Crawford he contributed to the development of American policy in many fields. But the times were changing. During most of Monroe's first term the country suffered in the grip of economic depression. To appease the clamor from the manufacturing states the protective duties which were to have expired in three years time were extended and increased in 1819. Imports declined, and as the balance of trade shifted, the British market for Southern cotton fell. The South began to see in this continued subsidization of industry her own economic ruin.

The tariff controversy came at a most critical time. In a series of leading cases between 1819 and 1824 the Supreme Court reasserted and amplified the doctrine of national supremacy. Opposition to the tariff had already taken the form of a denial by the cotton states of any constitutional power in Congress to protect industry at the expense of agriculture. The Missouri Compromise, which established in effect an internal balance of power, came in the midst of the tariff debates. It served to warn the planters of the South that their system of labor might also be in jeopardy at the hands of a Northern majority. How far, they asked, might Congress go in passing laws that fell with unequal weight on different sections of the country? And who was to say when the national legislature had gone too far?

By 1824, when the duties were again increased, the tariff had become in the eyes of its opponents a strictly sectional matter. The benefits accrued exclusively to the manufacturing states, while the cost fell with unequal burden upon those who produced staples for a foreign market. It was at this time that Calhoun began to side with his fellow Southern planters. As Vice President he gave the casting vote that broke a Senate tie and defeated a tariff increase on woolens in 1827, but it was no more than a delaying action. A year later the "tariff of abominations" raised the average level of duties to 45 per cent, and aggressive elements in the South began talking openly of rebellion.

Though Calhoun was the Democratic candidate to succeed himself as Vice President, he took little part in the campaign of 1828. The dilemma of the cotton states absorbed his full attention. Both wealth and population were increasing more rapidly in the North than in the South. If a majority in the two houses of Congress, with the concurrence of the President, were, indeed, the supreme and ultimate power in the land, then there was no hope for tariff reform. In the long run there was no hope of perpetuating the system of chattel slavery on which Southern agriculture was based. If the South intended to retain her slaves and to stay in the cotton business, she could not wait patiently until the free states held undisputed sway in national affairs. Unless, of course, the supremacy of the federal government could be successfully challenged!

In spite of the nationalistic attitude of the Supreme Court, the actual extent of federal power had not yet been settled. The states were politically strong, and they commanded a loyalty unknown to later generations. Could not their power be used to correct injustice at the hands of a Congressional majority? Following the precedent of the Virginia and Kentucky Resolutions, and of the Hartford Convention which had formalized New England's opposition to the War of 1812, Calhoun argued that in ratifying the Constitution the states had yielded none of their original sovereignty. They had merely delegated certain powers to a general government created by joint agreement among them. If that government exceeded its authority, its acts were to that extent not binding. In short, if Congress persisted in passing laws deemed unconstitutional, any injured state might interpose to arrest the execution of the law—to nullify it within her limits. It would then rest with the states (or the three-fourths of them required to amend the Constitution) to resolve the question.

Having formulated the doctrine, Calhoun awaited developments. The party failed to follow through on tariff reform, while old differences were exploited by designing men to create a breach between Jackson and his Vice President. Calhoun was excluded from the party councils at a time when all his influence was needed to quiet the rebellious discontent in his native state. For a little longer he held the hotheads in check, but again in 1832 Jackson failed to intervene for tariff reduction. The bill passed in that year —primarily with an eye to the election—was complex and confusing, but it was not satisfactory to the cotton planters of the South.

By this time the younger leaders in South Carolina were ready to take that state out of the Union, and things were threatening to get out of hand. So far Calhoun had not sided with the Nullifiers, although he had devised the constitutional doctrine they proposed to invoke. Now, however, he took the lead. A special convention was called to meet in the fall of 1832 which pronounced the tariff to be null, void, and unenforceable in South Carolina.

For a time an armed clash between state and federal forces seemed unavoidable. Calhoun resigned the Vice Presidency to return as a member of the Senate over which he had presided for eight years. There he joined with Clay, Webster, and a handful of other moderate and patriotic men who would not allow the Union to be destroyed over a difference of opinion. A compromise acceptable to both sides was worked out, and the crisis passed.

But another soon arose to take its place. A sweeping attack on the whole institution of slavery was gaining momentum and presently overshadowed all other points at issue between North and South. The turning point came with the annexation of Texas in 1845. As Secretary of State in the last year of Tyler's administration, Calhoun handled the negotiations, but the effect was the opposite of what he intended. The South saw in Texas additional slave states to balance Oregon and preserve an uneasy equality in the Senate. But Texas, and the territory acquired by the war with Mexico which followed hard upon the heels of annexation, brought the North face to face for the first time with the prospect of an actual extension of slavery. Politicians were forced to take sides. On so clear a moral issue, few hesitated long.

In the Senate once more, Calhoun's efforts were devoted to fending off growing attacks on Southern slavery, to battling for the symbolic right to carry slaves into the new territories, and to unifying the cotton states. The North had greater numerical strength as well as the better cause. There seemed no alternative, short of surrender, save to defend slavery as a positive good and to fall back upon constitutional guarantees, backed by sectional solidarity. So the states' rights dogma, refined and amplified, became the political creed of the Cotton Kingdom. Calhoun wielded the South as a powerful pressure bloc to obstruct the will of the majority. In his brilliant works, *Disquisition on Government* and the unfinished *Discourse on the Constitution* to which it is a preface, he has given us a reasoned statement of the conservative reaction to the equalitarian philosophy of the mid-19th Century. While Europe flamed into revolution, and Northern intellectuals toyed with the Socialist doctrines popular abroad, Calhoun rejected the major premise of democracy itself. In defense of slavery he denied the equality of men, and upheld the class structure of society as both necessary and good.

In his political writings he has left us a legacy that cannot be overlooked, for there will always be minorities which the democratic state must treat with equal justice and respect. It was Calhoun's tragedy that he could not compromise with change. His warning against arbitrary power, whether exercised by one man or by a majority, is as valid today as it was a century ago. But his example is a warning, too—that the static society will perish; that security is not an end in itself; and that democracy cannot endure apart from its moral moorings.

The Great Emotion

DAVID DONALD

About 1830 decisive change came into the South. Not only did a Cotton Kingdom advancing inland from the coastal areas as a result of Eli Whitney's invention enhance the economic foundations of slavery, but a change in the psychological climate occurred. Northern agitation to abolish slavery aroused in the South an attitude of you-keep-your-house-and-we'll-attend-to-ours, and the more violent the agitation grew, the more deeply entrenched the attitude became, feeding on fears of Negro insurrection, turning to human logic and divine gospel to prove that white supremacy was next to godliness, and creating a sectional emotionalism that coated itself with traditions of aristocracy and chivalry, kinship and love of soil. An example of the firm legal armor that was placed around the "peculiar institution" occurred in North Carolina in the case of State v. Mann—"the power of the master must be absolute to render the submission of the slave perfect"—and that was that. In books like Lincoln's Herndon *and* Divided We Fought: A Pictorial History of the War, 1861–1865, *Professor David Donald of Columbia University has demonstrated a firm grasp upon the forces underlying the fateful years of war; he has demonstrated as well gifts of narration which he now brings to relating how the agitation of the slavery question turned the course of the American Story.*

T HE stores in Boston were closed. State Street and Court Street were draped in black, and a huge coffin was suspended across State Street. On the sidewalks an immense crowd gathered angrily before the court house and milled about. It was June 2, 1854, the day when Anthony Burns, a runaway Negro slave from Virginia, was ordered to leave the free soil of Massachusetts and return to the slavery from which he had fled.

The machinery of the law had operated swiftly. Only nine days before the police had seized Burns, who was described as "a piteous object, rather weak in mind and body, with a large scar on his cheek, which looked like a brand, a broken hand from which a large piece of bone projected, and another scar on his other hand." His Virginia master had promptly identified him as a runaway, and a hearing was scheduled before the federal commissioner in Boston. It was "anniversary week" in Boston, a time when the antislavery societies turned out in full number for their annual meeting, and abolitionist leaders were horrified by the news. Protest meetings were summoned, and, inspired by Wendell Phillips and Theodore Parker, outraged citizens tried to rescue Burns from his cell. Thoroughly frightened, the mayor called for federal troops. Then, as a further precaution, he enrolled as a marshal's guard a force which was then called "the lowest villains of the community . . . bullies, blacklegs, convicts, prize-fighters, etc." The federal commissioner heard Burns's case behind four or five cordons of police and soldiers and ordered him to be returned to slavery.

It was easier to pronounce a sentence than to enforce it. As the church bells tolled mournfully and the citizens pressed about the court house, it became clear that only force could send a man from Massachusetts soil back to servitude. But with unqualified promise of aid from Washington, the city officials called out more than one thousand soldiers and police to escort "with shotted guns [this] one trembling colored man to the vessel which was to carry him to slavery." Down the streets which James Otis and Samuel Adams and John Hancock had walked, marched this "vile procession." The troops marched between stony faces, between volleys of muttered curses, between shouts of "shame!" and "kidnapers!" It was a triumph of force, and when they placed Burns on the waiting ship the swaggering soldiers sang the pre-Bland minstrel song, "Carry Me Back to Old Virginny."

It had come to this, then. After decades of discussion, after years of Congressional debates, after promises and compromises and adjustments, each of which had promised to be final, the issue of slavery proved once more to be fearfully alive. The case of Anthony Burns involved more than the fate of one shivering fugitive, for, after all, free-soil friends promptly took up a subscription and purchased the Negro's freedom. It involved more than the $100,000 it had cost the United States to secure his re-enslavement.

The significance of the affair lay in its revelation that the North and the South were no longer speaking the same language. To the Southerners the mob violence in Boston seemed an object lesson in Northern duplicity. The free-soil element, they believed, was unwilling to keep the Northern share of the sectional bargain. On the other hand, to the free men of the North the Burns case demonstrated that slavery was not just an abstraction, a remote evil existing in distant Florida or Texas; this hideous monster was extending its slimy tentacles into the very heart of the North. Throughout the free states men repudiated the idea of further bargaining with the South's "peculiar institution." After the Burns case they said: "We have endured all we ought; all we can."

In both sections there were moderates, but their soft voices of reason and conciliation were outshouted by the strident appeals of firebrands and agitators. Suspicious and distrustful, extremists in both sections found their prejudices bolstered by events in Kansas. North and South claimed equal rights to the Kansas-Nebraska region, one of the last bits of territory still owned by the federal government not yet divided into territorial or state units. The Missouri Compromise of 1820 had attempted to settle the issue of slavery in this area; so had the Compromise of 1850 and the Kansas-Nebraska Act of 1854. But the laws made in Washington did not prevent bloodshed in Kansas, where proslavery Missouri border ruffians fought a guerrilla war with Northern free-state immigrants. The proslavery forces sacked the free-soil capital of Lawrence. Then an antislavery gang descended upon some unsuspecting Southerners at Pottawatomie and butchered five defenseless settlers. Their leader was John Brown of Osawatomie.

The Congress and the President both attempted in vain to settle this tangled problem of slavery in the national territories, but they succeeded only in irritating tempers and raising new difficulties. In 1857 the Supreme Court stepped into the furiously controverted issue. Their decision concerned an obscure St. Louis Negro named Dred Scott, who had once been taken by his master to live in a territory where slavery was outlawed by Act of Congress. Long after he returned to Missouri and to bondage, interested friends brought suit for the Negro's freedom. In March, 1857, the Supreme Court tried to settle the confused and tangled case. Each of the nine Justices gave his own opinion, two of them dissenting sharply from the majority view. But the eighty-year-old Chief Justice, Roger B. Taney of Maryland, spoke for the Court in declaring two principles: (1) that a Negro, like Scott, could not be a citizen of the United States; and (2) that Congress had no power to prohibit slavery in any of the national territories.

In the furor that erupted, Scott himself quickly dropped out of sight. Voluntarily emancipated by his master, he spent the rest of his life as a porter in a St. Louis hotel. But if Scott himself was forgotten, the issues of the Dred Scott decision were long remembered. Northern antislavery opinion exploded in a denunciation of the Southern-dominated Court. (The *New York Tribune* announced that the Court "has abdicated its just functions and descended into the political arena. It has sullied its ermine; it has draggled and polluted its garments in the filth of pro-slavery politics.")

Southerners, on the other hand, greeted the Dred Scott decision as the simple statement of constitutional justice. The *Washington Union*, newspaper voice of President Buchanan's pro-Southern administration, believed that the opinion of the Court would "exert a most salutary influence throughout the United States" in quelling further agitation of the slavery question. But there was little rejoicing below the Mason-Dixon line. Already sectional cleavages had progressed so far that many Southerners completely distrusted their Northern fellow citizens and felt, with the *Augusta* (Ga.) *Constitutionalist,* that no court opinion could "take away the occupation of demagogues, nor cure the madness of the anti-slavery fanatics of the North."

Almost every day fresh incidents served to inflame sectional antagonisms. Bumbling President Buchanan did little to allay unrest, but instead promoted partisan squabbling. The struggle in Kansas flickered on fitfully. In the North, a convention of abolitionists at Worcester, Massachusetts, called the Union a failure and urged that the antagonistic people of North and South be divided into separate nations. In the slave states extremist leaders were secretly planning steps that would lead toward Southern independence. It would take only a few gusts to fan these embers into a raging flame of civil war.

In October, 1859, the gale struck. With an army of twenty-one men, John Brown seized the federal arsenal town of Harper's Ferry, Virginia, and renewed his private warfare upon slavery in the South. With hands still red from the Kansas forays, Brown had appeared in New England and had announced that murder of slaveholders had been "decreed by Almighty God, ordained from Eternity." This "grim, farmer-like looking man" persuaded Boston philanthropists to finance his new blow against slavery.

At eight o'clock on Sunday night, October 16, Brown ordered the advance on Harper's Ferry, and marching along as solemnly as a funeral procession his men stole across the Potomac bridge into the sleeping, unsuspecting Virginia village. Within a few minutes bridges, armory, and arsenal were captured and then Brown sent his aides into the countryside to capture hostages. Completely in control at Harper's Ferry, Brown now waited indecisively, hoping that the slaves of the Shenandoah Valley would desert their masters and flock to his side. The President ordered ninety U.S. Marines to the troubled area, under command of a Virginia brevet-colonel named Robert E. Lee. Lee found that the local militia had cornered the fierce old fanatic and his men in the fire engine house of the armory, and in the dim light of early morning beat down the door and captured the survivors. John Brown's raid was over.

John Brown was of no great personal consequence, any more than had been those two other obscure individuals, Anthony Burns and Dred Scott, and his Harper's Ferry adventure was of a piece with his entire career. Convicted of treason against the Commonwealth of Virginia, Brown was hanged on December 2, 1859.

But it was easier to put John Brown on a scaffold than to get him down again. That lean Puritan figure upon the gallows became a symbol of terror throughout the South. In his deepest heart the Southerner most dreaded an insurrection of his Negro slaves, and the fact that Virginia Negroes did not rally to Brown brought little reassurance. John Brown's raid was unsuccessful, but while fanaticism and abolitionism prevailed in the North would there not be another attempt? Southerners who had hitherto deplored talk of an "irrepressible conflict" now openly spoke of secession. A plain citizen of North Carolina summarized the Southern view: "I have always been a fervid Union man but . . . the Harper's Ferry outrage . . . has shaken my fidelity and . . . I am willing to take the chances of every probable evil that may arise from disunion, sooner than submit any longer to Northern insolence and Northern outrage."

In the North, too, the grim soul of John Brown could not be stilled, though his body lay a-moldering in the grave. While moderates like Abraham Lincoln deplored the wild recklessness of the raid, many antislavery men accepted Brown's own historically absurd claim of innocence, or condemned the Governor of Virginia for executing an insane man. From pulpits all over the North antislavery preachers proclaimed the glories of this saint "whose . . . martyrdom . . . will make the gallows as glorious as the cross." In North and in South the voice of moderation could not be heard through the din of fanaticism and agitation which magnified issues beyond their importance, misconstrued their significance, and militated against real solutions. Within eighteen months after the John Brown raid the Civil War had begun.

Abraham Lincoln

BENJAMIN P. THOMAS

So was the classic pattern of the war set, and the North that idolized Webster was arrayed against the South that reshaped Calhoun's political philosophy to fit the great emotion. Out on the prairies two men, running in a Congressional election, debated the issue of whether a house divided against itself could endure. With the Lincoln-Douglas debates, what slavery meant to the political and moral fiber of the country was clearly defined. Thereafter the "irrepressible conflict" developed under a kind of brute dynamics, and perhaps even with a kind of fundamental national logic that only could be perceived in retrospect.

Who was this Lincoln, suddenly thrust into the fore of the nation's thoughts? What was the background, the creed of this man who, as Philip Van Doren Stern has said, would become so much a folk hero in the land that a child, clutching a penny on the way to the store to buy candy, would be familiar with his image? Among our foremost biographers of Lincoln is Benjamin P. Thomas, author of Abraham Lincoln, A Biography *and* Portrait for Posterity, *a modern historical sage in the Old Springfield whence Lincoln came to fulfill a destiny without parallel in the American Story.*

THE United States was entering its darkest hour when Abraham Lincoln took the oath of office as President on March 4, 1861. Already seven states had renounced the Union and formed a new nation of their own. Eight more states were wavering and four of them would soon go out. Within six weeks the North and the South would be locked in bloody war.

No President ever entered office under more trying circumstances or faced more critical problems. None was so hated, so blamed, so reviled—and in the end so loved. For, despite the self-seeking politicians, the impatient abolitionists, the headstrong and unfit generals, and the venomous defeatists with whom Lincoln constantly had to deal, he remained patient, tolerant, and forbearing, and, above all, steadfast in his determination to preserve the American Union.

To the Founding Fathers—Washington, Jefferson, Madison, John Adams—the American Revolution had meant the beginning of higher and better things for all men everywhere. A similar vision of America had come to Lincoln very early in his life. About to assume office as President of the United States, Lincoln said to the New Jersey legislature: "I am exceedingly anxious that the thing which they [the Revolutionary patriots] struggled for; that something even more than National Independence; that something that held out a great promise to all people of the world to all time to come; I am exceedingly anxious that this Union, the Constitution and the liberties of the people shall be perpetuated in accordance with the original idea for which that struggle was made, and I shall be most happy indeed if I shall be an humble instrument in the hands of the Almighty, and of this His almost chosen people, for perpetuating the object of that great struggle."

Throughout the war Lincoln never lost sight of what he felt was the real issue—whether the nation, born so auspiciously in 1776, and dedicated to the proposition that all men are created equal and are alike entitled to life, liberty, and the pursuit of happiness, would live on to vindicate democracy in the sight of all mankind.

Lincoln's faith in democracy was buttressed by the facts of his own life. He was living proof of what a man, untrammeled, can make of himself if he will. Born in Kentucky of poor and illiterate parents, reared in backwoods Indiana, and migrating to the Illinois prairies when he came of age, Lincoln had been molded but not mastered by the lusty, primeval forces of the American frontier. Hard fare and hard toil had been his lot, until at last he broke away from family hindrances and struck out on his own. Striving against poverty and lack of schooling, he rose from laborer and flatboatman to surveyor and village postmaster. He served as a soldier in the Black Hawk War. He failed as a storekeeper. Through hard study he equipped himself to be a lawyer. He was elected to the Illinois legislature.

He learned from each new experience; he learned from his contacts with people. He became familiar with a few great works of literature such as the writings of Shakespeare and the Bible. From them and from patient self-teaching, he gained skill in using words. His mind moved slowly and cautiously, as the man himself seemed to move. That mind was logical and tenacious; it sought and demanded proof.

Intellect and temperament often seemed at odds in Lincoln; for along with his coldly logical mind he had a warm and tender heart. Honesty became his best-known attribute in politics, in his law practice, and in his personal dealings. He would break out of a chronic, haunting melancholy with droll quips and comic stories; it has been said of him that "perhaps no human clay-pot has held more laughter and more tears."

Lincoln's law partner described his ambition as "a little engine that knew no rest." At last, through unwavering service to his party, he gained a seat in Congress. But there he made a serious, if conscientious, misstep by opposing the Mexican War. Renounced by the people whom he represented, he despaired of a future in politics, and reconciled himself to the life of a country lawyer. He continued his self-teaching, determined to make himself a better lawyer and an enlightened man. For five years Lincoln applied himself assiduously to the law. Then came a moral awakening and the turning point in his life, when the repeal of the Missouri Compromise in 1854 again brought slavery to the fore as a flaming national issue.

For as long as Lincoln could remember he had reasoned "if slavery is not wrong, nothing is wrong." Yet, throughout his political career, he had been cautious about slavery, knowing full well the danger it held to national unity. In this issue, as in so many others, he had looked to the Founding Fathers, and if he correctly understood their attitude toward slavery, they had sought to keep it from spreading so that it would one day die for lack of growth. So their policy became Lincoln's policy too, even though toleration of human bondage violated his concept of America as the land of freedom and equality.

But the repeal of the Missouri Compromise opened new areas to slavery and might grant it indefinite life. To Lincoln, such a change in policy meant rejection of the goal of ridding America of a hypocrisy and making it a genuine democracy at the earliest practicable time. He was roused, he said, as he had never been roused before. Within four months he was back in politics, moved by a moral earnestness that gave his words new power, and thrust him forward as a leader. And six years later he was President.

Only in America could this have happened—and how well Lincoln knew it! "To the humblest and poorest among us are held out the highest privileges and positions," he told the men of an Ohio regiment. "The present moment finds me at the White House, yet there is as good a chance for your children as there was for my father's child." It would have been well for the country, in 1860, had people known better the thought pattern of this man, and the background of experience which fashioned it. He would not lightly allow a Union which he held so highly to be lost; he would not surrender easily the ideals that Union stood for.

With war upon the nation, Lincoln fumbled at first. He was haphazard as an administrator. He was plagued by bungling generals. And when they failed, he sometimes interfered mistakenly in military matters. Before long, however, Lincoln showed that notwithstanding his idealistic thinking, sound common sense controlled his actions. In formulating policy he demonstrated an uncanny skill in harmonizing the diverse factions in his party. He demonstrated his primacy over rivals in his Cabinet. He maneuvered adeptly against headstrong men in Congress. He handled the touchy slavery problem with the tact that it demanded; one misstep there and the loyal border slave states might have elected to leave the Union.

Lincoln knew that victory over the brave, determined people of the South, who were fighting for their families and their firesides and for the right as they saw it, could come only by vanquishing their armies, wasting their economic resources, and wearing down their will to win. It was not a task to his liking, nor did the Northern people like it. Lincoln's most challenging duty was to bring home to them the broader meanings of the conflict, to convince them that theirs was a cause worth dying for, and to persuade them that their sacrifices would lift themselves, their enemies, and all mankind toward a brighter, better future.

Lincoln's long schooling in politics had given him an almost perfect sense of timing. Knowing that the function of a leader in a democracy is not to impose his will but to encourage the people to choose wisely for themselves, he moved forward or waited as the nation's mood quickened or flagged. The exercise of power endowed him with new strength. Always he had shown a rare capacity to summon inner resources for whatever demands he had faced. Now, under the stress of war, his mind and spirit burgeoned. Tenderness and pity were entwined in his heart; his own soul writhed in torment as he hurled the thunderbolts of war. His face, etched deeply by the prairie years, took on new depths, new shades, new high lights, as the war years wrought upon it. His faith in the basic goodness of the people survived the harshest trials, and as the people saw him, steady and courageous, even when the cause seemed lost, they came to trust their simple, homespun President, and to call him "Father Abraham." They accepted his decisions because he epitomized their hopes. And so, with the people behind him, he brought the nation through.

As victory became certain, Lincoln turned his thoughts to binding up the nation's wounds. Renouncing vengeance toward an enemy whom he could never hate, he besought the people's mercy for their vanquished countrymen. To help lift the Southern people from the ruin of defeat, he was willing to offer payment for the slaves whom he had freed. At that moment an assassin struck him down. And the gentlest, and perhaps the most peace-loving of our Presidents, whose ironic lot it had become to launch the nation on a brothers' war, himself became part of the sacrifice.

Perhaps he himself has best summed up the meaning of it all. For as the signs began to look better and peace seemed less distant than before, he had written from a brimming heart: "Thanks to all. For the great Republic,—for the principles it lives by and keeps alive,—for man's vast future,—thanks to all."

The Emancipation Proclamation

P A U L   M .   A N G L E

When the first battles of the war went against the Union, Lincoln despaired. A memorandum reveals the torment which tore at the President's heart:

"The will of God prevails. In great contests each party claims to act in accordance with the will of God. Both may be, *and one* must *be wrong. God cannot be for, and against the same thing at the same time. In the present civil war it is quite possible that God's purpose is something different from the purpose of either party— and yet the human instrumentalities, working just as they do, are of the best adaptation to effect His purpose. I am almost ready to say this is probably true—that God wills this contest, and wills that it shall not end yet. By His mere quiet power, on the minds of the now contestants, He could have either saved or destroyed the Union without a human contest. Yet the contest began. And having begun He could give the final victory to either side any day. Yet the contest proceeds."*

At the moment Lincoln's mind debated one of the greatest decisions of his career, an act by which what had gone before in the war would bear a different relationship to the unforeseeable future. How Lincoln reached this decision, completely within his own essential character, is told by Paul M. Angle, director of the Chicago Historical Society, a leading Lincoln authority, and author of such memorable books as Bloody Williamson *and* By These Words.

THE Civil War was well along in its second year, and Northern victory seemed as unreal as a desert mirage. Only a few weeks earlier the Union general, George B. McClellan, had threatened to smash the Confederate armies defending Richmond and choke the city to death. But Robert E. Lee took command, counterattacked, and now McClellan was frantically demanding reinforcements and predicting disaster if they were not sent to him. Some months before, in the West, Grant had scored brilliant successes at Fort Henry and Fort Donelson, and in the bloody Battle of Shiloh had sent a Southern army into retreat. But since then, a stalemate had prevailed in that theater.

In fact, the war was going badly for the Union. On this point the lonely man in the White House had no illusions. The South appeared to be impregnable. As Lincoln thought about the elements of Confederate strength he could not ignore the slaves. To be sure, they were not in uniform, but thousands served in the Southern armies as teamsters and laborers, thus freeing white men for fighting. Behind the lines many more thousands worked in the fields and kept the enemy in food. If the slaves were freed, would they continue to work for their masters?

No one knew better than Abraham Lincoln that the North had not gone to war to free slaves. The masses had sprung to arms to restore the Union. Nor was the President himself an abolitionist. From earliest youth he had believed slavery to be wrong, but he had considered it to be a matter which, under the Constitution, each state had a right to decide for itself, and he would be satisfied if human bondage were put, as he phrased it, in the course of "ultimate extinction."

Still, by means of a proclamation of freedom issued as a war measure, a crippling blow might be struck at the South. In odd moments he drafted such a document. On the 22nd of July, 1862, he called the Cabinet together and read to them what he had written. Several members made suggestions. Then William H. Seward, Secretary of State, asked if he might speak. He favored the proclamation, he said, but he questioned whether it should be issued on the heels of military defeat. He feared the people would look on it as the desperate measure of a government driven to the wall, or, in his vivid phrase, "the last shriek on the retreat."

"I suggest, sir," Seward continued, "that you postpone its issue until you can give it to the country supported by military success, instead of issuing it, as would be the case now, upon the greatest disaster of the war."

Lincoln recognized the force of Seward's argument, and put the proclamation aside.

Although the President had made up his mind, he would allow

no inkling of his purpose to reach the public. One month to the day after the Cabinet meeting he wrote a letter to Horace Greeley, editor of the powerful *New York Tribune,* in which he argued the question of emancipation as if it were still an open one.

"My paramount object in this struggle," Lincoln said, "is to save the Union, and is *not* either to save or to destroy slavery. If I could save the Union without freeing *any* slave, I would do it; and if I could save it by freeing *all* the slaves, I would do it; and if I could save it by freeing some and leaving others alone, I would also do that." To which he added in conclusion: "I intend no modification of my oft-expressed *personal* wish that all men everywhere could be free."

In discussing emancipation with a committee of Chicago churchmen three weeks later, the President debated the question again. "What good would a proclamation accomplish?" he asked his visitors. To be sure, it would weaken the South by drawing off its laborers, but might it not also weaken the North by spreading disaffection in the border slave states which had remained loyal? "I have not decided against a proclamation of liberty to the slaves," he concluded, "but hold the matter under advisement; and I can assure you that the subject is on my mind, by day and night, more than any other. Whatever shall appear to be God's will, I will do."

Within four days Lincoln received the sign that he had been seeking. On September 17, 1862 the Army of the Potomac and the Army of Northern Virginia came to grips in the Battle of Antietam fought in northwestern Maryland. After a day as bloody as the war would offer, Lee withdrew his army. The North called it victory.

On September 22, Lincoln summoned the Cabinet to the White House. After the members had assembled he reached for a book— *Artemus Ward: His Book*—which Artemus Ward, a popular humorist, had sent to him, and read a chapter, "The High-handed Outrage at Utica," as if the amusement of these grave men were his sole end in life. Then he became serious. He reminded his heads of departments that he had broached the subject of emancipation to them in July, but had then deferred to the objection that the time was not propitious. Now the military situation had changed. He admitted that Antietam was not a clear-cut victory, but the Confederates had headed southward, and Pennsylvania was no longer in danger of invasion.

"When the rebel army was at Frederick," he continued, "I determined, as soon as it should be driven out of Maryland, to issue a proclamation of emancipation such as I thought most likely to be useful. I said nothing to anyone; but I made the promise to myself, and"—here the President hesitated—"to my Maker. The rebel army is now driven out, and I am going to fulfill that promise."

On that same day Abraham Lincoln, as President of the United States and Commander-in-Chief of the Army and Navy, issued the proclamation on which he had decided two months earlier. The war, he promised, would continue to be a war for the restoration of the Union, and he gave notice that he would urge Congress to reimburse the people of such loyal slave states as would voluntarily free their slaves. But he warned that on January 1, 1863, the slaves in any states which had not come back into the Union would be declared "then, thenceforward, and forever free," and that the military power of the United States would be used to enforce the declaration.

The Confederate states ignored the warning.

The first of January came, and with it came thousands of visitors to the traditional New Year's reception at the White House. For hours Lincoln stood in the receiving line. Late in the afternoon he quietly left for his own office. On the desk at which he seated himself lay the proclamation, awaiting his signature. For a minute or two he worked the fingers of his right hand which had been stiffened from prolonged hand shaking. Then, without ceremony, he took the pen and in a firm, steady hand wrote his full name.

The Proclamation of Emancipation simply carried out the warning of the preliminary proclamation of September 22, 1862, by declaring that hereafter the slaves in the rebellious states would be free. It was an official document and its language was necessarily formal and legalistic. But at the very end came the touch of the true Lincoln in these words: "Upon this act, sincerely believed to be an act of justice, warranted by the Constitution upon military necessity, I invoke the considerate judgement of mankind, and the gracious favor of Almighty God."

Contrary to what many people believe, the Proclamation of Emancipation did not bring about the immediate end of slavery in this country. Human bondage continued in Tennessee and in the loyal border states—all of which were exempted from the Proclamation's provisions—while in the states of the Confederacy where it did apply it could not be enforced until the armies of the South should be vanquished. Even then, since it had been issued solely as a war measure, it was of doubtful permanent validity. Nevertheless, it had tremendous moral influence. By ranging the

North on the side of freedom, it made it very difficult for any European nation to give open support to the Confederacy; it heartened the American opponents of slavery; and it made inevitable the Thirteenth Amendment to the Constitution, which banned slavery forever from the United States or any of its possessions.

Sherman and the Hard Hand of War

EARL SCHENCK MIERS

After the bloodless capture of Fort Sumter, some Southerners felt that the war would be a lark. Northerners were rudely jolted by the disaster at Bull Run. For both sides the war turned into a fearful ordeal. "Wait till you see the elephant," veterans warned new recruits eager for action, and after the first battle—after the elephant had been seen—only the grimness, the nastiness remained. The shock of Shiloh haunted dreams for weeks afterward: that was but one instance. In time, we would understand that the world never had known a war quite like this, and one of the men who would bring this lesson home to the American people, both North and South, was William Tecumseh Sherman. Earl Schenck Miers has written a number of books about the war, among them The General Who Marched to Hell *and* Web of Victory; *more recently, with Paul M. Angle, he edited* The Living Lincoln.

THE red-headed colonel was in a fight up to his neck. A dozen years later the Battle of First Bull Run still lived vividly in his memory. With the discomfort of a soldier whose old wounds are itching with a change in climate, William Tecumseh Sherman remembered ". . . the affair at Blackburn's Ford, when for the first time in my life I saw cannonballs strike men and crash through the trees and saplings above and around us, and realized the always sickening confusion as one approaches a fight from the rear; then the night-march from Centerville, on the Warrenton road, standing for hours wondering what was meant; the deployment along the edge of the field that sloped down to Bull Run, and waiting for Hunter's approach on the other side from the direction

The passion of the Southern cause—with all its overtones of sentiment and fervor, with its touches of optimistic humor and defiance—are movingly exemplified in these almost-forgotten popular Confederate songs. One verse ends: "Sons of the South awake! Strike till the brand shall break, Strike for dear Honor's sake. Freedom and Life!"

In both the North and the South, great masses of
people believed that the Civil War would last no
longer than ninety days. Northern optimism and
idealism is seen in this 1861 lithograph . . . and
again, below, in the Currier and Ives print of a
soldier who would soon rejoin the "beloved ones
who gathering come, to bid their hero, husband,
father welcome home."

As the war closed, the feeling that swords would become plowshares and that all wounds would be healed was a fervent one for many, and is apparent in this lithograph commemorating the $2,000,000 gift of philanthropist George Peabody "to promote education in the southern states," thereby easing Reconstruction. But (*below*) Andrew Johnson never had a chance to help heal the wounds. Radical Republicans in Congress went on an orgy of restrictive and revengeful legislation—and impeachment proceedings, "Black Codes," scalawags, and carpetbagger rule ensued.

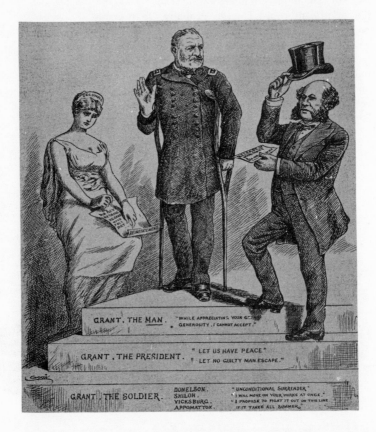

GRANT, THE MAN.   "WHILE APPRECIATING YOUR GREAT
                   GENEROSITY, I CANNOT ACCEPT."

GRANT, THE PRESIDENT.   " LET US HAVE PEACE"
                        " LET NO GUILTY MAN ESCAPE."

GRANT, THE SOLDIER.   DONELSON.   "UNCONDITIONAL SURRENDER"
                      SHILOH.   "I WILL MOVE ON YOUR WORKS AT ONCE."
                      VICKSBURG.   "I PROPOSE TO FIGHT IT OUT ON THIS LINE
                      APPOMATTOX.   IF IT TAKES ALL SUMMER."

Throughout his career Grant was plagued
by associates with a propensity for bribe-
taking and embezzling. While he was President, his Secretary of Treasury resigned
under fire; his personal secretary was involved in the Whisky Ring; his Secretary of
War quit office to avoid impeachment for
bribe-taking. In later years his partners in a
banking house perpetrated fraud, and he
was bankrupted. But Grant himself remained a beloved figure, as this cartoon
tribute indicates.

of Sudley Springs, away off to our right; the terrible scare of a poor Negro who was caught between our lines; the crossing of Bull Run, and the fear lest we should be fired on by our own men; the killing of Lieutenant-Colonel Haggerty, which occurred in plain sight; and the first scenes of a field strewed with dead men and horses."

Characteristically, the dry humor of Sherman added: "Yet, at that period of the battle, we were the victors and felt jubilant." Two hours later the tide had turned heavily against the Union forces. Sherman, commanding in his first battle, confessed that he had no idea the North was beaten. He didn't need to ask what to do, however. When a retreat started moving, even a red-headed colonel rolled along with it—at First Bull Run, at any rate, where the soldier boys, both North and South, were more boys than soldiers in the shrewdest estimate of the war god Mars.

In time, Sherman would learn to fight like a tiger; they almost all did. In time, Sherman would become "Uncle Billy," the idol of the swaggering, cocky, unkempt Western army that bragged it couldn't be licked and seldom had to back down on that boast. In time, to pick one of the less feral titles, Sherman also would become "the Brute," the one Northern general whom the South hated and feared to the bottom of its passionate heart.

The various nicknames applied to Sherman during the course of his military career tell the story of his evolution from scared rabbit to terrible avenger. In the beginning, he was plain "Cump" Sherman, the name he took with him in 1832 when, he said, looking like "an untamed animal just caught in the Far West" (as Ohio was sometimes considered in those days), he entered West Point. After First Bull Run, sent to command in Kentucky, troops mistook his nervous temperament for irritability and called him "Old Pills"; but experience soon demonstrated that he was a soft touch under the gruffness and they re-named him "Old Sugar-Coated." Sherman always had distrusted his ability to command; in Kentucky, one reflection of his exaggerated defensiveness was a suspicion of newspapermen amounting to a neurosis; and another was the steady deterioration of his mental health under the strain of preparing to fight overwhelming forces that existed only in his imagination. An antagonistic press wasted no sympathy in characterizing him. As "Crazy" Sherman his part in the war might have ended, except that first Halleck and then Grant recognized his latent abilities and coaxed him back to a confidence that set him at last on the high road to fame and infamy.

Truly it was a meager military experience that Sherman carried into the Civil War. At West Point he had excelled in engineering, geology, rhetoric, mental philosophy—and demerits. Afterward, in Florida, he had learned to waltz but he never opposed a hostile Indian. A hitch at Fort Moultrie, within easy reach of Charleston, found him an eager captive of Southern hospitality. When the Mexican War came along Sherman was shipped to California; doubtless there were Mexicans there, but he never found them in the mountainous mists surrounding him; and so while Grant and Lee, Joe Johnston and a host of other military contemporaries were learning war in actual combat, Sherman was fighting nothing but boredom.

In one way this fact was a handicap, but in another it wasn't. As the Civil War built momentum it began to assume an individuality. Then the war began to make its own rules, to forget that the rival knights were brothers in a tradition of ancient gallantry (a tradition that more or less had its last fling at Gettysburg), and to get on with the dirty business of breaking a people's will to resist. It was at the old-style war that Sherman was no great shakes, but in the new style he emerged as a general to be reckoned with, and whether that result was derived from luck or design or temperament or circumstances doesn't detract from what he came to represent. Sherman is realist or devil, depending on whether your sympathies are blue or gray; in either case, he is scarcely dull.

We have tended, these long years afterward, to sentimentalize the Civil War and thus to obscure the reality of how horribly men died; moreover, had the war continued another year, men would have died even more horribly. In the early Sixties we were on the mere brink of the machine age, yet we glimpsed the volcano of death that this age contained, and its frightful new tools of destruction were within our grasp. When, on Little Round Top, the Rebels encountered a hundred or so of Berdan's Sharpshooters and described them as "two Federal regiments," it was small wonder; those Yankee rascals were using the only machine guns at Gettysburg and firing an average of ninety-five rounds each in one twenty-minute action. The breech-loading rifle, the rifled cannon, balloons for aerial reconnaissance, iron-plated warships, deadlier types of the pug-nosed howitzer are innovations of the war familiar to its current legions of armchair strategists; but not so well known is what the testing grounds were teaching us about armored vehicles, incendiary rockets, flame-throwers, submarines, explosives. Modern combat was emerging, for all the obstacles an unimaginative ordnance staff could put in its way. With good reason a disturbed Henry Adams wrote his brother: "Some day science may have the existence of mankind in its power, and the human race commit suicide by blowing up the world."

If Sherman possessed, as it was said, a "nervous-sanguine temperament," so did the war in this state of flux. What, after all, had been learned by those who had fought in Mexico? Certainly a country without railroads had taught precious little about logistics. The flank attack, based on diligent reconnaissance and all possible surprise, was about the nub of the strategy that had been taught there. Develop lines of communication, direct intelligent reconnaissance, ascertain the precise position of the enemy, bring sufficient units into the right position at the right time—there, in essence, was the art of command as Grant and Lee and the others had observed it in Mexico and Sherman had not. It was all standard, all sound—as far as it went.

For the American Civil War, however, it did not go far enough. The old West Point notion that trenches made the troops cowardly remained to be exploded, and both Sherman and Grant realized that fact after bloody Shiloh came within a whisker of costing them their necks. At Vicksburg, Sherman learned another lesson— again quite against his will. Grant's ultimate decision to abandon his base of supplies scandalized Uncle Billy into voluble complaint. It was all right to read in Jomini how Napoleon had fought and subsisted on the country, but Napoleon had used an organized system of requisitions. Grant smiled and went his own way—to victory. Thus the vistas of a new kind of war unfolded, sometimes in the theater where Sherman fought, sometimes elsewhere. Another example was the use of cavalry as mobile infantry, and poor old Rosecrans kept nagging army ordnance for the machine guns that would give such a unit a real bite; actually, in this air-borne age, imagination does not have to be stretched too far to substitute planes for horses and to call these mobile warriors paratroopers.

Sherman reached Atlanta, the crazy man who had become a genius in nurturing the fighting morale of his raucous, high-spirited Western boys. When he told his officers that he intended to march to the sea, Major James Austin Connolly of the 123rd Illinois spoke for his comrades: ". . . There is to me something romantic in the conception of this campaign, and I am really charmed with it. Nothing in military history compares with it except the invasion of Mexico by Cortez, the Spaniard, who, landing on its hostile shore, burned his ships, destroyed all means of retreat, and turning to his army told them they must rely on God and their own right arms; that they must conquer or die."

There had been more plunder, a greater lust for personal glory in the heart of Cortez, however, than existed in the heart of Sherman. Part of the unremitting hatred leveled against Sherman has stemmed from the belief that, finding no better adversary, he waged war on defenseless women and children. "For these deeds," cried old Wade Hampton, meaning every scorching word, "history will brand him as a robber and incendiary and will deservedly 'damn him to everlasting fame' "—but history hasn't been so harsh on Sherman as that fine old Southern gentleman expected. On the march to the sea Sherman fought the material and human resources supporting the Confederacy at war, and in telegraphing Lincoln that Savannah was his for a Christmas present it was no idle after-thought that led Sherman to include the 25,000 bales of captured cotton (which turned out to be 38,500 bales). Today we accept calmly the concept of war that carried Sherman through Georgia; in Europe stand the ghosts of cities bombed repeatedly and mer-cilessly during World War II as legitimate means to the same necessary end; and at Hiroshima and at Nagasaki atom bombs were dropped because, as Sherman said on entering South Caro-lina, ". . . we are not only fighting hostile armies, but a hostile people, and must make old and young, rich and poor, feel the hard hand of war."

Sherman bears the distinction of being the one Northern general whom the South twice learned to hate. In early post-bellum years Uncle Billy was a sharp critic of carpetbaggers, Radical Republi-cans in Washington, and the 15th Amendment; the wounds of war, he believed, could only be healed by "natural influences," which was exactly what the South believed; and when he characterized President Johnson as "Lear roaring at the wild storm, bareheaded and helpless" he paralleled Southern sentiment. On the point of almost forgiving Uncle Billy, Southerners began reading *Memoirs of General W. T. Sherman Written by Himself*. Pride in Southern generalship was the little that the South retained from its long years of bleeding sacrifice; and Southern tempers bristled as Sherman presented many of its military heroes as neither over-bright nor especially effective on or off the battlefield. That Northern generalship fared no better by Sherman's appraisal seemed quite beside the point.

So, in the end, Sherman's pen proved at least as mighty as his sword in bringing down everlasting enmity and scorn upon the red head which, as a boy, he had tried to dye only to have his hair turn a sickly shade of green. For fifty years thereafter fires that destroyed houses in Georgia and South Carolina were somehow his responsibility. Yet no one could deny that Sherman had fulfilled his mission in history. The hard hand of modern war is, indeed, very hard.

Southern Yeomen in the Civil War

BELL IRVIN WILEY

With the exception of a few months in 1861 the North was generally prosperous throughout its conflict with the South, and the very nature of its government made it better suited for fighting a total war. In contrast the Confederacy had to contend with limited gold reserves, with a blockade that disrupted its export of cotton, with depleted inventories of many important civilian commodities, and with a principle of states' rights that often worked against an efficient prosecution of the war. Yet despite these handicaps the Southern military forces fought doggedly and even brilliantly. In part the credit belonged to Southern generalship, but in larger measure an explanation of stubborn Rebel resistance had to be found in the almost unique individualism of the Southern soldier. In two books that now are classics in their field—The Life of Johnny Reb and The Life of Billy Yank—Professor Bell Irvin Wiley has demonstrated a rare ability for writing with wit and wisdom upon this subject.

Fʀᴏᴍ the historical standpoint one of the most important aspects of the Civil War is the insight that it affords into the character and attitudes of Southern yeomen. During the war this normally reticent class—small landowners and tenant farmers for the most part—became articulate in a large degree. The call to arms in 1861 took large numbers of yeomen away from their homes for the first time in the South's history, and caused them to write many letters, keep diaries, and become the subject of newspaper notices and official reports. Since they regarded their war experience as far and away the most momentous episode of their lives, lowly Rebs and their families tended to preserve the letters and diaries written in camp when other personal papers were lost or destroyed. Because censorship, to all practical effects, was non-existent in the 1860's, most Rebs wrote fully and without restraint of what they thought and did in camp and battle; and in so doing they revealed much of themselves. On the basis of their own documents, which are to be found by the thousands in public depositories and private possession, the historian is able to form a fairly accurate estimate of what Southern yeomen of a century ago were like, and of the forces that determined their conduct during the Civil War.

Studies of manuscript census schedules made by Professor Frank Owsley and others have provided valuable information about the number and status of Southern yeomen on the eve of the Civil War. In 1860 this class comprised five-sixths of the total Southern population. Four-fifths of them owned no slaves, and most of the remainder owned only one to five Negroes, and none more than ten. (Despite the reiteration of historians, the fact is still commonly overlooked that three-fourths of all white Southerners neither owned slaves nor belonged to slave-owning families.) Most of the yeomen in 1860 owned land, and many landless ones derived modest incomes from livestock pastured on the public domain or from crops grown on rented property. The shiftless, down-at-the-heel element, deserving the designation "po' white," comprised only a negligible part of the Southern population.

The overwhelming majority of Johnny Rebs came from this rural, non-slaveholding group, and they possessed both the virtues and the weaknesses of the class from which they sprang.

A substantial portion of them—perhaps as many as one to three —were illiterate. And the spelling and grammar of those who could read and write left much to be desired. Letters of common soldiers abound with such usages as "I seen," "nary," "hain't," "hit," "fiten," "wonst," "tords," "sity," "nuse," and "bin."

The following, though a composite rather than an actual communication, is a typical Johnny Reb letter:

> "Dear Wife:
>
> I seat myself and take pen in hand to drap you a few lines . . . (*Note: One Reb got confused and wrote, "I pen myself and take seat in hand*) . . . I am well at this time and hope that you are enjoyin a like blesson. I was in the orful fite at Chat a noo ga and was wonded wonst in the foot but otherwise I com out saft. I am now in the horsepittle and gitting along as well as could be expected, though I hant sadisfied. When I git out of here I am agoing to try to git a trance fur to the comma

sary for I have seen the elephant and had my fill of fiting. So no more for the present. John Jones to Elvira Jones Yore husban ontell deth do us part.

> *When this you see remember me,*
> *though many miles a part we bea*
> *My pen is bad my ink is pale*
> *my love for you shall never fale."*

As might be expected, Southern yeomen in gray were provincial in their outlook and prejudiced in many of their views. They looked askance at urban folk, referring to them as city slicks, parlor soldiers, and kid glove boys. Some Western Rebs looked down their noses at Virginians and Carolinians, and the disesteem was abundantly reciprocated by the Easterners. Soldiers from other states nicknamed Virginians the "Buttermilk Brigade"; South Carolinians, "Sand Lappers"; Alabamians, "Yellow Hammers"; and Georgians, "Goober Grabbers." Rebs who followed Joe Johnston sometimes referred to Lee's troops as "Jeff Davis pets," and attributed Eastern victories to feeble Yankee resistance on the Virginia front. Similarly, some of Lee's soldiers regarded men of the Army of Tennessee as inferior fighters. One of Marse Roberts's boys, after denouncing the surrender of Vicksburg as shameful, stated: "If I live to be one hundred years old, I shall always be proud to know that I once belonged to the Army of North Virginia."

One of Johnny Reb's most frequently manifested and pungently expressed prejudices was that with which he regarded his officers. A Louisiana sergeant wrote his wife that General Pemberton was "the most insignificant puke I ever saw." A Mississippian declared that "our General Rube Davis . . . is a vain, stuck up, illiterate ass." An Alabamian stated that "Col. Henry is [an ignoramous] fit for nothing higher than the cultivation of corn." A Floridian said of officers in general: "[They] are not fit to tote guts to a bear."

Much of this disparagement of officers was a mere blowing off of the steam created by the restraints of regimentation and the discomforts of soldiering. But the same cannot be said of the denunciatory comments made by Rebs about their foes. Owing largely to the unreasoning diatribes during ante-bellum years of Southern politicians, editors, and preachers, most Rebs and their folk at home regarded Northerners as Godless, grasping, hypocritical, meddlesome people, obsessed by a fanatical determination to destroy the South's chosen way of life. This extreme attitude was not held by all Rebs, and the frequency of fraternizing

of those who wore the gray and the blue indicates numerous lapses
of hostility along the fighting front. Even so, bias and hatred were
the general rule. In general, the women manifested deeper and
more enduring hatred of the Federals than did the men. But the
Reb who stated that Yankees were "thicker than lise on a hen and
a dam site ornrarier" was reflecting a sentiment fairly general
among the soldiers.

Another outstanding quality of the Southern yeomen as they
revealed themselves in the Civil War was humor. Indeed, I have
encountered no richer humor in the whole of American literature
than that displayed in the letters and diaries of Johnny Reb. Soldiers would write teasingly of how women whom they encountered
in far places showered them with attention. A young Tar Heel of
Lee's Army boasted to his homefolk of winning fifteen Virginia
sweethearts by "telling thim som sweete lies . . . stating that five
of my negroes had runaway and ten of Pappies But . . . [we] had
plenty more left and then they would lean to me like a sore eyed
kitten to a Basin of Milk."

A married Reb from Georgia, whose character was such as to
preclude the slightest suspicion of flirtation, wrote his wife on one
occasion: "If I did not write and receive letters from you I would
forgit that I was marrid. I don't feel much like a maryed man but
I never forgit sofar as to court enny other lady. But if I should
you must forgive me as I am so forgitful."

Their irrepressible humor caused Rebs to joke even about their
hunger and raggedness. One of them wrote of the cows that were
killed to provide the meat ration: "It takes two soldiers to hold
up one beef to shoot it." And a Mississippian wrote from near Atlanta in June, 1864: "In this army one hole in the seat of the
britches indicates a captain, two holes a lt., and if the seat of the
britches is all gone, the individual is a private."

Rebs, like the class from which they came, were an earthy people, in whose nature the genuine reverence of God was rivaled by
the attraction of the world, the flesh, and the Devil. Many of them
were deeply and consistently religious. Periodically, and especially
after 1863, great revivals spread through the camps like wildfire.
But usually the effects in terms of reformed conduct were short-
lived. As a general rule, evil was far more apparent than righteousness, and in most camps profanity, gambling, drinking, and ob-
scenity were notoriously frequent.

But these lowly men who marched to the strains of "Dixie" and
"The Bonnie Blue Flag" were possessed of many admirable quali-

ties. As a rule they were generous to the point of sharing their last bit of cornpone with less fortunate comrades. They were deeply devoted to their families. Their most frequently and earnestly expressed desire, regardless of their own attainment, was that their children might not grow up in ignorance and Godlessness. Many of them had an esthetic sensitiveness that caused them to write appreciatively and even eloquently of the beauties of mountains, streams, and flowers of the country through which they marched.

In the crucible of war, and especially in the ordeal of combat, many of them rose to heights of greatness. In battle, or on the march, at home or in the field, they were, despite their weaknesses, solid, dependable, lovable people. In general, they acquitted themselves more admirably in the crisis of the 1860's than did their more privileged neighbors.

The question often arises: why did a group which was predominantly non-slaveholding espouse so enthusiastically and support so stubbornly a cause that was tied inextricably to the perpetuation of human bondage? The answer, as revealed in the letters and diaries of Johnny Rebs, is simple. Most of the common soldiers were not deeply concerned about the basic issues of the war. They tended to accept at face value the arguments of their leaders that the North was attempting to subvert in its own interest the original character of the government as established by the Constitution. They did not consider themselves as fighting primarily for the perpetuation of slavery. But they believed that slavery was beneficial to both whites and Negroes, and that it was sanctioned by the Bible. Their chief interest in the institution was as a means of social control. To them, emancipation meant "race equality," and that was something too terrible for their contemplation. Moreover, they were convinced that slavery was a peculiarly Southern institution and that Yankees had no business sticking their noses in Southern affairs and saying what should or should not be done about them.

In the final analysis, ideological considerations had very little to do with the Southern yeomen's course. At the time they made their decision to don the uniform, the South was threatened with invasion and most of them needed no other incentive than the protection of their homes and hearths against the incursions of a sectional foe. Once they were in service an additional incentive, and the one that probably did most to keep them there in the face of ever increasing peril and hardship, was pride—in themselves, their units, their leaders, and their families.

Grant and Lee: A Study in Contrasts

BRUCE CATTON

"When in doubt, fight," said Ulysses S. Grant, reducing to a simple equation the secret of his military success. Yet Lee could fight also —tenaciously and brilliantly, but not without the resources of war: the men, the materials, the food. With a magnificent self-possession Lee sustained the Lost Cause beyond a point that seemed believable—sustained it because he sought nothing for himself, except that he remain true to his love for Virginia. As Mr. Catton's title indicates, Grant and Lee are a study in contrasts—the one an ancestor and the other a descendant, a distinction that ran far deeper in its meaning to the country than the flipness of an epigram ever could indicate. Editor of American Heritage, *Pulitzer Prize winner for* A Stillness at Appomattox, *the third of the volumes in his revealing study of the Army of the Potomac, Mr. Catton looks again at the two generals who met on a quiet Palm Sunday.*

W HEN Ulysses S. Grant and Robert E. Lee met in the parlor of a modest house at Appomattox Court House, Virginia, on April 9, 1865, to work out the terms for the surrender of Lee's Army of Northern Virginia, a great chapter in American life came to a close, and a great new chapter began.

These men were bringing the Civil War to its virtual finish. To be sure, other armies had yet to surrender, and for a few days the fugitive Confederate government would struggle desperately and vainly, trying to find some way to go on living now that its chief support was gone. But in effect it was all over when Grant and Lee signed the papers. And the little room where they wrote out the terms was the scene of one of the poignant, dramatic contrasts in American history.

They were two strong men, these oddly different generals, and they represented the strengths of two conflicting currents that, through them, had come into final collision.

Back of Robert E. Lee was the notion that the old aristocratic concept might somehow survive and be dominant in American life.

Lee was tidewater Virginia, and in his background were family,

202

culture, and tradition . . . the age of chivalry transplanted to a
New World which was making its own legends and its own myths.
He embodied a way of life that had come down through the age
of knighthood and the English country squire. America was a
land that was beginning all over again, dedicated to nothing much
more complicated than the rather hazy belief that all men had
equal rights, and should have an equal chance in the world. In
such a land Lee stood for the feeling that it was somehow of advantage to human society to have a pronounced inequality in the
social structure. There should be a leisure class, backed by ownership of land; in turn, society itself should be keyed to the land as
the chief source of wealth and influence. It would bring forth
(according to this ideal) a class of men with a strong sense of obligation to the community; men who lived not to gain advantage for
themselves, but to meet the solemn obligations which had been
laid on them by the very fact that they were privileged. From
them the country would get its leadership; to them it could look for
the higher values—of thought, of conduct, of personal deportment
—to give it strength and virtue.

Lee embodied the noblest elements of this aristocratic ideal.
Through him, the landed nobility justified itself. For four years, the
Southern states had fought a desperate war to uphold the ideals
for which Lee stood. In the end, it almost seemed as if the Confederacy fought for Lee; as if he himself was the Confederacy
. . . the best thing that the way of life for which the Confederacy
stood could ever have to offer. He had passed into legend before
Appomattox. Thousands of tired, underfed, poorly clothed Confederate soldiers, long-since past the simple enthusiasm of the early
days of the struggle, somehow considered Lee the symbol of everything for which they had been willing to die. But they could not
quite put this feeling into words. If the Lost Cause, sanctified by
so much heroism and so many deaths, had a living justification, its
justification was General Lee.

Grant, the son of a tanner on the Western frontier, was everything Lee was not. He had come up the hard way, and embodied
nothing in particular except the eternal toughness and sinewy fiber
of the men who grew up beyond the mountains. He was one of a
body of men who owed reverence and obeisance to no one, who
were self-reliant to a fault, who cared hardly anything for the past
but who had a sharp eye for the future.

These frontier men were the precise opposites of the tidewater
aristocrats. Back of them, in the great surge that had taken people

over the Alleghenies and into the opening Western country, there was a deep, implicit dissatisfaction with a past that had settled into grooves. They stood for democracy, not from any reasoned conclusion about the proper ordering of human society, but simply because they had grown up in the middle of democracy and knew how it worked. Their society might have privileges, but they would be privileges each man had won for himself. Forms and patterns meant nothing. No man was born to anything, except perhaps to a chance to show how far he could rise. Life was competition.

Yet along with this feeling had come a deep sense of belonging to a national community. The Westerner who developed a farm, opened a shop or set up in business as a trader, could hope to prosper only as his own community prospered—and his community ran from the Atlantic to the Pacific and from Canada down to Mexico. If the land was settled, with towns and highways and accessible markets, he could better himself. He saw his fate in terms of the nation's own destiny. As its horizons expanded, so did his. He had, in other words, an acute dollars-and-cents stake in the continued growth and development of his country.

And that, perhaps, is where the contrast between Grant and Lee becomes most striking. The Virginia aristocrat, inevitably, saw himself in relation to his own region. He lived in a static society which could endure almost anything except change. Instinctively, his first loyalty would go to the locality in which that society existed. He would fight to the limit of endurance to defend it, because in defending it he was defending everything that gave his own life its deepest meaning.

The Westerner, on the other hand, would fight with an equal tenacity for the broader concept of society. He fought so because everything he lived by was tied to growth, expansion, and a constantly widening horizon. What he lived by would survive or fall with the nation itself. He could not possibly stand by unmoved in the face of an attempt to destroy the Union. He would combat it with everything he had, because he could only see it as an effort to cut the ground out from under his feet.

So Grant and Lee were in complete contrast, representing two diametrically opposed elements in American life. Grant was the modern man emerging; beyond him, ready to come on the stage, was the great age of steel and machinery, of crowded cities and a restless, burgeoning vitality. Lee might have ridden down from the old age of chivalry, lance in hand, silken banner fluttering over his head. Each man was the perfect champion of his cause, drawing both his strengths and his weaknesses from the people he led.

Yet it was not all contrast, after all. Different as they were—in background, in personality, in underlying aspiration—these two great soldiers had much in common. Under everything else, they were marvelous fighters. Furthermore, their fighting qualities were really very much alike.

Each man had, to begin with, the great virtue of utter tenacity and fidelity. Grant fought his way down the Mississippi Valley in spite of acute personal discouragement and profound military handicaps. Lee hung on in the trenches at Petersburg after hope itself had died. In each man there was an indomitable quality . . . the born fighter's refusal to give up as long as he can still remain on his feet and lift his two fists.

Daring and resourcefulness they had, too; the ability to think faster and move faster than the enemy. These were the qualities which gave Lee the dazzling campaigns of Second Manassas and Chancellorsville and won Vicksburg for Grant.

Lastly, and perhaps greatest of all, there was the ability, at the end, to turn quickly from war to peace once the fighting was over. Out of the way these two men behaved at Appomattox came the possibility of a peace of reconciliation. It was a possibility not wholly realized, in the years to come, but which did, in the end, help the two sections to become one nation again . . . after a war whose bitterness might have seemed to make such a reunion wholly impossible. No part of either man's life became him more than the part he played in their brief meeting in the McLean house at Appomattox. Their behavior there put all succeeding generations of Americans in their debt. Two great Americans, Grant and Lee—very different, yet under everything very much alike. Their encounter at Appomattox was one of the great moments of American history.

Johnson and the Radicals

H O W A R D   K.   B E A L E

"With malice toward none; with charity for all; with firmness in the right, as God gives us to see the right, let us strive on to finish the work we are in; to bind up the nation's wounds; to care for him who

shall have borne the battle, and for his widow, and his orphan—to do all which may achieve and cherish a just, and a lasting peace, among ourselves, and with all nations."

With these words, on the fourth day of March in 1865, Abraham Lincoln, who once had wanted to write poetry, closed his Second Inaugural. A month and six days later, speaking to a cheering crowd on the lawn of the White House following Appomattox, Lincoln asked for one prize of war: "I have always thought 'Dixie' one of the best tunes I have ever heard. Our adversaries over the way attempted to appropriate it, but I insisted yesterday that we fairly captured it." At the President's request, the band played "Dixie." Four days later John Wilkes Booth shot Lincoln, and the nation, to which the South was returning, never had lost so grievously as in the death of the leader whose heart at the war's end was still unembittered.

So to Andrew Johnson in the American Story came a responsibility to discharge that might well have staggered the soul of any man. He was a son of the frontier, once a slaveholder, who had knocked around and come a long way from those days when he had sat cross-legged, plying the trade of a tailor. He had been a Congressman and governor of Tennessee; and he had been six weeks the Vice President when Lincoln was assassinated. Johnson's contemporaries judged him harshly and all but removed him from office; history deals much more gently with the tailor catapulted into the Presidency. Howard K. Beale, professor of history at the University of Wisconsin, and author of The Critical Year: A Study of Johnson and Reconstruction, *places Johnson in proper perspective and finds a man to respect.*

Wʜᴇɴ the Civil War ended, chaotic conditions prevailed in the South and in the nation. Both North and South were torn by internal dissension. Government within the Southern states had collapsed. Political ties between Southern states and federal government had been sundered. Slave institutions that had provided social controls in the South were abolished. And economic disaster threatened. Half the country was booming with a war-induced prosperity which the end of the war-demand now threatened with collapse. The other half lay prostrate in the wake of war, its social system and means of livelihood as badly damaged as its railroad equipment and its looted plantation houses. The only large-scale effort to overthrow our government by force had been put down by superior arms. The great problems of the late 1860's were what the government should do with those who had sought to destroy the nation, and how it could best restore loyalty, prosperity, and national well-being.

Lincoln had determined upon principles and put a program into operation even before the war ended. Andrew Johnson, who succeeded him as President, tried to carry out those plans. Lincoln believed that magnanimity and fair treatment of a defeated foe would best recreate a united and happy nation. He believed that to make the Union serve them well was the best way to lead back to loyalty men who had been disloyal. He was willing to forgive past disloyalty in return for future loyalty. He believed the Negro could not be protected and given a chance through coercing with military rule the Southern white with whom the Negro lived, but only by persuading those whites to treat him well.

In pursuit of what he knew Lincoln would have done, Johnson offered amnesty with restoration of full civil rights and property (except slaves) to all but fourteen excepted classes, on condition that everyone take an oath of future loyalty. Even to the excepted groups, whom he considered the responsible leaders of rebellion, he offered, with a handful of exceptions, individual pardons whenever they were asked for, provided investigation showed intent of future good citizenship.

In each state Johnson appointed a provisional government and provided for choosing first a convention to adopt a new constitution and then elected officials and legislature. He refused to permit important leaders of the attempt to overthrow the government to vote or hold office until they had sought and obtained pardon. Otherwise men voted and held office freely, regardless of past effort as soldiers or civilian officials to destroy the nation. Three actions he urged: (1) repeal of the ordinances of secession, now invalidated anyway by military defeat; (2) ratification of the Thirteenth Amendment freeing the slaves; and (3) repudiation of state and Confederate debts contracted for war against the government. He urged the Southern states to protect the civil rights of Negroes, but felt protection could not legally or effectively be imposed by the central government. Johnson could re-establish governments in Southern states but he could only advise Congress to admit loyal Senators and Representatives elected under the new constitutions.

In Congress were men of ideas and spirits far different from Lincoln's or Johnson's. Radical Republicans were radical in nothing but their determination to control the South or make it over on a Northern model, but in that they were extremists indeed. "Traitors" must be punished, they insisted. Any past association with the effort to set up a separate Confederacy left, in their minds, a permanent taint of treason. Besides, Southerners in Congress had voted against things which Northern industrialists and representatives of Northwestern areas aspiring to become industrialized wished the government to support. If Southerners were readmitted they would, as agrarians, again oppose these things that Republican leaders wanted, and Southern and Northwestern farmers by uniting could control Congress. Indeed, at the end of the war the industrial element was not even certain of controlling the Republican Party, the Western wing of which was still composed mainly of farmers. During the war, under plea of wartime necessity and with Southerners gone from Congress, businessmen of the Northeast had won many favors: high tariffs to offset war taxes, a national banking system, large grants from the public domain, freedom from government regulation of business. To many, "a return of rebels to power" actually meant a successful opposition to still higher tariffs; to government subsidies to railroads; to the national banking system; to deflation of the currency, which bankers and industrialists sought. It might mean cutting off grants of the rich public domain to private enterprise, effective regulation of railroads and other business, and taxes favorable to the majority of people and less satisfactory to the wealthy. It might even mean serious further inflation of money. But President Johnson, a majority of Northern and Western voters, and even a majority of the Republican Party agreed with Southerners on these issues. Hence the minority group that controlled the Republican party, and through it the United States government, had to avoid economic issues and find a means of winning support for keeping Southerners out of Congress, and keeping the South Republican when Southerners did return.

The result was mass propaganda rivaling 20th Century propaganda techniques. The vital economic issues of the day were evaded by name-calling, demagoguery, talk about protecting the Negro, about preserving the Union against subversives bent on overthrowing it. Some men like Charles Sumner were sincerely devoted to the Negro. Many Republican leaders, however, cared nothing for the Negro except as an emotional appeal convenient in evading issues and winning votes. As after any war, there was some sheer vindictiveness among leaders and voters alike. Radical Republicans played upon sympathy for the Negro and popular fears and hate. By a trick they lumped three other provisions into a constitutional amendment along with a clause guaranteeing the federal debt, and then persuaded voters that everyone opposed to the other more questionable provisions was trying to make government bonds bought for patriotic purposes worthless. They seized control of Congress in 1865 before it was organized, refused seats to loyal Southerners duly elected, forced through a mandate referring all measures concerning the South and reconstruction to a famous Joint Committee of Fifteen packed with extremists. This Committee summoned witnesses and used its hearings not to obtain information but to persuade the voters that all who opposed Radical Republican policies were "traitors." Radical Republican leaders branded the Democratic Party as the party of treason. Even moderate Republicans and the President of the United States were denounced as traitors seeking to overthrow the Government—the words "subversive" and "communist" were used but only rarely—and the big lie was so oft repeated that it came to be believed. Clergymen who had been antislavery were won by their concern about the Negro. Much of the press and the federal patronage were controlled by the reckless agitators eager to hang onto power in defiance of democratic principles. The campaign of abuse and misrepresentation and the appeals to fear were so successful that a people overwhelmingly ready in 1865 to forgive and let the South return to participation in democratic government was persuaded by November, 1866, to elect a Congress controlled by the extremists.

Through their own shortsightedness, both Democrats and Southerners helped put the Republican extremists into power. Southerners, like Northerners, were divided. Most Southerners were ready to admit not defeat, but the results of defeat and return loyally to their old citizenship. But in the stubbornness born of defeat and in despair over solving the problems left by war devastation and the sudden freeing of slaves, many of them did and said foolish things. Furthermore, while the war had made the Negro a freeman, it had not solved the problem of mass ignorance. Laws had forbidden slaves to learn to read or write lest they read dangerous ideas, such as those of the Declaration of Independence, for instance. Slavery had prevented their becoming civilized or responsible. It had denied them even morality or the sanctity of marriage and the family. But it had controlled them harshly. Now the controls were removed, and ignorance, inefficiency, the necessity of working out a new labor system and accustoming both

workers and employers to free labor were left to be settled by a
South suffering from the devastation of war. To meet the situation
severe and foolish "Black Codes" were enacted which played into
hands of Radical Republican agitators. Democrats, on their part,
had long been out of power and were hungry for office. A great
convention of moderates of both parties was held with enthusiasm, but it did not form a party organization nor name candidates for office. Men of both parties, like politicians of all times,
hesitated to break old party ties and risk forming a new party.
Democrats, seeing a hope of return to power, were unwilling to
support for the sake of principles a moderate Republican. Hence
moderate candidates were not nominated, and at the polls voters
faced a choice between an extremist Republican and a Democrat
associated by campaign oratory with treason. Faced with this
choice moderates voted against what they were told was treason in
sufficient numbers to elect a two-thirds majority of Radical Republicans in Congress, though in many contests the vote was close.

With power to override all Johnson's vetoes the Radical Republicans, who had been afraid to advocate such measures in the campaign, quickly moved on to military rule of the South, Negro suffrage, and disqualification of Southern leaders. An "ironclad oath"
barred from office everyone who had ever fought or held office
under the Confederacy or had in any way supported it. Johnson's
moderate governments were overthrown by a bitterly resented
army of occupation. Then, with Negroes voting and Northern
soldiers supervising, conventions were chosen to draw new constitutions, and new governments were elected.

President Johnson actually was neither a traitor, drunkard, nor
the incompetent he was pictured. He had more than average ability. He was devoted, industrious, indomitably courageous. He had
an almost religious faith in democracy. In a period of hysteria he
showed calm judgment, and later historians came to regard his
program as the wise one. Yet he did not control the party he
headed. Actually he was a Democrat elevated by Republicans to
the Vice Presidency to win a wartime election. Lincoln would have
been attacked as bitterly, but with advantages of personality and
experience that Johnson lacked, might have won out.

Ultimately Congress passed a law limiting the President's power
over the army of which the Constitution made him commander-in-
chief, and forbidding him to dismiss his own executive subordi-
nates. All Johnson could do was write able veto messages. In 1868
impeachment proceedings began. In his Senate trial the only

"crime" that was proved was disagreement with Congress. Even with seven Republicans supporting him, only one more vote would have removed him from office. Had he been ousted, Senator Wade, president pro-tem of the Senate, would have become President, and Ben Wade had said: "There is no doubt that if by an insurrection [the colored people] could contrive to slay one half of their oppressors, the other half would hold them in the highest respect and no doubt treat them with justice."

Had Johnson been removed, the President would have become a mere tool of Congress, and the Supreme Court would next have been stripped of its powers. The aim of the Radical Republicans was to destroy the states except as administrative divisions, and then to make Congress omnipotent within a highly centralized government, under which checks and balances had been abolished.

But now the tide turned. Beginning with 1869, conservative whites in Southern states regained control. They often did so by destroying democracy through fraud and violence, even murder, to terrorize Negroes and their white friends, but they did regain control when Northern troops were withdrawn. Radical Republicans, never really interested in the Negro, deserted him when using him ceased to serve them. A reaction against corruption that affected North as well as South, national government as well as states, and Democrats as well as Republicans diverted men's attention from controlling the South. Men became preoccupied with a serious depression and, before and after it, with unparalleled opportunities for profit from developing industrialism or exploiting the rich public domain. As war emotions died and "waving the bloody shirt" became less effective, Democrats with little interest in the war or the Negro regained power. A Northern people learned that an army of occupation could not coerce men into changing their ideas. Northerners themselves refused longer to tolerate military rule. Hence the last of the troops were removed in 1877 by President Hayes, and concern for the Negro and the attempt at reconstruction collapsed. What remained?

In the South the bitterness of war was greatly increased by the Reconstruction experience. The Negro was left with no protection of his civil rights, ultimately without any but a theoretical right to vote, socially inferior, economically exploited, and with little chance of improving himself or his status. The white South was left too concerned about "keeping the Negro in his place" to divide on other important issues, and with little voice in national affairs.

The nation inherited the political handicap of a "solid South." Industrial forces which would easily have been outvoted in 1865 managed to keep an agrarian majority from uniting to overthrow it. Through long years a new social and economic order was nurtured to maturity by tariffs and other government favors made possible by keeping the South impotent. When uncontrolled representatives of the white South finally united with agrarians from the West, modern industrialism was too powerful to be effectively controlled. Reconstruction did, however, bring considerable economic rehabilitation, and it gave birth to the "New South." Good state constitutions laid the basis for greater democracy for poorer white folk as well as for Negroes, and for universal education. Though national civil rights legislation was repealed or invalidated by an unfriendly Supreme Court, and the war amendments were long ignored or violated, they did remain in the Constitution. The Thirteenth Amendment guaranteed the Negro's freedom, the Fourteenth provided federal protection of his civil rights, and the Fifteenth gave him the right to vote. They remained ready for use in the mid-20th Century when a greater concern for democracy recreated a popular will to make these theoretical rights genuine.

SIX

Darwin

and Politics

THE HERO of the war, Ulysses S. Grant, followed Johnson as President, and with the "uncommon common man" at the helm of the Union he had helped to save, everyone expected the American ship of state to sail smoothly toward shores of greater abundance. Eight years of Grant in the White House changed that hope for many. Grant was woefully naive in politics; he played favorites who in turn played him; and, gradually, there were those who saw America changing from the land of opportunity into a seeming tight-fisted monopoly of the influential few.

Southerners who believed that the unjust rule of the carpetbaggers left them the chief victims of postwar dislocations now dominating the American scene had neither the time nor opportunity to understand what was happening almost everywhere to the man who toiled on farm or in factory for his daily bread. More and more the farmer and the laborer felt backed against an economic wall, while their resources of strength and productivity were ruthlessly exploited and their prospects grew gloomier.

If political revolt was in the making, it was small wonder. Out in the West one reformer cried that what Kansas needed was to raise less corn and more hell, and not alone in Kansas did that new war cry apply. Henry George, who became the key spokesman of his age (and, indeed, its most influential thinker), railed bitterly

213

against an America where "The gulf between the employed and the employer is growing wider; social contrasts are becoming sharper; as liveried carriages appear, so do barefooted children."

A raw, bruising struggle was in the making, and the social and economic foundations of America would be shaken (and not infrequently toppled) in the battle that followed. Those who held power and wealth borrowed from Darwin and Herbert Spencer to transfix biological laws into social laws, calling the new creed Social Darwinism, and shrugging shoulders at the downtrodden masses who were victims of an evolutionary process in which no sane man would meddle by proposing corrective social legislation. In retrospect a neater package of complacency toward want and underprivilege could not have been devised. Nothing could be done—evolution worked against the masses, with, apparently, the sanction of the clergy, press, and higher education; "the Moral Governor," wrote the Reverend D. S. Gregory, "has placed the power of *acquisitiveness* in man for good and noble purpose,"[1] and those who wished to argue with the Moral Governor could burn their breeches in brimstone for the trouble.

A few at first, and ultimately a great many Americans, were willing to run that risk, however. They assumed many labels and wore many faces. They, too, looked Darwin squarely in the eye, and decided he was a political asset. Said the Reform Darwinists, in essence, if evolution (which meant environmentalism) was the root of all evil, why not kick out the corrupt political bosses, unseat the trust magnates, and thus create a better environment? Into the battle charged Henry George, with his *Progress and Poverty*, nailing the issue to the precise cross the Reform Darwinists chose to bear. "The injustice of society," stated George, "not the niggardliness of nature, is the cause . . . of want and misery."

All sorts of people were to read George, skim over his single tax as the panacea to all social ills, and retain the deeper significance of his revolt. The brilliant Brandeis would read George and change—into a traitor to his former benefactors, if one listened to Back Bay bitterness. The country lawyer, Clarence Darrow, would be awakened by George; and so, too, would Bryan and Tom Johnson and others in the American Story whom you will be meeting in the next few pages. Using the stirring melody of the "Battle

[1] The quotations in this and the succeeding paragraph are drawn from Eric Goldman's absorbing *Rendezvous With Destiny*, now available in a paperback edition (New York, 1956).

Hymn of the Republic," delegates to the Populist Convention in 1892 sang lustily:

> They have stolen our money, have ravished our homes;
> With the plunder erected to Mammon a throne;
> They have fashioned a god, like the Hebrews of old,
> Then bid us bow down to their image of gold.

In the end, America wasn't bowing.

The Gilded Age

L E L A N D   D.   B A L D W I N

In Pudd'nhead Wilson's Calendar, *Mark Twain remarked: "If you pick up a starving dog and make him prosperous, he will not bite you. This is the principal difference between a dog and a man." The greatest humorist of the often humorless postwar age poked his own fun at the human stuffiness on which Social Darwinism thrived. In* What Paul Bourget Thinks of Us *Twain again ribbed his fellow Americans with twinkling insight: "In Boston they ask, How much does he know? In New York, How much is he worth? In Philadelphia, Who were his parents?" In a more critical vein the distinguished author, editor, and historian, Professor Leland D. Baldwin of the University of Pittsburgh, author of many historical volumes, including* The Stream of American History, *looks at America as it tries "to disinherit its pioneers."*

THE NAME Gilded Age was given by Mark Twain to the period that followed immediately upon the Civil War, but we can now see that the aspects which he regarded as typical of that period applied also to the entire era from the Civil War to World War I. The Gilded Age was the heyday of the middle class, and was marked by all the virtues and the vices that accompany a middle-class civilization. It was the germinal season of the remarkable progress which we have seen in the last generation, but it must also be recognized that in retrospect certain unlovely characteristics were far more in evidence.

It was an age of materialism in which religion and art frankly kowtowed to wealth; in which size was a synonym for significance, and in which the sentimentality of the pre-Civil War generation was transformed into a popular glorification of superficiality and mediocrity. The "plain people"—those without social or intellectual pretensions—were vaguely conscious of the conflict and confusion of the age, but their confidence that they were in tune with the divine order was little affected by what was going on around them. We must look to the newly rich and the great middle class for the traits which are most characteristic of the Gilded Age.

The philosophical clichés of the Gilded Age were contributed by Herbert Spencer, whose influence in the United States was so great that he was sometimes called the "Apostle to the Americans." He was responsible for the rise of Social Darwinism, which extended the biological struggle for survival to the social sphere, and proclaimed that in the long run a man prospered or suffered as he deserved. In effect, Spencer was giving the approval of nature and morals to the changes which were occurring in Western civilization as it applied the lessons of technology to industry. He was, moreover, giving encouragement to those who sought to arrest American moral progress at the status quo in order to free their hands to promote material progress and to amass property. Thus his doctrine superficially seemed to fall into line with American experience and to justify so many things we wished to do. William Lawrence, proper Bostonian and Episcopal bishop, proclaimed that "in the long run, it is only to the man of morality that wealth comes . . . Godliness is in league with riches."

This channeling of American energy into material lines was natural. The problem of conquering a continent was a material one and it called for material measures. The man who did the most to solve material problems was the acknowledged leader and his prosperity, in the Calvinist tradition, became the proof of righteousness. Van Wyck Brooks has called him the "inspired millionaire," and, as he labored and disported himself, education, art, literature, politics, and the church played soft accompaniments. These forces were engaged in an unconscious conspiracy to preserve the economic status quo and they sought this end by a campaign to preserve proper moral attitudes which, of course, must approve the economic status quo.

Americans were engaged in three quests—for wealth, for respectability, and for culture. The search for respectability found one outlet in the exhibitionism which has been called the cult of conspicuous consumption. No aspect of the Gilded Age was so clearly gilded rather than golden, snobbish rather than sound. Devotees of this cult made their headquarters in the brownstone mansions of upper Fifth Avenue in New York, but summered at Newport and wintered in the rising playground of Florida or the baroque palaces of the Mediterranean. Perceptive individuals, even among the wealthy, warned of the social and political effects of this flaunting of waste, but it did not die down until the progressive movement and World War I brought in a new social consciousness and high taxes. In a sense the cult of conspicuous consumption flourished because rich men's tastes were those of the class from which they had sprung: simple, garish, untrained, and finding pleasure in a kind of juvenile display of superiority.

Another and more valuable aspect of the search for respectability is found in what we may call the cult of respectability. There was considerable danger that slickness and love of power would become more prominent as American traits than the sense of ordered responsibility—that is, devotion to duty—which we call character. The task of subduing this wildness and of making character a part of the American grain was an absorbing interest of the Gilded Age.

Reliability and predictability became the watchwords of the cult of respectability. Appearance, manners, and behavior became all important. The seamy side of life was ignored or covered with a genteel veneer; indeed there was a tendency to identify the appearance of respectability with character. It was not so evident then as it is now that respectability without character may fail in its aim, and produce a rascal or a stuffed shirt. Still, it was in the spirit of the English motto—"Manners maketh man." The attempt to teach respect for the humdrum virtues was a healthy sign and a necessary step to the building both of culture and of socially conscious wealth. It was also necessary in preparing the nation for the responsibilities which were to descend upon it in the 20th Century.

There was something almost pathetic in the American desire for culture, and it was perhaps natural that the United States should tamely accept European dictates in art, music, architecture, and women's fashions. Even public taste in literature frequently waited on the British verdict. Women were most active in the pursuit of culture. Men were accused of being more uncouth: perhaps they were, but on the other hand it may well be that they saw that European cultural dictates were out of step with the necessities of the coming age. There was a saying at the turn of the century that the United States imported art and exported artists. It was tragically true that most Americans were unable to recognize the creative pioneers in their midst, especially if they had not studied in Paris, Munich, or Rome.

The facade of respectability did not effectively cover the confusion and oppression beneath, nor the clash and din of the changeover from agriculture to industry, from the culture of the few to the culture of the many. Too many of the potentially creative artists could not see beyond the vulgarity and the brutality of their time and despaired of the American future. With the exception of certain hardy souls who were to become the cultural parents of the present, they fled in distaste or alarm: some into a sullen silence; some into the arms of the brute they feared; some to the tradition-haunted cities of Europe. Even the sincerest artist was sometimes tempted into flight by the feeling that he could never set down in writing or in paint or carve in stone that sprawling giant, America, with all its turmoil, confusion, and contradictions. Again with certain honorable exceptions, creative artists failed to see the age-old connection between conquest of physical problems and intellectual and aesthetic growth. "We're the disinherited of art," cried Henry James of the American expatriates, who failed to see that Europe also was striving, even more bitterly, to disinherit its pioneers.

It was the architect Louis Sullivan who laid his finger on the unease of the expatriate when he issued his declaration of independence in the words, "Form follows function." Forms had followed functions in the past, and those forms had become fixed in modern minds as necessary to the good life. Without disparaging traditions, for it is clear that new cultural forms must build on old ones, it must be observed that aesthetes of the Gilded Age resisted the demand of the Machine Age for new forms to accompany new functions. They hated the machine less for what it was doing to the masses than for what it did to the old forms of art which they had accepted as unalterable.

To them must be attributed at least in part the failure of the United States to play a mature role in the drama of the first decades of the 20th Century. They had fallen short in the mission of the creative artist, which is to interpret society to itself and thus to call forth self-understanding and a sense of responsibility, but more, to point out the direction which progress should take. As it was, Americans saw that the artists' portrayal of the American way was false because it was based upon European standards which could not apply to the democratic and industrial civilization which was emerging in the New World. The call to support and defend the Old World was understood by some Americans to mean the preservation of an outmoded, even obstructive way of life. There was no real understanding of the historical continuity which makes tradition contribute its building stones to the structure of the future.

Creative artists have long claimed that where they lead culture will follow. Without completely denying their claim one may venture to propose on the basis of the American experience that they may have been too smug and exclusive. Certainly the American way is in large part the creation of the capitalists, engineers, artisans, politicians, clergymen, schoolmasters who were demanding that cultural and material resources should no longer be the property of a chosen few but should become the property of all. They saw the triumph of spiritual advancement, and they sought to fit the evolution of that idea to the moral values which they believed are eternal.

This we must remember in summing up the Gilded Age, with its glorification of the smug, the conventional, and the mediocre. At the very moment when the self-styled creative artists were proclaiming the doom of America, other men, who would never have dreamed of calling themselves artists but who, nevertheless, were imbued with the authentic fire of artistry, were planning a social structure more magnificent than the world had ever seen. And this is the structure on whose threshold we stand today.

The Farmer Protests: Populism

J. D. HICKS

That Irish firebrand of Populism, Ignatius Donnelly, strode to the platform on a hot July 4 in Omaha to deliver the keynote address of the 1892 convention. Corruption, shouted Donnelly, dominated "ballot-box . . . legislatures . . . Congress . . . even the ermine of the bench." Homes sagged under mortgages; labor was denied the right to organize for self-protection; and "a vast conspiracy against mankind has been organized." The fighting Irish in Donnelly cried that this conspiracy must be "met and overthrown" unless "terrible

*social convulsions" were to produce the "establishment of an ab-
solute despotism." The convention hall rocked with cheers; Donnelly spoke the gospel of the common man's protest against Social
Darwinism and the injustices it sired. A long struggle, now almost
twenty years in the making, had led to this new Declaration of
Independence in Omaha, and John D. Hicks, professor of history
at the University of California, and author of* A Short History of
American Democracy *and other books, traces its origins and
whither it led.*

THE ECONOMIC revolution that occurred in the United States
during the 19th Century deeply affected both industry and agriculture. Railroads rapidly connected every part of the nation with
every other part; steamship lines amplified immeasurably the
means of foreign trade; new machines cut down the amount of
hand work required of workers, whether in the factory or on the
farm. The population more than doubled. Cities grew immoder-
ately, especially in the Northeast, where industry became paramount. Increasingly the ascendancy of agriculture was pushed to
the South and West. But at the same time the West also grew; the
western half of the nation, virtually unexploited by agriculture
before the Civil War, now came vigorously into production.

In general, the new dispensation brought relatively greater
benefits to the manufacturing than to the farming interests. The
former concentrated steadily in strategic centers, increased the
size and efficiency of its plants, and with the aid of a dependable
protective tariff exploited to the full the sales possibilities of the
nation. The latter could not be concentrated or organized. It still
remained in the hands of hundreds of thousands of individual
farmers, each in competition with every other, not only throughout
the nation but also throughout the world. For the farmers a protective tariff was practically valueless, since the produce of American farms exceeded the capacity of the American people to consume, and the excess had to be sold abroad.

In the disposal of his goods the American farmer was thus dependent upon a world market. The price of wheat, for example,
was set by what buyers would pay in Liverpool, England. But
when it came to purchases, the farmer must buy on a noncom-
petitive home market. The price of farm machinery was fixed by
the implement trust, to which high tariff rates gave full protection.

This discrepancy was the more serious because of the great

change that had come over farming itself. Once each farmer had counted on producing the essentials of life for himself and had to buy very little, but now he raised crops principally for sale, and depended on the profits he made for the means with which to meet his needs for outside purchases. One or more staple crops, usually cotton and tobacco in the South, or small grain, corn, livestock, and dairy products in the West, accounted for most of the farmer's income. The farmer also made greater use of credit than ever before—credit to help him buy his land, which especially in the newer sections was often mortgaged for all it was worth; credit to buy the improved machinery without which his production would be inadequate; credit to build houses and barns; credit for household supplies until his crop could be sold.

Furthermore, he faced the problem of marketing his goods at long distance. He must pay handling charges to elevators, warehouses, and railroads—particularly to the railroads, whose tendency before the days of regulation was to charge all the traffic would bear. Everyone farmed the farmer—the land speculators, the railroads, the middlemen, the bankers, the storekeepers, and, whenever tenancy existed, the landlords. The problem of tenancy was at its worst in the South, where crop liens were legal and the sharecropper was perpetually in debt. But even in the more prosperous Northwest the farmer was lucky, indeed, if at the end of the year he owed less than he received.

Under such circumstances it was inevitable that in some manner or other the farmers would protest. Their great problem was how to unite their forces, since by instinct and tradition they were utter individualists and had, in addition, the burden of achieving intersectional accord. Farm leaders took courage from the record of organized labor, which was equally aggrieved at the unrestricted supremacy of industry and had tried to do something about it. If labor could unite, why not the farmers? During the decades that followed the Civil War the spokesmen of agricultural discontent raised at least four separate standards of revolt, and large numbers of farmers gathered under each.

First came the Patrons of Husbandry, or the Grange, a kind of farmers' lodge which grew to respectable strength both in the South and the West. Designed by its founders to be an educational order which would teach the farmers to farm better, it developed, especially in the Northwest, into a political movement with the curbing of railroad extortions as it principal purpose. Eventually a set of Granger laws, held constitutional by the United States

Supreme Court in 1877, established the right of the states to reg-
ulate the railroads, even to the extent of setting maximum rates.
And a decade later Congress, through the Interstate Commerce
Act, accepted the same responsibility for the nation as a whole.

Next in order came the Greenbackers, who pointed to the in-
adequacy of the currency and the steadily appreciating value of
the dollar as the principal causes of the farmer's woes. What this
country needed, they said, was more money and a cheaper dollar.
Congress should oblige with new issues of greenbacks. This frank
appeal to money inflation kept the Greenbackers from winning
any substantial victories, but at least they called attention to an
alarming situation. The nation's monetary system was obsolete; it
did stand in grave need of overhauling.

Then came the Farmers' Alliances, one in the Northwest and
another in the South, but both equally determined to unite the
farmers in their own defense. In the South the one-party system
stood guard against the formation of a separate farmers' party,
but Southern Alliance men flocked to the Democratic caucuses,
took over the Democratic Party machinery in state after state,
elected their candidates to state offices and to Congress. In the
Northwest, however, the Alliance by the early 1890's had begun to
take on the character of a third party—the People's, or Populist
Party, which speedily took the lead in the battle for farmers' rights.

Western enthusiasm for the Populist revolt, the fourth in the
series of farmer movements, had certain special encouragements.
Along the Middle Border—that area west of the western boundary
of Missouri but east of the arid High Plains—the inrush of population had come during a series of wet years when the rainfall was
adequate. Then, toward the end of the Eighties, the cycle changed
and one dry season succeeded another with devastating monotony.
The farmer had troubles enough in good times, but crop failures
meant mortgage foreclosures, want, and despair. Poor crops did
not even mean good prices, for the world supply was scarcely
affected by the conditions of a given region. But the hapless farmers were unwilling to blame all their troubles on the weather. They
had been sinned against by the railroads, the bankers, and the
middlemen; the government must do something about it. Into
politics they went with a fervor and earnestness they had never
shown before.

It was a religious revival, a crusade, a pentecost of politics in
which a tongue of flame sat upon every man, and each spoke as
the spirit gave him utterance. The farmers, the country merchants,

the cattle-herders, they of the long chin whiskers, and they of the broad-brimmed hats and heavy boots, had also heard the word and could preach the gospel of Populism. Women with skins tanned to parchment by the hot winds, with bony hands of toil and clad in faded calico, could talk in meetings, and could talk to the point.

Third party tickets won substantial victories in the elections of 1890, but it was not until the election of 1892—after three great conventions—that the People's Party was ready to compete in the national arena. To the disappointment of its leaders, few Southerners were willing to risk a break from the one-party system which had created the "solid South," so that the movement became far more Western than national. Also, the new and powerful American Federation of Labor refused to co-operate. The third party was thus in reality more a Farmers' Party than a People's Party.

Nevertheless, at their Omaha convention, held early in July, 1892, the Populists nominated James B. Weaver,[2] of Iowa, for the Presidency and James G. Field, of Virginia, for the Vice Presidency. They wrote a long platform that incorporated Granger, Greenback, and Farmers' Alliance reforms; urged changes in the land, transportation, and financial policies of the nation that would make the government supreme over business instead of business over government; and demanded also certain political reforms, such as the initiative and referendum, that would enable the people really to take control of the government.

Weaver and Field won twenty-two votes in the electoral college, all from Western and mountain states. The interest of the latter came from the more or less incidental espousal of the "free silver" issue by the Populists. To the Western silver miner, "the free and unlimited coinage of silver at the ratio of sixteen to one" meant higher prices for silver; to the farmers it came to mean primarily money inflation. Greatly to the disappointment of genuine reformers, the silver propaganda carried everything before it. According to Henry Demarest Lloyd,[3] free silver was the "cow-

---

[2] Weaver, Ohio-born lawyer, a brigadier-general of volunteers in the Civil War, editor of the *Iowa Tribune* of Des Moines, member of Congress in 1879–81 and 1885–89, had been the Greenback candidate for President in 1880.

[3] Lloyd, born in New York and educated at Columbia, went West to join the editorial staff of the *Chicago Tribune;* his most notable book was *Wealth Against Commonwealth.* He was also author of such works as *A Strike of Millionaires against Miners, or the Story of Spring Valley* and *A Country Without Strikes.*

bird of the sacrifices and labors of others, who laid its eggs in their nests, pushing out their eggs which lie smashed on the ground." Free silver, rarely understood by its advocates, became an unreasoning passion, a panacea that according to true believers would cure every ill and right every wrong:

> The dollar of our daddies,
> Of silver coinage free
> Will make us rich and happy,
> Will bring prosperity.

First free silver captured the Populist Party; then the Democratic Party, by embracing free silver, captured Populism. When the Populists in 1896 nominated as their candidate for President William Jennings Bryan, who became the Democratic candidate, their day of independence was done.

But many of their ideas lived on and greatly altered the course of 20th Century American history. The Populists helped prepare the way for Theodore Roosevelt's conservation policy, for the closer regulation of railroads and trusts, for the Federal Reserve Banking system, for a series of reforms that greatly promoted popular control of the government, both state and national, even for parity prices. As a political revolt, Populism was a failure; the Populist Party lived only to die. But Populism was good on diagnosis even when it was faulty on prescription. As an educational movement it was a great success.

Labor Protests: The Pullman Strike

H E N R Y   D A V I D

In 1894 a depression swept the country. Now a new voice of dissent roared through the land—that of a badly constricted labor—and new apostles of discontent and reform appeared, among them Eugene V. Debs. Crowds screamed and whistled, and flung hats in the air as Debs spoke the new rising protest the depression had bred:

"The forces of labor must unite. The dividing lines must grow dimmer day by day until they become imperceptible, and then labor's hosts, marshalled under one conquering banner, shall

The Gilded Age: A typical one-family residence—provided the family was Vanderbilt,
and the period one in which the conspicuous
consumption of wealth was the custom. The
fashionable Sunday parade of carriages was
de rigueur.

Industrial unrest: Depression, strikes, and unemployment became part of the pattern of living toward the end of the 19th Century. The Pullman Strike of 1894 was crushed when President Cleveland ordered federal intervention, and sent infantry troops (*above*) to patrol the trains. At about the same time, (*below*) groups of the unemployed formed "armies" of protest. The best-known was led by Jacob S. Coxey of Ohio; when he and 400 of his band reached Washington, the leaders were promptly arrested.

Cartoonist G. Y. Coffin in the Washington *Post* perceptively spoofed the support enjoyed by William Jennings Bryan in the first of his three unsuccessful campaigns for the Presidency. In 1896 Bryan was supported by the agrarian South and West, opposed by the commercial and industrial interests of the Northeast.

New York City has always been the chief
portal for European immigration. This photograph, made in 1900, graphically shows
the crowding and slum conditions prevalent
in many Eastern cities when the influx was
approaching its zenith.

march together, vote together and fight together, until working men shall enjoy all the fruits of their toil. . . ."[4]

Debs spoke of the dream; the reality was still far off, with the United States government quickly aligned on the side of the strikebreakers. An early focal point of crisis was the Pullman Strike, and Henry David of Columbia University's Graduate School of Business brings to an examination of this episode in the American Story the authoritative background he has demonstrated as an editor of the eight-volume Economic History of the United States.

I N JULY of 1894, newspaper headlines screamed of mob rule, terror, and insurrection in the city of Chicago, and of a conspiracy by the American Railway Union against the government of the United States. A Chicago dispatch to the *Washington Post* of July 7 reported: "The situation tonight is more alarming than at any time since the trouble began. War of the bloodiest kind in Chicago is imminent, and before tomorrow goes by the railroad lines and yards may be turned into battle fields strewn with hundreds of dead and wounded."

The frightening picture projected by such newspaper headlines and stories was false. It did not convey the real issues of one of the most dramatic episodes in American labor history—the Pullman Strike—and it grossly exaggerated and misrepresented the violence which marked that struggle.

The Pullman Strike grew out of the soil of a major depression—as severe as any the nation experienced—which began with a financial panic early in 1893. By the close of that year, some five hundred banks had closed; major railroads were in receivership; industrial production fell off sharply; and business enterprises worth more than a quarter of a billion dollars had failed.

Widespread suffering marched hand in hand with growing unemployment and wage cuts. At the height of the depression the unemployed were estimated at three million, or roughly one-fifth of all those gainfully employed outside of agriculture. Private charitable and relief agencies and emergency relief measures were unable to cope with the deprivation and misery which it caused.

A novel, and to the well-to-do and conservative-minded, an ominous protest against unemployment appeared in the so-called

[4]Quoted in Ginger, Ray: *The Bending Cross: A Biography of Eugene Victor Debs* (New Brunswick, 1949), p. 115.

"industrial armies." These groups of unemployed workers set out from different parts of the nation to make their way by foot and rail to Washington, where they planned to urge Congress to take remedial action. In the West they frequently commandeered trains when they failed to secure free transportation. The most famous of these "armies" was headed by Jacob S. Coxey, a reform-minded successful businessman from Massillon, Ohio. He proposed that the jobless be employed on highway and other public construction financed by the federal government. Coxey's "army" of four hundred was prevented by the police from presenting its "petition in boots" to Congress after arriving in Washington in April, 1894, as were the remnants of other "industrial armies" which later reached the city.

While the jobless begged for work, the employed were faced with severe wage cuts. In a flooded labor market, in the absence of strong unions, and in the face of employer attitudes which rejected collective bargaining, a strike against wage cuts was essentially an act of desperation. Yet more than 690,000 workers were involved in strikes in 1894, a greater number than in any preceding year, and wage issues played a key role in most of them.

The impact of the depression upon the employees of the Pullman Palace Company followed an all too common pattern. This extremely successful enterprise, created by George Mortimer Pullman, was pre-eminent in the manufacture and operation of sleeping cars. In 1893, it employed 14,500 workers and had total earnings of $11,400,000 on assets of sixty-two millions.

The production of cars was centered in Pullman, a model town on the outskirts of Chicago, where five and a half thousand workers were employed in 1893. This unique industrial community was founded by George Pullman thirteen years earlier. It boasted of handsome public buildings, excellent sanitation, shaded walks and gardens, parks and playgrounds. But it was a company town and its inhabitants lived in the shadow of an unfeeling paternalism. Its political life was dominated by the company. Unions were not tolerated after an unsuccessful strike in 1886. Charges for rent, gas, and water were substantially higher than in neighboring communities. "We are born," declared one worker, "in a Pullman house, fed from the Pullman shop, taught in the Pullman school, catechized in the Pullman church, and when we die we shall be buried in the Pullman cemetery and go to the Pullman hell."

When new orders fell off, the Pullman Company first reduced its work force drastically. Then to keep the shops going, it cut its prices for new construction, and balanced that move by slashing wages. On the average, the wages of the thirty-three hundred workers employed in the spring of 1894 were about a fourth lower than they had been a year earlier. Some workers, however, were compelled to take wage cuts of 40 per cent. At the same time, the company's policy of staggering employment further reduced weekly earnings. The company's financial position, however, was quite strong, for income from the operation of the Pullman cars remained high enough to permit it, had it so desired, to absorb losses in new car construction, pay the regular 8 per cent dividend, and still enjoy a surplus of two million in 1894.

Behind in rent and short of food, the workers in the Pullman shops turned to collective action, for which a new vehicle was available in the American Railway Union. This industrial union was founded in June of 1893 under the leadership of Eugene V. Debs—far from being a Socialist at this time—and was open to all white workers in the railroad industry. The union's membership grew very rapidly, and its successful strike against the Great Northern Railroad in the spring of 1894 promised a bright future. Four thousand of its 150,000 members were recruited from the shops in Pullman.

On May 11, after the company had denied a request for wage increases and rent reductions and had fired three members of the workers' grievance committee, three thousand Pullman employees went out on strike. About a month later, the American Railway Union, meeting in convention in Chicago, carefully considered the dispute and the plight of the strikers. Leaders of the union and rank-and-file delegates wanted the strike to be settled by negotiation or arbitration. But the company knew that the strikers could not endure a protracted struggle, in spite of the contributions which they received from trade unionists and others, and Pullman bluntly declared that there was "nothing to arbitrate." Finally, the convention decided that if the company refused to arbitrate by June 26, the members of the American Railway Union were to refuse to handle Pullman cars. This action was designed to cut off the company's chief source of revenue and force a negotiated settlement.

The resulting boycott of Pullman cars by members of the American Railway Union quickly developed into a strike which affected the major railroads of the country in twenty-seven states and territories and virtually paralyzed some lines. When the railroads fired workers for refusing to handle trains containing Pullman cars, members of the American Railway Union countered by going out on strike. Thus, the strike at Pullman was transformed into a struggle on national scope between the American Railway Union and an organization made up of twenty-four railroads entering Chicago called the General Managers' Association.

At stake now was the very existence of the American Railway Union, which the General Managers' Association sought to destroy. The Association planned the strike strategy and tactics of the railroads. It secured strikebreakers. It made certain that the strike would be marked by violence. It showed how to manipulate the law and the courts against the strikers. And, far more important, it brought the federal government into the struggle on the side of the railroads.

In this connection the Association was aided by the antiunion sentiment of the period and the destruction of railroad property and the occurrence of mob violence, for which tramps and hoodlums and not the strikers were overwhelmingly responsible. The strike interfered with interstate commerce and disrupted the mails and this made it possible for the Attorney General of the United States, Richard Olney, to become a powerful ally of the Association. Olney had been a leading railroad lawyer, and his heart and able mind were dedicated to the protection of property rights. He promptly appointed as special assistant to the federal attorney in Chicago a man suggested by the Association who was attorney for the Chicago, Milwaukee & St. Paul. It was Olney who worked out the grounds for securing an injunction against the strikers and the union leaders and who influenced President Grover Cleveland to order federal troops into Chicago. Through Olney, in short, the resources of the United States government were used to ensure that the strike would fail.

On July 2, the federal district court in Chicago issued an injunction forbidding all persons to refrain from interfering with the operation of the railroads. Its terms were so broad that it even prohibited efforts to persuade employees to stop work. Similar injunctions were issued against strikers in other parts of the country. Meanwhile, five thousand deputies, many of them strikebreakers, had been sworn in by United States marshals in Chicago.

The decisive step came on July 3 when President Cleveland ordered federal troops into Chicago, even though local and state authorities had not requested assistance to maintain peace and order. There was, in fact, more violence in Chicago after the appearance of federal troops than before. Governor John P. Altgeld of Illinois, who had himself ordered out the state militia to prevent disorders, castigated the President's action as unnecessary and unconstitutional. Other governors into whose states federal troops had been dispatched also protested Cleveland's course.

On July 10, Debs and other union leaders were indicted and arrested for conspiracy to obstruct the mails. Similar action was taken against strikers elsewhere. Then Debs and his associates were arrested again and charged with contempt of court in having disobeyed the original injunction. They were later found guilty of this offense and served a jail sentence.

By the last week in July, the struggle was practically over, and on August 2, the American Railway Union called the strike off with the knowledge that the union itself would not long survive. Before that date, the forgotten strike in the Pullman shops had also collapsed.

From today's vantage point, the Pullman Strike represents a valiant protest against the consequences of a major depression and the bold use of governmental power to determine the outcome of a labor dispute and the life of a union. It also illuminates a hostility to unionism and collective bargaining and an indifference to human rights and well-being which American society has long outgrown.

In Words of Fire

E R I C   F.   G O L D M A N

The name of Ignatius Donnelly is remembered today by only the historical specialist; and as Socialism has faded from the current political scene, so also has the memory of Debs dimmed. Perhaps some day a similar fate will befall William Jennings Bryan, who burst upon the American scene with the awesome brilliance of a comet in the sky. Bryan had read his Henry George and had harkened to the new gospel of the common man. Opposing the principles of Social Darwinism, he also disbelieved in nothing so strenuously as the whole blasphemous theory of evolution. So Bryan, who was to be a great American symbol in many ways, also epitomized two generations at war intellectually and emotionally. But that was later—much later than the dazzling day in 1896 when the young marvel from Lincoln, Nebraska, addressed a political

*convention. Eric F. Goldman, associate professor of history at
Princeton University and winner of the Bancroft Prize for his
brilliant book,* Rendezvous With Destiny, *tells the story.*

A̶LL ACROSS America emotions ran high. The years after the Civil
War brought a miracle of industrial growth in the United States,
but they did not produce a contented population. By the 1890's,
workingmen were angrily demanding an eight-hour day, higher
wages, and a more respected place in society. Farmers bitterly
charged that Wall Street was cheating them out of a decent living
by keeping the prices of manufactured goods high and keeping
low the prices of agricultural products. Businessmen and white-
collar workers, nervous at the mounting discontent, irritably told
each other that the Republic was threatened with revolution.

Out in Lincoln, Nebraska, a young lawyer watched it all, and
his big, powerful body tingled with excitement. William Jennings
Bryan knew his America as he knew every expression on the face
of his beloved wife Mary. He knew that every so often the nation
reaches a state of feelings when a bold, decisive voice can swing
men with the force of a typhoon. Bryan had no doubt which way
he wanted the swing to go. He was a product of the farms and small
towns of the Midwest, with a Jeffersonian suspicion of the lusty
corporations that had become so influential in America. He had
even less doubt that he was the man to lead an assault on all policies which favored the rich and the powerful.

Bryan had scarcely left his father's farm when he was preparing
himself for this leadership. At little Illinois College he was far less
interested in the regular courses than in oratorical contests, where
he declaimed away on such subjects as "Labor" and "Justice." Once
out of college, he practiced law for a few years and established
quite a reputation, but his heart was not in the work. Soon he was
giving full time to the bitter political battles of the day, winning
election to Congress as a radical Democrat in the early 1890's,
practicing his voice and his arguments as he barnstormed the Midwest. When the Democratic National Convention assembled in
1896, Bryan was invited to deliver an address, and he was ready.

American political conventions had heard many a great orator,
but they had never heard anything like this thirty-six-year-old
Nebraskan. Bryan assailed conservatism with every skill that the
public speaker can command. He was expository, and then this
handsome face was all earnestness and the words rippled out in

the cadence of good teaching. He was sly and insinuating, and the fervid eyes lit up his paleness as the voice twisted its way under the arguments of those who favored big business. He was, above all, apostolic, his big frame vibrant, the long, black hair thrown back, the great golden baritone cascading over the audience. All through the speech, cheers kept rolling through the hall. When Bryan finished, there was for a long moment an electric silence. Then the convention broke into one vast roar of sound, with the delegates laughing, crying, praying, hugging each other, beating on tin pans, and yelling, always yelling, for more than thirty minutes.

Bryan, despite his youth, was named the Democratic candidate for the Presidency of the United States. Pouring his deep religious and political feelings into the effort, he turned the campaign of 1896 into a drive of unprecedented intensity. Day after day Bryan campaigned, praying to his God on the floor of his sleeping car at night, sleeping soundly, rising refreshed to speak to twenty or thirty meetings before another sundown. And after the speeches, observers noted, "the poor, the weak, the humble, the aged, the infirm" would rush forward by the hundreds, holding up "hard and wrinkled hands with crooked fingers and cracked knuckles to the young great orator, as if he were in very truth their promised redeemer from bondage."

Bryan lost the election of 1896. Nominated twice more, in 1900 and 1908, he lost twice again. Yet Bryan in defeat was a good deal more important than many victorious political leaders have been. The United States at the turn of the 20th Century had to make a series of fateful decisions. Millions of poor Americans plainly were no longer willing to accept their low lot, and even many of the middle classes were growing fearful that they would be crushed by selfish forces of wealth. Either industrial and political leaders would recognize this situation and move to bring greater prosperity and more confidence in the future to the lower groups, or the United States was headed for the bitter class divisions which were already racking Europe. By giving an eloquent voice and powerful leadership to the discontented, Bryan did an enormous amount to teach the top groups the wisdom of reform.

He campaigned for some things—most notably, inflation of currency by the unrestricted coinage of silver—which were never accepted by the country. But he lived to see written into law most of the policies which he advocated—among them the direct election of United States Senators, a federal income tax, governmental aid in providing cheap loans for farmers, an eight-hour day for industrial labor, enforced publicity for campaign contributions, and federal control of the currency.

Year after year, the Republican Party which was defeating Bryan in elections took over more and more of his program. Year after year, the Democratic Party, which had a wing that loathed Bryan, also swung toward the kind of thinking which he represented. By 1912, the two leading candidates were the Republican, Theodore Roosevelt, and the Democrat, Woodrow Wilson, and both men campaigned ardently for economic and political reforms. When Wilson won, he promptly named Bryan to the No. 1 post in his Cabinet, Secretary of State. "This is only natural," the new President declared, "for the man who had led in the transformation of the national attitudes."

Bryan was fifty-three when he took office as Secretary of State. Unfortunately, he was becoming a creature of a past generation, out of tune with his times while still in the prime of life. However forward-looking Bryan had been in his social and political program, he was essentially a spokesman of the old agrarian America, where men assumed that the United States was an island unto itself and where they measured ideas by prescientific standards. All the while, the world and the nation had raced ahead into a new phase, in which the United States was entangled with events happening thousands of miles away, and the American people were adopting attitudes which fitted the flood of scientific findings.

Bryan lived on into 1925, but his final decade was hardly distinguished. As Secretary of State, he was confronted with the problems produced by World War I, and he could bring to them only a simple pacifism and a still more simple plea that the United States should remain neutral by turning its back on the world. When Bryan refused to sign a strong note denouncing the sinking of the *Lusitania*, President Wilson and his Secretary of State could no longer work together. Bryan resigned from the Cabinet, and once more the applause rang. But this time it came not from millions who were looking forward but from a small band whose eyes were turned to the past.

The period after World War I was still more melancholy. At a time when the nation was hurrying the adaptation of its ideas to modern science, Bryan emerged as the fervid spokesman of a century gone by. Soon he was making dismal headlines with attacks on Charles Darwin's theory of evolution, which had long since been accepted by educated Americans. Sinking to the level of cracker barrel bravado, Bryan announced that he offered a hundred dollars in cash to any professor who would sign an affidavit stating that he was personally descended from an ape.

The final stage came in a steaming courthouse at Dayton, Tennessee. Bryan had made himself the leader of a movement which sought to ban the teaching of evolution in the public schools, and his opponents rightly insisted that this was the opening wedge in an attempt to keep all modern science and learning out of education. Enlightened Americans were outraged. They determined to make a test case in Tennessee, and a brilliant galaxy of legal talent, led by the redoubtable Clarence Darrow, descended on Dayton.

Since Bryan rested his case on the argument that a literal interpretation of the Bible should be the heart of education, Darrow concentrated on this point. He aimed to show that Bryan did not understand the Bible; his cross-questioning was devastating (and Bryan made a poor showing under Darrow's barrage in defending his statement that everything in the Bible should be literally interpreted).

"Mr. Bryan, do you claim that everything in the Bible should be literally interpreted?"

"I believe what the Bible says."

"I suppose you mean that the earth stood still?"

"I accept the Bible absolutely."

"Do you believe that the men who wrote it thought that the day could be lengthened or that the sun could be stopped?"

"I believe that what they wrote was inspired by the Almighty."

"Now, Mr. Bryan, have you ever pondered what would have happened to the earth if it stood still suddenly?"

"No."

"Don't you know it would have been converted into a molten mass of matter?"

"You testify to that when you get on the stand."

"You believe the story of the flood to be a literal interpretation?"

"Yes, sir."

"When was the flood?"

"I would not attempt to fix the day."

"But what do you think that the Bible itself says? Don't you know how it was arrived at?"

"I never made a calculation."

"What do you think?"

"I do not think about things I don't think about."

"Do you think about things you do think about?"

"Well, sometimes."

Derision swept over the United States. Will Rogers expressed what millions were thinking. "I like Bill Bryan," Rogers said, "but he is making a fool out of himself and out of religion."

Five days after the trial came to an end, Bryan lay down to have a nap. He never awakened. Darrow, who had just used every conceivable legal weapon to annihilate Bryan, spoke the proper epitaph.

"I used to listen to him in the great days," Darrow said, "and I will never forget the experience. Today he may have missed the boat, may not even know where the boat is heading. But at the turn of the century, when it most needed to be said, when it took real courage, he spoke the meaning of America in words of fire. He kept insisting—and history will remember him for it—that America is not really America unless the lowliest man feels sure in his bones that he has free and equal opportunity to get ahead."

The City and The Muckrakers

ARTHUR M. SCHLESINGER, SR.

The rise of the city posed still another problem, and added to the vocabulary of an America that now spoke of the Gilded Age and the Age of Enterprise, Populism and Greenbackers and Free Silver and Reform Darwinism; it added a word that perhaps would outlast them all—Muckraker. When one day S. S. McClure told Lincoln Steffens to get out of New York if he wanted to learn how to edit a magazine, neither knew what he was starting; but Steffens hadn't spoken very long to the district attorney in St. Louis, who was determined to circumvent the bosses, before the journalist began to sense that he had come upon something big. The conditions that brought Steffens to his moment, and some of the consequences that resulted, are analyzed by Arthur M. Schlesinger, Sr., professor of history at Harvard University, recipient of many academic honors, and editor of the thirteen-volume History of American Life.

WILLIAM JENNINGS BRYAN was a product of the great Western prairies. Theodore Roosevelt, who absorbed many of his ideas, was a child of the urban East. The eclipse of the rural type of national leader by city-bred statesmen marked a significant turning point in our political history.

Cities, however, were far from new in the United States when this occurred. Even our colonial forebears, though primarily farmers, found it necessary to establish settled communities to carry on trade with one another as well as with the Old World. Today these places would seem hardly more than overgrown villages; yet they played an important role both politically and economically in the life of the times.

The Revolution, for example, was largely an uprising of the principal seaports from Boston to Charleston, South Carolina, against the burdensome restrictions which the English government had imposed on commerce. It was a famous tea party in the New England metropolis of 15,000 people that led directly to the War for Independence.

Nevertheless, rural ways and interests continued for many years to dominate the tone of American life, as the population surged westward and the pioneers occupied one new frontier after another. Most Americans seemingly shared Thomas Jefferson's view that populous centers were "pestilential to the morals, the health and the liberties of men." "True," the great Virginian went on, such places "nourish some of the elegant arts, but the useful ones can thrive elsewhere, and less perfection in the others, with more health, virtue and freedom, would be my choice."

Besides, with agriculture still the chief source of national wealth, the need for great hives of humanity was lacking.

Following the Civil War, however, cities began to multiply both in number and in size, and even to approach in magnitude those of the Old World. Between 1860 and 1900 the urban population increased almost five-fold, while the sum total of rural inhabitants hardly doubled.

In the year 1860 only one out of every six Americans lived in towns of eight thousand or more; but in 1880 the proportion was one in four and, as the century closed, one in every three. By 1890 greater New York, with its two and a half million souls, had about caught up with Paris, the world's second city, while Chicago and Philadelphia outranked all but five European centers.

In the Far West, Los Angeles jumped from less than five thou-

sand in 1860 to one hundred thousand in 1900, Denver from nothing at all to one hundred and thirty-four thousand. In the postwar
South, Memphis, Tennessee, leaped from a bare twenty-three thousand to more than one hundred thousand.

This astonishing growth rested on an expansion of manufacturing such as mankind had never before known. Men residing in the
cities led the world in creating new products and launching vast
new industries. The enterprise and resourcefulness which had
earlier gone into conquering the wilderness now turned to these
newer domains of achievement. As a result, the United States became one of the leading industrial countries of the earth, standing
second only to Great Britain.

The challenging opportunities for work and wealth in the cities
attracted hordes of people not only from the American countryside but from all over the globe. Within the United States, many
of the rural districts suffered severe losses of population. In New
England, for example, the drain of inhabitants left silent witnesses in abandoned farms and deserted hill villages whose
crumbling ruins still remind the passer-by of once busy communities. From abroad, thirteen and a half million immigrants came
to our shores between 1865 and 1900, considerably more than the
entire population of the United States in the year 1830. Most of
the foreign newcomers also thronged into the towns and cities.
Horace Greeley, who had once advised, "Go west, young man!"
was now writing, "We cannot all live in cities, yet nearly all seem
determined to do so."

These agglomerations of humanity confronted the American
people with problems of government without parallel in their
history. They had developed their democratic institutions under
simple rural conditions for a widely scattered population. Now,
suddenly, they had also to govern fearfully-growing congested
centers that required such essential daily services as sewerage,
waterworks, street paving, rapid transit, lighting, fire and police
protection, and all the other provisions of modern municipalities.

It is hardly surprising that crooked politicians and grafting officials, joining with unscrupulous businessmen, projected themselves into the situation, reaping enormous gains at the public's
expense from municipal franchises, contracts, subsidies, and tax
concessions.

A notorious instance was the Tweed Ring, which ruled New
York in the late 1860's and early 1870's. Boss Tweed, in effect,
owned the district attorney, the courts, and most newspapers;

within the short period of two and a half years he and his confederates defrauded the city of $100,000,000 or more by means of
dishonest bond issues, the sale of franchises and official favors, and
by other corrupt methods. Upon being exposed, Tweed fled
abroad but was eventually brought to justice. Most of his ac-
complices escaped, however, and later years saw New York again
wallowing in municipal misrule.

Some of the exploiters of the rising cities operated on a country-
wide basis. One group of capitalists, known as the Big Six, controlled the street railways of New York, Philadelphia, Pittsburgh,
and a hundred other communities in the East and Middle West.
They also dominated the gas and electric lighting companies of
about eighty towns and cities. In practically every case, such men
acquired their ascendancy by bribing or browbeating mayors and
municipal councils. Sometimes, to protect their special privileges,
they found it necessary to buy governors and legislatures. In
nearly all instances the citizens suffered from undue charges or
inferior service.

Hardly less detrimental to the public interest were the landlords who, unrestrained by law or conscience, spawned some of
the worst slum districts in all the world. Human misery became
as characteristic of American cities as ostentatious wealth. One
visitor compared New York to "a lady in ball costume, with dia-
monds in her ears, and her toes out at her boots." The same figu-
rative description might have been applied to other great centers.
Little wonder that James Bryce, a sympathetic English critic of
America, in 1888 called the government of cities "the one conspicuous failure of the United States." Thomas Jefferson's darkest
fears earlier in the century seemed to have been realized.

But already individuals were beginning to cry out against the
malpractices and demand reform. One of the earliest was Jacob
A. Riis, a crusading reporter in New York, who exposed the sickening conditions of tenement life and in 1890 won a nationwide
hearing for his cause with his book, *How the Other Half Lives.*
A few years later young Theodore Roosevelt as Police Commissioner of New York succeeded temporarily in ending the alliance
between the supposed guardians of the law and the forces of vice
and criminality.

Then, shortly after the turn of the century, Lincoln Steffens, the
greatest of the so-called muckrakers, wrote a series of widely
read books and articles on *The Shame of the Cities,* which
awakened the American people to the national extent of the dis-

ease. Most of the other muckrakers pounded away at the evils that confronted the federal government, such as the overweening power of Big Business, but Steffens unceasingly preached that reform, to be lasting, must begin at home—at the citizens' own doorsteps.

In the meanwhile a group of progressive mayors, mostly in the Middle West, showed that grit and determination could repair the bitter mistakes of the past. Among the outstanding leaders were Hazen S. Pingree in Detroit, "Golden Rule" Jones and Brand Whitlock in Toledo, Emil Seidel in Milwaukee, Mark Fagan in Jersey City, and Tom L. Johnson in Cleveland.

Johnson, the best remembered of this band, was a self-made man, a wealthy and successful manufacturer, and the owner of numerous street railways in different localities. But he changed the whole course of his life upon reading Henry George's writings on the single tax, and thereafter he devoted his time and energy single-mindedly to the public weal.

As Mayor of Cleveland from 1901 to 1909, he conducted a continuing campaign of education to acquaint the citizens with the needlessly bad conditions and to stir them into supporting enlightened measures for their own welfare. Like his colleagues in the other municipalities, he had first to arouse the voters from their long sleep before he could bring about constructive action. Accordingly, he used a circus tent, moving it about from place to place in the city, and holding meetings in which the humblest member of the audience could ask questions and freely express his own views.

Realizing that some of Cleveland's difficulties arose from restrictive state legislation, Johnson carried his fight into the state at large, and in 1910 he succeeded in obtaining a constitutional amendment which granted Ohio municipalities the right of home rule so that Cleveland and all the other cities of the state could henceforth deal with their own problems in their own way without external political interference.

Johnson's methods paid rich dividends. Though he did not achieve all that he sought, he rooted out graft, placed the street railways under firm municipal control, improved the service while reducing the fares, and brought about a more equitable assessment of real estate. At the same time he planned an imposing civic center and inaugurated an extensive park system. Lincoln Steffens hailed Tom Johnson as "the best mayor of the best governed city in the United States."

To these courageous men and their like in the early years of the century is due much of the credit for the civic renaissance that has occurred since. Their example inspired municipal reformers everywhere, leading to such improved devices of government as the city-manager plan, nonpartisan local elections, and the almost universal practice of civil service qualifications for appointed officials. The old-time political boss, deprived of most of his accustomed props of power, has accordingly found the problem of survival increasingly difficult.

Along with these changes has come an increase of municipally-owned waterworks and other public utilities, and also widespread programs of slum clearance and public housing for the poor. Equally important has been the adoption of systematic city planning in order to provide the people with safer, more convenient, and more attractive surroundings.

Lord Bryce, were he still living, could no longer call municipal government "the one conspicuous failure of the United States." But he would undoubtedly warn the citizens that, unless they are eternally vigilant, these hard-won gains can easily be lost.

The Age of Enterprise

ALLAN NEVINS

The discontent of the farmer that grew into the national movement of Populism, or the ills of labor that were so baldly and so boldly dramatized by the Pullman Strike were not quite the whole story. Harsh, cruel abuses arose, and were fought with a mighty tenacity, but it is easy to cloud the picture, to overemphasize cause and effect, to fit fact to creed. In time reforms came, rather more doggedly than precipitately; writer Ray Stannard Baker said he was always sure reform would sweep the country "until I talked to the man next to me on the street car."

Rather, a cycle was repeating, as once it had been experienced when Bacon's Rebellion planted the seed of the tree of liberty—a conflict between overlapping generations, of men on both sides who were neither all right nor all wrong, all good nor all bad, and who were carried along by a dynamics of history that bent their strength and resources and intelligence and spirit to national

necessity. Only a historian-philosopher can delve into such mean-
ings of an age with quick, clear insight, and Allan Nevins, professor
of history at Columbia University, three-time winner of the Pulitzer
Prize, and teller of distinction of many phases of the American
Story, now makes that essential evaluation.

AT THE end of the Civil War, James Russell Lowell wrote in his
Commemoration Ode that America, calling her sons back from
battle, awaited "the morn of nobler day, enthroned between her
subject seas." What did idealistic Americans, facing the future in
1865, prophesy about this nobler day? They said that the Union
was now saved; that with three million square miles of farm, forest,
and mineral wealth, Americans would count on security and prosperity; and that since their worst faults had been burned away in
the war, they would soon cultivate the fine flowers of life. Politics
would become purer. Letters and art would rise to rarer heights.
Who foresaw the real nature of the postwar era?

Let us take an illustration of what really happened from the
career of Charles Francis Adams, Jr. He came out of the Civil War
at thirty, this grandson of John Quincy Adams, full of ideals and
ambition. He had to begin somewhere. "The change was something terrific," he wrote later. "I had been a full colonel, in command of a regiment. Within the beat of his sentries there is no
one on earth more of a despot than a colonel commanding a regiment. He is supreme . . . Now, I found myself an office-boy—a
mere tenderfoot!" He looked about for ways of making himself
useful. He tried to become a writer. And then he yielded to the
spirit of the age. Where was this Adams in old age? "For over forty
years," he wrote in 1916, "I have been at the head of the Kansas
City Stock Yards Company, directing its policy and development.
When I became President, it was a concern of $100,000 capital . . .
From this I . . . have built it up, always its President, until today
it is capitalized at ten millions, and earns annually over $1,200,000
gross." No longer was an Adams President of the United States;
he was president of the Kansas City stockyards—and justly proud
of it.

Who, we repeat, foresaw the postwar Age of Enterprise? The
answer is, Nobody. In the generation after 1865, did the American
genius burn brightly in politics? On the contrary, no political
leader except Grover Cleveland rose above mediocrity. Did it

flame in literature and art? With all due credit to Howells, Henry James, Mark Twain, to Augustus Saint-Gaudens and Winslow Homer, we fell far short of European achievement. The field in which America excelled was industrial enterprise. Carnegie, Rockefeller, Westinghouse, Duke, Armour, Swift, Havemeyer, Leland Stanford, Harriman, James J. Hill—these were the famous figures. The masses in Europe and South America who had never heard of James A. Garfield or Stephen Crane became as familiar with the names of Rockefeller and Carnegie as with those of Bismarck or Gladstone. For thirty years such men typified America—a very different America from that which Lowell had foreseen.

Why did the advent of the Age of Enterprise take most Americans by surprise? Why was the dismay so great? What were the real achievements and the real faults of that age? What was its legacy to our own time?

It took America by surprise because it bloomed so rapidly and with so little precedent. In 1860 the country had no big business. But the Civil War applied a forcing draft to our Industrial Revolution just as the Napoleonic Wars had applied a bellows to the Industrial Revolution in England. The war furnished capital in fat government contracts, new habits of popular investment, and abundant paper credit. In 1860 the United States had no national market. Only local markets existed for meat, for flour, for clothing, for tools, supplied by local dealers and makers. But after 1865 the country was swiftly covered with a railroad network, which provided a true national market. Great national manufacturers—Armour for meats, McCormick for farm implements, Studebaker for wagons—arose to supply it.

In 1860 the business habits of the country were conservative. After 1865 they were radically progressive, for the war broke the cake of custom, brought aggressive young men to the front, and made people ready to accept bold innovations in technology. In 1860 immigration came in moderate volume. After 1864 it rose to great heights, providing an ample pool of cheap labor. Our Jeffersonian principles of government meanwhile aided big business; for the central government remained weak, and kept its hands-off attitude toward private enterprise. The government's willingness to sell minerals, forests, and lands at rock-bottom prices, and the westward movement of population, made our rich natural resources available to those with capital and energy to grab them. All these factors were focused on American business after 1861. The speed of the ensuing development took men aback.

Indeed, the velocity of the growth, the size of the fortunes accumulated, the power of the trusts, the rapidity with which natural resources disappeared, appalled observers. By 1900 E. L. Godkin was speaking of robber barons; the muckrakers were about to loose their wrath on the oil combine, sugar combine, and meat packing combine; Theodore Roosevelt was ready to launch his reform program. This was natural and healthy. But the real sins of the Age of Enterprise were not at all what the muckrakers thought them. The real achievements were equally misread.

The sins did not grow out of greed for great wealth, as muckrakers said. Carnegie, Rockefeller, Jim Hill became very rich, but they were not greedy men. All three were astonished by the final size of their fortunes. Rockefeller said again and again that it was unforeseen and undesired. Carnegie and Rockefeller devoted their later years to giving away, with system and wisdom, most of their wealth. Nor did the real sin of the Age of Enterprise lie in conscious brutality. Ida Tarbell sternly indicted Rockefeller, J. H. Bridge indicted Carnegie, and Lewis Corey indicted Morgan for brutal activities. But the forces making for industrial concentration were really impersonal economic forces. The necessities of the people called for great business aggregations. We could not do without powerful trunkline railroads, huge steel mills, or a strongly organized system for refining, piping, and marketing petroleum. In short, small units had to be merged into great units. And it cannot be too often said that far more men were bankrupted by the old-time excesses of competition, by the cutthroat business methods of small manufacturers desperately trying to undersell each other, than were bankrupted by the rise of the pools, trusts, and holding companies organized to put some limit on competition. More men were ruined in the chaotic early years of the oil industry, for example, when many hundreds of refineries fought each other tooth and nail, than were ruined by the rise of Standard Oil in the 1870's.

But the main point is that neither conscious greed nor conscious cruelty evoked the huge business concentrations which remade the United States. They were evoked by economic necessities—the necessity for large-scale production to meet the needs of the fast-growing population; the necessity for seizing the economies of quantity manufacture; the necessity for putting some curb upon a price-slashing competition ruinous to everybody.

No, the real sins of the Age of Enterprise have to be stated in different terms. One basic fault of the age was that it applied the methods of the old unco-operative age to a new period which required increasing attention to social ends. The conditions of American life ever since John Smith set his Jamestown settlers to work had produced more individualism than the civilized world had before seen. On the frontier, David Harum's motto applied: "Do unto others as they would do unto you, and do it fust!" Much of the individualism was unsocial. But the small grocer sanding his sugar, the small butcher selling diseased pork, the stagecoach line doubling its rates as soon as ice stopped the canalboats, harmed only a few. One great fault of the Age of Enterprise was that much big business from 1865 to 1900 clung to the old ways. Its heads took the view that the service they gave, the prices they charged, the tricks they played within the law, were their own affair—"The public be damned!"

Actually the time had come when bad food, shoddy cloth, excessive prices harmed tens of millions at a time. Carnegie felt more social responsibility than Frick, Rockefeller had a better social conscience than John D. Archbold. But the general level was too low. The piratical Bet-a-Million Gates said: "I only do openly what Morgan does behind closed doors." Morgan retorted: "That is what doors are for"—which was not an answer.

Another glaring flaw in the Age of Enterprise lay in its relation to government. Big business took control at many state capitals. The trusts grew so powerful that they regarded Washington much as medieval barons long regarded weak kings. By 1900 it seemed a fair question whether government would control business, or business control government. Theodore Roosevelt said in his famous speech at Osawatomie, Kansas: "Exactly as the special interests of cotton and slavery threatened our political integrity before the Civil War, so now the great business interests too often control and corrupt the men and methods of government. We must drive the special interests out of politics." The struggle to make business truly subordinate to government, led by T.R. and Woodrow Wilson, was long and grueling. By 1915 the battle had been decisively won. The task of writing wise economic legislation, however, so that government controls can be effective without crippling free enterprise, will present new problems to every generation.

What is the legacy of the Age of Enterprise? In its early years, public opinion regarded its leaders as builders. The spirit of the time was with them. Few doubted that Singer had been a benefactor in filling the world with sewing machines, McCormick in making reapers abundant, Carnegie in bringing the Bessemer process to America, Rockefeller in standardizing kerosene and giving American oil a world market against Russian competition, Westinghouse in popularizing electrical equipment.

In the muckraking years opinion changed; the Age of Enterprise came under the fiercest criticism. Now that big business is fairly tamed and most heads show a proper social sense, the pendulum has swung back again. On a few men, like Jay Gould, a lasting stigma has been placed. But we can see that a majority of the Great Enterprisers were builders. They gave the country an industrial plant which became indispensable to our high standard of living, and to our victory in two World Wars. Their Age of Enterprise raised our economy to the point where we produce 60 per cent of the wealth of the world. They enabled America to become the bulwark of the free world. That Age—the Age of the Great Moguls—belongs to history. For all its mistakes and sins, it accomplished its mission. How else could this have been done more quickly and efficiently? How else could it have been done with less human strain and suffering? It will be a bold man who essays an answer.

The Immigrant in America

C A R L   W I T T K E

Discontented elements in America were not always satisfied with focusing on the corrupt politicians and the trust magnates as the sole source of their despair. The Know Nothing Party that had flourished in the 1850's as a strongly anti-Catholic movement revealed one of the unpleasant tendencies that could creep into the American character. The farmers who dominated the 1892 convention of the Populists could not rise above their suspicions toward newcomers in general, or newcomers of foreign extraction in particular, and a statement in their platform emphasized "the fallacy of protecting American labor under the present system, which opens our ports to the pauper and criminal classes of the world." Even the rising young Socialist Party split into wings, the more "American" Western sector displaying an open contempt for the Eastern branch of the party. In such books as Refugees of Revolution, *Carl Wittke, professor of history at Western Reserve Uni-*

versity, has, with sound scholarship, explained what the immigrant has meant to America, and with keen sympathy shows what he sometimes has been made to suffer.

I t is a solemn decision to bid farewell to one's native land forever, but some 35,000,000 made that decision in the years before World War I. They turned with hope in their hearts to the great Republic across the sea, confident that it would give them both freedom and bread. Many more millions of present-day Americans, who are listed in the census as natives of this country, had parents or grandparents born in foreign lands, and are descended from a half dozen nationality groups and perhaps as many religious denominations. The grand central motif of United States history has been the impact of successive immigrant tides upon a New World environment. This country has been a mother of exiles, the cradle of a new race of men, and a young nation with Old World memories.

Over forty languages and dialects are still spoken in the United States, and each has supported its own press. The roster of our city governments, as well as in the field of sports, reads like the roll call of the United Nations. The famous "Lost Battalion" of World War I was made up of Yiddish pushcart men and garment workers from New York's lower East Side. Boston is one of the largest Irish cities in the world, and on Patriot's Day the modern Paul Revere begins his ride in the city's Italian quarter.

The blood of 1776 already was a mixed blood, and descendants of Dutch, Swedes, French, Germans, Jews, Scots, Welsh, and Irish are eligible for membership in the Sons and Daughters of the American Revolution. Their ancestors came over in crowded immigrant ships, and often as indentured servants who sold themselves into service because they could not pay for their passage. In the colonial period, the Germans and the Scotch-Irish were the most numerous and the most important of the immigrant groups, and today, "Pennsylvania-Dutch" is the oldest immigrant language still in daily use in the United States.

In the 19th Century, four and a quarter million Irish crowded the shanty towns of our Eastern cities; built many of our canals and railroads; became masters of the game of American politics; and furnished the largest single element in the Catholic Church, which grew rapidly a century ago as essentially an immigrant church. For several decades, the social habits and the religious allegiance of the Irish profoundly disturbed many of their native American neighbors, who believed the newcomers from the Emerald Isle could never be properly Americanized.

About five and a third million Germans arrived before 1914, and introduced the German social and cultural pattern wherever they went. Many went West to farm; others were skilled craftsmen and professional men. Their number included a substantial proportion of intellectuals, the refugees of the German revolutions of 1830 and 1848, who were able to provide the cultural leaven for the whole German group. They organized Turnvereins, singing societies, dramatic performances, libraries, schools, and lecture series; they contended for the liberal Continental Sunday as opposed to American Sabbatarianism; they published more newspapers than any other foreign-born group, and they played a significant role in the politics of the 1850's. They made an outstanding record in the Civil War.

By 1900, over a million Scandinavians had scattered over the American West. They were the vikings of the Western prairie country; their culture was essentially Teutonic, and they came to stay. They were rapidly assimilated and buttressed every worthy American institution with the rugged virtues of the tillers of the soil. Swiss, Welsh, Dutch, French, and Jews continued to come throughout the 19th Century, and each made their contribution in the areas where they settled.

The last quarter of the 19th Century saw a shift in the immigrant tide from northern and western to southern and eastern Europe. Some 14,000,000 so-called newer immigrants arrived before 1920, and provided a sharp contrast with the older stocks in language, customs, political experience, and living standards. Much of the new immigration was a male exodus by men who either had no families or left them at home until they could return with their pockets bulging with American dollars. These "birds of passage" were an entirely new phenomenon in our immigration history. The newcomers represented a score of nationality groups, and each supported its own press and societies. The majority settled in the industrial areas of America, where many of their neighbors were disturbed by the conditions under which they were forced to live. When they established families, their amazing fecundity caused further concern as to what would become of the older stocks in the American population. Comparisons between the new and the old immigration always turned out in favor of the old, but time has proved that in this case also, the processes of Americanization and amalgamation were far stronger than the separation of any national or ethnic group. Today some of the most distinguished Americans in public life and the professions are the descendants of people whom the champions of Nordic supremacy once called barbarians. It is well to recall also that many of the derogatory remarks made in recent times about the newer immigrants were made in almost identical language about the Germans and the Irish a century ago.

A lot of culture has been brought to the United States in immigrant chests, and the immigrant has left his mark on the whole range of our civilization. He helped to build America in industry, business, the professions, politics, art, and music, and provided the inexhaustible labor supply so necessary for America's phenomenal industrial growth. Europeans who came here because they sought political and religious freedom, or greater economic opportunities, have fully repaid the nation which opened its doors to them. There is no difference between the descendants of those who came by Plymouth Rock, or through Castle Garden and Ellis Island, as to their loyalty and devotion to the life of this Republic.

The gates stood open, and virtually unguarded, for a long time, and most Americans believed this country should be a haven of refuge to anyone who wanted to come and share in their democratic experiment. But there has never been a time in our history as a nation when American politics has been free of a nativist agitation against the foreign-born. The high point in the movement to restrict immigration and make it more difficult or impossible for the newcomer to acquire citizenship and participate in public affairs, was reached in the Know Nothing movement of the 1850's. It was marked by violence and hatred, and was not much different in spirit from the later Ku Klux Klan.

It was directed against all foreign born, but mainly at the Irish because of their religion, some of their habits, and their extraordinary activity in American politics. It ended in rioting, bloodshed, and the destruction of property, and, to a large extent, was the product of sheer bigotry and intolerance. On the other hand, some nativist agitation stemmed from lax immigration laws and bad voting procedures, and many Americans believed that the melting pot was boiling over from new ingredients that could not be properly absorbed.

After the Civil War, the United States government began to impose restrictions upon prospective immigrants, intended to keep out criminals and the physically and morally unfit. Men and women in trouble because of their political or religious views were specifically to be exempted from such restrictions, however, and were not to be considered as offenders against the law. World War I and its aftermath produced the climate of opinion which resulted in a complete reversal of an immigration policy which had prevailed since the founding of the Republic. The literacy test was passed over President Wilson's veto in 1917, and was followed by the various quota laws and the National Origins law of the 1920's, which reduced the immigrant tide to a mere trickle in comparison with earlier years.

With this change in fundamental policy, which amounted to a virtual closing of the door either by rigid quotas or other new requirements for immigrants, we came to the close of an era in the history of the United States; it is inconceivable that the doors should ever be opened again as widely as they were for several centuries. Each census shows a steady decline in the number of foreign-born; the fusion of the many nationality groups goes on rapidly, and will eventually produce a typically American amalgam. Many of our people have forgotten that their ancestors came in steerage, but it is well not to forget that they found in America new hope and new opportunities for lives frustrated by unhappy experiences abroad. And they provided for their children, out of the bounty of this new and hospitable land, good things of life which would have been impossible for them at home.

Booker T. Washington: "Up from Slavery"

SAMUEL R. SPENCER, JR.

In 1838 the son of a Negro slave and a white father fled from Baltimore to freedom in the North. His name was Frederick Augustus Washington Bailey—a name he shortened to Frederick Douglass after his escape from bondage. Douglass became one of the most ardent voices of militant abolitionism: lecturer for the Massachusetts Antislavery Society, editor of an abolitionist newspaper, vigorous campaigner for Negro regiments to join in the struggle against the South, an unyielding proponent of Negro suffrage and civil rights. He was the outstanding Negro spokesman of his time; appointed Recorder of Deeds in the District of Columbia, he later became minister to Haiti, and dined in the White House with President Cleveland. He saw members of his race in the South assume political power—at one point, during the years between 1868 and 1873, Negroes were in the majority in the South Carolina House of Representatives. But he also saw the Negro lose many of his new citizenship rights again, in the North as in the South.

In 1895 another son of a Negro slave and a white father rose to leadership—Booker T. Washington, speaking before a white audience in Atlanta and enunciating a conservative doctrine for race relations in the South. "In all things that are purely social," he said, "we can be as separate as the fingers, yet one as the hand in all things essential to mutual progress." Booker T. Washington gave his race two guides: belief in the innate goodness of the white man, and strength through acquiring proficiency in useful labors. He implemented these two guides as an educational leader, as a writer and lecturer, and as an interracial statesman who worked closely with Presidents and industrialists and party politicians.

"Up from slavery" was the thrust of Booker T. Washington's message to the Negroes of America in 1895. Now Samuel R. Spencer, Jr., dean of students at Davidson College, in Davidson, North Carolina, and author of Booker T. Washington and the Negro's Place in American Life, *shows us the will, the intent and the philosophy which made it possible for Washington to help his race begin the hard climb up from bondage.*

ATLANTA was "delirious with excitement and joy" on the evening of September 17, 1895. Eagerly the city awaited the opening of the Cotton States and International Exposition, which would demonstrate to the world the achievements of the New South.

The following day, with a booming of cannon and blowing of whistles, the great event got under way. The uncommon sight of a tall, heavy-set Negro mounting the speaker's platform occasioned no surprise, for the press had announced well in advance that Professor Booker T. Washington would deliver one of the addresses.

Most of the audience knew that Washington was Principal of Tuskegee Institute, an industrial school for Negroes in the Black Belt of Alabama. Starting in 1881 with thirty students and a blind mule, Washington had built his school into a pilot project for Negro education throughout the entire region. Already well-known as an educator, he set forth that day in Atlanta a race relations program which established him as the leading spokesman for Negroes until his death in 1915.

Any plan for easing the race problem, which complicated every other problem of the South that had emerged from the war, would have found an eager audience. During these years the nation's black stepchildren could see little hope and less promise in their future. Economically they were barely better off than before Appomattox, for most had remained on the farms as virtual slaves to the sharecrop and crop-lien systems. Abandoned by Northern friends, Negroes were helpless in the face of a sweeping tide of legal restrictions which relegated them to second-class citizenship.

Booker Washington himself had been a wanderer in the wilderness of freedom. Born a slave on a back-country plantation in the Virginia hills, he was nine years old when he set out with his mother, sister, and brother in a wagon for his post-war home in West Virginia. Here he worked with his stepfather in the salt and coal mines. Here, on a part-time basis, he received the taste of "book learning" which whetted his educational appetite. Here, too, he worked as houseboy for a "hyper-strict" Yankee woman who instilled in him the New England gospel of thrift, propriety, cleanliness, and hard work.

Determined to further his education, he set out in 1872 for Hampton Institute, far across the mountains on the historic peninsula between the York and the James Rivers. The young Negro took all Hampton could give him. He learned most from General Samuel C. Armstrong, who had founded Hampton "to train selected Negro youths who should go out to teach and lead their people." When a letter came from Tuskegee, Alabama, asking for a man to head a new Negro school, General Armstrong recommended Booker T. Washington.

Washington took with him to Tuskegee Armstrong's "industrial education" philosophy, which combined character development and elementary learning with the mastery of mechanical and agricultural skills. Undaunted when he found the new school nonexistent, he met the situation in characteristic fashion. If there were no school, he would create one. If there were no students, he would seek them out. After begging the use of an old church and a dilapidated shanty, he spent a month tramping the hot countryside to meet Negro families and to advertise Tuskegee Institute. The school opened as scheduled—on the Fourth of July, 1881.

Following the Hampton model, Washington proposed to take

young men and women from the farms, train them in agriculture or trades, and send them out to become the backbone of a prosperous citizenry. In industry, he insisted, the foundation of the future must be laid. On such a foundation would grow "habits of thrift, a love of work, economy, ownership of property, bank accounts." These in turn would help to produce moral and religious strength.

Despite some misunderstanding of his project, Washington had the good will of most whites and Negroes. Well-wishers of both races contributed to the purchase of a nearby farm as a permanent site for the school. Many gave pies, cakes, and other products for sale at festivals and bazaars. "Mr. Washin'ton," said one seventy-year-old woman, "I ain't got no money, but I wants you to take dese six eggs, what I's been savin' up, and put dese six eggs into the eddication of dese boys and gals."

Despite local generosity, the growing school demanded larger gifts. An old employee recalled years later that he went each morning with a wheelbarrow to the office where Washington opened the mail. "If there was money in the mail," he testified, "then I could go along to the town with the wheelbarrow and get provisions. If there was no money, then we'd just eat what we had left." By dint of weary pavement-pounding in the cities of the North and East, Washington stimulated a trickle of financial support which eventually flowed in a steady stream.

Meanwhile he and his students were building—always building, for he insisted that the school, as it grew, should be constructed by the students themselves. As early as the second year, Tuskegee citizens who rode out in their buggies for a look at the new school could see evidence of substantial progress. By 1895 the enrollment had reached eight hundred, the staff numbered fifty-five, and the Institute owned property worth more than two hundred thousand dollars.

The fame of Tuskegee brought Washington his invitation to speak at the Atlanta Exposition. This address, later dubbed the "Atlanta Compromise" by his critics, gave him national prominence. He became the friend of the great and near-great. Rising from the social level of the slave cabin to acceptance at the White House and the Court of St. James, he captured the imagination of thousands who read his autobiography, *Up From Slavery*.

His program of race relations, enunciated at Atlanta, rested on the conviction that Negroes should rely on moral and economic means to advancement rather than political. Brains, property, and character were more useful weapons, he said, than statutes. Furthermore, progress must come through cooperation with Southern whites and a recognition of mutual interest. "I quit hating the white man," Washington said, "because it did not do him any harm, and it certainly was narrowing up my soul and making me a good bit less of a human being."

Washington believed that his program would bring lasting, if not immediate, results. On behalf of the Negro he accepted, for the time being, the place assigned him by Southern custom. He asked in return that the Negro be judged not by his color, but by his worth as an individual. Primarily he wanted assurance of economic opportunity, the right to compete with the white man on even terms in agriculture and the rising industries of the New South. Predecessors like Frederick Douglass had taken their lead from Thomas Jefferson; Washington took his from Benjamin Franklin. By over-emphasizing industrial education he high lighted economic progress as a means to full integration and bulwarked future resistance to the lure of Communism.

As Washington's prestige grew after 1895, more militant Negroes took issue with his apparent bargaining-away of Negro rights. Resentful of his political influence and his control over the Negro press, they bitterly attacked his policy of moderation. There were indeed chinks in his armor; but his despotism was benevolent, and his position so well established that the challenge to his leadership was ineffective during his lifetime.

Furthermore, Washington was not blind to restrictions which were crowding in upon Negroes. "I do not overlook," he stated emphatically, "the wrongs that often perplex us in this country." Discrimination in public education particularly galled him. "As no color line is drawn in the courts in the matter of punishing crime," he argued, "neither should any color line be drawn in the opportunity to get education in the public schools." That Washington looked forward to the day of liberty and justice for all cannot be doubted. He accepted half a loaf, not as a permanent settlement, but as a means to the whole loaf later. He did what was possible, given the time and place in which he lived, and did it to the utmost.

Despite his many activities, his heart was always at Tuskegee. Idolized by his students, he was just as interested in the families from which they came. At his annual Tuskegee Conferences he taught scientific farming and home economics to thousands who came on foot, in wagons and buggies, on horseback, and by rail-

road. Tuskegee became the lighthouse of better living for a widening circle which encompassed not only nearby counties but even
the states beyond.

A Northern visitor to the South was asked on his return home
if he had seen Booker T. Washington's school. "School!" he replied.
"I have seen Booker T. Washington's city." By 1915 Tuskegee's
massive brick buildings, neatly landscaped grounds, up-to-date
shops and barns, and twenty-four hundred acres of farmland were
worth the time of any tourist. Almost two thousand young men
and women, neatly uniformed in blue and white, attended as regular students; an equal number benefited from special courses and
extension work. Daughter institutions, founded by Tuskegee graduates, dotted the map of the Southern states.

Both Negro and white Southerners who knew him learned by
example as well as precept the lessons of self-reliance, integrity,
and consideration for one's fellow man. "More and more," he said
late in life, "we must learn to think not in terms of race or color or
language or religion or political boundaries, but in terms of humanity." Such vision belonged not to the past, but to the future. In
an age which was just learning that the color of a man's skin has
nothing to do with his potential contribution to society, the entire
human family benefited from the life of such a man as Booker T.
Washington.

The Frontier Disappears

RAY A. BILLINGTON

*The dreadful bloodletting of the Civil War, the tragedy of the
South under the rule of carpetbaggers, the struggle of the Negro up
from slavery, the impassioned efforts of farmer and laboring man
to wrest legislative cures for social and economic maladies were
spectacular events of the last half of the 19th Century. Yet a quiet
phenomenon was taking place, a powerful catalyst in shaping these
other cataclysms. Out of the controversy of Free State vs. Slave
State in the undeveloped territories had come war; and in the forty
years following, many of America's new problems grew out of the
fact that the frontier, which once had been the symbol of the common man's bountiful opportunity to get ahead through pluck and
persistency, had simply disappeared. To this fascinating subject*

Ray A. Billington now turns; he is professor of history at North-western University and his books include Westward Expansion: A History of the American Frontier *and* The Far Western Frontier.

THE DIRECTOR of the census made a dramatic announcement in 1890. The nation's unsettled area, he revealed, "has been so broken into by isolated bodies of settlement that there can hardly be said to be a frontier line." These words sounded the close of one period of America's history. For three centuries before men had marched westward, seeking in the forests and plains that lay beyond the settled areas a chance to begin life anew. For three centuries they had driven back the wilderness as their conquest of the continent went on. Now, in 1890, they were told that a frontier line separating the settled and unsettled portions of the United States no longer existed. The West was won, and the expansion that had been the most distinctive feature of their country's past was at an end.

The story of that westward march begins in the early 17th Century, when Englishmen began their assault on the deep forests of America at Jamestown and Plymouth. For the next years the advance was slow, as Europeans learned the technique of subduing a wilderness; by 1776 the line of settlements extended only to the crest of the Appalachians. With independence won, and a sympathetic national government ready to provide the frontiersman with self-government and cheap lands, the pace of migration accelerated. Across the broad valley of the Ohio and along the Gulf plains the pioneers marched, until by 1850 their settlements filled the first tier of states lying beyond the Mississippi. There they halted, for ahead lay the unfamiliar environment of the Great Plains, a giant grassland that provided neither timber for homes nor adequate rainfall for crops. Yet so strong was the expansionist urge that even now bolder frontiersmen leaped across this barrier to fill the interior valleys of California and the Oregon country. After the Civil War, when railroads and other man-made devices allowed the conquest of the semiarid plains country, the march was resumed, this time to end only with the West occupied and the continent settled.

Opportunity was the magnet that drew men westward during those three centuries, for nature's untapped riches promised pioneers the fortunes that fate had denied them in older societies. There, where a king's ransom in furs could be had for the taking, where lush grasslands beckoned the herdsman, where fortunes in gold and silver lay scarcely hidden, where virgin soils awaited only the magic touch of man to yield their wealth, men and women could begin life anew with only their brains and brawn and courage to sustain them. There they could realize the social equality that was the goal of every democratically-inclined American. These were the lures that drew the frontiersmen ever westward toward the Pacific.

They moved in an orderly procession. The fur trappers came first, roaming far in advance of the settled areas as they gathered the bales of shiny beaver peltry that would gladden the hearts of Europe's elite. Then came the miners, who also left civilization far behind as they prospected mountain streams and desert wastes in their endless quest for gold or silver. Behind them were the cattlemen, seeking the grassy pastures where their herds could graze without the confinement of fences. Cowboys were a familiar sight on the frontiers of Virginia or Kentucky or Illinois long before they won their place in the sun and cinema on the High Plains of the Far West. These shock troops of civilization made little impression on the wilderness; instead they adapted themselves so completely to the forest environment that they altered the face of the country but slightly.

Not so the farmers who moved westward on the heels of the cattlemen. To them nature was an enemy; every tree was a barrier that stood before the advance of civilization and must be removed. This process was begun by the "pioneer farmers." Nomadic, restless men, they half-cleared the forests, built their cabins, raised a few crops, and then moved on again as neighbors came uncomfortably near. When they moved, they sold their improvements to "equipped farmers" with some capital, who continued cutting away the forests until their clearings met. Behind them came the frontier of villages and towns, where adventuresome merchants and editors and lawyers completed the transformation of the wilderness into a civilized land.

The civilization emerging in this way, however, differed from that of Europe or even of the eastern United States, for as the pioneers moved westward they found that the habits, the institutions, and the cultural baggage of the older societies they had known were out of place in their primitive forest clearings. Highly developed political institutions designed to operate in compact cities were unnecessary in a tiny frontier outpost; complex economic controls were useless in an isolated community geared to an econ-

omy of self-sufficiency; rigid social customs were outmoded in a
land where prestige depended on skill with the ax or rifle rather
than on hereditary glories. So there occurred in each of these
frontier communities a reversion toward the primitive. The settlers
met together to provide such governmental controls as existed;
each man cared for his own economic needs without dependence
on his fellows; cultural progress halted as the frontiersmen concentrated on the primal tasks of providing food, clothing, and
shelter for their families. In this reversion toward a state of nature,
the habits and customs of older civilizations were momentarily
forgotten.

Gradually, newcomers drifted in to swell the population of each
wilderness outpost. As their numbers increased, the community
began a slow climb back toward civilization once more. Governmental controls were tightened and extended, economic specializa-
tion set in, social stratification began, and cultural activities quickened. The process continued until eventually a fully developed
society evolved. This new society, however, differed from the old
from which it had sprung. The accident of separate evolution, the
borrowings from the different lands represented among its founders, the influence of the physical environment in which it developed, all played their part in creating a unique social organism.
It was similar to but different from the older civilizations that lay
to the east.

As this process went on, over and over again, during the three
centuries required to settle the continent, these minute societies
slowly merged to form a nation as unique as the units from which
it was formed. The characteristics of its people and the nature of
its institutions reflected their primitive origin long after the frontier
had passed on westward. An "Americanization" of both men and
society had taken place. The distinctive traits that are associated
with the American people today stem at least partly from the
frontier experience of our ancestors.

This fact does not mean, of course, that our characteristics and
institutions are solely the result of that frontier heritage. The
United States of today is the product of a variety of forces: its
European origins, the continuing impact of ideas from abroad, the
constant mingling of peoples, and the changes wrought by the
Industrial Revolution. Yet none of these forces was more significant than the frontier in endowing the Americans with the traits
that distinguish them from other peoples of the world. Down to

the present time many of our basic attitudes toward society and the world around us reflect that pioneer background.

What are the characteristics that are traceable to this unique feature of our inheritance?

We are a mobile people, constantly on the move, and but lightly bound to home or community. If you were to ask any group of Americans today how many live in the homes where they were born, or where their parents were born, only a handful would reply in the affirmative. If you asked that same question of a group of Englishmen or Frenchmen or Italians, an opposite answer would be given. Like our frontier ancestors, who shifted about so regularly that mobility became a habit, we are always ready for any change that promises to better our lives.

We are a wasteful people, unaccustomed to thrift or saving. The frontiersmen established that pattern, for nature's resources were so plentiful that no one could envisage their exhaustion. Within a few years of the first Virginia settlement, for example, pioneers burned down their houses when ready to move west; thus they were allowed to retrieve nails, and none gave thought to the priceless hardwoods that went up in smoke. As a people we still destroy much that others would save. I had this driven home to me when, during a year's residence in England, I received a letter from one of that nation's largest banks, enclosed in a second hand envelope that had been readdressed to me. Such saving would be unthinkable in the United States, where even the most insignificant bank would never address a client save on elaborately engraved stationery, usually with the names of all twenty-eight vice presidents parading down one side of the page.

We are a practical, inventive people on whom the weight of tradition rests but lightly. In many lands of the world, people confronted with an unpleasant situation will quietly adjust themselves; in the United States, a man's first impulse is to change things for the better. This willingness to experiment came naturally to the pioneers, who had no precedents on which to build. It has remained a trait of the industrial pioneers whose ability to adapt and change has laid the basis for America's supremacy as a manufacturing nation.

We are individualistic people, deeply resentful of any intrusion into our affairs by government or society, also a basic attitude among frontiersmen. Aware that they were living in a land where resources were so abundant that only their own energies were necessary for success, they wanted to be left alone above all else. This trait has persisted in American thought, even though the passing of the frontier has forced the government to adopt a more positive social role. Even today such activity is more resented in the United States than elsewhere; and this resentment also helps explain the almost fanatical American hatred of political systems such as fascism or communism that are based on the subjugation of the individual.

We are a democratic people. Our pioneering forefathers originated neither the theory nor the practice of democracy; the western world was well on its way to political equalitarianism when the continent was settled. But conditions in frontier communities vastly stimulated this trend. There nature reduced men to equality by dimming the importance of wealth or hereditary privilege. There poverty served as a great leveler. There the demand for self-rule was particularly strong, for frontiersmen knew that their problems were unique and must be solved locally. And so on the frontier the democratic tradition was strengthened, until it became a part of the American creed. The undying hatred of the United States for all forms of totalitarianism only mirrors the strength of this faith.

Thus has the frontier placed its stamp on America and its people. In the continuing rebirth of civilization during the three centuries required to settle the continent, nature modified the characteristics of its conquerors, even in the midst of their conquest. There emerged a new people, robust and strong, with an unwavering faith in the merits of the individual and an unswerving allegiance to the principles of democracy. The frontier is no more, but its heritage remains to give strength as well as individuality to the civilization of the United States.

SEVEN

From McKinley

to Wilson

As WINE and ringing bells ushered in the year 1900, Henry James wrote sourly to his old friend, Henry Adams: ". . . of course the past that was our lives is at the bottom of an abyss— if the abyss *has* any bottom . . ." James, at this late date, was rarely that perceptive, and it remains a moot point whether he actually intended saying what he did. But passed by indeed had been those American expatriates who had disinherited their own pioneers while they themselves sought refuge in Europe. At home America seemed to begin in the dying years of the 19th Century to gather a new tempo; it talked "Manifest Destiny" and "Cuba libre" and remembered the *Maine;* it burst headstrong and cocky into the 20th Century, and found, after a time, that it had bitten off more than it had ever wanted to chew.

The three great political figures of these years would be as colorfully diverse as the American contradictions they symbolized. First there was William McKinley, the finest political triumph of Mark Hanna, spoiling the whole wonderful game Hanna had created by falling before an assassin's bullet. Then out stepped the bustling Teddy Roosevelt, so eager to get things moving that he was out of the White House sooner than he wished to be; but still etching his image forever upon the American scene—the flower of progressivism, who dined with a Negro, put a Jew in his Cabinet, and muckraked the muckrakers. Finally the scholarly

259

Wilson emerged, brimming with academic wisdom and cussed-
ness.

Turning these pages in the American Story still brings the excitement of the change, and reveals, despite a good deal of mud-
ding through, that a decent sort of national courage dominated
the era. True, as old struggles blended with new struggles, old
cynicisms bred new cynicisms. It was not within the nature of
human nature for everyone to feel so cock-sure, so full of confidence and hell's-the-other-way optimism as Teddy. Certainly
Mark Hanna seldom felt it after the madman from Oyster Bay
moved to Washington.

McKinley and Manifest Destiny

JULIUS W. PRATT

*Centuries in historical terms rarely begin by the calendar, any
more than William McKinley as the twenty-fifth President of the
United States entered the White House intending to add the
Hawaiian Islands, Puerto Rico, Guam, and the Philippine Islands
to the possessions of the United States. But McKinley, a man of
tact and charm, could be stubborn about a belief once he grasped
it—and stubbornly honest too, along with that political sixth
sense that knew when to compromise a minor issue for a major
gain.*

*Scotch-Irish in background, McKinley worked hard and clung
to his purpose, thus blending the two strains in him. The McKinley
Tariff, going into effect in 1890, placed tariffs on tin plates, not
then manufactured anywhere in the United States, and if one
could be more high-protectionist than that, McKinley wanted to
know how. Defeated for Congress, he served four years as governor of Ohio, and for Mark Hanna—Cleveland's wealthy indus-
trialist and the Republican Party's national boss, who thrived on
charges of "rule with the rich"—here was the man to turn back
Bryan. McKinley conducted a front-porch campaign from his
home in Canton and piled up a popular plurality of some 600,000
votes. Hanna's cup overflowed; prosperity had been made permanent; and those who felt their noses were out of joint could try*

their luck at the gold rush then flourishing in Alaska. The worst throes of the panic of 1893 had been erased; the country was ready to get ahead with new business, and in "Manifest Destiny" it did precisely that. So America had what John Hay called "a splendid little war," and Julius W. Pratt, professor of history at the University of Buffalo and author of Expansionists of 1898 *and* America's Colonial Experiment, *examines that little war and some of its big consequences.*

MEN WERE dying in Cuba with Cuban insurgents and Spanish soldiers shooting each other in guerilla fighting. Women, children, and old men were dying too, huddled in concentration camps where were harbored the supposed friends of the government, not its enemies. Cubans who refused to come into the camps were held to be hostile and shot on sight. Those who came in were promised safety, but food, shelter, sanitation, medicine, and medical care were all lacking. According to some accounts, starvation and disease carried off 200,000 of these people in two years.

What was it all about? Spanish government in Cuba was harsh and undemocratic. Taxation was heavy, and 90 per cent of the taxes collected went to pay Spanish officials, Spanish troops, and a debt resulting from earlier insurrections. Little was left for roads, schools, hospitals, or other public services. Discontent was chronic, but to add to the island's woes, in 1893 came a worldwide depression. The demand and the price for sugar, Cuba's chief product, fell off so sharply that workers in the cane fields and the sugar mills lost their jobs or were put on starvation wages. In February of 1895, thousands of them joined with leaders who raised the cry of Cuban independence. They formed an insurgent government and army. They burned cane fields and sugar mills to make the island valueless to Spain.

Spain countered by sending more troops and a new Captain General, Valeriano Weyler ("Butcher" Weyler he was nicknamed in the United States). Weyler tried to end the rebellion by herding loyal Cubans into the concentration camps and shooting those who stayed out. For three years the war dragged on. Agriculture and industry were at a standstill. A shocking number of Cubans had died; many more were incapacitated by famine or disease. Yet there was no sign of victory for either side.

Cuba lay at the very door of the United States. The struggle of the Cubans for independence, and the suffering of innocent civilians in the concentration camps, made a strong appeal to the sympathy of the American people. Terrible as they were, these sufferings were made to appear even worse by sensational American newspapers, the so-called "yellow press." The American Red Cross sent food and medicines; its head, the venerable Clara Barton, went in person to Cuba to supervise the work in a great effort to relieve the sufferings of the Cuban civilians.

But relief of suffering was not enough. There was a growing demand in the United States that this government should intervene, by force if necessary, to secure independence for Cuba. Newspapers, Senators and Congressmen, clergymen of all the large Protestant churches, were soon crying out in the name of humanity and Christianity that it was the duty of the United States to put an end to this abuse on its doorstep. On the other hand, many conservative people, many businessmen, some politicians like President McKinley's friend and confidant, Mark Hanna, opposed intervention. They doubted the ability of the Cubans to govern themselves, and they feared the effect of a war with Spain on American business.

Grover Cleveland, President till March 4, 1897, held out against intervention. So did his successor, William McKinley, during his first year in office. Then the pressure on him became irresistible. In December, 1897 there were riots in Havana, and as a safeguard for American lives and property, McKinley sent the battleship *Maine* to Havana harbor. There, on the night of February 15, 1898, a terrific explosion sank her at her anchorage. Two hundred and sixty American bluejackets died in the explosion or were drowned in their quarters.

Who or what caused the destruction of the *Maine* has never been certainly revealed. Two boards of American naval officers concluded that she had been sunk by a mine or torpedo exploded under her hull. There is, on the other hand, a possibility that the only explosion was an internal one. Spain made a reasonable offer to submit the whole question to arbitration. But the American public, led by the yellow press, assumed that the *Maine* had been deliberately sunk by an agent of Spain. "Remember the *Maine!*" became the popular watchword.

President McKinley yielded to the pressure, and late in March in 1898 sent Spain an ultimatum. She must agree to an armistice and revoke her concentration camp policy. Spain grudgingly yielded on both points, but too late to satisfy the American President or Congress. On April 20, Congress formally demanded that

Spain give up Cuba, and five days later formally declared war.

A strange war it was, and a one-sided war. Both contestants were unprepared, but Spain's lack of preparation was much worse than ours. Supposedly the purpose of the war was to make Cuba free—Cuba libre, as the Cubans said. Yet the first serious blow was struck half-way around the world from Cuba at Manila Bay in the Philippines. There, on May first, Commodore George Dewey led his ships through the mine fields at the entrance to the harbor. In a few hours the antiquated naval vessels of Spain's Asiatic squadron had been destroyed—all without loss of an American life.

Why did the war for Cuba libre begin in the Philippines, thousands of miles from Cuba? First, because the Spanish ships there, if not destroyed, might attack and damage American commerce. But there was a deeper reason. To some Americans, Spain's empire in the Philippines, rich in sugar, hemp, and coconut products, with a wonderful harbor at Manila, looked like a rich prize. To some Americans it seemed that the United States had kept too long within its continental boundaries. The time had come, they thought, when it should reach out for distant naval bases and colonial possessions in competition with other great powers.

Several lines of thought led to this conclusion. American devotees of Charles Darwin's theory of evolution pointed out that upward progress came through a "struggle for existence," in which "the fittest" survived and passed on their victory-giving qualities to posterity. Let the United States, they said, join the international struggle. Surely the American people have what it takes to survive and conquer. That way lies progress.

A second line of thought, a racialist line, acclaimed the political genius of the "Nordic" races, especially the Germans and Anglo-Saxons. These Nordics were adept at government. Let them, therefore, bring good government to the ill-governed regions of the world.

A third line of reasoning, spearheaded by the scholarly naval officer, Captain Alfred Thayer Mahan, emphasized the important role of sea power in making a nation great and strong. And sea power included not only a navy and merchant marine, but colonies and naval bases in distant quarters of the globe.

All of these ideas were brought to a focus and given practical application by the coming of the war with Spain. Here was the opportunity, all at once, to join in the international struggle for power, to extend the blessings of American government to colonies long misgoverned by Spain, to acquire a rich colony in the Philippines, and naval bases from among Spain's other possessions in the Caribbean and the Pacific. An old phrase of the Mexican War period was revived. "Manifest Destiny" pointed to American expansion in the Caribbean and the Pacific.

And so the war to free Cuba became a war of expansion, of "Manifest Destiny," though William McKinley was hardly aware of the transformation till it was all over. Among the men who shaped the new policy of expansion were Theodore Roosevelt, Assistant Secretary of the Navy before the war began and later lieutenant colonel of the "Rough Riders" in the war in Cuba; his friend, Henry Cabot Lodge, Senator from Massachusetts; and Captain Mahan. It was Roosevelt who had planned the attack on Manila Bay and had picked Commodore Dewey to lead it.

Two months after Dewey's victory at Manila, the main Spanish fleet was destroyed in a running fight near Santiago, Cuba. The city of Santiago was under attack from the landward side. On July first "Teddy" Roosevelt led the footsore "Rough Riders" (their horses had been left in Florida!) in a charge up San Juan Hill, or more accurately its neighbor, Kettle Hill. Other outer defenses were taken on the same day, and on July 17 the city was surrendered. Spain now asked for peace. An armistice was signed on August 12, and in October, American and Spanish commissioners met in Paris to write a treaty.

President McKinley, slowly feeling his way, at last adopted the program of the "Manifest Destiny" boys, who insisted that we must follow up Dewey's victory by keeping the Philippines. He was under several kinds of pressure to do so. Businessmen, who had been reluctant to go to war with Spain, now saw in the Philippines a guarantee that the United States should have its full share of trade with China. The Protestant churches sensed a divine call to mission work among the Filipinos even though most of them were Catholic Christians. It was argued too that if we did not keep the islands, the alternative was their misgovernment by Spain or their seizure by some rival power, like Germany or Japan.

So McKinley decided. The commissioners in Paris were told we must have the Philippines—for which we paid Spain $20,000-000; also the little island of Guam in the Pacific and Puerto Rico in the Caribbean. Hawaii, an independent republic, had joined us voluntarily during the war. Cuba would become free, but held for a while with leading strings by the United States.

So, in the treaty signed on December 10, 1898, and ratified a few weeks later, the United States took its place as a great power on the world stage. It accepted the imperial mission to which, as people like Theodore Roosevelt believed, "Manifest Destiny" called it. That mission, as we now know, was to be one not of perpetual empire, but of preparing colonial peoples for self-government or independence. Its chief fruits are seen today in the self-governing commonwealth of Puerto Rico, remaining of its own choice under the Stars and Stripes, and the independent Philippines, the most dependable outpost of the free world in the Far East.

The Incomparable Teddy

ELTING MORISON

A friend of the Roosevelt family told of a walk with Teddy and his wife. "We came to a hill," he said. "Teddy charged up. His wife did not change her gait, and the remarkable thing is that they both reached the top at about the same time."

But Theodore Roosevelt simply had to release the abundant energy he possessed; at the age of forty-two he became the youngest man ever to occupy the White House. It was said the same overactive glands stimulated all sorts of worries, and Teddy was surely the biggest worry Mark Hanna faced in a political lifetime. With young Roosevelt in the Presidency, the nation's big business interests shivered. "I shall go slow," Teddy assured Hanna; and at first he did.

Elting Morison, a member of the faculty of the School of Industrial Management at the Massachusetts Institute of Technology, and editor of the eight-volume The Letters of Theodore Roosevelt, *frankly admires Teddy and recaptures the buoyant spirit of one of the most deeply loved men ever to play a climactic part in the American Story.*

EVERYBODY knows that Washington couldn't tell a lie and had false teeth, that Franklin flew a kite, that Lincoln had a mole on his face and dreamt bad dreams, that U. S. Grant drank whisky, and that Calvin Coolidge didn't talk much. It is interesting to wonder why we remember these things and forget, for instance, equally remarkable things about other men in our history—such as the fact that Daniel Webster had eyes that burned like coals of fire, that Henry Clay probably drank as much whisky as Grant, or that John Randolph rode a horse in the black of night shouting, "Macbeth doth murder sleep."

This mental shorthand sometimes obscures our recollection of big things. Take the case of Theodore Roosevelt: what comes to mind are the teeth, the grin, the spectacles. Maybe some will recall his days in the Badlands of the Dakotas, where he worked as a cowboy; maybe a few will remember the Rough Rider, the words "delighted" and "Bully"; others will remember the days in 1912 when he stood at Armageddon, fighting for the Lord (his way of saying he was willing to start a new political party that would nominate him for the Presidency of the United States).

These things are all true enough; they are the outward visible signs of a tremendous personality that for a time laid a kind of spell over the country. They are, taken all together, some of the things, certainly, that made Theodore Roosevelt one of the great vote-getters in our history. But they do not explain in themselves what Theodore Roosevelt actually did for his country. They do not describe why he deserves to be remembered in our history.

What, then, did he do? One must begin far back in his life to find the start of his public service. As a very young man, just graduated from Harvard College, he stood for election to the state legislature in New York. There, for four years, he got the foundations of his political education, learning how to carry his own ward, how to frame a bill, and how to mobilize support for his views by persuasion, necessary compromise, and sound argument.

Some years later, in 1889, he became a Civil Service Commissioner in Washington. For four years he talked, argued, and fought to eliminate undue political influence in the appointment of men to the federal offices. His aim was to obtain, by careful selection, the ablest and most honest officials to run the complicated machinery of our government. From this post he went back to New York City to become Police Commissioner, and from there, in 1897, he traveled again to Washington, to become Assistant Secretary of the Navy. In that post he did his best to prepare the navy for the war with Spain in 1898, in which he himself fought bravely as a lieutenant colonel of the Rough Riders.

His dramatic part in this war attracted so much attention that, upon his return from Cuba, he was elected governor of the State of New York. During the next two years he made a fine record—by the selection of very able men in state offices, by his quick and efficient action to eliminate fraud in some departments, and by the support he gave to sensible legislation protecting labor and ordering industrial enterprise. In fact he did so good a job that in 1900, the political boss of the state, T. C. Platt, "kicked him upstairs to the Vice Presidency" to get him out of the way. Another boss—Mark Hanna—who was the intellectual power behind the McKinley Administration, was not so pleased as Platt by this maneuver. "Don't you realize," he said, "that there is but one heartbeat between the White House and this madman?"

And when McKinley's heart stopped beating, Theodore Roosevelt—"that madman," "that cowboy"—became President of the United States. His preparation for the job was excellent—a state legislator and governor, a city official, a two-time officer in the federal government, a soldier. What then were the results in actual practice of such training?

Let us look at some of these things. First there are some specific acts that are worth noting—the construction of the Panama Canal, the building up of the navy, the enlargement of the civil service, the insistence upon honest administrators in all parts of the government, the attraction of first-rate minds and characters to government service, and the development and maintenance of honorable, progressive, decent government in our island possessions.

These acts are all substantial contributions to the ordering of this country's affairs. But the greater importance of Theodore Roosevelt lies in his efforts to increase his own and his countrymen's understanding of the kind of world they lived in. He was the first President to recognize clearly the meaning of industry. He was the first man in his office to describe clearly not only the problems but the possibilities presented by industrial energy. When he assumed office, there was the growing probability that the wealth and power concentrated in the hands of a few corporations would create grave and dangerous imbalances in our national life, that the accumulated power of some industrial organizations would in time be greater than not only the power of individual citizens or communities to protect themselves, but also greater than the power of the national government itself.

By words and actions, Theodore Roosevelt strove to explain the nature of this grave danger and to provide by dissolution of the "bad" trusts and control of the "good" ones sensible solutions for

the problem thus presented. But he tried equally hard to find a
useful balance in suggesting his solutions. He recognized more
clearly than most of his contemporaries that this was, as he said,
an industrial society whose future depended upon the good health
and development of our industrial enterprise. Therefore he tried,
throughout his term of office, to establish sensible regulations
within which our industry could flourish without damaging the
social fabric. Today these attitudes toward our industry and ourselves are commonplace. But the progress we have made in this
area rests, in considerable part, upon the wisdom and intelligence
Theodore Roosevelt brought to the task of educating himself and
his constituency.

A second educational contribution lay in his attempt to explain
that this country was no longer an island unto itself, but a working
member of a community of nations. The cruise of the battle fleet
around the world, the Portsmouth treaty between Russia and
Japan, the prompt action in the Venezuela crisis, the participation
in the Algeciras Conference[1] were all efforts to demonstrate, at
home and abroad, that this country lived in the world as an important part of the whole.

There is something else one should mention in casting up these
accounts—not a dramatic action, a sound political decision, or
a wise foreign policy—not any of these, but simply an attitude
toward life. Wherever Theodore Roosevelt was there was also a
kind of brightness in the atmosphere. This brightness he com-
municated to the whole people; during his terms of office there
was a feeling that life was fun, and that governing oneself was
exciting. Because he believed in himself, he made most men believe in themselves. One person who lived through those times said,
"We woke up every morning wondering what new adventure we
were off on when Roosevelt was President." And Roosevelt, of
course, was always off on adventures of his own—on the plains
and mountains of this country, on the rivers of South America,
in the jungles of Africa, and in the palaces of Europe.

He was, as we remember, fascinating; he was exciting with a
wonderful way of finding just the right word for his purpose. He

[1] In 1905 war in Europe seemed to hang in the balance as Germany demanded
a share in the control of Morocco. Great Britain had secretly agreed that
France should be the dominant power in Morocco and that in exchange Britain
should not be disturbed in exploiting the Egyptian Sudan. Germany had been
handling about a fifth of Morocco's trade and wanted her interest recognized.
Roosevelt backed Germany's opponents, and at the suggestion of the Kaiser
arranged a conference at Algeciras, Spain, to pacify the contending parties.

did have big teeth and thick glasses, and he did fight both at San Juan Hill and Armageddon, but he belongs permanently in our gallery of great men because, as President, he recognized that America was an industrial society with extraordinary opportunities to build an industrial civilization that would satisfy its members; because he recognized that America could no longer live in solitude; and because he gave his countrymen a feeling that to live in such a society, and take part in the affairs of the world, was a great and worthwhile adventure.

Passage to India—at Long Last

JAMES SHENTON

Under Teddy, things happened. In 1903 the Pacific cable was completed, wireless communication had been proven practical, the Wright brothers made their successful flight at Kitty Hawk, and the Department of Commerce and Labor was established. In the next few years the Pure Food and Drug Act was passed, the United States Forest Service was created, Oklahoma brought its corn as high as an elephant's eye into the Union, and whereas other business leaders had grave doubts about an automotive industry, Henry Ford organized the Ford Motor Company, and six years later would produce the first "Model T." And in 1906, construction of the Panama Canal as a lock canal began, fulfilling a dream which, as James Shenton, historian at Columbia University, tells us, realized one of man's oldest dreams.

ALTHOUGH Columbus did not realize it when he made his first journey in search of a Passage to India in 1492, he had discovered two vast continents. These, for more than four centuries, were to remain effective barriers to the numberless explorers who followed him in search of a similar passage. Only the explorer with the courage of a Magellan dared the turbulent waters of Cape Horn. Truly the passage around the Horn brought the traveler into the calm Pacific, but so often did the perilous journey end in disaster that the search for a safer route continued unabated. Up the Mississippi and the St. Lawrence, along the wide Amazon men journeyed, only to learn that they had penetrated into the hearts of vast continents rather than to the wealth of fabled India. Later men were to realize that the wealth concealed within the new continents was greater than any India could offer. But the promise of India was immediate; the promise of the Americas was future.

Only along the narrow waist of the Isthmus that divided the Pacific from the Caribbean did a route exist which involved less than forty miles of land travel. Almost from the moment of Balboa's discovery of the Pacific, the idea of a man-made passage to India began to agitate men's imaginations. One of Balboa's lieutenants had, between 1517 and 1529, conducted extensive surveys in order to determine the best route for a canal across the Isthmus, but his efforts came to naught. The explosive Spanish energy successfully created a vast empire, but it burned itself out in the effort. The proposed canal remained nothing but a grandiose dream. During the three centuries of Spanish dominance, the treasure and produce of western North and South America was laboriously shipped across the stone-paved highways that the Spaniard cut through the jungles of the Isthmus.

As the Spanish grip upon Middle and South America loosened, a new nation began to take form far to the north. With ever-increasing speed, it began to lay claim to the almost uninhabited northern reaches of first the Spanish Empire, and then the Mexican Republic. An eminently practical people, the Americans believed that possession represented at least 99 per cent of the law. Convinced it was their "Manifest Destiny" to rule a continent, they did not allow their consciences to quibble over the petty details of rightful possession. They brought together their ever-expanding continental empire with railroads. Across the vast Western prairies and the massive Western mountains, they built steel passages to India. Possessed of the richest third of a continent, the Americans turned with longing eyes toward the tropical remnants of the fast-crumbling Spanish Empire. The fate of Middle America, they were convinced, was indisputable; it was to be theirs. The only question left for settlement was whether they would conquer peacefully or with the sword.

Mexico had fought to maintain itself against the onslaught of the Yankee but had lost. Upon Mexico's surrender, the Polk Administration had divided over the issue of how to settle with the defeated Mexican. President Polk had insisted that divesting Mexico of Texas, California, and New Mexico was enough, but his fiery Secretary of the Treasury, Robert Walker, had demanded "total annexation" of Mexico. Denied all of Mexico, Walker, who preached that the American destiny was "continental," insisted the Americans receive the right to build a canal across Mexico's Tehuantepec Peninsula. The Mexicans conceded the right, but the tangled wilderness of Tehuantepec proved too much even for the dynamic Yankee.

But having once been accepted by the American imagination, the idea for a canal recurred with increasing frequency. As the conservative politician attempted to prevent the coming of civil war, increasing attention was paid to the possibility of American expansion into the tropical regions of Middle America. Here, if anywhere, the Southerner might find new lands able to support his peculiar institution of slavery, and privately-backed invasions of Central America by American citizens left the region in perpetual turmoil. Schemes for canals across Honduras or Nicaragua were broached with increasing frequency. If will had been enough, the region would have been crisscrossed with canals.

However, will was not enough. The mysterious yellow fever and malaria made life hazardous, and equipment capable of cutting through the jungle and hills of Central America did not exist. Above all, the European powers, England and France, refused to allow the Americans to dominate the Isthmus. Reluctantly, in 1850, the Americans agreed to the Clayton-Bulwer Treaty which stipulated that neither Britain nor America would "ever obtain or maintain for itself . . . exclusive control" over any ship canal built across Nicaragua. The two countries also agreed to extend jointly their protection over any canal or railway built . . . "across the Isthmus . . . especially . . . by way of Tehuantepec or Panama." That treaty endured until 1901. Only after American power had become overwhelming did the United States assert its right to build a canal independently of foreign interference.

Although the right of a sovereign power to build a canal across the Isthmus was held in abeyance during the latter half of the 19th Century, nothing kept private enterprise from attempting the feat. Ferdinand de Lesseps, flushed from his successful construction of the Suez Canal in 1869, agreed to assume the leadership of a project to build a canal across Central America. An international congress which met at Paris in May, 1879 agreed to construct a sea-level canal across the narrow waist of Panama. The prospect of foreign control, even if private, brought a storm of protest from the United States. President Hayes insisted that "an interoceanic canal across the American Isthmus . . . would be the great ocean thoroughfare between our Atlantic and our Pacific shores, and virtually a part of the coast line of the United States."

Despite American protests, de Lesseps' company, amply backed by an eager French public, began construction on a large scale in 1883. Although considerable work on the canal was completed by 1889, the original estimate of $240,000,000 proved woefully inadequate. In February, 1889, the French courts placed the company in receivership. Scandals rocked France as it became apparent that fraud and bribery of public officials had characterized the company's activities. An aged de Lesseps died in disgrace, having been sentenced to a five-year prison term.

The defrauded French stockholders, eager to salvage something from their investment, sought to sell their rights to the partially built canal. The New Panama Company was formed out of the wreckage of the old company, and substantial holdings were transferred to American investors. Especially interested were the stockholders of the Panama Railroad Company. Representing this group was William Nelson Cromwell, a corporation lawyer, who was described as having ". . . an intellect that works like a flash of lightning, and it swings about with the agility of an acrobat." Philippe Bunau-Varilla, de Lesseps' engineer, although possessed of substantial holdings in the new company, supported the project out of a profound conviction that a canal could and ought to be built across the Isthmus. Despairing of any further French support, he turned to American aid and found his strongest supporter in Mark Hanna, the Republican Party boss. Hanna acknowledged "the operation of canals was one of the few subjects with which in my business life I had become acquainted in all directions." Less friendly sources suspected that Cromwell's reported $60,000 contribution to Republican campaign funds had whetted Hanna's interest in canals.

Over the opposition of supporters of the Nicaragua Canal route, Hanna pressed his campaign for the Panama route. The almost bloodless victory of the United States over Spain in 1898 had placed the Americans in control of an overseas empire for the first time. As continental "Manifest Destiny" had demanded the building of transcontinental railroads to bind together the vast territories of the United States, so imperial "Manifest Destiny" made the construction of a canal connecting the Atlantic and Pacific imperative. Nor had the meaning of America's new empire escaped the attention of the outside world. Britain abandoned her insistence that America abide by the provisions of the Clayton-Bulwer Treaty. On November 18, 1901, Secretary of State John Hay and the British ambassador, Lord Pauncefote, concluded a new treaty which gave the United States the right to build and operate a canal across the Isthmus.

The Hay-Pauncefote Treaty signaled that the United States had committed itself to the construction of a canal. The supporters of a canal across Nicaragua, fortified with the knowledge that their route had fewer obstacles to a successful conclusion, pressed their case in Congress. The New Panama Company, fearful of finding itself burdened with a white elephant investment, vigorously fought back. It offered its entire property to the United States canal commission for $40,000,000. On January 28, 1902, Senator Spooner proposed a compromise solution to the conflicting claims of the Nicaragua and Panama Canal supporters, authorizing the President to purchase the Company's properties, provided a satisfactory treaty guaranteeing American rights in Panama could be obtained from Colombia within a "reasonable time." The compromise was, in fact, offered by Spooner as a direct result of Theodore Roosevelt's decision to support the Panama route.

Once Teddy had made up his mind that the canal was to use the Panama route, he proposed to allow nothing to stand in his way. When Colombia, of which Panama was then a province, proved stubborn in the negotiations which were meant to secure the American rights to the Canal Zone, he calmly informed Hay, "I am not inclined to have any further dealings whatever with those Bogotá people." His final decision was put with even greater bluntness to Mark Hanna, in a letter that concluded, "I feel that we are certainly justified in morals . . . in interfering summarily and saying that the canal is to be built and they must not stop it."

By October, 1903, Roosevelt was thoroughly aware of the fact that the Panamanians, eager to benefit from the construction of a canal, were prepared to revolt against Colombia if the treaty granting the United States construction rights was not approved. Guns and other munitions of war were ". . . smuggled into the city of Colón in piano boxes and merchandise crates" until ". . . nearly every citizen of Panama had some sort of rifle or gun in his posession with ammunition . . ." Nor did Roosevelt propose to allow a successful Colombian counterattack. Ships of the navy were ordered to Panamanian waters with specific orders to prevent the landing of Colombian troops ". . . if in your judgment this would precipitate a conflict." The result was a foregone conclusion. On November 6, 1903, the United States extended recognition to the new Panamanian government. Theodore Roosevelt had fathered a new nation. In gratitude, Panama granted the United States all the rights it desired for building a canal.

Not until 1914 did Columbia express its willingness to recognize Panamanian independence. The uneasy American conscience had persuaded itself that paying a $25,000,000 indemnity to Colombia, and an apology expressing sincere regret that any unfortunate incident ". . . should have occurred to interrupt the . . . cordial friendship that had so long subsisted between the two nations" would prove proper atonement for an improper act. An angry Roosevelt, who had in 1911 boasted that he "took the canal zone," argued "Either the course we took in 1903 was right, in which case it is worse than an outrage now to pay blackmail, or it was wrong, in which case we have now no right to be on the Isthmus." If the latter were the case, he concluded, "it would be a shameful thing for us to celebrate the opening of the Canal." Roosevelt's protests were sufficient to prevent any final settlement. Not until 1921 did the Colombians receive their $25,000,000 indemnity; the apology remained unspoken.

In August, 1914, the canal was opened to traffic. The long-sought passage to India had been built with the sweat of men's brows. In the more than four centuries of man's search for the legendary route, continents had been subdued, and men and women by the millions had come in search of a better day. That such should have happened was only right, for what was the passage to India but humanity's search for a better future? Walt Whitman had summed it all up in his passionate poetry when he wrote:

> Passage to India!
> Lo, soul, seest thou not God's purpose from the first?
> The earth to be spann'd, connected by network,
> The races, neighbors, to marry and be given in marriage,
> The oceans to be cross'd, the distant brought near,
> The lands to be welded together.
> . . . , not for trade or transportation only,
> But in God's name, and for thy sake O Soul.

Knowingly or not, the men who had built the canal had made the world smaller, and brought it closer to the day when it had to reckon with whether it would be as one or many, whether it would live or die.

Realism in American Literature

HOWARD MUMFORD JONES

Tolstoy, Zola, Ibsen . . . in Europe's turbulent struggle between the forces of environment and economics, these were the realists who had arisen to fashion a literature that would have meaning to their generation at home and abroad. Howells, Garland, Norris . . . in America, too, the realists were emerging to dissect American life, to probe the American character, to reveal the resources of the American spirit. Among our authorities on the intellectual history of the United States, none surpasses Howard Mumford Jones, professor of English at Harvard University, whose numerous books include The Theory of American Literature.

In any discussion, such as "American Writers Look at American Life: Realism in American Literature," there are two elements that offer some difficulty. In the first place, no matter how you define "realism," it must not be thought that only realists look at American life. Romantic writers look at it also; for example, Longfellow, in *The Courtship of Miles Standish;* and though Longfellow's poetry is just now out of fashion, the sentiment, the color, the motivation of this love story are quite as representative of American things as are the novels of William Dean Howells or Frank Norris. The second difficulty lies in the word "realism." Realism is one of those words, the meaning of which everybody more or less understands and the definition of which nobody can give.

When the term "realism" is used in literary discussion, it may have a number of meanings. I shall discuss two. In a general sense it can be said that all works of literature are either classical, romantic, or realistic; and it has long since been established that classical literature tends to picture man as he ought to be, romantic literature pictures man as he would like to be, and realistic literature pictures man as he is. These are vague, yet helpful distinctions. Probably no one was ever so ideally heroic as Hector appears to be in the *Iliad*, so perfect, so brave, so adventurous, so witty as D'Artagnan in Dumas' *The Three Musketeers*, a perfect example of a romantic personage. But if you read a novel like

Barchester Towers by Anthony Trollope you are in a world populated by ordinary human beings who are not very good, and not
very bad, who do not die heroically, who do not have brilliant
adventures, but whose thoughts and emotions are even as yours
and mine.

This type of art came to dominate much American writing in
the last quarter of the 19th Century. Its best theorist was the novelist, William Dean Howells, who practiced what he preached. In
an influential book entitled *Criticism and Fiction,* published in
1891, he applied the general principles of realism to the American
novel. Romantic writing as commonly practiced he thought was
false to our way of life. He compared the romantic writer in
America to somebody who had manufactured an artificial grasshopper out of wire and cardboard and who said to the scientists:
"I see you are looking at a grasshopper there which you have found
in the grass, and I suppose you intend to describe it. Now don't
waste your time . . . in that way . . . The thing that you are proposing to do is commonplace." Howells argued that the way to
find out about grasshoppers was to study and describe real grasshoppers, not artificially perfected imitations; that is, to write of
the American people as they are, not as they ought to be, or as
they dreamed of being.

What are the Americans? Well, said Howells, they "are really
a mixture of the plebeian ingredients of the whole world." But this
is far from being a bad thing. It gives them a certain strength, a
certain cheerfulness. "It is worth while," he said, "even at the risk
of being called commonplace, to be true to our well-to-do actual-
ities." "Such beauty and such grandeur as we have," he said further, "is common beauty, common grandeur"—and those of you
who know Emerson's "American Scholar" address will see that
what Howells is doing is to continue Emerson's injunction to embrace the common, to explore and sit at the feet of the familiar,
the low. Howells argued that the conditions of American life,
which lack an aristocracy, invite the artist to study and present
ordinary, democratic life. He wrote: "The arts must become democratic, and then we shall have the expression of America in art."
For Howells, democratic life was essentially the life of the American middle class.

His best-known novel, *The Rise of Silas Lapham,* issued in 1885,
exactly fulfills his formula. Silas and his wife are both middle-
aged and middle-class, with the habits and tastes, the defects and
virtues of their tradition. Howells takes you into their home, lets

you overhear their speech (no one had a better ear for American talk than this novelist), and compels you to undergo with them both the moral and the financial crises of their lives. Silas sinks in the financial scale, but he rises in the moral scale; and although it is not literally true that this is the first time a middle-aged pair had appeared importantly in an American book, this is the first time such an American family had been made central to an important American novel.

In *The Rise of Silas Lapham* Howells accepts the society in which this couple lives, and does not find fault with it. But beginning with *A Hazard of New Fortunes,* in 1889, Howells sought likewise to expose the weaknesses of American society and to suggest ways of improving it. During the next twenty years more and more of his fiction was devoted to inquiring why middle-class America did not work according to plan. Howells thought we ought to swing more and more in the direction of Socialism. This combination of sympathetic insight into ordinary American lives with a zeal for social and political changes intended to enrich ordinary American life, characterized not only Howells in his later books but also the group of writers one associates with him.

Prominent among these are Hamlin Garland and Frank Norris. In a series of short stories, the best collection of which is *Main-Traveled Roads* (1890), and in various novels, long and short— for example *Rose of Dutcher's Coolly* (1895)—Garland, himself a farm boy from the Middle West, portrayed the lives of American farm folk before the telephone, the radio, electricity, the automobile, and mechanization had brought city comforts to the farm.

Frank Norris took for his principal subject life in California, and the implications of large scale farming there. An early novel of his, *McTeague* (1899), concerns the life of a fake dentist, who is also a huge brute of a man; the characters in the novel are each motivated by a single dominant desire; and though *McTeague* contains some of Norris's most powerful writing, including vivid descriptions of life in San Francisco, because of the influence of Zola it is less characteristically American than are *The Octopus* (1901) and *The Pit* (1903), parts of an unfinished trilogy concerning the growing, marketing, and shipping of the wheat crop.

In both novels Norris's contention is that bad business practices have American life by the throat; in *The Octopus* a railroad monopoly so frustrates the wheat growers that they rise in armed rebellion—a futile rebellion, it proves; and in *The Pit* the inhuman practices of the Chicago grain pit wreck the hero's career and almost wreck his marriage. Both books pass beyond Howells's contentment with ordinary life. They tend to be epic in dimension, and even a little mystical, but they are nonetheless part of the literature of realism by virtue of their interest in processes, their exact (and exacting) pictures of contemporary America.

An element that Howells tended to soft-pedal is important in the work of both Garland and Norris. These novelists give much attention to sexual energy. Howells recognized the importance of biology, but he thought it could not be permitted in books for a reading public mostly composed of women. Accustomed as we now are to the much franker portrayal in contemporary fiction, the treatment of this theme by Garland and Norris may seem to us today rather timid and genteel. These matters are, however, relative. In Norris, women are not pictured as soul mates, but they are pictured as a kind of athletically perfect beings, who in union with their husbands are to produce a superior American race. How far this parallels the growth of physical training for women as well as for men is an amusing question; and how far this attitude toward women is an "American" attitude is a point endlessly under debate.

Of course there were other realistic novelists—Gertrude Atherton, H. H. Boyesen, Harold Frederic, Henry B. Fuller, Robert Grant, Robert Herrick—even Mark Twain, in such a book as *Pudd'nhead Wilson.* In another sense of realism—this time, having to do with human psychology—Henry James was perhaps the best realist of the age. And of course Edith Wharton, Ellen Glasgow, and Willa Cather followed where James led. And realism is very much with us today, sometimes in the extreme form of naturalism, represented by Theodore Dreiser or James T. Farrell, or in the extreme form of psychological naturalism, as in such a book as Salinger's *The Catcher in the Rye* (1951) or parts of William Faulkner's work—for example, *The Sound and the Fury* (1929). But by the term "realism" one commonly refers to the writing done by the generation of Howells, Garland, and Norris.

What did realism accomplish for American life? Despite the contradiction that theories of realism were invented in Europe before they were in the United States, one of the principal effects occasioned by the realists was to increase American independence from European writing. The careful treatment given a particular scene, the conscientious description of things and persons as they actually are in the United States, the noting of American speech habits, American ways, American traditions inevitably concentrated attention upon life here and now. In the second place, for better or worse—and there is constant discussion of the problem—American realists tended to diminish the appeal of idealism to artists and their public. At the beginning of the 19th Century a group of writers in Connecticut were still struggling to begin American literature with epic poetry comparable to Homer and Virgil. Ideally, that is the way a national literature ought to begin. The realists had no truck with this nonsense, so to speak; they more or less ended the search for the Great American Epic and for the Great American Novel. But in so doing they also diminished the sense that literature is something that is good in proportion as it reaches an ideal form, or depicts the failure of men because they do not follow moral ideals. Part of the present bewilderment of Americans as to what the country is and what it ought to be is probably due to the successful attack upon all forms of idealism begun by the realists. But finally, and most importantly, in their best novels, the realists have left us trustworthy and unforgettable pictures of average American life as it actually was during the latter part of the 19th Century and subsequent years.

The Birth of The Ash Can School

J A M E S T H O M A S F L E X N E R

And what of our artists at this period? What influences sent them scurrying off to Europe, certain that otherwise they must die creatively—and what influences, with the beginning of the 20th Century, kept them here for the same purpose? Why the Art Students League and the Society of American Artists? Why could technical proficiency remain sterile to a Robert Henri? What were the stimulants behind the painting of Ryder, of Eakins? These are just a few of the questions that James Thomas Flexner answers as he leads us to the birth of the Ash Can School in American art. Mr. Flexner teaches at Columbia University, and among his many distinguished books on American culture is American Painting: The Light of Distant Skies.

THROUGHOUT the history of our nation, American painting has been confused and impeded by physical and cultural isolation. First-class, old master canvases have always been rare in this land, available only in a few cities. Although examples of the European art then contemporary have been imported in every generation, the men who created them and the studios in which they were created have remained across three thousand miles of ocean. Foreign traditions have never been assimilated in the United States. Yet no intelligent man can deny that these traditions have, down the ages, created a greater art than our own.

From the beginning, this situation has placed our painters in a dilemma. The America that was their birthright was an exciting land, and, in any case, it was irrevocably built into their personalities, by environment even if not by heredity. On the other hand, the masterpieces which seemed in every lifetime to be signposts pointing the way to immortality were created in distant lands, under different conditions, to express another way of life. Blending European skill with American experience has always been a most puzzling labor. Most artists have found it easier either to forget the great traditions, or to forget the United States. As time has passed, these two solutions have been accepted alternately, in a sort of rough pendulum swing.

Although American painting dates back to at least 1660, not till 1760 did an important American painter set foot in Europe. The art of the colonial period was, of necessity, largely a native growth. However, the same increase in power and prosperity that inspired the American Revolution propelled our painters abroad. For two generations, American artists played a role on the world stage. The first of these generations adhered to native roots and prospered; the second attempted to become completely Europeanized, and failed so dismally that the pendulum suddenly leapt to the other extreme. In the 1820's, the members of the Hudson River and related schools became passionately dedicated to depicting American life and landscape; they based their painting techniques on the crude sources that were easily available to them in the United States. Again there were two generations. At the outbreak of the Civil War, the second was in the ascendant. American exhibitions were dominated by huge canvases—they would not get through the door of a modern apartment—which showed the natural wonders of our continent. These brought greater prices than were paid for imported European art.

When peace returned, the majority of the young painters arising throughout the land looked at these pictures with new eyes and saw only their faults. They noticed a lack of subtlety without noticing strength; they noticed a dry literalness of technique which contrasted unfortunately with such European canvases as they had seen. Paying little attention to such sophisticated workmen among their elders as George Inness, completely ignorant about the native painters of previous epochs, they told each other that there had never been an American art. The opportunity to create an American art they believed to be their own, and they thought they knew how to do it—import everything from Europe. One by one, the young men sailed abroad.

The Mecca that attracted many was Munich, in the 1870's a fashionable art center, although the work done there was not to stand the test of time. Among the many arrivals at the Bavarian city, two men from the Middle West attracted particular attention. William Merritt Chase of Indiana and Frank Duveneck of Ohio became expert at painting professional models posed in clothes hired from a theatrical costumer, and in giving the resulting pictures an allover yellowish tinge which approximated the effect of age on old masters. Since flashing brushwork was the trade-mark of the Munich School, they dashed their paint-loaded brushes against canvas as if fencing with an invisible opponent. That nothing they were doing in any way connoted their native land, made it all seem the more exciting, the more valuable for reforming American art.

Duveneck stayed for a time in Munich, where he instructed his young compatriots who continued to flock there. Chase joined the flood of students who were returning home, each clutching a favorite formula. They had worked not only in Munich, but had shopped around among European traditions, like bargain hunters in a department store. They picked up something here and something there until their styles, which were lightly felt, were polyglot. Eager to share their discoveries, they organized a school in New York, the Art Students League, and, when the older painters who controlled the National Academy slighted their pictures, in 1877 they formed an academy of their own, the Society of American Artists. Their ranks swelled yearly, as more young men sailed in from abroad. Since Paris was becoming increasingly ascendant in European art, French influence gradually replaced that of Munich as dominant in the Society of American Artists.

The painters of the new movement generally avoided depicting American life except in its most refined and idealized aspects. Subscribing to the doctrine of "art for art's sake," they insisted that subject matter was of secondary importance as compared to technique. Indeed it was basically in the realm of technique that their contribution to our culture lay. To some extent, they narrowed the gap between American crudeness of execution and the knowledge that enabled Europeans to express brilliantly in paint what they saw and felt. But the leaders of the Society of American Artists refused, in their reaction against what they considered the crudeness of their environment, to see and feel. They created superficial pictures.

Today we regard as our greatest artists of the late 19th Century three men who never tried by an act of will to cut themselves off from their American roots. Building through personal experimentation in early training as a magazine illustrator, Winslow Homer became one of the world's greatest water-colorists, and a majestic painter, in oil, of the ocean as it battered the coast of his beloved Maine. Albert Pinkham Ryder, a gentle, gigantic, bearded hermit, invented for himself the weird technique with which he gave substance to the visions that floated naturally through his mind as he prowled New York City streets. And Thomas Eakins exemplified the most fruitful way for an American to use European study. In France, Eakins selected techniques that were peculiarly suited to his temperament. After his return to Philadelphia, he matured slowly an individual art, based on his convictions concerning the Pennsylvania world he knew so well.

These great creators stayed apart from the fashionable artistic life of their time: the Society of American Artists created the loudest buzzing in critical and social circles. Little by little, its leaders were elected to the National Academy, and, in 1906, they merged the two organizations. But already the pendulum of taste had started to move in the opposite direction.

After studying in the leading art schools of the United States and Europe, Robert Henri reached the conclusion that even the greatest technical proficiency was sterile unless it was mated with life. In Philadelphia, he accepted as students a group of newspaper illustrators—John Sloan, George Luks, William Glackens—and he took the revolutionary step of advising them that the street scenes they drew for their commercial employers were suitable subject matter for serious art. The resulting canvases of gaslit bars, shopgirls hurrying home, and ragged urchins dancing in the gutter shocked the exponents of art for art's sake who now controlled the National Academy. Again secession became a necessity.

In 1907, the painters of city scenes joined with other advanced artists to form "The Eight" and to hold their own exhibition. Although they were mocked as "The Ash Can School," their pictures were in keeping with a time when writers were increasingly concerned with realism, economists with the problems of urban life. Their reform showed signs of sweeping everything before it when the greatest artistic revolution in six hundred years roared into a much louder explosion.

Since the end of the Middle Ages, the ideals of Renaissance art had dominated Western culture. But at the beginning of the 20th Century, men of many nations, including a few Americans, developed in Paris what has been called modernism: an art with very different ideals. The wave of confusion and achievement thus set up moved slowly across the ocean to reach the United States in 1914. Even leaders of "The Ash Can School" were caught up in the wave that washed American painting into new and strange directions.

Woodrow Wilson

ARTHUR S. LINK

Mark Hanna's not-so-private belief that if Teddy Roosevelt were given enough rope he would hang the Republican Party (as Hanna defined that party) finally came true. The new American political hero, as a consequence, was the steely-voiced man of books and ideas, Woodrow Wilson, governor of New Jersey after a stormy session as president of Princeton University.

The turning point in Wilson's career came when his fight with Dean Andrew West was ended by the bequest of a Princeton alumnus who left several millions to the Graduate School with the proviso that Dean West remain in control. Wilson needed a change and James Smith, the Democratic boss of New Jersey, needed a candidate who would satisfy the anti-Bryan wing of the party. Wilson looked safe and pliable; but Smith never made a worse guess in his life. The scholarly Wilson was progressive and unyielding, and Smith lost his long-coveted chance for a seat in the U.S. Senate.

Under Wilson, New Jersey secured a primary election law, a corrupt practices act, a public utilities act, an employers' liability act, school reform laws—the state had never moved ahead so quickly, nor carried a governor with the same long strides into the White House. Arthur S. Link, professor of history at Northwestern University, is the author of Wilson: The Road to the White House *and* Woodrow Wilson and the Progressive Era.

W HEN Theodore Roosevelt took the leadership of Republican progressives in opposition to William Howard Taft, and then disrupted the party in the spring of 1912, the chief result was to ensure the election to the Presidency of a newcomer to politics— Woodrow Wilson, governor of New Jersey. Who was this man, to whom the voters entrusted leadership of the United States in November, 1912—this man who made such a strong impression upon his period that historians call it the Wilson Era?

Born in Staunton, Virginia, in 1856, Woodrow Wilson grew up in a Presbyterian manse in a South undergoing Civil War and Reconstruction. Educated at Princeton, the University of Virginia, and at Johns Hopkins University, he taught political science in the 1880's, and acquired considerable reputation as a critic of the Congressional system of government. Elected president of Princeton in 1902, he drove forward in a series of educational reforms until he tried to abolish the undergraduate eating clubs, and became involved in a bitter personal controversy over the control of a new Graduate College.

Wilson's defeat at Princeton set off a political chain reaction of enormous consequence to America and the world. Because the Princeton situation had become personally intolerable, Wilson accepted the Democratic nomination for governor offered to him in the summer of 1910 by the New Jersey party bosses, who thought they could use him as a respectable front. But Wilson rallied the reform forces of both parties, and won the governorship by a surprising majority in November, 1910. He then went on during the spring of 1911 to push through the legislature practically the entire program for which New Jersey progressives had been fighting for a decade.

The country was startled and pleased. It was even more startled when Wilson began a campaign to win the Democratic Presidential nomination in 1912, and succeeded after a grueling battle at the Baltimore convention. When Theodore Roosevelt organized the Progressive, or Bull Moose, Party in Chicago, and entered the Presidential race in August, the stage was set for one of the great battles of the 20th Century. Calling his program the New Nationalism, Roosevelt spoke for advanced progressives and social reformers who wanted to commit the federal government to comprehensive regulation of business and industry in behalf of the masses. In contrast, Wilson was more cautious and willing to undertake a limited program. What he called the New Freedom aimed only at eliminating special privilege, and destroying the nearly monopolistic power of big business and finance. Wilson won the election and clear control of Congress largely because Roosevelt divided the majority Republican vote with Taft. Knowing that he spoke for a vast majority of Americans, however, the new President proceeded to give the country a new lesson in leadership. Calling Congress into special session in April, 1913, he fought off the lobbyists and spokesmen of special privilege, and forced the enactment of two major reform laws before the end of that year. The first was the Underwood Tariff Act, which destroyed the system of high protection that the special interests had carefully erected since 1861. The second was the epochal Federal Reserve Act, which completely reorganized the national banking system, and provided a money supply geared to the needs of a great industrial and business economy. In addition, during 1914 Wilson obtained passage of the Clayton Antitrust Act to tighten existing prohibitions against monopoly, and establishment of the Federal Trade Commission, which was empowered to preserve competition in the business world.

This, then, was Wilson's New Freedom—a middle-of-the-road reform program designed only to destroy monopoly and special privilege in order to unleash the creative economic energies of the American people. But it was not enough to satisfy the demands of social reformers and other advanced progressive groups who wanted to convert the federal government into the guardian and helper of workers, farmers, and underprivileged groups everywhere.

Although Wilson made necessary concessions in order to keep a Congressional majority, on the whole he successfully withstood the demands of the advanced progressives before 1916. He prevented passage of a bill to establish a federal system of long-term credit for farmers, and refused to give labor unions immunity from prosecution for violating the antitrust laws. He would not support woman suffrage, or a measure to outlaw child labor. By the autumn of 1914, many progressives doubted that Wilson could meet the great domestic challenge of his time—that of consolidating the forces of discontent in a new drive for social and economic justice.

But a political revolution was brewing even as they spoke. Roosevelt had taken a large majority of progressive Republicans and many independents with him into the Progressive Party in 1912, but that party virtually vanished during the Congressional elections of 1914. By themselves a minority, the Democrats could win again in 1916 only if they gained the support of a large number of former Bull Moosers. Perceiving this necessity with customary wisdom, Wilson executed a daring strategy during the months preceding the election of 1916. In brief, he changed from a cautious liberal into an advanced progressive, and a champion of the New Nationalism instead of the New Freedom.

Wilson carried out his campaign with dramatic swiftness. It began with the appointment of Louis D. Brandeis,[1] a leading progressive lawyer, to the Supreme Court in January 1916. Next, the President won approval of a rural credits measure that satisfied the demands of farm spokesmen, of federal child labor and workmen's compensation bills, of an act establishing the eight-hour day on the railroads, and of similar legislation. And by the time the campaign of 1916 was in full swing he had, through Congress, enacted into law virtually every plank in Roosevelt's Progressive platform of 1912.

Wilson won a second term in 1916 in a narrowly contested battle against the Republican nominee, Charles Evans Hughes, precisely because he won enough independent and former Bull Moose votes to give him a bare majority. Important though his victory was, in the long run the meaning of his and the Democratic Party's conversion to advanced social and economic pro-

[1] Brandeis emerged as the hero of the progressives when in 1908 he defended Oregon's ten-hour law for women before the Supreme Court. "The argument Brandeis made was as unconventional as a six-foot judge in a two-foot robe . . . The existing law, Brandeis said, made clear the right to purchase or sell labor was part of the 'liberty' protected by the Constitution and that this liberty was subject to such reasonable restraints as a state government might impose, in the exercise of its police power, for the protection of health, safety, morals, or general welfare." Goldman, Eric F.: *Rendezvous With Destiny* (New York, 1956), p. 107.

gressivism was even more significant. For by their legislation in 1916, Wilson and his party leaders set the United States upon the road that would lead straight to the New Deal and the Fair Deal. Because he saw the necessity for meeting the challenges of an urbanized and industrialized society, and because he provided leadership in meeting those challenges through democratic action, Wilson's claim to greatness is large indeed.

President during a time when the United States was emerging from the chrysalis of isolation, Wilson's role in world affairs was perhaps even more significant than his part in helping to shape the course of the progressive movement at home. In dealing with Mexico, which was torn by bloody revolutions from 1913 to 1917, he helped give the reform groups a chance to begin their slow progress toward democracy.[2] But twice he intervened with military force which embittered Mexican-American relations for years to come. In dealing with the Central American and Caribbean republics, Wilson talked idealistically of the equality of small states. Yet, he carried on the Roosevelt-Taft policy of securing American supremacy by military and diplomatic interventions in Nicaragua, the Dominican Republic, and Haiti. In his Far Eastern policy, he acted strongly to prevent Japanese encroachment against Chinese sovereignty. But whether naive or wise, his actions reflected the fact that the United States was a world power.

However, Wilson's most decisive role in world affairs lay in the manner in which he shaped American policy toward Europe during the first three years of the First World War, from 1914 to 1917. Sharing the then-dominant American view that the United States had no vital stake in the outcome of the war, he proclaimed and tried hard to preserve American neutrality in the face of increasing assaults against American neutral rights by both the British and Germans. He accepted British control of the seas and allowed the United States to become a financial and industrial arsenal for the Allies because he had no other practical alternative, and perhaps because he privately believed that an Allied victory would not endanger American security. He successfully resisted, before 1917, the German attempt to control the seas by using the submarine—in part because he shared the American revulsion at the seeming inhumanity of submarine warfare, with its indiscriminate

---

[2] When Madero was shot, Victoriano Huerta became president, and rich Mexicans continued to grow richer at the expense of the people. Wilson denied the right of "government by assassination," and declared: "We hold that just government rests always on the consent of the governed."

killing of noncombatants, in part because he recognized that German control of the Atlantic would gravely imperil future American security. At the same time, he worked hard to end the war on terms that both sides could accept. He began to dream of a postwar world organization to maintain the peace, in which the United States would play a leading role.

The Germans wrecked Wilson's bright hopes for mediation just when he thought he was making real progress toward bringing the war to an end. By launching unlimited submarine warfare against American as well as Allied shipping in January, 1917, the German government forced Wilson to make the choice for war that he had so long evaded. He chose war, not to save America's alleged economic stake in an Allied victory, but because acceptance of the German campaign meant the total destruction of everything for which he had fought. He saw in it the almost inevitable triumph of an expansive power governed by a ruthless military clique. But the decision was forced upon him, and he made his war address to Congress on April 2, 1917 in agony, little realizing that he was determining not merely American history, but also the future destiny of the world.

During the next eighteen months, Wilson rallied the American people to a Great Crusade to make the world safe for democracy. Their contribution came in time to tip the balance in Europe and make an Allied victory possible in the autumn of 1918. And as the months of American participation passed, the war President caught the vision of a future free of international rivalries and fratricidal wars. Whether he could lead the nations at war to a just and lasting peace, and carry his own people into active leadership in the postwar era—this would be the great challenge of the future and the ultimate test of Woodrow Wilson as a man of destiny.

Failure After Versailles

J O H N A. G A R R A T Y

Under Wilson's leadership, Americans sailed off to World War I singing about "K-k-k-katie" and how the doughboys weren't coming back till it was over "Over There." Black Jack Pershing was reported to have visited the tomb of Lafayette and to have said,

"I wish to preach, not the doctrine of ignoble ease,"
said Teddy Roosevelt, "but the doctrine of the
strenuous life." He lived it—personally and politically,
whether as a North Dakota rancher (*above*) or as
President. In the political cartoon (*below*, from
"Harper's Weekly") he is seen meeting "strenuous"
Senate rejection of a debt-payment agreement with
Santo Domingo.

As early as 1523 men were considering ways to cut a canal between the two American continents. Yet it was August of 1914 before the Panama Canal was opened to traffic. The Gates of Pedro Miguel are seen in this contemporary lithograph by Joseph Pennell, whose etchings included many devoted to American industrial subjects.

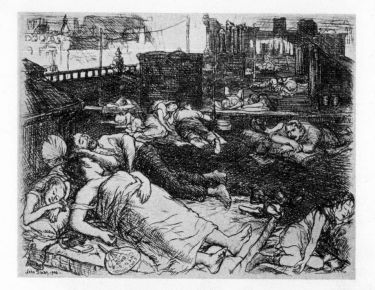

One of the American artists who during the years after 1900 were known variously as "The Eight," "The Black Gang," and "The Ash Can School," John Sloan was a leader in the realistic revolt against formalism and conservatism in art. *Above* is a reproduction of "Roofs, Summer Night" (1906); *below,* "Fun, One Cent."

Woodrow Wilson's reelection in 1916 followed a campaign in which he stressed the need to keep America out of the war. But it was not long before neutrality became impossible. Germany—not the President, and not Congress—"rocked the boat," and American soldiers went "Over There." In 1919 Woodrow Wilson and General Pershing stood at attention on a French battlefield while victorious fighting men marched in review.

"Lafayette, we are here!" (Someone else said it.) It was a cruel war, for the volcano of death that the Machine Age had contained was now in full eruption. The Marne, Belleau Wood, Chateau-Thierry, Saint Mihiel, the Argonne Forest . . . grim were the battles for which the names stood, brave were the Americans who died in those distant fields and dells, and all too soon forgotten by many were the heroism and the idealism that lifted America to one of its most magnificent hours. At last came that beautiful November morning in 1918 when the moment of Armistice arrived. This is the point at which John A. Garraty, assistant professor of history at Michigan State College, and author of Henry Cabot Lodge: A Biography, *brings us back to the second half of the Wilson story.*

At the approach of the long-awaited moment, an electric tingle ran through the troops. Thousands of doughboys glanced anxiously at their watches, sweating out the last minutes of a long, brutal, and dirty war. Precisely at eleven o'clock, all along the front from Sedan to the Moselle, the big guns fired a thundering salute. As the echoes reverberated, the final shells whined across No Man's Land to explode in a chaos of mud, steel, splinters, and human flesh. Then silence. The war was over.

But for the grey, long-jawed, one-time professor in the White House, November 11, 1918 was not an end but a beginning. As countless helmets, grey and olive drab, rose warily from the opposing trenches in the strange stillness of the battlefields, as bold black headlines proclaimed the end of Armageddon, as hysterical civilians stormed and shouted in the streets of Paris, London, and New York, Woodrow Wilson realized that the peace was but a prelude. Ahead lay the vast task of rebuilding battered Europe and establishing a world order that would make another tragic conflict impossible.

No one could say he was not ready. Long months beforehand he had formulated his "Fourteen Points," outlining his blueprint for the better world that was to come with victory. If the plans were somewhat vague, they also vibrated with a high idealism: national self-determination for Europe's oppressed minorities; an end to diplomacy behind closed doors; freedom of the seas and a freer world trade; disarmament; a new colonial policy based on justice to native peoples; and, above all, a League of Nations to guarantee "political independence and territorial integrity to great and small states alike."

To convert this blueprint into a concrete structure, Wilson broke the tradition that no President should leave the country while in office, and ventured in person to Paris, where the world settlement was to be made. At the palace of Versailles, with its vast cobblestoned courtyard, its miles of corridors, its acres of parks and gardens, he met with Britain's Lloyd George, France's Clemenceau, and Italy's Orlando, pitting his idealism and faith against their cynicism and self-interest.

Sitting around a table with these three stocky, white-moustached Europeans, each devoted to the goals of his own nation, Wilson faced an almost impossible task. Clemenceau, "the Tiger," remembering two Germanic invasions of his homeland and determined there must never be another; Lloyd George, "as direct as a zigzag, as unwavering as a weathercock," with one eye on the European balance of power and the other on the ebb and flow of British public opinion; Orlando, silent and almost ignored during the Conference, but stubborn enough to quit it when Italy did not get what he thought was her due—these men had little confidence in Wilson's dreams. Yet by determined adherence to his principles, by pure personal force, Wilson emerged from the grueling Paris discussions with an agreement generally in line with his "Fourteen Points." National self-determination, if not completely carried out, was largely achieved. According to Winston Churchill, the treaty left only 3 per cent of the people of Europe under governments they disliked. A system of international supervision of the former German colonies was set up. And a League of Nations was organized as an integral party of the treaty.

To Wilson, this last was the key to the future hope of the world. To attain it he had sacrificed part of China to Japan, allowed Italy to swallow up some former Austrian territory, and made other concessions. "The structure of peace," he said in a speech, "will not be vital without the League of Nations." But through the League, the principles of disarmament, free trade, freedom of the seas, and open diplomacy—those parts of his fourteen-point program which he had not won in Paris—could eventually be realized.

Wilson returned to America in July, 1919. Though the backbreaking work of treaty making had brought him to the edge of physical collapse, his spirits were high, buoyed up by his bright visions of a new day. The cheering throngs that greeted him in New York and Washington, and the widespread newspaper support for his League of Nations idea, were most encouraging. But trouble loomed ahead. A treaty, as Wilson well knew, was not really a treaty until two-thirds of the Senate had approved it. And Senate approval was not to be easily won.

First of all, a narrow majority of the Senators were Republicans who would be tempted to balk at the work of any Democratic President. Wilson had made a bad mistake in failing to take some important GOP Senator to Paris, thus missing an opportunity to gain bipartisan support for his handiwork. Now success for the treaty might add to the prestige of the Democrats alone, an outcome to be avoided at all costs in Republican eyes. This political difficulty was reinforced by barriers of principle. Membership in an international organization meant abandoning America's "traditional" isolationism and surrendering some measure of the sovereign authority of the United States, so dearly won in the Revolution and enshrined in Jefferson's immortal Declaration of Independence. Some Senators (and a few Democrats were among them) were unalterably opposed to any League of Nations. Led by the shaggy-browed William E. Borah,[3] these so-called "irreconcilables" intended to fight it to the death with every weapon of logic, politics, and emotionalism at their command.

But despite these difficulties, the prospects of Wilson's treaty were not entirely hopeless. The "irreconcilables" were only a small minority. Nearly all the Democrats would back the President, and most Republicans accepted the League idea in principle, arguing only about details. Wilson's driving leadership, the basic sympathy of the people for a plan to promote world peace, and the universal desire to bring a formal end to the war by signing the treaty, all worked in its favor.

Yet there was sure to be a fight. The Republicans were led by Henry Cabot Lodge[4] of Massachusetts. Possessed of a keen intel-

[3] Borah, "The Lone Lion of Idaho," was consistently a Senator who embraced causes that pleased his own conscience, so that he would be best known (aside from helping to create the Department of Labor) for his advocacy of Woman Suffrage and Prohibition and for his opposition to the internationalism of Wilson and Franklin D. Roosevelt. Told Borah had gone horseback riding, Coolidge looked dubious. "I have always understood that a horseback rider has to go in the same direction as the horse," Coolidge said, a mild-mannered man having a bit of mild-mannered fun.

[4] Lodge, Republican leader of the Senate Foreign Relations Committee, had lectured at Harvard and won recognition as an historian at the age of thirty. He was one of the group whom Wilson castigated as "a little group of willful men, representing no opinion but their own." Curiously, and with history's rare sense of humor, Lodge's grandson and namesake became the American representative to, and stanch supporter of, the League's successor organization, the United Nations.

ligence and great oratorical powers, Lodge had an absolute mastery of the ins and outs of parliamentary procedure. His greatest
weakness as a statesman was his extreme partisanship. Throughout
his career he came perilously close to arguing that the only good
Democrat was a dead one. His attitude in 1919 was further colored
by his antipathy to Woodrow Wilson, the result of a long series
of clashes before and during the war. He once said to Theodore
Roosevelt: "I never expected to hate anyone in politics with the
hatred I feel towards Wilson." Though Lodge claimed to believe
in a bipartisan foreign policy, this hatred was bound to distort his
views. Further, as leader of his party his chief aim was to keep it
united, which involved concessions to its isolationist wing.

Lodge had little faith in the effectiveness of a world organization. But he was not opposed to the experiment if it were given a
Republican stamp, and modified to protect American rights. He
therefore proposed a series of reservations, spelling out the obligations of the United States to the League, and the right of Congress to decide just when these obligations should be met.

Some of these reservations were mere quibbles over wording.
One, for instance, exempted the Monroe Doctrine from League
control, although the treaty had already done so. Others, such as
the provision that the United States would not endorse Japan's
seizure of Chinese territory, were added only to embarrass Wilson
by pointing up compromises he had been forced to make at Versailles. The most important reservation stated that America's obligation to guarantee the territory and independence of League
members against aggression could not be invoked "unless in any
particular case . . . Congress . . . should by act or joint resolution
so provide."

But the President would not agree even to minor modifications.
Already some of his Fourteen Points had been lost at Versailles;
he had made his last concession. As sentiment for further changes
developed he resorted to a desperate step. Against the advice of
his doctors, who told him he must not submit his already exhausted
body to further strains, he embarked on a nationwide tour to rally
the people to his cause. But before he had carried his campaign far
enough to test its effectiveness, the predictions of the physicians
came to pass. After making a speech in Pueblo, Colorado, Wilson
collapsed, and suffered a crippling stroke. For months thereafter
he was confined to his bed, inaccessible to friend and foe alike.

Thus the Democrats, already a minority, were deprived of his
leadership in the battle over reservations. One by one, under the

masterly hand of Lodge, the Republicans tacked their reservations to the Covenant. That accomplished, all but the "irreconcilable" die hards were ready to ratify it. Then, as the final vote approached, Wilson stirred himself. To vote for the treaty now, he warned the Democratic Senators, would not be to ratify it but to nullify it. "I trust that all true friends of the treaty will refuse to support the Lodge resolution."

On November 19, 1919, before packed galleries, in an atmosphere charged with tension, the Senators responded to the calling of the roll. When it was over, the treaty had failed—the Democrats had joined with the "irreconcilables" to defeat it.

So perished Wilson's dream of American participation in the League of Nations. An effort to revive the treaty a few months later met a similar fate. We shall never know what course history might have taken had the United States joined. But looking back from our present position of international leadership, this much is clear. Without America, the League failed. Millions of lives were sacrificed in a second catastrophe, which real international co-operation could have prevented.

Who must bear the blame? Certainly the "irreconcilables," who set their faces against the march of progress and spread prejudice and hatred among the people. Certainly also Lodge, who put his party above patriotism and cynicism above hope. But also Woodrow Wilson. When every responsible leader—Democrat and Republican alike—urged compromise, he alone stood stubbornly against Lodge's reservations. Former President Taft, who worked harder for the League than perhaps any single American, summed up the situation in a sentence: Wilson and Lodge, he said, "exalt their personal prestige and the saving of their ugly faces above the welfare of the country and the world."

The Changing Status of Women

AGNES ROGERS ALLEN

When the Civil War ended the cause of militant abolitionism, Susan B. Anthony had no difficulty in finding her next crusade. Her diary entry for December 11, 1865 read: "Commenced Women's Rights work in earnest" and that Christmas she and

Elizabeth Cady Stanton spent the day "writing and folding and addressing petitions." From such humble beginnings the struggle for equal rights for women built momentum, and though Wilson might turn a cold, scholarly shoulder to the movement for woman suffrage, by then a gale was blowing. Agnes Rogers Allen, associate editor of Reader's Digest, *reiterates a theme she developed so delightfully in her popular book,* Women Are Here to Stay.

THE WOMEN who met at Seneca Falls, New York, in 1848 would be very much astonished to see how far the feminist movement which they spearheaded there has carried. The women who cast their votes in November, 1956, would be equally amazed if they could be miraculously transported back in time—say, fifty years—and see what it was like to be a woman then. For the emergence of the American woman from within the walls of her own house to the world outside has been one of the most striking phenomena of our day.

Many forces have contributed. The revolution was not effected solely by the efforts of the militant workers for woman suffrage, but also by a variety of other factors, among them the great upheavals caused by world wars, the automobile, the changing pattern of family life, mechanization of the home, and many other influences.

The declaration of independence for women that was formulated by Elizabeth Cady Stanton and Lucretia Mott at the historic convention at Seneca Falls demanded full legal equality, full educational and industrial opportunity, equal compensation, and the right to vote—none of which then existed. Little by little the educational and industrial barriers crumbled, and property rights were slowly granted. By 1913 twelve states had granted women the right to vote on matters within their borders, but it was not until 1920 that the ratification of the 19th Amendment to the Constitution gave women nationwide suffrage.

It is difficult for us today to realize the bitter opposition to woman suffrage with which the early workers in the field had to contend. Even so moderate a man as Grover Cleveland wrote in the *Ladies' Home Journal* in October, 1905, "sensible and responsible women do not want to vote. The relative positions to be assumed by man and woman in the working out of our civilization were assigned long ago by a higher intelligence than ours."

This statement expresses the general estimate of woman's position at the turn of the century, and, indeed, with some modifications, up until World War I. The ideal American woman was the sheltered lady who lived at home, protected from the rude world by her husband. She concerned herself with the care of children, management of the household, supervision of the servants, and arrangements of family entertaining. Her intellectual interests were limited to reading romantic novels and poetry; and she was supposed to appreciate music and art, and to have a modest ability to perform—strictly as an amateur—at the piano or easel.

This is not a picture of the average American woman of the time: it is the ideal which was generally admired, and to which most women aspired. There were, of course, exceptions—as there always are. Not everybody agreed with Cleveland's definition of woman's brains. A notable exception was a hard-headed, successful businessman of Poughkeepsie, New York, who, in 1861, expressed his reasons for endowing a college for women as follows: "It occurred to me that woman, having received from her Creator the same intellectual constitution as man, has the same right to intellectual culture and development." Thus spoke Matthew Vassar, and Vassar College was opened in September, 1865 with 353 students from twenty-two of the thirty-six states. By 1888, Mount Holyoke, Elmira, Wellesley, Smith, Bryn Mawr, Radcliffe, and Barnard were well established in the East. West of the Alleghenies, a policy of coeducation permitted women to share with men the facilities of most of the state universities.

But for a long time the college girl was regarded as suspect—she must be radical, or a bluestocking, or a man hater, or in some way peculiar. As more and more colleges opened for women, and more and more universities welcomed women to their graduate schools, and more and more parents submitted to the desire to give their children—daughters as well as sons—the education they never had, the oddness wore off. Today it is, of course, the rule rather than the exception for girls who can afford it to go to college. In 1900 there were only 8,108 women college graduates in the country. In 1950, the fall enrollment of women in higher education institutions was 727,270.

At the turn of the century there were few occupations open to women which were socially acceptable. If a woman was unfortunate enough to be unmarried, and had no money and no close male relative to support her, she could enter the professions of teaching or nursing without losing caste. If widowed and living in a house large enough, she could take in boarders. For the very few women of exceptional talent who could write, there were handsome rewards. The theatre was very dubious, and only a handful of well-born women defied convention and became noted stage and opera stars.

During the first decades of the 20th Century a new fold opened, that of the social worker. To be sure, there were thousands of women who couldn't afford to think about social status when it came to earning a living. The great majority of wage earning women were domestic servants. Women worked in factories, too, and here it was the immigrant who filled most of these jobs. When the typewriter replaced the letter press in business offices, another avenue was opened to working women—and how they swarmed in! In 1900 there were 200,000 women stenographers in the country. Thirty years later there were two million.

The 1920's saw a drastic change in the status and attitude of women in the United States, especially among the younger ones. Not only had women won the vote, but in certain areas of business and industry, doors once locked against them were opened. For the first time, numbers of women were working alongside of men, not as inferiors or rivals, but in partnership. With this sweeping change the old social taboos melted away.

The statistics on American women wage earners today would have seemed fantastic to the early feminists. In 1952 about one-third of the 58 million adult women in the country, or close to 20 million, were at work or looking for jobs. The figures continue to mount—of the 451 occupations listed by the Census Bureau in 1940, there were only three in which no women were employed— locomotive engineer, fireman, and firefighter.

World War II drew women by the thousands into the war effort on a paid basis, besides volunteer workers. They were taken into the armed forces, Red Cross, munitions factories, and the mushrooming government agencies. Many others took civilian jobs, such as taxi driving, to release men for fighting. It was expected that most of these newcomers to the labor force would return home after the war. But they didn't. The proportion is still as high as in the war years—32 per cent of all workers. And more than half of them are married!

From a strictly feminist point of view, the picture is not quite so rosy as it appears from these figures. Women hold high-level jobs in many fields, but in some of the professions they still lag far behind men. They number less than 5 per cent among doctors, dentists, engineers, architects, and lawyers. And their over-all earnings are less than men's. In 1949, the working alumnae of a group of eastern women's colleges reported an average salary of $3,790, as opposed to a comparable group of men whose average salary was $9,800.

It was generally believed that when women won the vote they would rush in to seek political office. This did not follow; indeed, there is no such thing as the "women's vote." To be sure, there have been a sprinkling of women Cabinet members, ambassadors, and there are eleven women in Congress—but in world terms these figures are not impressive. In contrast to Denmark, where 10.7 per cent of the seats in the national parliament are held by women, our figure is only 1.3. But the record in state legislative bodies is higher and this presents, perhaps, a fairer comparison, since in our vast country many of our states bear a resemblance to the smaller countries of Europe.

It is difficult, if not impossible, to track down statistics to support any assertions of social changes in the daily lives of American women during the past thirty-odd years since the granting of universal suffrage, but the changes are there. Take, for example, the relaxation of the Victorian code of propriety that governed women's drinking—a little wine at dinner, a glass or two of champagne at a fashionable ball was all that was permitted a respectable woman. The use of tobacco—taboo to women or at least extremely rare before World War I—was adopted gradually at first and with increasing speed until in 1948 the percentage of women smokers was estimated at 38 per cent. Minor conventions such as mourning attire, the dinner call, and various others vanished. A major convention, that of the chaperone, disappeared with the enormous use of the automobile.

In the past twenty or thirty years the pure mechanics of domestic living have changed almost beyond recognition. Rising costs have necessitated smaller living quarters, and the shrinking of the domestic servant class to almost the vanishing point, have been balanced by the general mechanization of the home. Household machinery—vacuum cleaners, washing machines, gas and electric equipment of all kinds, frozen foods and deep freezes in which to keep them—have revolutionized the business of housekeeping. And the ever-growing cult of informality has set up new and simplified standards of entertaining as well as of daily living.

The pattern of young married life today reflects this new concept of daily living in that the husband assumes many of the domestic duties as a matter of course. The young father who is unable to prepare a meal or tend the baby is a rarity in this day and age.

In a number of fields the earlier distinctions between women's interests and men's interests are increasingly blurred. As women in greater numbers take an active or passive part in sports and games, so are they yielding their traditional role as sole guardians of "the finer things of life." Men today may acknowledge an interest in painting and music as easily and naturally as they wield the dishcloth—or the baseball bat.

In short, not only has the American woman entered what was once a man's world, but the American man, in some areas, at least, is participating in what was once strictly a woman's world.

Back to Normalcy

Q U I N C Y   H O W E

Harding and Teapot Dome, Silent Cal who didn't choose to run and Hoover who did . . . with these leaders an age rushed to its giddy climax, sometimes soaked in bathtub gin, sometimes breathless from flapping after women enjoying their equal rights. It was the age of fabulous heroes—Babe Ruth, Bobby Jones, Jack Dempsey; the age of fabulous villains—Capone et al.; the age of fabulous faith and fabulous cynicism. It was America on a grand spree before the big bust. It was the age of the tender years for most Americans in their prime today. Quincy Howe, well-known to radio and television audiences for his scholarship and skill as a news analyst, evaluates those roaring Twenties, as so many of us do, with bitter-sweet memories.

THE AMERICAN people elected Warren G. Harding as President in 1920 because he promised to lead them "back to normalcy." But Harding did not lead. The American people moved forward, not backward, and they never arrived at normalcy. Politics offered few attractions to men of honor or ability. Men of ambition turned to private business rather than to public service, and the center of national power shifted from Washington to Wall Street.

Yet the burden of the Presidency soon crushed Harding. He died after barely two years in office, and within a few months of his death some of his closest associates and highest officials were revealed as common thieves. Harding had surrounded himself with bad men, notably Albert B. Fall, the only Cabinet officer in American history sentenced to jail for corruption in office. Harding's hometown folks in Marion, Ohio, said of him: "George Washington could not tell a lie. Harding could not tell a liar." After Harding came Calvin Coolidge, a dour New Englander, whose midnight swearing into office by his justice-of-the-peace father thrilled the nation.

During the six years that Coolidge occupied the White House, he slept more than any other President, whether by day or by night. He retired by ten almost every night, and took a two-hour nap almost every afternoon. "Nero fiddled, but Coolidge only snored," wrote H. L. Mencken, the leading literary critic of the 1920's. But Coolidge paid no heed to literature. An inquiring reporter once asked him why he limited his White House guests to men of business, and never invited any artists, musicians, actors, and poets, as Wilson, Roosevelt, and others had done before him. "I knew a poet once when I was in college," Coolidge replied, "class poet, name of Smith. Never heard of him since."

Coolidge not only walled himself off from one of the most creative decades in the history of the United States—or, indeed, of any country—he symbolized that Puritan tradition which was collapsing all around him. The attempt to enforce national Prohibition created the bootlegger, the highjacker, the crooked official. Scott Fitzgerald, who recorded the history of the jazz age in fiction, created the gangster hero of the time in the greatest of his novels, *The Great Gatsby.* Ring Lardner's short stories depicted the professional athletes, the popular song writers, the vaudeville hoofers—all those gaudy practitioners of *The Seven Lively Arts,* as Gilbert Seldes called them in his book that bears that title. Charlie Chaplin on the motion picture screen, Al Jolson in musical comedy, and such popular composers as Irving Berlin, George Gershwin, Jerome Kern, and Cole Porter gave birth, through their combined if unorganized efforts, to a new, distinctive, and wholly American art.

The literary 1920's began with the publication of Sinclair Lewis's *Main Street,* and closed with Thomas Wolfe's *Look Homeward, Angel.* In the middle of the decade, Theodore Dreiser produced his masterpiece, *An American Tragedy.* The dramas of Eugene O'Neill also dwelt on the darker sides of American life. American scholars presented past and present with new perspective. Charles

A. Beard and his wife, in their *Rise of American Civilization,* showed the part that economic forces had played in American history. Vernon Parrington's *Main Currents in American Thought* treated American literature in the same fashion. And Robert and Helen Lynd's *Middletown* dissected a typical American community of the mid-1920's as an archaeologist might dissect the remains of an ancient culture. President Coolidge had said, "The business of America is business," and the Beards, Parrington, and the Lynds took him at his word. That is, they addressed themselves to describing how Americans had made and still continued to make their livings, only to discover that their findings conflicted with the hopes, beliefs, and assumptions of the business community.

The American people had come out of the First World War with a magnificent industrial plant. Ten years later they stepped up the efficiency of that plant 50 per cent. Americans in the 1920's did not chase dollars any harder than Englishmen chased pounds or Frenchmen chased francs. What set the American of the 1920's apart from the people of other countries was his capacity to produce wealth; the force that drove him throughout the decade was the determination to sell. As Will Rogers, the humorous cowboy philosopher, put it: "One-third of America promotes; two-thirds of America provides." And it was the promoting third that gave the Twenties their special character. Installment buying financed the industrial boom and spread the wealth more widely. Government debt declined, but not so fast as the borrowings of the public from the banks increased. And the American businessman tried to pyramid his profits by borrowing ten times as much ready cash as he actually possessed in order to speculate in the stock market. President Coolidge and Secretary of the Treasury Mellon did nothing to stop the speculative boom. Just the opposite. They encouraged its further development.

Herbert Hoover, Coolidge's Secretary of Commerce, foresaw trouble, but he could not stop the trend. As prices of common stocks went up and up, Governor Roy A. Young of the Federal Reserve Board laughed helplessly as he told a friend, "What I am laughing at is that I am sitting here trying to keep a hundred and twenty million people from doing what they want to do." Mr. Young exaggerated. At no time did more than a million Americans ever speculate in the stock market, but those who did caused enough commotion to produce world-wide effects. Coolidge's proverbial luck served him well. He left the White House in March,

1929, and Hoover succeeded him with the largest popular vote and the largest electoral vote ever accorded a President up to that time. The boom continued until Labor Day. It faltered in September. On October 24, over twelve million shares of stock changed hands. On October 29 came the deluge. More than sixteen million shares were thrown on the market for whatever they would bring, and within the space of a few weeks, the paper value of American common stocks dropped thirty billion dollars.

President Hoover vainly attempted to combat the collapse by using the same methods that had created the boom. "The Wall Street crash means nothing in the welfare of business," he declared. But as Will Rogers put it, "Confidence hasn't left the country; confidence has just got wise." Most Americans had not bought or sold any common stocks throughout the entire decade of the 1920's, so President Hoover's assurances therefore appeared reasonable. And Secretary of the Treasury Mellon ushered in the new decade with the prediction, "The speculative flurry is over. The nation will make steady progress from now on." But Hoover, who had deplored the speculative boom that Mellon had encouraged, had little contact with the American realities of the time. The lords of creation, whether they exercised their rule from Wall Street or from Washington, had lost touch with the mass of the American people who produced and consumed the bulk of the country's wealth.

The nation that invented mass production failed in the 1920's to solve the problem of mass distribution. American big business gloried in the absence of political constraint—to its own hurt. The wiser men of business always wondered when the speculative boom would end. The leading intellectuals felt themselves the virtual enemies of society. No common spirit possessed the people. The individual felt isolated, and thus, lacking national leadership and national purpose, Americans tended to split into rival groups. Fundamentalists fought modernists. Children rebelled against their parents. The divorce rate doubled. The American people during the 1920's dissipated their ever-growing vitality, yet the whirling dynamo of their prosperity served to stabilize many distant lands. It remained for the 1930's to show how the sudden end of that prosperity shook the world.

EIGHT

The

Modern Era

W HEN the big bust came, America wondered why once again it was lifting itself by the bootstraps. Vachel Lindsay gave a poet's answer. Ah, Babbitt, he cried, you tried to sell Judas and you tried to sell Christ, but your infamous day has ended, Babbitt, and the Virginians are coming again. This reaching back toward Jeffersonian aspirations fitted a pattern; in the 1870's, shocked by the spirit of gambling adventure behind Grantism and Tweedism, the patrician Samuel Tilden had emerged as a reformer in the same spirit. But Grant hadn't been a bad man nor had Babbitt; and even if Harding couldn't tell a liar when he met one, that fact wasn't the answer, either.

When Babbitt was placed under a microscope, he became in a way the commonest sort of common man history ever had produced. Forces had pulled at him, changed him, confused him, and very definitely had betrayed him. If in making a fast buck he forgot his own immigrant background and groped for a cultural identity that was distilled in the same bathtub with his gin, then in the kind of dizzy inebriation that possessed him he succeeded in knocking out the stopper and the tub ran dry. With the crash, the apple sellers, and the depression, Babbitt sobered up in a hurry. Stunned and shocked, if he wasn't a penitent, he was at least wide-awake.

What has Babbitt learned since those days when we had to be reminded that the worst we could fear was fear itself? From "Manifest Destiny" through isolationism to global responsibility is certainly a big about-face for a single generation. An awareness of what pro-Marxism really is, that social morality is basic to law, order, and prosperity, that in the grudging compromises and political shifts inherent in the free man's struggle of Conservatism vs. Reform come the process by which a democratized government works and hopes for a better tomorrow . . . these, too, are big lessons and big questions. Or the lessons and the questions as to which is the more effective offensive weapon—the bombs dropped on Hiroshima and Nagasaki, or the cornucopia of a Marshall Plan inverted over the hard-up-against-it sections of the world? Or labor vs. automation? Perhaps what Babbitt is learning best is to beware of extremes as man continues to oppose man. Mob rule does not solve desegregation; it adds another problem. Witch hunting does not reduce political naivete; it adds another problem. Angry words do not restore peace; they destroy hope.

And hope is the thing that America is seeking most earnestly in this, its modern era.

FDR and the New Deal

FRANK FREIDEL

"The legitimate object of government," Lincoln had said, "is to do for a community of people, whatever they need to have done, but cannot do, at all, or cannot, so well do, for themselves—in their separate, and individual capacities." The most controversial figure to occupy the White House since Lincoln was Franklin D. Roosevelt, who probably would have argued that, balanced against the exigencies of the times, everything he did squared with Lincoln's definition. But never had the national government entered more directly into the lives of individual Americans; at almost every social and economic level Uncle Sam essayed a paternalistic influence that wrote the uneasy term, "welfare state," into the nation's vocabulary. Where Teddy Roosevelt had been the idol of the liberal who called himself a Progressive, Franklin Roosevelt became the darling of the liberal who renamed himself the New Dealer; and where big business distrusted the first Roosevelt as the madman from Oyster Bay, it generally hated the second Roosevelt as "that man" from Hyde Park.

Yet even the austere Samuel Tilden had not been more patrician than FDR. Educated at exclusive Groton School, and then at Harvard and Columbia Law School, Roosevelt had grown bored as a junior member of a distinguished law firm and had turned to politics. A Democrat in a solid Republican district, his jaunty enthusiasm carried him into the New York State Senate in 1910, and he was quickly marked thereafter as a "comer" who had no need to kowtow to the political bosses. As Assistant Secretary of the Navy under Wilson, then as an unsuccessful Vice Presidential candidate, his stature grew. When infantile paralysis afflicted him during the summer of 1921, the fighting edge of the man's spirit became more sharply honed than ever; between 1928 and 1930 he served as governor of New York, with his eyes and those of Louis Howe, his chief adviser, never wavering from the sights they had set on the White House. In 1932, against Hoover and depression, FDR made it easily—the electoral vote was 472 to 59—and thus began quietly and in large part unconsciously an American revolution. Frank Freidel, professor of history at Harvard University, is currently at work on a six-volume biography of the second Roosevelt.

The year 1932 was a grim one in the United States. The gaudy balloon of jazz age prosperity had split at the seams three years previously, plummeting the American people to the depths of privation and despair. Millions were out of work in the summer of 1932, and millions more worked or farmed for a pittance. In the Middle West, farmers receiving two cents a quart for milk resorted to a desperate measure to restore prices: they began dumping milk bound for the market. In Washington, veterans rioted for immediate payment of a bonus not due until 1945. For millions of Americans, the only sign of hope on the horizon lay in the election of the Democratic candidate for President, Franklin D. Roosevelt, with his promise of a New Deal.

The New Deal which unfolded in the next six years was a complicated bundle of measures and agencies designed above all to rescue the United States from the depression. While it did not succeed completely in bringing recovery, it did introduce a number of significant changes into our government and way of life. It went far beyond the earlier American idea of the limited role of government to establish among many people a feeling that their government was responsible for their personal well-being. Twenty years later this feeling still precipitates political debates, and hot arguments still rage as to whether the New Deal saved American capitalism or took the first major step toward a welfare state.

Certainly the chief New Dealer, President Roosevelt, the living symbol of gay self-assurance in the face of disaster, had been able to capture the confidence of a punch-drunk nation. The country followed willingly while he tried first one remedy and then another for the national ills. He was able to hold together in his administration men representing many shades of political and economic belief. As he put their widely differing plans into operation, either simultaneously or separately, the resulting New Deal looked like a chaotic hodgepodge. Now, from the perspective of twenty years, we can see in that tangle strong lines of major design.

Roosevelt's first aim upon taking office was to restore national morale, and in his inaugural he proclaimed, "The only thing we have to fear is fear itself." In the famous hundred days following, his bold, persistent experimentation did much to drive fear away. Congress acted swiftly to pass the legislative program he framed to stimulate recovery, relieve hunger, and bring about reforms. This very speed itself did much to reassure a people psychologically keyed to meet crisis with free-swinging action.

It was not a radical program, and it was not a program aimed at benefiting one class at the expense of others. Roosevelt felt strongly that he was President of all the American people. Therefore he tried to meet the demands of each of the main blocks of voters. He bridged over strong oppositions between their goals with generalities and compromises, for he wanted to maintain a balance among conflicting interests. For bankers there were moderate reforms to enable their banks to reopen; it was only later that Federal Deposit Insurance came. For propertied people who wished to see government expenditures cut there were sweeping slashes, which lasted only long enough to betoken his good will. For the hungry there was federal relief. For conservationists there was the Tennessee Valley Authority. And thus Roosevelt proceeded, like a father dividing favors among clamoring children, hiding contradictions with a smoke screen of swift action and radiant confidence.

Throughout the new legislation ran one strong theme: recovery. Two agencies above all were set up to bring it about: the National Recovery Administration for business, and the Agricultural Adjustment Administration for farmers. Their purpose was to block and reverse the destructive downward spiral of deflation by immediately raising prices and wages, and by putting an end to overproduction. The N.R.A. enabled businesses to band together and establish codes of fair practices, an operation quite contrary to the spirit of antitrust laws. These codes, which had the force of federal law behind them, fixed industry-wide standards of quality and price. Labor received protection through a floor on wages, a ceiling on hours, and the right to collective bargaining. At first many business leaders, who had themselves proposed similar legislation, hailed this union of business and government with enthusiasm. But too many smaller businessmen were hurt by some of the regulations; too many others found loopholes; and the great mass of detailed codes were basically unenforceable. Laboring men, failing to benefit very much, began calling the N.R.A. the "National Run Around."

The Triple A succeeded better in its goal. The government paid farmers for growing less grain or cotton or pigs through funds raised by a processing tax on the produce when it reached the processor. But the drought which burned a large farming region into the parched dust bowl of the Thirties did more than government could to cut production and raise prices. And many small farmers, especially Southern sharecroppers, were more hurt than helped by the New Deal farm program.

By 1934, Roosevelt was rapidly losing the unified support he had enjoyed in the honeymoon days of '33. Conservatives feared the mounting debt, the concessions to labor, and the threats of reform legislation. Businessmen complained that they needed a breathing spell from the constant tinkering, and issued dire warnings that the nation was headed for dictatorship and statism. One of their leading spokesmen was Al Smith, who joined the Liberty League.[1] But to the masses which had adored him and formed the base of his political support, Smith seemed to have turned his brown derby in for a top hat. Even though the masses were dissatisfied with the New Deal, they voted for it in landslide proportions in the Congressional elections of 1934. "Thunder on the left," Charles Beard called it, but this thunder was to New Dealers more threat than reassurance. The potential storm it heralded was the growing danger that leaders of what Roosevelt called "the lunatic fringe" would steal from the New Deal the votes of underprivi-

[1] Smith joined with such self-styled "Jeffersonian Democrats" of property as W. R. Hearst and the 1924 standard-bearer, J. W. Davis, to support the Presidential candidacy of Alfred M. Landon, whose one claim to political strength was the fact that he had been the only Republican governor re-elected in 1934.

leged millions. Huey Long loomed on the horizon of the South; in the North, Father Coughlin; and in the West, Dr. Townsend. At the same time, during 1935 and 1936, the Supreme Court was dealing knockout blows to key New Deal laws: first the N.R.A. code system, then the Triple A processing tax.

Threatened from both sides, Roosevelt slipped from between the twin pressures like a squeezed grape and shot in the very direction the conservatives had feared—toward greater aid for the underprivileged. On the eve of the Supreme Court decision destroying the N.R.A. codes, he endorsed the Wagner Act, which gave labor unions strong government protection in the collective bargaining they had demanded. For the unemployed, he instituted a large-scale work relief program, the W.P.A. For small farmers, the new Triple A, based on soil conservation, together with other legislation held out hope of greater benefits. For old people, he produced the Social Security Act, which had already been long in the planning. As a final clincher to convince the underprivileged he had taken their side, he sponsored a measure which newspapers promptly labeled the "soak the rich" tax. It seemed destined more to provoke rage from the wealthy than produce dollars for the treasury.

The political product of all this activity was Roosevelt's overwhelming re-election in 1936, an election which changed the folk saying, "as Maine goes, so goes the Nation," into "as Maine goes, so goes Vermont." Except for these two stubborn New England holdouts, Roosevelt was at last armed with what he considered a sweeping vote of confidence. Therefore he dedicated his second administration to a fight for the salvation of what he described in his second inaugural as "one-third of a nation ill-housed, ill-clad, ill-nourished." Yet each measure he launched on behalf of the submerged third seemed destined to break on the rocks of the Supreme Court. To dynamite this obstacle, which he felt was perpetuating outmoded interpretations of the Constitution, he dropped an unexpected bomb in February, 1937: a plan to add as many as six new Justices to the Court. This maneuver stirred up a violent, months-long fight in Congress and throughout the country. Before Congressional debate reached any conclusion, the Supreme Court eliminated the problem by handing down decisions approving several key New Deal measures. So far as the Court was concerned, Roosevelt had lost the battle but won the war. The effect upon Congress was quite the opposite. The court fight marked the beginning of a coalition of conservative Democrats and Republicans who closed ranks against Roosevelt and his New Deal. They drew strength from the indignation of many middle-class people exasperated with sit-down strikes and other disputes between labor unions and industrialists. In spite of this, Roosevelt had still sufficient momentum to push further reform legislation through Congress.

In the summer of 1937, the country seemed so well on the way to recovery that Roosevelt tried to balance the budget by a sudden curtailment of public spending. By early autumn such a serious recession set in that within a few months business had declined 27 per cent, while unemployment was rising alarmingly. There seemed no answer except a return to priming the pump with new billions of government spending, which sent the national debt zooming upward again. By the fall of 1938, the recession was over.

While businessmen blamed this recession upon higher labor costs and the unsettling effect of the New Deal, Roosevelt just as vociferously blamed it upon big business. He claimed that concentration of economic power in a few huge corporate monopolies had enabled them to make vast profits at the expense of consumer buying power. Acting on this theory, he persuaded Congress to establish a Temporary National Economic Committee to devise the solution: modernized antitrust legislation. Thus the New Deal had swung full circle from the N.R.A., which in effect was government-sponsored monopoly, to the T.N.E.C. antimonopoly proposals. But Congress never enacted this program. After the election of 1938, in which Roosevelt sought vainly to purge several anti-New Deal Democrats, Congress was firmly under the whip of the conservative coalition. President Roosevelt himself was turning his attention from domestic reform to the increasing menace of the totalitarian countries.

In January, 1939, when the failure of the Munich pact made European war appear imminent, the President, in his message to Congress, delivered a valedictory of the New Deal. He pointed to the great gains that had been made in conservation, in aid to youth, the aged, and the needy, and in putting the credit system, agriculture, and labor relations on a sounder basis. All these, he said, had made the United States a stronger nation, so that in the "race to make democracy work . . . we may be efficient in peace and therefore secure in national defense."

There was a new thunder in the air, keyed to the phrase "national defense," that required the nation to be at its top economic strength. And waiting in the future, like an ironical footnote to the President's jaunty opportunistic idealism, was a frenzy of billion-dollar spending. It was demanded—not by the laws of a recovery-minded Congress—but by the harsh law of war necessity, and it would rocket both national debt and national prosperity up to heights never dreamed of by even the most visionary New Dealers.

American Labor Organizes

IRVING HOWE

In 1886 the Knights of Labor were making a respectable fight for an eight-hour day when on May Day in Chicago disaster struck. Who threw the bomb into the Anarcho-Communist mass meeting in Haymarket Square no one knows; eight anarchists were subsequently convicted, on extremely shaky evidence, and when the Knights asked clemency for the condemned men, although disavowing the dynamiting, public opinion turned against the trade union movement.

In this dark hour for organized labor, however, a new force already had risen, and, in fact, had waged a militant opposition to the Knights on the principle that the future of unionism in America rested with the skilled craftsman. Originally called the "Federation of Organized and Labor Unions of the United States and Canada," after the Haymarket incident this group renamed itself the "American Federation of Labor." More than any other factor that brought the AFL to the fore was the leadership of Samuel Gompers, who would serve as its president thirty-seven times.

Born in London, Gompers came to America at the age of thirteen and a year later became the first registered member of the Cigar-Makers' International Union. Devoted to principles of industrial arbitration and legislative action in behalf of labor, he gave unionism in America the kind of leadership it needed. Gompers' gains were many—in influencing the creation of a separate Department of Labor and in framing or supporting laws for an eight-hour day for government employees, for limiting the use of injunctions in labor disputes, in regulating punishment for contempt of court. During World War I his influence was used against strikes; unquestionably, under his direction of the AFL, labor achieved a new respectability.

Actually what was afoot was the creation of a "big labor" to deal with "big business" in striking a balance of power in industrial America; a climax (not the last, but one of the most important) would come in the 1930's, with FDR in the White House. Irving Howe, professor at Brandeis University and author of The UAW *and* Walter Reuther, *traces labor's story through this turbulent period.*

T HE HISTORY of labor unions in the United States reaches back to the early 19th Century, yet only fifty years ago American unionism was a puny affair. In 1900, the labor movement had organized only about 5 per cent of the wage and salaried workers of the nation. During and shortly after the First World War union membership boomed; but at the high point of this boom, in 1920, only about 17 per cent of all wage and salaried workers had put their names on union cards. The years of prosperity led to a slump in union membership, and even the early years of the depression brought no sudden growth. By 1935 less than 10 per cent of the American workers were union members.

Then something extraordinary happened. By 1938, membership climbed to nearly eight million; by 1944, almost 35 per cent of all wage and salaried workers were enrolled in the trade unions. Why this sudden, dramatic upsurge of American unionism?

Before the 1930's, the labor movement was essentially based on craft unions. The American Federation of Labor, formed in the 1880's, abandoned the idealistic schemes of its predecessors; it would have nothing to do with general ideas, politics, reform. Essentially, the AFL was a tough-minded alliance of skilled crafts; the printers, cigar-makers, brewers, mechanics, and others—all concerned with maintaining their craft monopolies. These craft unions charged high dues, paid good benefits, engaged in shrewd collective bargaining. In the main, the AFL was an organization for the defense of an "aristocracy" of skilled labor; it did not concern itself with the millions of unskilled workers. The unskilled workers—so ran the AFL argument—were too easily replaceable and too divided by national feelings brought over from Europe to permit them to be organized. Scoop up the cream of skilled labor and leave the rest alone, was the AFL attitude.

It worked well enough for a time; the AFL grew rich and powerful, gaining many benefits for its members until the great depression of the 1930's came along and made its cautious, conservative methods seem inadequate.

During the fifty years since the AFL was founded, American industry had been completely transformed. Mass production had come into its own, and small-scale employers had increasingly been replaced by giant corporations. As a result, it was almost impossible to preserve the craft distinctions in the great industrial plants. Yet only the miners and needle trade workers were organized along industry-wide lines; everywhere else the AFL still tried to organize the workers of large industrial units into as many as ten or twelve craft unions, each jostling the other. It just couldn't work. By the early Thirties, the American labor movement was in a bad way. Membership had dropped, funds were low. But then came a lifesaver—Franklin D. Roosevelt and the New Deal.

In his program for counterbalancing the power of big business and for saving American capitalism through reform, FDR found that he needed a strong labor movement as a prop. His administration quickly introduced and passed legislation that encouraged a new wave of union growth. In June, 1933, the National Industrial Recovery Act (soon known as the NRA) was passed, and its famous Section 7A provided that "employees shall have the right to organize and bargain collectively through representatives of their own choosing. . . ." On the Labor Advisory Board of the NRA, Roosevelt appointed John L. Lewis, head of the miners; Sidney Hillman, head of the Amalgamated Clothing Workers; and, of course, William Green, president of the AFL.

Green and the craft unions were not too happy about all this. They suspected the whole idea of mass organization. Green even went so far as to tell Gerard Swope, head of General Electric, that the AFL couldn't undertake to organize GE unless it could divide its workers into fifteen separate craft unions—which was preposterous on the face of it.

But soon the new mass, industrial unions began to spring up, stimulated by a yearning for better conditions among the workers and sparked by the government's legislative green light. The mine and garment unions more than doubled their memberships between 1933 and 1935. In the coal towns placards appeared saying, "The President Wants You To Join Unions."

By 1934, the flood tide of industrial unionism was almost irresistible. The AFL convention of that year was deluged with resolutions favoring industrial organization. John L. Lewis, Sidney Hillman, David Dubinsky and other leaders of the proindustrial union group pressed for immediate organization drives in rubber, steel, auto; and by the next annual convention the fight grew still more bitter. The few industrial unions that had sprung up in the interim had been hampered and cramped by the AFL hierarchy. When the minority of industrial unionists was again defeated, John L. Lewis and his friends decided to go on their own. They set up the Committee for Industrial Organization "to encourage and promote organization of the workers in the mass production and unorganized industries. . . ." In his usual laconic fashion, Lewis sent Green a one-sentence resignation as AFL vice president.

For a time the CIO was a splinter within the AFL. But when the top AFL leadership ordered the CIO to stop organizing the mass industries, and the CIO refused to obey this order, there came the inevitable showdown: late in 1936 the CIO separated from the AFL, and a second major federation of the union, later calling itself the Congress of Industrial Organization, was set up.

But here we have to shift our camera a little so as not to gain the impression that the growth of the new trade unions was essentially the result of government fiat. In the plants of Detroit and Akron, Chicago, and Pittsburgh, history was also being made— perhaps more decisively than in Washington. The Roosevelt Administration made the new unions possible, but the hard work was undertaken by thousands of nameless young men in the plants who were swept by the excitement and idealism of a new labor movement.

The original CIO strategy called for the organization of steel first, and then for concentrating on the satellites of steel. This plan seemed logical, but the course of events had a logic, or a passion, of its own. Late in 1936 a series of spontaneous strikes broke out in the automobile industry. The United Automobile Workers had been organized earlier in the year and within a few months its membership had grown from thirty thousand to one hundred thousand. The corporations bitterly resisted the sprouting young union, and its members soon agreed that only strike action could bring recognition.

The first sit-down strike in auto—there had been sit-downs earlier in rubber—occurred at Bendix in South Bend: the workers simply refused to leave the plants until their union was recognized. They won. Encouraged by this victory, the UAW pushed ahead to the giant of the industry: General Motors. The strike against GM began with a walkout of some eight thousand workers at the Cleveland Fisher Body plant on December 28, 1936. By the first day of the new year it had spread to the two other Fisher Body plants in Flint. By January 11, it had overwhelmed most GM plants. One hundred and thirteen thousand men were on strike. By the end of January, the strikers captured the strategic Chevrolet Plant #4 in Flint. A few days later the corporation beat a retreat, and recognized the UAW as the bargaining agent of its workers. To win recognition, the auto workers had had to resort to a revolutionary new device—revolutionary and new in America —the sit-down, a device labor soon repudiated.

In the days of the sit-downs, Detroit and Flint looked like armed camps. More than four thousand National Guardsmen "occupied" Flint alone. Vigilante groups were organized in the name of "law and order." But the solidarity of the strikers was unbroken. When the settlement finally came and the union, after weeks of desperate struggle, was recognized, people poured through the streets of Flint crying, "You can join now, you can join now." This spontaneous outburst had a certain symbolic significance. It expressed a realization among the industrial workers that, for the first time, they were now in a position to help determine their own destinies.

A few months after the GM settlement, sixty thousand workers in the Chrysler plants occupied the factories in the biggest of all sit-down strikes. Soon the Chrysler management agreed to accept the union. Organization of the Ford plants came later, and was far more difficult; but by the end of 1937 the bulk of the automobile industry, a traditional stronghold of antiunion practices, was organized. The victory for industrial unionism was far greater than even the fabulous mushrooming of the auto workers' union to nearly four hundred thousand members would indicate, for it was a victory that set a pattern and a precedent for many other industries.

Soon steel fell into line. The United States Steel Corporation, which had always resisted efforts to unionize its employees, recognized the union, established an eight-hour day, and began to institute the complex collective bargaining machinery which is now standard in most mass production industries. Some bitter struggles remained. Strikes against the Little Steel companies were, for the moment, unsuccessful; yet in a few years steel was almost completely unionized.

By 1940 only 9 per cent of the total membership of American trade unions was still in craft unions; the remainder was divided, almost equally, between industrial and amalgamated unions. Even the AFL, the traditional enemy of industrial unionism, has in practice had to accept this form of organization, if only as a means of ensuring its survival.

No one has yet been able to measure the full consequences of the rise of the CIO in America. In its own way, it has meant a kind of social revolution—largely peaceful—in American life. Millions of Americans who had previously been dormant in the social and economic life of the nation now began to play a major role. The unions provided a new means of political expression for factory workers who had often been politically mute. They gave the workers—especially those members who were more active in their ranks—a sense of belonging, a sense of their own value and integrity. In short, they gave the workers a means of expressing their collective needs and desires—a voice now made more powerful by the merger of America's two mightiest labor organizations.

Many problems still remain for industrial unionism. Whole industries, like textile and mining, fall sick, and there seems little that a union can do to cure this sickness. A major and increasingly industralized area of America, the South, still resists union organization. Some unions which have become too strong or too complacent tend to lose their original spirit, declining into bureaucratic machines in which the members have little to say. But on the whole, it seems fair to conclude that the mass organization of millions of industrial workers in America during the 1930's was a significant step toward extending and enriching democracy in every corner of our life.

FDR and Global War

NATHANIEL PEFFER

From 1937 to 1940 the face of the world became pockmarked with what Franklin D. Roosevelt described as the contagion of war. The vulgar, barbaric Nazi military machine under Hitler seized Austria, subdued Poland, Denmark, and Norway, swept over Belgium and the Netherlands, all but trapped three hundred thousand British and French troops on the beaches of Dunkirk, whipped France to her knees, and terrorized Hungary, Rumania, and Bulgaria into an abortive submission, conquered Greece and much of North Africa. In Asia, the Japanese warlords, always masters at imitation, followed a similar pattern of arrogant strut and savage subjugation.

In December of 1940, FDR enunciated a historic decision for America: "We must be the great arsenal of democracy." The following August the President and Britain's Winston Churchill met in Placentia Bay, Newfoundland, aboard the battleship Prince of Wales, *to frame the Atlantic Charter; less than four months later the Japanese struck at Pearl Harbor. America braced to defend "the last best hope of earth," to use Lincoln's phrase; and to tell this chapter in the American Story we turn to Nathaniel Peffer, a resident of China for many years, now professor of international relations at Columbia University, and author of such authoritative books as* Basis for Peace in the Far East *and* America's Place in the World.

On DECEMBER 7, 1941, one chapter in American history closed, another began. Indeed, the United States may be said then to have come into a new life. On that day the United States entered the Second World War, forced into it by the Japanese attack on Pearl Harbor. Yet, that was only its formal entry. In effect it had been participating in the war before then, not as a belligerent, but committed in its feelings, its convictions, its realization of where the national interest lay. The exchange of American destroyers for British bases in the West Indies, lend-lease, increased help to China—these all marked stages on the road to war, the most far-flung, the most perilous war in American history.

This action marked, too, the formal, final renunciation by the American people of the fundamental principle that had guided their thought, policy, and action since 1787—nonparticipation in foreign politics and wars, or what is commonly and erroneously called isolationism. True, the United States had entered the First World War, but that was without recognition of the consequences, or willingness to accept them, as shown by refusal to join the League of Nations.

Participation in the First World War may be called episodic; in the Second it was final. And it was indicative and symbolic that, for four years, American boys were to be found on guard or fighting in every quarter of the planet, however remote—in the jungle swamps of New Guinea and Burma, on barren, sun-scorched islands off the Persian coast, in the deserts of Africa and Australia, in the Arctic north, on tiny, pinpoint atolls in the mid-Pacific, in France and Italy and Germany. And whether American boys were physically to return home from those remote points after the war or not, America as a country was never to do so. Never again would there be a spot on the globe where America would not be concerned, nor where, in small measure or large, it would not have to play a part and have a voice in decision. This, indeed, was the second American revolution.

How had such a revolution come about? It was no doubt moving on the tide of history, a tide that the American people had been trying, futilely, to sweep back since 1920. Europe had been left prostrate by the First World War and disjointed in all its parts by the Treaty of Versailles. Central Europe had been in ferment since the late 1920's, a ferment violently stirred by the world depression. In 1933 the Nazis seized control in Germany. Goaded by Nazi fascism and the incomprehensible perversion of a people till then counted on as one of high civilization, the old German militarism reasserted itself. Massed, goose-stepping boots thundered again; the raucous, bellowing summons to conquer the world was heard once more. By 1937 Germany was on the march. In early 1938 it swooped down on Austria; in autumn, 1938, it took most of Czechoslovakia, after the capitulation at Munich. The Teutonic horde was on the prowl again.

But this was not all. On the other side of the globe, a primitive force of the same kind was in motion. Japan had begun conquest in Manchuria in 1931, and within five years made clear that it meant to have north China too. Like Hitler's Germany, it had resolved on taking one bite at a time. Chinese resistance stiffened, however, and Japan had to choose between renouncing its grandiose ambitions or making an end of China altogether. It chose, and in 1937 its army invaded China. A year later it enunciated the East Asia Coprosperity Sphere, meaning that China would become an outright Japanese colony.

It was impossible for the United States to avoid drawing provisional conclusions. In the West, a frenzied fascist system was threatening to impose a barbaric dominion over all Europe, stretching from the border of Russia, its ally, to the Atlantic. In the East, a semifascist regime was threatening to impose a kind of modernized tribal warrior rule on half of Asia. Either would imperil American security; the two together would mean immediate, dire peril.

There was another force, even stronger, impelling America to turn a sterner face to the world: a moral force. The barbarous excesses of the Germans in Europe, their contemptuous repudiation of the accumulated sanctions and decencies of centuries of Western civilization, were revolting to Americans. Even those Americans who still clung to the rule, "let Europe stew in its own juice," could not stomach what they saw. In Asia, the excesses of the Japanese, some of them bestial, were no less revolting.

Something more than military security and political interest began to work in the American consciousness. A moral question was posed. It was a growing sense of the distinction between good and evil. To numbers of men, for whom security and political interest were subordinate considerations, it became impossible to blot out, suppress, or ignore the question: could one, *did* one want to live in an evil world even if one were personally safe? And against that stark moral issue the warnings of the isolationists, having nothing but cold and brittle arguments to sustain them, seemed pallid and bloodless and somewhat ignoble. The Great Debate was drawing to a close. The cumulative horror of fascist warmaking was giving unofficial decision.

The result began to be manifest in acts rather than pronouncements. Help to Great Britain increased; the injunctions of international law as to neutrality were quietly waived; a higher law, though not invoked, was in effect. Much the same was true in Asia. Japan, driven to insensate foolhardiness by its militarists and dazzled by German successes, had cast in its lot with the Axis, reveling in dreams of dividing up the world. In midsummer, 1941, Japanese troops invaded south Indochina, from which they could spring at will into Thailand, Burma, and India. Recognizing the portent, in July, 1941, the American government issued a decree freezing Japanese assets in the United States; it was followed in this action by Great Britain, the Netherlands, and the British Dominions. Again Japan had to choose: reverse its course, starve or fight. In Washington, diplomatic negotiations between the two governments dragged on inconclusively through the spring, summer, and autumn. The issue could not be compromised. The Japanese would not give up their hold on China. On the contrary, they pressed the United States to cease helping China and induce the Chinese to accept subjection. The American government held as firmly to the principle that without an independent China there could be no peace in the Far East, and therefore Japan would have to withdraw from that country. Both sides stated their position unequivocally in November. Later it became known that Japan had already come to a decision in October: America must yield or Japan would go to war. And on December 7, without declaration of war or warning, Japanese planes swooped down out of the air over Pearl Harbor and sank or damaged nearly all the American fleet assembled there. The American people were at war. Four days later Germany and Italy declared war on the United States.

The bombs that fell on Pearl Harbor spread ruins in that base, but they were a consolidating force on the American mainland. Within three hours the American people were bound in firm and unbreakable unity as never before. The Great Debate was stilled. Angered by the foul blow and goaded by humiliation, America girded itself for retribution. Men were called up. Plants for manufacturing ships, guns, and munitions sprang up where cornfields had been. The nation's manpower, wealth, energy, resourcefulness, and technical ability were mobilized for the most gigantic effort in its history—first to protect itself from invasion, then to purge the world of fascist power and poison. Results began to be visible in a few months: the Battle of the Coral Sea, the Battle of Midway, the landing on Guadalcanal, the campaign in New Guinea and the leap from island to island in the Pacific, the expedition to North Africa and Italy and, finally, the historic landing on the Normandy beaches. The tide had turned. Germany surrendered on May 8, 1945, Japan on August 14, 1945, eight days after a new epoch in the history of mankind had been ushered in by the explosion of the atomic bomb over Hiroshima—probably the most dramatic and lasting product of the war.

The bombs that wrecked Pearl Harbor also buried in its ruins the traditional principle of American foreign policy—nonparticipation in foreign politics. Two wars had testified that America could no longer stay out of the world; the issue was dead. The danger we had faced and the wealth and power we had demonstrated proved alike that the United States could not do without the world nor the world without the United States. Long before Germany and Japan surrendered, the idea of the United Nations had crystallized and taken substance; and just as Germany was gasping its last breath the United Nations was formally organized at San Francisco. This time there was no popular controversy; there was no opposition in the Senate; American membership was voted almost as a matter of routine. No voices were raised in opposition, even among the most casehardened isolationists. It was significant that whatever mental reservations they had, they recognized that American opinion had moved so far that the old arguments would fall on deaf ears. Without formal declaration, America had made its decision—an irrevocable decision in the sense that whatever might happen to the United Nations itself, America would never again be able to withdraw from the world. This destiny, too, is a lasting product of the war.

New Hope at San Francisco

VIRGINIA C. GILDERSLEEVE

By 1944 we could glimpse the ultimate military triumph, but we understood in our hearts that it was not enough. The dimensions of the world had shrunk, the tools of war had grown too terrible, and a revitalized morality was necessary if any nation were to live in peace and hope hereafter. So at San Francisco the Charter of the United Nations was adopted, and President Harry S. Truman exclaimed, "What a great day this can be in history!" One member of the United States delegation at the San Francisco Conference was Virginia C. Gildersleeve, dean of Barnard College, Columbia University. Dean Gildersleeve knows intimately the aspirations that motivated the adoption of the Charter, and she knows, too, that we have made real gains toward fulfilling this dream of a workable world brotherhood.

THE San Francisco Conference which gave birth to the Charter of the United Nations grew out of the bitter need felt by men and women everywhere in our broken world. The Second World War was then raging—the most terrible of all wars. As its horrors sank into the minds and hearts of Americans, they began to wish with an increasingly desperate eagerness that something could be done to prevent such horrors in the future. The world, they now sensed, had become a small place, the interests and the emotions of the various nations entangled with one another. Obviously, it was no longer possible for America to wrap its oceans about itself, withdraw from international affairs, and retreat to comfortable isolation.

The great national organizations that had felt intense interest in the League of Nations and hoped for our country's membership in it now began again to demand some world organization for

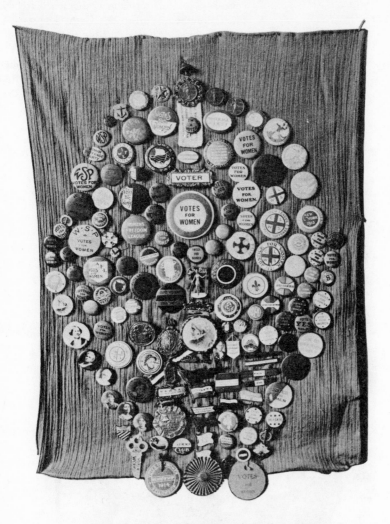

At 4:00 A.M. on August 26, 1920, the Secretary
of State of the United States received word
that Tennessee had just become the 36th state
to ratify the 19th Amendment—and votes for
women became the law of the land, some fifty
years after "equal suffrage" had been introduced in the Territory of Wyoming. This collection of buttons urging woman suffrage was
made by Mrs. Alice Park.

Out of work—but willing to work for one dollar a week—these laborers and craftsmen marched down Broadway during the Great Depression of the Nineteen Thirties, unable to find a single employer. The low point was March, 1933. Unemployment was 15 million, industrial output was almost halved, farm mortgage foreclosures were widespread, and one-third of the nation's railroad mileage was in bankruptcy.

Section 7 of the National Labor Relations Act
(1935) upheld the right of labor to join organizations and bargain collectively through
representatives of their own choosing—and also
created a Board to supervise elections to choose
those representatives. Here the NLRB is seen
conducting an election at the River Rouge Ford
Plant.

Two views of Franklin D. Roosevelt—the first reflecting the soaring will-to-fight he brought to an ailing nation, the other demonstrating the bitterness aroused by his plan to reorganize the Supreme Court. Below, FDR is seen as he discussed plans for a Channel crossing with General Dwight D. Eisenhower.

peace and security. They found a ready response in the hearts of parents whose sons were facing death on the battlefields and on the oceans. The cry of our people for some stupendous effort to stop future wars rose in a mighty crescendo. By the time the United States delegation went to San Francisco in April, 1945 for the conference that was to create a definite Charter of the United Nations, we felt carried forward on a great wave of support and of prayers from our fellow countrymen.

President Franklin Roosevelt and his advisers planned with considerable astuteness to avoid at least some of the difficulties which had wrecked the possibility of United States membership in the League of Nations. He wanted to keep the new project out of and above party politics; and he wanted to make the people of the country at large feel that their ideas and wishes were being consulted and followed. His success in raising the issue above party politics was largely due to the personality and influence of that remarkable man, Senator Arthur Vandenberg. A stanch Republican, very influential in his party, Vandenberg had been an isolationist. He had, however, come to see clearly that it was impossible for our country to stand aloof from world affairs, and that we must now lead some co-operative effort for peace and security among all nations.

The delegation which represented our country at San Francisco was constructed on a bipartisan basis. Besides its leader, Secretary of State Stettinius, it included the Democratic Chairman, Senator Connally, and the Republican Minority Leader, Senator Vandenberg, of the Senate Committee on Foreign Relations; the Democratic Chairman, Congressman Bloom, and the Republican Minority Leader, Dr. Eaton, of the House Committee on Foreign Affairs; and two members at large: Commander Harold Stassen of the United States Navy, formerly governor of Minnesota, a Republican, and the one woman member, a Democrat, Dean Virginia C. Gildersleeve of Barnard College, Columbia University. This setup of the committee was successful in keeping the Charter free from party politics.

To make the people at large feel that they had some hand in this vital work, many national organizations were invited to send representatives to San Francisco to serve as "consultants"—to hear reports of the progress of the Charter discussions and to make suggestions. Thus the whole population of the country had a chance to feel close connection with what we, their representatives and spokesmen, were doing in building a new world organization to keep the peace. All this contributed to producing general approval of the Charter and its almost unanimous ratification by the Senate of the United States.

The other forty-seven nations whose representatives assembled at San Francisco seemed as eager as we were to stop future wars. Many of them had suffered far more terribly than we had during the war still raging. The four great powers which "sponsored" the conference—China, the United Kingdom, the United States, and the Union of Soviet Socialist Republics—had already prepared a draft of a Charter to serve as a basis of discussion.

At San Francisco, we agreed without much difficulty that our general purpose was to maintain international peace and security, to develop friendly relations among nations, and to promote human welfare and respect for human rights and for fundamental freedoms for all without distinction as to race, sex, language, or religion. And we agreed that nothing in the Charter should authorize the United Nations to intervene in matters essentially within the domestic jurisdiction of any state.

In order to achieve our purposes, we had to set up some definite machinery. To reconcile disputes between countries and stop wars the machinery had to have, as we expressed it, "some teeth in it." The Security Council, as we designed it, had this. It is the only organ of the United Nations that has authority to enforce its decisions. It consists of the five great powers (France had been added to the original four), and six other nations elected from time to time by the General Assembly.

It is required to try in every possible way to bring about peaceful settlements of disputes that arise and that may lead to war. But if these efforts fail, the Security Council has, according to the Charter, armed forces provided by the different nations, and immediately available national air force contingents for combined international enforcement action. However, these weapons of enforcement never came into being as planned. The great powers could never agree in the Military Staff Committee on the setup of these armed forces. An army to act for the United Nations in stopping aggression in Korea was improvised, but the Security Council, for the greater part of these years, has had to function without any "teeth"—without weapons to enforce its decisions.

This vital, central organ of the UN has been handicapped also by the veto power possessed by each of the Big Five, which, as used by Russia, has seemed a hindrance and a curse. People ask:

Why did we ever adopt it at San Francisco? There were really two reasons. First, it seemed no decision could ever be carried out unless the five great powers were in unanimous agreement. Since this was so, why not recognize it by giving each a veto? The second reason was a practical one. Russia and the United States both insisted on having a veto. Our delegation was told that there was no chance of our getting the United States Senate to ratify the Charter unless the United States had a veto.

The smaller nations under the leadership of Australia fought long and violently against the veto. They accepted it finally because without it they could not have had a Charter, and they preferred some world organization, even with the veto, to a complete failure of the Conference.

Publicity about the United Nations has been so centered on the conflicts in the Security Council, and the headlines which people see have so vividly portrayed the political disputes and deadlocks there, that we have tended to overlook the really great constructive work for human welfare carried on by the United Nations. This concern for the well-being of humanity, for a good life for every man, woman, and child everywhere, is what is sometimes called "the soul of the Charter." It centers in the Economic and Social Council.

This Council consists of eighteen nations elected by the General Assembly of the United Nations. It works largely through commissions concerned with economic affairs in different parts of the world, social affairs, and human rights; and also through a large number of specialized agencies or affiliated organizations concerned with such vital matters as food and agriculture, the health of the world, banking and finance, educational and cultural relations, labor conditions, and the very terrible problem of refugees. If you could regularly read the *United Nations Bulletin,* and get a picture of the wonderful work for human welfare which is being done through this multitude of agencies, your hopes for the future would become brighter. In it you would learn, for example, about the joint effort of the World Health Organization and the Food Agriculture Organization to remedy the tragic deficiency in the diets of millions of children in various countries. Milk is what they acutely need. How to produce more milk under the agricultural conditions in the different lands the W.H.O. and the F.A.O. are effectively teaching; and in the places where milk can not be produced, what substitutes are best and how they can be obtained.

The Economic and Social Council is the center for all these activities, guiding and co-ordinating them. It has no authority what-soever to enforce any of its decisions on the nations belonging to the organization. It can only recommend. It is like the community welfare councils with which we are familiar in a thousand towns in our country. They too have no power to enforce decisions, but when the various groups that come together realize that the plans will work for their good, they agree voluntarily. So it is with countries.

The General Assembly, sometimes called "The Town Meeting of the World," is the organ where each member nation—now seventy-six in all—has one vote. All problems and plans can be aired and discussed here. The General Assembly, however, is not like Congress or Parliament, a legislative body with power to enforce its decisions. It has some power over the Trusteeship Council and the administration of countries under this guidance, and it does elect members of the Security and Economic and Social Councils. Otherwise it can only make recommendations. Most people do not realize this. They think a decision of the General Assembly has all the authority and force of the United Nations behind it. This feeling has caused some grave misunderstandings.

Because of the failure of the Security Council to function satisfactorily, our country has tended to throw more and more emphasis on the General Assembly and get it to act on critical questions. But if the General Assembly is ever to become that body of fundamental authority and power which some people wish, it will have to be drastically reorganized so that the Republics of Costa Rica and Liberia will not have as much voting strength as the Soviet Union and the United States of America. How would votes be allotted? If it is to be merely by population numbers, should we be willing to have India, for example, cast two or three times as many votes as the United States?

One very great difficulty is, of course, the possession of the veto power by the five great powers. Must that continue, and how? When at San Francisco we chose China, France, Britain, Russia, and the United States as the five great powers, how could we tell how long this would last? Who are the five great powers today? Who will they be a hundred years from now?

In the present state of our globe, where the nations live elbow to elbow, it is obvious that there will have to be some sort of world order. Perhaps it will all be under the domination of one great power. Let us devoutly hope not. But if this fate is not to befall us, we must have some general organization of nations, but with each retaining its own individuality and control over its internal affairs. Should our present United Nations fail and be discontinued, as some isolationists now hope it may be, then we should just have to start all over again and build up painfully a new world organization. It seems infinitely better for us to fix our minds upon the many good things that our United Nations is now doing, build upon them, and try to remedy, as the years go on, the shortcomings that inevitably develop in a human machine faced with such an intricate and delicate task.

Cold War and Communist Containment

DAVID J. DALLIN

"We must cultivate the science of human relations—the ability of all peoples, of all kinds, to live together and work together in the same world, at peace."

These were the last words written by Franklin Delano Roosevelt, the first statesman of the Atomic Age. The uneasy conscience of America, of the world, made us wonder, however, about man. Could he grow in spiritual stature as quickly as he could grow in scientific knowledge and technological achievement? Specifically, could he resist the threat of Communism, so intent on conquering the world by blotting out the spirituality of man and reducing him to slavery by a new name?

Little hot wars became the deformed progeny of the big cold war thus thrust upon us. We faced up to the Russian colossus, recognizing that he was spawned by revolution, death, and murder, that his fears arising from national youthfulness drove him into patterns of delinquency—in brief, that his environment in a national sense contained dangerous psychotic symptoms that led him to lie, to cheat, to bully, to steal, to kill. So time, time for the slow process of growth and mental healing, became the agonizing need of an age that had all but shattered time in every other way.

One of the foremost authorities on American foreign policy, especially as it applies to Russia, is David J. Dallin. His eight books on Soviet Russia have all been published by Yale University Press, and include Forced Labor in Soviet Russia *and* Soviet Russia's Foreign Policy.

THE ERA of peace which descended on the world with the silencing of the last guns in the Pacific was not of long duration. Within a short five years the American army was facing a new enemy. Once again American soldiers were shedding their blood thousands of miles from home in a conflict which, had it occurred a few decades earlier, would never have required American intervention. This was the Korean war of 1950–53.

The aggression from the north against the little-known and impoverished country was warded off by the hastily mobilized power of the United Nations. The American contribution in men and resources bulked large in an effort to halt the advance of Communism in Asia. America's course of action in the Korean war was part of a new conception of international policy. The United States had advanced during World War II to first place among the great powers, and was carrying a greatly increased responsibility in world affairs. Additionally, this country was operating in a world in which unprecedented technological achievements implied unprecedented destruction in case of a new war.

Betraying the hopes of the world, breaking treaties and commitments, the Soviet government after World War II embarked on a new course of forcible expansion and aggression. In 1945 and 1946 Russia's neighbors in Europe and the Far East, their territory occupied by the Red Army at the end of the fighting, were transformed into a new kind of dependencies, so-called satellites, with the Communist Party in power. Soon a belt of such satellites (with a gap only at the comparatively less important Iran-Afghan frontier) girded Russia from the Baltic Sea to the Pacific Ocean. Although the United States and her Western allies protested this course, Moscow remained adamant, fully aware of the inability of the Western allies to prevent this process of expansion.

Now, with military bases at the Elbe and the Kiel Canal in Germany, in Austria, in Manchuria, and in Korea, the Soviet Union was threatening not only the western part of the defeated Reich, but England, France, and Japan as well. Long-range bombers of the huge Soviet Air Force were capable of reaching the capital of any of these nations in less than two hours.

Setting up of satellite governments in adjoining nations was the Soviet way of expanding the political and economic system of Communism. But now the satellites themselves embarked on a similar course in regard to their own neighbors. They extended their ties with Communist underground organizations, assisting them with arms, leaders, advisers, and experts. East Germany, for instance, was trying to strengthen Communism in West Germany; Manchuria, taken into the Soviet fold in 1945–46, later extended its activity into neighboring Korea; Bulgaria and Yugoslavia, both Soviet satellites up to 1948, had to take care of the Communist uprising in Greece; China, transformed into a Communist satellite, extended help to Indochina. Thus the Soviet Union's immediate neighbors, the original satellites, were fathering new satellites. This method of expansion, recognizing no limits, threatened every free nation of the world.

In these circumstances a new conception of American foreign policy emerged, the essence of which was to stop the progress of Communism. Trying to avoid the extremes of a world war on the one side, and acquiescence in Soviet expansion on the other, this policy of containment meant many things to many countries—in some cases financial aid; in others, arms and supplies; in others, military alliances; and in still others, even military activity, as was the case in Korea.

The United States realized, of course, that the Communist movements which developed after the war in various countries had not been artificially generated or created from without by Russian propagandists or Russian gold. The roots of these movements, which in some countries embraced millions of men and women, lay in the economic poverty, famine, and distress which existed in these countries. Material help on a grand scale was required—not modest charity to the neediest, but billions of dollars in agricultural, industrial, and other aid. The meeting of this need was the essential purpose of the large American grants and loans since 1946. Later these became integrated into the one huge system known as the Marshall Plan, which was announced in germinal form by Secretary of State George Marshall in his Harvard speech of June 5, 1947.

The same idea in another form lay at the roots of President Truman's so-called Point Four program—a grand-scale project of technological and medical aid to backward nations over the world.

Both the Marshall Plan and the Point Four program had one serious shortcoming, however: they could not work very fast. Many months are needed to produce, accumulate, and deliver goods to a nation in need; it takes years for the stormy political movements in the impoverished countries to quiet down; and a further long period of time ensues before the effects of gradual amelioration begin to tell in international affairs. As a long-range measure the Marshall Plan was an excellent one, but it was a plan of strategy rather than of tactics, occurring precisely at a time when the Communist offensive was already on the march in both the East and the West, when every lost day was tantamount to a lost battle. Strategy had to be supplemented by tactical moves of swift and striking effectiveness.

One such policy was enunciated by President Truman on March 12, 1947. The immediate concern was the plight of Greece in the Communist-led civil war and the difficult situation of hard pressed Turkey. But going beyond the narrow problems of the Balkans, President Truman outlined a new concept of American foreign policy which was to last for a long time. The President said:

". . . totalitarian regimes imposed upon free peoples by direct or indirect aggression, undermine the foundations of international peace and hence the security of the United States. . . . At the present moment in world history nearly every nation must choose between alternative ways of life. The choice is too often not a free one.

"One way of life is based upon the will of the majority, and is distinguished by free institutions, representative government, free elections, guarantees of individual liberty, freedom of speech and religion, and freedom from political oppression.

"The second way of life is based upon the will of a minority forcibly imposed upon the majority. It relies upon terror and oppression, a controlled press and radio, fixed elections, and the suppression of personal freedoms.

"I believe that it must be the policy of the United States to support peoples who are resisting attempted subjugation by armed minorities or by outside pressure."

In accordance with the new policy, the United States appropriated large funds for aid to Greece, where the resistance of the Communist guerrillas was stubborn and prolonged. Almost three years elapsed before President Truman could report to Congress that the civil war in Greece had been won, and the defense of Turkey substantially strengthened.

Another inevitable consequence of the tense world situation, and a component part of the containment policy, was the great increase in United States military forces. Having been reduced to about 12 billion dollars in 1947, the military budget rose to 19 billions in 1950, 39 billions in 1951, and 44 billions in 1952. New weapons had been introduced and new inventions tested. Progress in the development of the atomic bomb reached the stage of widened production, particularly after September, 1949, when Russia exploded the first of her own atom bombs. Combining her own forces with those of other powers, the United States initiated the North Atlantic Treaty Organization, an alliance of at first twelve and later fifteen nations, and helped these nations materially in their rearmament. To protect Japan from a Communist onslaught which otherwise would certainly have taken place, the United States established military bases in Japan, as well as on a number of other islands in the West Pacific. For the same reason it has kept a sizable army in Germany and Austria.

Up to the time of Stalin's death in March, 1953, mounting Soviet aggressiveness and Soviet antagonism to the United States had kept the world in a state of continuous tension. In addition to the conflicts over great issues, such as the fate of Germany and China and the war in Korea, there were the petty irritating moves made by Stalin against the United States. These, it seemed, were calculated to aggravate the bitterness of the conflict to the point of intolerable intensity. After Stalin's death, however, the bitterness of the conflict began to subside. The Korean war was brought to an end; United States citizens, imprisoned on fictitious charges, were released; old prisoners of war were sent back to their homelands; the language of the Soviet radio and press became less offensive.

This new situation, which had given new hope to the world of an era of real and enduring peace, lasted only half a year. Gradually the old goals of Soviet policy were restored. Old techniques and methods were again applied. It became evident that the Bulganin-Khrushchev-Shepilov trio was as great a menace to the free world as had been their malevolent and vindictive predecessor in the Kremlin.

This fact explains why the policy of containment could not be discarded. On the contrary, the increase in Russian military might and Communist aggression against various countries have made containment a permanent principle of American policy at this stage in world history. If it is successful, it will mean security for all nations, large and small, and liberation for all subjugated peoples.

The Great Dilemma

WALDEMAR KAEMPFFERT

On an August day in 1939 Albert Einstein, living quietly in exile in Princeton, New Jersey, wrote a letter to President Roosevelt:

"In the course of the past four months it has been made probable . . . that it may be possible to set up a nuclear chain reaction in a large mass of uranium, by which vast amounts of power and large quantities of new radium-like elements would be generated. Now it appears almost certain that this could be achieved in the immediate future."

Other portions of Professor Einstein's letter indicated that a bomb conceivably could be constructed through this new phenomenon—and "a single bomb of this type, carried by boat and exploded in a port, might very well destroy the whole port together with some of the surrounding territory." Moreover, Professor Einstein said, Germany had confiscated the uranium mines of Czechoslovakia and in Berlin scientists were working along the same principles. Thus was the creation of the Office of Scientific Research and Development stimulated, and when the Atomic Age was unveiled at Hiroshima we had the word of President Truman that "we have spent two billion dollars on the greatest scientific gamble in history—and won."

Just how much we have won, however, and how we are to utilize that victory is the Great Dilemma of the modern era. It is difficult to place national boundaries around human intelligence; given the result, in time minds almost everywhere devise means to that end—and perhaps beyond. Again, we are forced to gamble both on science and the growth in man's spirituality.

Perhaps no person is better acquainted with the background of the growth of science and technology in the United States than Waldemar Kaempffert. Former editor of Scientific American, *now science editor of* The New York Times, *Mr. Kaempffert also has practiced patent law. Among his fascinating books are* Explorations in Science *and* Science Today and Tomorrow.

IN THE vast wilderness that was North America two centuries ago, the pioneer with ax and gun was more at home than the man with test tube and microscope. The early settlers of the United

States, English for the most part, were far more interested in tools and machines than in the chemical composition of coal or the nature of light.

It must not be inferred from this interest in the practical that there was an utter disregard of pure science in colonial times. Benjamin Franklin; David Rittenhouse, the astronomer; Benjamin Rush, a leader in medicine as well as a signer of the Declaration of Independence; Benjamin Thompson, the Tory who later became Count Rumford; and, somewhere later, Nathaniel Bowditch, the mathematician, were all pure scientists.

Important, too, in their influence on the development of science in America were the learned societies. Franklin founded the American Philosophical Society for the promotion of "useful knowledge." The word "useful" is significant, indicating as it did the temper and needs of 18th Century America. The Royal Society of England, on the other hand, was founded to promote "natural knowledge." But the strongest influence on the development of American science was the Smithsonian Institution, which was founded in 1846 with a bequest by James Smithson, an embittered Englishman who never saw this country. Joseph Henry was the Institution's first secretary—that is, its director. He was the leading experimental scientist of his time, a man about whom we should know more.

The individualistic Yankee whittler, long regarded as ingenuity incarnate, forerunner of the inventor of remarkable automatic machine tools, printing presses, and textile machinery, profited by liberal policies which were incorporated in the Constitution and early legislation. What enabled the inventor to develop technology on a grand scale were social and economic opportunity, enormous natural resources, a patent system of unprecedented liberality, and the freedom to think and act that is inseparable from democracy. The bent of his thinking was determined by the social environment. Since the growing country had long been short of labor it was natural that he became the inventor of labor-saving machines: just as it was natural for Germany to develop chemistry because of her lack of raw materials.

Though the debt of industry to technology was always obvious, it was not until Thomas A. Edison appeared that inventing became a profession. Edison was a practical man with more inventions to his credit than any man who ever lived, with the possible exception of Leonardo da Vinci. He organized and directed a laboratory which was the prototype of the industrial research laboratory of today. Yet he was as individualistic as any in the Yankee whittler tradition. He may well have been the last of the heroic inventors on whose contrivances whole industries have been founded.

Though Germany had demonstrated by the end of the last century that organized research in chemistry could wring from coal tar hundreds of dyes, drugs, scents, flavors, explosives, and photographic developers, the United States was slow in learning the lesson. American businessmen preferred to wait for something to turn up in the form of a useful machine or process. The passage of the antitrust laws spurred them into action—a fact that many historians of industrial technology have failed to note. The antitrust laws forbade price-fixing and other monopolistic restraints of trade. Under the patent laws, as interpreted until very recently, there were no such restrictions. Obviously it paid to develop, patent, and then monopolize new machines and processes.

Patents imply research and development. The industrial laboratory came into being. Research and development became as much a part of industry as manufacturing and selling. About half the patents now granted by the United States are applied for by the salaried scientists and engineers of industrial laboratories. The garret inventor of the Goodyear type will probably never disappear, but he has been supplanted by groups of scientists in magnificently equipped laboratories—a transformation that was inevitable with the advance of science and technology. The farm mechanic who can invent a reaping machine would be baffled by the intricate problems presented by electronics, organic chemistry, and the utilization of atomic energy. The machines and processes of today are so complex that they can be designed and built only by trained engineers. Indeed, invention is now so much a phase of engineering that there has been a decline in the rate of patenting all over the Western world.

What distinguishes industrial research is not only the highly specialized training of those engaged in it, but its methods. In the past, invention was haphazard. Today industrial research is systematic, carefully planned, and continuous. Time is telescoped. Pacinotti, an Italian cultivator of grapes, invented the dynamo and buried it in an obscure publication. Gramme, an energetic Belgian, reinvented it and introduced it. These anomalies can hardly occur in an industrial research laboratory that develops electrical machinery. Radio, television, plastics, synthetic fibers, electric lighting, long distance electric communciation, and other achievements of organized group research are subject to ceaseless scrutiny and improvement.

Whether they come from individualists like Eli Whitney and Cyrus McCormick, or from industrial laboratories, inventions are usually based on fundamental theories and discoveries. The classic example is the discovery of induction, on which rests the colossal structure of electric engineering. Scientists of the United States have distinguished themselves in astrophysics, medicine, genetics and psychology, but on the whole, American industrial technology has exploited the basic theories and discoveries of Europe. We have still to produce mathematical physicists who rank with Clerk Maxwell, Einstein, de Broglie, Schrödinger, and Heisenberg. Josiah Willard Gibbs, who created what he called "statistical mechanics," is the only American scientist who belongs in that class. The topmost physicists who developed the atomic bomb were European refugees for the most part.

This defect of American science and technology became apparent during and after World War II. We scraped the bottom of the barrel for basic theories and discoveries that could be applied for military purposes. Europe had been crippled. Her universities could produce little of importance. There was nothing for it but to plunge into basic research through the National Science Foundation. In a sense, the Foundation continues an old tradition, and emphasizes the important part that military necessity has played in the evolution of science. Our National Academy of Sciences was created by Lincoln to meet needs that arose in the Civil War, and our National Research Council was created by Wilson under military pressure. Even though the National Science Foundation operates basically on military problems, it is bound to become a potent factor in developing basic science.

We seem at last to have learned that there is nothing so impractical as the practical businessman, that nothing works so well as a sound theory, and that so terrible a weapon as the atomic bomb comes out of the equations of a dreamy Einstein, and radio out of the mathematical ruminations of Clerk Maxwell on the electromagnetic nature of light. An analysis by Alfred B. Stafford on patent trends leaves little doubt that there will have to be more research in what is called theoretical science if we are to have fundamental inventions in the future.

Despite our belated admission that we have been too dependent

on Europe for basic theories and discoveries, the trend of research
and development is still heavily in the direction of applied science
and technology. According to the Steelman report on "Science and
Public Policy," nine-tenths of the research money spent in the
United States in 1947 (excluding atomic energy) went for applied science; there is no sign that the trend is less marked today
than it was then.

A half century ago federal expenditures for research and development amounted to about ten million dollars annually. By
1930 they were ten times as great. They are now about two billion annually, exclusive of funds at the disposal of the Atomic
Energy Commission. Moreover, industry is spending on its own
account nearly three times as much for research and development
as it spent in 1941. The federal government provides nearly two-
thirds of all the money spent on research and development in the
United States. About nine-tenths of these federal appropriations
go for military purposes.

There is no doubt that the exigencies of war determine the
course that science seems destined to pursue. From the earliest
days of the Republic to our own there have been federal scientific
agencies and bureaus. To these we have added commissions of
experts to study specific problems and give advice which may or
may not be heeded by Congress. In World War II it became necessary to weld university, industrial, and government science into
a huge system. The Office of Scientific Research and Development created the new pattern. Contracts were made by the Office
and other government agencies with universities, industrial laboratories, and research institutions.

Today the Department of Defense is the principal support of
scientific research in the United States. This pattern of government supervision of contract research, no matter where it is conducted, is likely to persist. Since the results of much contract research must be kept secret it is no longer possible for university
professors to follow the old principle of giving their knowledge
freely to all the world. Scientists have changed with the intrusion
of the government. They can no longer hold themselves aloof from
the market place, no longer ignore pressure from without. Their
loyalty is a matter of government concern. If they are security
risks they may not engage in certain kinds of research with government grants-in-aid. Once while England and France were at
war, Sir Humphry Davy was invited by the French Academy of

Sciences to deliver a lecture on his researches. Such an incident could not occur today. Science and technology have changed social conditions and folkways. It is for mankind to match these strides with comparable advances in social organization.

CONTRIBUTORS

Agnes Rogers Allen

Distinguished author and editor; Associate Editor of the "Readers' Digest"; author of *Women Are Here to Stay*.

Paul M. Angle

Director of the Chicago Historical Society since 1945; historian, author of many Lincoln books, including (with Carl Sandburg) *Mary Lincoln, Wife and Widow*.

John Bakeless

Winner of two Guggenheim Fellowships; author of *Lewis and Clark, Partners in Discovery*, *The Eyes of Discovery*, and other books.

Leland D. Baldwin

Editor and historian; author of many historical volumes, including *The Stream of American History*; State Department lecturer in Pakistan, India and Ceylon, 1953–54.

Howard K. Beale

Professor of History, University of Wisconsin; co-author of *Theory and Practice in Historical Study*; editor, *Charles A. Beard: An Appraisal*; author, *The Critical Year: A Study of Johnson and Reconstruction*.

Whitfield J. Bell, Jr.

Research Associate Professor of History, University of Pennsylvania, since 1954; assistant editor, *The Papers of Benjamin Franklin*; author of *Needs and Opportunities for Research in the History of Early American Science*.

Ray A. Billington

William Smith Mason Professor of History, Northwestern University; Harmsworth Professor of American History, Oxford University, 1953–54; Guggenheim Fellow, 1944; author of *Westward Expansion* and *The Protestant Crusade.*

Claude G. Bowers

Writer and Jefferson authority; awarded the Jefferson Medal for his work; served as U.S. Ambassador to Spain, 1933–39, and to Chile, 1939–53; his books include *Jefferson in Power—The Death Struggle of the Federalists.*

Irving Brant

Formerly editorial writer for some of the nation's leading newspapers; now at work on a five-volume life of James Madison, most recently published of which is *James Madison, The President, 1809–1812.*

Carl Bridenbaugh

Margaret Byrne Professor of American History, University of California at Berkeley; first director of the Institute of Early American History and Culture, Williamsburg, Virginia; author of *Cities in Revolt* and *Seat of Empire.*

Carl Carmer

Author of *Stars Fell on Alabama, Listen for a Lonesome Drum, Rebellion at Quaker Hill,* and other books; editor of the "Rivers of America" series.

Bruce Catton

Editor of the new magazine of history, "American Heritage"; winner of the Pulitzer Prize in History in 1953 for *A Stillness at Appomattox;* winner of the National Book Award in 1954.

Thomas C. Cochran

Professor of American History, University of Pennsylvania; author of *The Railroad Leaders, 1845–1890,* and co-author of several other books on American industry.

Arthur C. Cole

Long Chairman of the History Department, Brooklyn College; Chairman of the Academic Freedom Committee of the American Civil Liberties Union; author of many books and articles on American history, including *Irrepressible Conflict, 1860–1865.*

David J. Dallin

Writer on political and economic questions; author of many books, including *The Rise of Russia in Asia, The New Soviet Empire,* and *Soviet Espionage.*

George Dangerfield

Writer, lecturer; Pulitzer Prize winner in American History, 1953; awarded the Bancroft Prize for distinguished writing in American history, 1953; author of *The Era of Good Feelings* and *Victoria's Heir*.

Henry David

Educator and labor specialist; since 1954, Professor in the Graduate School of Business, Columbia University; Executive Secretary of the National Manpower Council since 1951; author of *Labor Problems in America*.

Philip Davidson

President of the University of Louisville since 1951; author of *Propaganda and the American Revolution*.

David Donald

Professor of History, Columbia University; author of *Lincoln's Herndon;* editor of several history books, including *Inside Lincoln's Cabinet* and *The Civil War Diaries of Salmon P. Chase*.

James Thomas Flexner

Lecturer on the history of American art and civilization; winner of a Guggenheim Fellowship and of the Life in America Prize; author of biographies of Gilbert Stuart and John Singleton Copley, and of histories of American painting.

Frank Freidel

Professor of History, Harvard University; currently at work on a six-volume biography of Franklin D. Roosevelt, the most recently published of which is *The Ordeal*.

John A. Garraty

Assistant Professor of History, Michigan State College; author of *Henry Cabot Lodge: A Biography* and *Woodrow Wilson: A Great Life in Brief*.

Virginia C. Gildersleeve

Dean Emeritus of Barnard College, where she served as Dean and Professor of English, 1911–1947; author of *Many A Good Crusade*.

Lawrence H. Gipson

Research Professor Emeritus, Lehigh University; President and Managing Director, The Caxton Printers, Greeley, Colorado; author of *Coming of the Revolution* and *The British Empire Before the American Revolution*.

Eric F. Goldman

Guggenheim Fellow, 1955–56; Professor of History, Princeton University; author of several books, including *Rendezvous With Destiny*, for which he was awarded the Bancroft Prize, and *The Crucial Decade*.

Robert Selph Henry

Author of *The Story of the Mexican War, The Story of the Confederacy, This Fascinating Railroad Business;* Vice-president of the Association of American Railroads.

J. D. Hicks

Professor of History, University of California; Visiting Professor of American History and Institutions, Cambridge University, 1950–51; author of *A Short History of American Democracy* and other books.

Irving Howe

Professor of English at Brandeis University; author of *The UAW and Walter Reuther* and *Sherwood Anderson.*

Quincy Howe

Noted author, radio news analyst and historian; Associate Professor of Journalism at the University of Illinois, 1950–54; author of many books, including *The News and How to Understand It* and *World Between the Wars.*

Marquis James

Late Pulitzer Prize winner in Biography (in 1930 and 1938); author of *The Raven: The Life Story of Sam Houston* and *Andrew Jackson: Portrait of a President,* as well as other books on historical subjects.

Howard Mumford Jones

Professor of English, Harvard University; author of many books on literature and history, including *The Theory of American Literature* and *The Bright Medusa.*

Waldemar Kaempffert

Science editor, "The New York Times"; former editor of "Scientific American"; author of *Explorations in Science, Science Today and Tomorrow,* and other books.

Bernhard Knollenberg

Author of *Washington and the Revolution, A Reappraisal; Samuel Ward,* and other books; Divisional Deputy of the OSS, 1944–45.

Oliver W. Larkin

Professor of Art, Smith College; winner of the Pulitzer Prize in History for his *Art and Life in America;* contributor on art and related subjects to journals and periodicals.

Irving A. Leonard

Professor of Spanish American Literature at the University of Michigan; editor since 1935 of the *Handbook of Latin American Studies,* and former editor of "The Hispanic American Historical Review"; author of *Books of the Brave.*

Jay Leyda

Author, educator; authority on Herman Melville, about whom he has written several books, including the notable *The Melville Log;* a Guggenheim Fellow, he is completing a biography of Emily Dickinson.

Arthur S. Link

Professor of History, Northwestern University; author of several books on Wilson, among them *Wilson: The Road to the White House,* and *Woodrow Wilson and the Progressive Era.*

Dumas Malone

Professor of History, Columbia University; author of a five-volume series on Thomas Jefferson, the first two books of which are *Jefferson the Virginian* and *Jefferson and the Rights of Man;* Managing Editor, the "Political Science Quarterly."

Earl Schenck Miers

Editor and publisher; formerly editor with Alfred A. Knopf and the World Publishing Company, among others; author of *The General Who Marched to Hell* and *Web of Victory: Grant at Vicksburg.*

Nathan Miller

Professor of History, Rutgers University; contributor to many historical journals and periodicals, particularly on economic history.

Elting Morison

Educator and historian; Professor of History, Massachusetts Institute of Technology; author of *Admiral Sims and the Modern American Navy;* editor of the eight-volume *The Letters of Theodore Roosevelt.*

Richard B. Morris

Professor of History, Columbia University; Guggenheim Fellow, 1947–48; editor of the *Encyclopedia of American History* and author of *The American Revolution: A Brief History.*

Allan Nevins

Professor of History, Columbia University; twice winner of the Pulitzer Prize in Biography; recipient of the Scribner Centenary Prize and the Bancroft Prize in 1947; author of *Statesmanship of the Civil War, Study in Power,* and many other works.

Nathaniel Peffer

A leading authority on the Orient; Professor of International Relations, Columbia University; author of *The White Man's Dilemma, Basis for Peace in the Far East,* and *America's Place in the Far East.*

Dexter Perkins

John L. Senior Professor of American Civilization at Cornell University; long head of the History Department, University of Rochester; author of *The Evolution of American Foreign Policy,* and many other books, notably on the Monroe Doctrine.

Julius W. Pratt

Professor of History at the University of Buffalo; author of many books, including *Expansionists of 1898* and *America's Colonial Experiment.*

Max Savelle

Professor of American History, University of Washington; author of *Seeds of Liberty: the Genesis of the American Mind* and *Foundations of American Civilization: History of Colonial America.*

Nathan Schachner

Late famous attorney; author of *Alexander Hamilton, Nation Builder; Church, State, and Education;* and *The Founding Fathers.* Founder and first president of the American Rocket Society.

Arthur Schlesinger, Sr.

Historian and writer; Professor Emeritus of History, Harvard University; author of many history books, including *Approaches to American Social History, Land of the Free,* and *Harvard Guide to American History.*

Arthur Schlesinger, Jr.

Professor of History, Harvard University; winner of the Pulitzer Prize for his historical study, *The Age of Jackson;* author of *The Vital Center,* and other books on politics and history.

James Shenton

Assistant Professor of History, Columbia University; author of *The Life of Robert John Walker, Nineteenth-Century Governor of Mississippi.*

Odell Shepard

Author and editor; awarded the Pulitzer Prize in 1937 for his biography, *Pedlar's Progress, the Life of Bronson Alcott;* author also of many other biographies and historical novels.

Samuel R. Spencer, Jr.

Dean of Students, Davidson College, Davidson, North Carolina; author of *Booker T. Washington and the Negro's Place in American Life* and *Decision for War, 1917.*

Benjamin P. Thomas

Noted biographer; author of several books on Lincoln, including *Abraham Lincoln, A Biography;* and *Portrait for Posterity: Lincoln and His Biographers.*

Thomas J. Wertenbaker

Professor in the History Department, Princeton University, 1910–1947; visiting professor at many educational institutions; winner of Medal for Service in the Cause of Freedom; author of the three-volume *The Founding of American Civilization,* and many other books.

Bell Irvin Wiley

Professor of History, Emory University, since 1948; Rockefeller Foundation post-war Fellow, 1948–49; author of *The Life of Johnny Reb: Common Soldier of the Confederacy* and other books on the Civil War.

George F. Willison

Writer, historian, educator, public information officer; author of *The Pilgrim Reader, Saints and Strangers, Here They Dug the Gold,* and *Why Wars Are Declared.*

Charles M. Wiltse

Historian; author of a three-volume definitive biography of Calhoun, titled *Calhoun: Nationalist, Nullifier,* and *Sectionalist.*

Carl Wittke

Professor of American History and Dean of the Graduate School, Western Reserve University, author of many books, including *Refugees of Revolution* and *The Utopian Communist: A Biography of Wilhelm Weitling.*

Louis B. Wright

Director of the Folger Shakespeare Library; author of *The Atlantic Frontier: Colonial American Civilization, 1607–1763; Religion and Empire;* and *First Gentlemen of Virginia.*

INDEX

345

699 provincialism, and denouncing officers